Translation of the

Ratno Yizkor Book

The Story of the Destroyed Jewish Community

Dedicated To the Memory Of A
Vanished Jewish Town In Ukraine

Original Yizkor Book Published by
THE FORMER RESIDENTS OF RATNO IN ISRAEL
TEL-AVIV 1983

Published by JewishGen

**An Affiliate of the Museum of Jewish Heritage—A Living Memorial to the Holocaust
New York**

Translation of the Ratno Yizkor Book
Translation of: Ratne; sipura shel kehila yehudit she-hushmeda
Story of a Destroyed Jewish Community (Ratno, Ukraine)

First Printing: June 2020, Sivan 5780

Translation Project Coordinator: Lynne Siegel
Editors: Nachman Tamir
Layout and formatting: Jonathan Wind
Cover Design: Nina Schwartz
Name Indexing: Jonathan Wind

Published by JewishGen, Inc.
An Affiliate of the Museum of Jewish Heritage
A Living Memorial to the Holocaust
36 Battery Place, New York, NY 10280

Printed in the United States of America by Lightning Source, Inc.
Library of Congress Control Number (LCCN): 2020938061
ISBN: 978-1-939561-89-3
(Hard cover: 590 pages, alk. paper)

Cover photograph: Chait (or Chayat) tailor shop, Ratno, circa 1927-8. Left to right: Yitzchak (Icko), Leibel, and Srul Chait, other 4 unknown. Photo: courtesy of Myron Hyman. Photo correction: Nina Schwartz.
Back Cover Credit: Ratno Volunteer Firemen march with their band in a local parade, circa 1920. Leibel Chait at far left, playing trumpet. Photo courtesy of Myron Hyman
Bottom of back cover: A formerly Jewish house in Ratno, 2011. Photo courtesy of Mady Land
Front and Back Cover: Map of the German Empire in 1939, Courtesy of Map Archive of Wojskowy Instytut Geograficzny, http://english.mapywig.org

JewishGen and the Yizkor Books in Print Project

This book has been published by the **Yizkor Books in Print Project**, as part of the **Yizkor Book Project** of JewishGen, Inc.

JewishGen, Inc. is a non-profit organization founded in 1987 as a resource for Jewish genealogy. Its website [www.jewishgen.org] serves as an international clearinghouse and resource center to assist individuals who are researching the history of their Jewish families and the places where they lived. JewishGen provides databases, facilitates discussion groups, and coordinates projects relating to Jewish genealogy and the history of the Jewish people. In 2003, JewishGen became an affiliate of the **Museum of Jewish Heritage—A Living Memorial to the Holocaust** in New York.

The **JewishGen Yizkor Book Project** was organized to make more widely known the existence of Yizkor (Memorial) Books written by survivors and former residents of various Jewish communities throughout the world. Later, volunteers connected to the different destroyed communities began cooperating to have these books translated from the original language—usually Hebrew or Yiddish—into English, thus enabling a wider audience to have access to the valuable information contained within them. As each chapter of these books was translated, it was posted on the JewishGen website and made available to the general public.

The **Yizkor Books in Print Project** began in 2011 as an initiative to print and publish Yizkor Books that had been fully translated, so that hard copies would be available for purchase by the descendants of these communities and also by scholars, universities, synagogues, libraries, and museums.

These Yizkor books have been produced almost entirely through the volunteer effort of researchers from around the world, assisted by donations from private individuals. The books are printed and sold at near cost, so as to make them as affordable as possible. Our goal is to make this important genre of Jewish literature and history available in English in book form, so that people can have the personal histories of their ancestral towns on their bookshelves for themselves and for their children and grandchildren.

A list of all published translated Yizkor Books in the project with prices and ordering information can be found at:
http://www.jewishgen.org/Yizkor/ybip.html

Binny Lewis, Yizkor Book Project Manager
Joel Alpert, Yizkor-Book-in-Print Project Coordinator

JewishGen
Yizkor Book Project

This book is presented by the
Yizkor Books in Print Project
Project Coordinator: Joel Alpert

Part of the
Yizkor Books Project of JewishGen, Inc.
Project Manager: Lance Ackerfeld

These books have been produced solely through volunteer effort of individuals from around the world. The books are printed and sold at near cost, so as to make them as affordable as possible.

Our goal is to make this history and important genre of Jewish literature available in English in book form so that people can have the near-personal histories of their ancestral towns on their bookshelves for themselves and for their children and grandchildren.

Any donations to the Yizkor Books Project are appreciated.

Please send donations to:
Yizkor Book Project
JewishGen
36 Battery Place
New York, NY 10280

JewishGen, Inc. is an affiliate of the
Museum of Jewish Heritage
A Living Memorial to the Holocaust

Notes to the Reader:

We apologize ahead of time for the poor quality of images in the book. Often these images had been scanned from the original Yizkor books which were of poor quality to begin with, being copies of old photographs. Each transfer results in loss of quality. We have done the best we could, given the original material and the resources and technology at hand. Even though images often appear of higher quality on computer screens, that does not transfer to high quality images in print. A reader can view the original scans on the web sites listed below.

Within the text the reader will note "{34}" standing ahead of a paragraph. This indicates that the material translated below was on page 34 of the original book. However, when a paragraph was split between two pages in the original book, the marker is placed in this book after the end of the paragraph for ease of reading.

Also please note that all references within the text of the book to page numbers, refer to the page numbers of the original Yizkor Book.

The original book can be seen online at the New York Public Library site:

https://digitalcollections.nypl.org/items/3bb3f420-9fbf-0134-4a3a-00505686a51c

or at the Yiddish Book Center web site:

https://www.yiddishbookcenter.org/collections/yizkor-books/yzk-nybc313959/tamir-nachman-ratnah-sipurah-shel-kehilah-yehudit-she-hushmedah

In order to obtain a list of all Shoah victims from Ratno, the reader should access the Yad Vashem web site listed below; one can also search for specific family names using family name option. These lists are continually updated by Yad Vashem, so it is worthwhile to periodically search these lists.

There is much valuable information available on this web site, including the Pages of Testimony, etc.
http://yvng.yadvashem.org

A list of this book and all books available in the Yizkor-Book-In-Print Project along with prices is available at:
http://www.jewishgen.org/Yizkor/ybip.html

Geopolitical Information:

Ratne, Ukraine is located at 51°40' N 24°31' E 274 miles WNW of Kyyiv

Alternate names for the town are: Russian: Ратно, Ukrainian: Ратно, Yiddish: Ratne ראטנע, Polish: Ratno

Period	Town	District	Province	Country
Before WWI (c. 1900):	Ratno	Kovel	Volhynia	Russian Empire
Between the wars (c. 1930):	Ratno	Kowel	Wołyń	Poland
After WWII (c. 1950):	Ratno			Soviet Union
Today (c. 2000):	Ratne			Ukraine

Jewish Population: 2129 (in 1897), 2140 (in 1937)

Nearby Jewish Communities:

Dubechne 10 miles SW
Kortelesy 14 miles NNW
Shchedrohir 15 miles NE
Datyn' 15 miles SE
Kamen Kashirskiy 19 miles E
Malaryta, Belarus 20 miles WNW
Divin, Belarus 21 miles N
Mala Hlusha 22 miles ENE
Nesukhoyezhe 23 miles SE
Velyka Hlusha 25 miles ENE
Charniany, Belarus 26 miles NNW
Shatsk 27 miles WSW

Ratno located in Ukraine

Hebrew Title Page of Yizkor Book

רטנה

סיפורה של קהילה יהודית שהושמדה

העורך: נחמן תמיר

יו"ר המערכת: משה דרוג

חברי המערכת:
משה גוטמן ז"ל, שמואל גולדמן, זאב גרבוב, יעקב גרבוב,
שמחה לביא, שלמה פרלמוטר, פרל קרש־ורניק

בהוצאת אירגון יוצאי רטנה בישראל תל־אביב, 1983

Translation of the Title Page of Original Yizkor Book

Ratne

The Story of a Destroyed Jewish Community

Editor: Nachman Tamir

Editorial Board Chair: Moshe Droog

Published by the former residents of Retna in Israel **Tel-Aviv, 1983**

Translation of the Title Page of Original Yizkor Book

Ratna

The Story of a Destroyed Jewish Community

[illegible]

[illegible]

[illegible]

Published by the former residents of Ratna in Israel Tel-Aviv [illegible]

Table of Contents

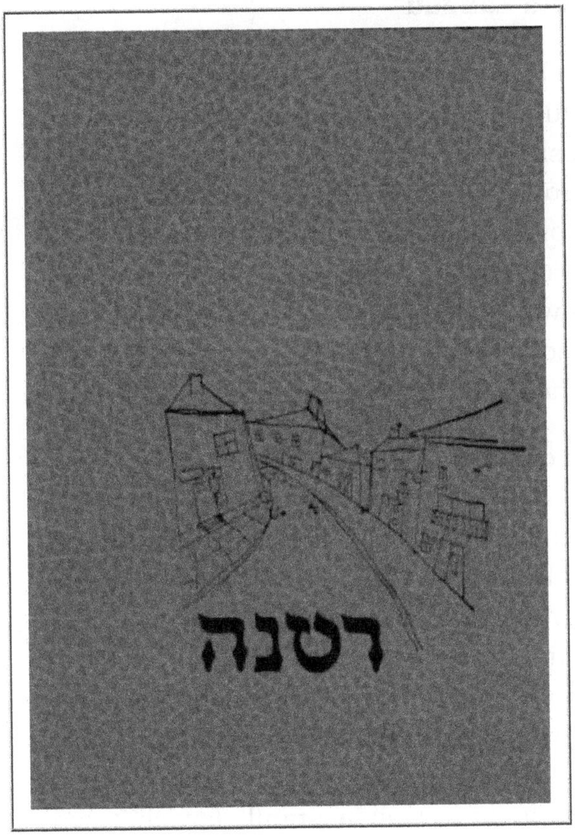

רטנה

סיפורה של קהילה יהודית שהושמדה

העורך: נחמן תמיר

יו"ר המערכת: משה דרור

חברי המערכת:
משה גוטמן ז"ל, שמואל גולדמן, זאב גרבוב, יעקב גרבוב,
שמחה לביא, שלמה פרלמוטר, פול קרשרוויץ

בהוצאת אירגון יוצאי רטנה בישראל
תל־אביב, 1983

Cover and Title Page of the Original Yizkor Book

Preface to the Book

Moshe Droog

Translated by Jenni Buch

Edited by Jerrold Landau

This book is primarily for you – our children and grandchildren. We, the adult natives of Ratno living in Israel, would perhaps have been satisfied with the Ratno Yizkor book that was published in Argentina in Yiddish -- a language that we know very well. This book contains the entire story of our town Ratno from its beginnings until its bitter end. If we saw the need to add this book to the literature of Jewish martyrdom -- it is because of our wish that you too will also get to know this town and through this be able to find our roots, that are also your roots, and so that you would come to know the well from which we drew during our childhood and adolescence.

Once there was Ratno. Even if you do not succeed in finding it in your geographical maps or atlases -- it existed. It was a town forgotten by man and G-d, as they used to write in the Volhynia district of Poland. It had a population of approximately 4,000, the majority of whom were Jews and the minority Ukrainians. The houses were built of timber, and the roofs were constructed of straw. The sidewalks along the streets were made of wooden planks, and after every rain, the mud would be neck deep. There were no great millionaires in her homes and yards, and the poverty oozed from every corner. No great spiritual leaders were found wandering her streets and famous industrialists also kept their distance from it. It was a small Jewish town similar to those that have been well portrayed by Mendele, Sholem Asch, and Shalom Aleichem, and about which you have learnt in school.

Moreover, what a wonder – our Ratno was also a rich, vibrant, dynamic town, abundant in creativity, Jewish values, Torah, wisdom, ideas, and accusations. Everything that existed in the larger Polish cities, those with the honored places in the maps and atlases, also existed in our little town. The doors in our little wooden houses were open to assist every person that needed it – one did not even have to knock or ring on the door before entering. Their hearts were also open. The mutual assistance of one Jew helping another Jew was their primary concern. This primarily took the form of giving charity anonymously, without the recipient knowing who had helped him in his hour of distress, and also without others knowing. The essence of Jewish life prevailed in the town and its customs were quite evident in the Jewish homes and on its streets. It is the essence of this life that we are trying to depict for you in this book.

In addition, the social and political life of the town was not inferior to that of any other large Polish town. Everything that existed there – existed also in our little town: Zionists from all the factions and parties, the anti – Zionists, zealous Hebraicists, and radical Yiddishists, left and right Poale Zion, Communists, General Zionists, Revisionists, the supporters of "Agudas Yisroel" and the supporters of the "Mizrachi", "Hashomer Hatzair", "Hehalutz Hatzair", "Brit Trumpeldor", and the Zionist Youth.

Basically, there was nothing lacking from what exists in these areas today in Israel.

In view of all this "abundance," you will not be surprised if we say to you that there was much social agitation by the young in its small streets and small homes of our town Ratno. Stormy public meetings and arguments that "reached the heavens", controversial ideological disputes within the same family, an abundance of parties, in which each one is obviously convinced that its way is the only path for the salvation of the Jewish race and the Jewish youth, etc.

In addition, our Ratno also had Hassidim and Mitnagdim, although the Hassidim always were the stronger, they were divided between different rabbinical courts and dynasties. In Ratno, there were Trisk Hassidim, Stolin-Karlin Hassidim, Niskiz-Stepan Hassidim, and Lubavitch Hassidim. Each of these factions had its own synagogue, prayer rite, and melodies

If you ask how this was all arranged and sorted out between the 450 Jewish families? This puzzle shall remain a puzzle.

Most of all, we did not forget the Land of Israel in Ratno. Believe it or not, in the atmosphere of tiny Ratno, thousands of miles from the Land of Israel, the breath and spirit of the Land of Israel, with its essence and experience, was felt. The Jews of Ratno were proud of every Zionist achievement, of every dunam that was redeemed in the Land of Israel, of every new settlement that was established. They sat on the banks of the Pripyat, but their heart was between the Kinneret and the Jordan. They were surrounded by Ukrainian folk songs but their souls overflowed with songs of Zion. The gentile boys and girls danced the Russian Kozachok[1] dances in the forests and near the surrounding lakes, but the Jewish youth came out and danced the Hora, the stormy Israeli folk dance with a longing that never left them for one second --

the longing to go there and to build their homes there. Every departure of a young person to Israel was accompanied by the whole town coming out with tears in their eyes and fervently wishing in their hearts that they could join them. Every decree against Zionist endeavors, every "White Paper" that was published in Palestine evoked waves of protests in the streets and synagogues, in the youth movements, and inside the little houses. Every Zionist envoy that came to the headquarters, and certainly every one that came from the Land of Israel itself, brought a celebration to the town, lifted the hearts and souls of the small town that never let up its guard.

Naturally, we cannot forget the Tarbut School – this was modeled after an Israeli school, very much like the schools at which you yourselves studied. Its teachers faithfully nurtured the devotion to Israel, and it was this school to a large extent that inspired us, your parents and grandparents, to immigrate to Israel – and therefore is how you all came to be here...

We hope that now you will understand what motivated us to write this book for you, what moved us to write an epitaph or memorial for this little town that is not to be found on a map. We certainly realize that many things in this book will seem peculiar or strange to you, as will be many of the names and terms in this book that you will read in this book. You are permitted to gloss over anything that does not make sense to you and that you cannot absorb. However, there is one chapter in this book that you are not permitted to skip -- the final chapter, about the Holocaust. You, the children and grandchildren of the Ratno natives in Israel, must not skip over this chapter that was written with our blood and the blood of our dear ones who perished in this terrible Holocaust. You often asked us, and you often wanted to ask and we prevented you from doing so: how did this frightful and terrible event take place? How did we go "as sheep to the slaughter?" You certainly thought in the recesses of your heart: these Jews of the exile... weak in body and weak in spirit... Why did they not rise up as one person to stand for their lives and to defend themselves? Where was your bravery and initiative? Where was this value of

"Sanctification of the Divine Name" about which we were educated and have educated others? In this manner, you spoke to your friends, and thought in your hearts after you heard what you had heard or read what you had read about the terrible Holocaust. Therefore, in that chapter, the final chapter of the book that we have published for your sake, we attempt to answer the questions that you have asked or have kept hidden. Without paint and a comb, without concealing anything, those who passed through this terrible

Holocaust, those who survived, one of a city and two of a family, those who found hiding places with the farmers in the villages and those who fought against the Nazi enemy in the forests with the partisans, those who were in the vale of murder, will relate to you in that chapter how things unfolded, and how everything happened. They do not tell these things to denigrate, not to sweeten the bitter pill -- and indeed it was bitter -- not to cast accusations, but rather as a factual accounting, for they see the need to tell you about everything that was there. You will make deductions and reach conclusions based on this, which you will then transfer to your descendants. Let the deductions and conclusions be as they are.

Sons, daughters, and grandchildren, with awe and trepidation we give this book into your hands. Search out your roots. This is a "visitor's ticket" to the town of Ratno, which you did not succeed in identifying in your maps and atlases.

We were assisted greatly with this book with the material from the "Ratno" anthology published in Yiddish in 1954 in Argentina. Many of the articles and sections from that anthology are included in this current book in Hebrew translations. Our sincere gratitude is extended to those who worked on and edited the Yiddish Anthology.

A street from Ratno. Store on left is labeled Kawiec

Origins and History of the Jewish Community

Translated by Jerrold Landau

Early Ratno in Historical Sources

We are not pretending to research the fundamental history of Ratno from the time of its founding, and it is doubtful if any of our readers would be interested in such research. What interests us and you are the Jews of Ratno, and everything that took place with them in that town. To our sorrow, the sources on this topic are very few, and all we have to rely on is brief articles in various encyclopedias or books that were published in Poland during various times. It seems to us that the most reliable information about the beginnings of Ratno is found in the book by Michael Balinski and Tadeusz Lipinski that was published in Warsaw in 1885. This book tells the following about Ratno:

"Ratno is an open city whose houses are built of wood and are erected between the bogs. A palace surrounded by large bogs is located on a hill near the town, next to the Pripyat River. The Tur River also streams through. Ratno is approximately 20 parasangs (miles) from the city of Chelm and 14 miles from Lubomyl.[1]

In the first half of the 14th century, Ratno and the surrounding region was conquered by the Lithuanian Duke Gediminas. This was after the kingdom of Halycz broke up and the State of Poland was weakened as a result of the wars with the Crusaders. Following this, the area was ruled by the heirs of Duke Gediminas: Liubartas, the Duke of Volhynia, (the Prince from Wladymir) and the ruler of the district of Chelm. After he had overcome the Lithuanians, who were also engaged in battles with the Crusaders, King Kazimierz the Great arranged a peace treaty with the great Lithuanian Duke Algirdas. According to this treaty, the district of Ratno and all of the surrounding land passed to the government of Poland, and thereby the district (Starostowo) of Ratno was formed.

According to the census of 1569, there were 278 houses in Ratno that year. The tax on each house was 3 groszy, plus 6 groszy for the bathhouse. Aside from this, there were 25 empty lots that year, as well as 33 people who lived in rented dwellings and paid a tax of 1 groszy, and 1.5 groszy for the bathhouse. The bath fees were not for the landowner who lived in a palace, but rather served as the salary of the bathhouse overseer Mebolbir, who also received 6 florins from the palace of the landowner. Since the auditors wrote that Mebolbir the overseer only received 4 florins, we have taken the latter to be accurate.

In earlier investigations, it was written that there were 24 pasture meadows and gardens in Ratno, but we only have found 19 of such. The payment for salt was not made despite the fact that no less than 1,000 pounds of salt were produced that year, the price of each being 10 groszy. There are 7 butchers here, each of them paying a tax of 15 groszy."

The first mention of Jews in Ratno in the middle of the 15th century can be found in the book "Chadashim Gam Yeshanim" (New as well as Old) by the historian A. A. Harkavy, Section I, page 10. The following is written there:

"The sixth witness (to the expulsion of Lithuania) was the Karaite physician Reb Avraham, the son of Yoshiahu of Truki. In his book of cures that is found here in manuscript (the manuscript in the Spanish Caesar collection of St. Petersburg), the following article is written:

'The expulsion of our ancestors (that is the Karaites) from the land of Lithuania and the Jews (i.e., the rabbinical Jews) who were found in the Kingdom of Lithuania took place in 5255 (1495). The name of the king who expelled them was Alexander. His brother, Olbrecht King of Poland, received them, and they remained there in the city of Ratno until the year 5263 (1503). That year, Olbrecht sent them back after the death of this aforementioned brother.'"

Harkavy adds the following to these words: "There is a degree of uncertainty about these words, for King Olbrecht of Poland died in the year 5266 (1506), and Olbrecht had no dominion over Lithuania. However, the Karaite is correct about the time of the expulsion, which took place between the years 5258 - 5263."

It is evident from these articles that Ratno served as a place of residence for the Karaites who were expelled from Lithuania for a duration of eight years. There is support for this, because Karaites lived in the city of Luck in Volhynia until the most recent period.

We find information about that era of the early period of Ratno in the annual publication of Volhynia (Roozwik Wolynsus) published in Rowno in 1931, pages 3-4: "The peace treaty between the Lithuanian Duke Liubartas and the Polish King Kazimierz the Great from 1366: According to the treaty, King Kazimierz received Belz, Chelm and Ludmir (Wladymir) and received a row of settlements located on the east of the Turia (Tur) River: Horodlo, Lyubomil, Turisk, Ratno, Kamen, Chachersk, and Oblucyn."

On page 9, it says: "Zygmunt, the son of Kistut the Duke of Lithuania transferred to Poland, in accordance with the treaty settlements on the border of Volhynia, such as Ratno and others, on October 15, 1432."

On page 10: "The Lithuanian Duke Sangoshki attempted to take by force the Volhynia cities Ratno and Lubomyl from Poland in the year 1440."

On page 13: "Again, in the year 1443, the Lithuanians attempted to cut Ratno off from Poland. A similar attempt was made in 1454."

We find the first exact and trustworthy information about Jews in Ratno in the Lustracja (registry) that was maintained in the Starostowa of Ratno, from 1565:

Among the citizens and householders in Ratno, we also find the following Jews: Shmerker, Shachna, Leibka, Zelig Shmulewicz, Zalman, Yakush, Yidl, Yosef Abramowicz, Mordish, Moshe Aharon Lewkowicz, and Immanuel Lewkowicz. There is also a Jewish synagogue. The Jews pay 3 groszy for every house, and also a bath tax of 3 groszy per house. The Jew Zalman also has a grazing pasture, for which he pays a tax of 3 groszy per year.

A Jew leases the right to sell liquor, for which he pays 120 zloty per year. The Jews pay to the palace (that is to the landowner / poretz) a royal tax of 15 zloty per year that is called "Sachosz."

In another source, "Jurajska Encyclopedia," Dr. Philip Friedman, who was searching for information about Ratno in all sources in response to a request from the editor of the book on Ratno that was published in Yiddish in Argentina, found the following lines:

"Ratno -- a city in the district of Chelm during the time of the Polish Republic. According to the Lustracja of Ratno from the Starostowo in the year 1565 (quoted above), there are 12 Jewish householder in Ratno, as well as a synagogue. In the Hebrew sources, we find a note that the Karaite Jews who were expelled from Lithuania in 1495 settled in Ratno and lived there until it was returned to Lithuania in the year 1503."

A general census took place in Volhynia 200 years later, in the year 1756. According to that census, we find that there were 210 Jews in Ratno. In the year 1847, the Jewish community of Ratno already numbered 1,065 souls. Fifty years later, in the year 1897, there were 3,098 residents in Ratno (according to the general population), including 2,219 Jews.

In the geographical dictionary that was published in Warsaw in 1888, we find the following definition of Ratno on pages 542-43:

"Ratno -- a town on the Pripyat River, at the place where the Tur River empties into the Pripyat, in the district of Ratno (the third district) in the province of Kowel, in the Horniki government. The town is located a distance of 6.5 verst (a verst is an old Russian unit of distance) from Horniki, 19 verst from Zablotja, 48 verst northwest of Kowel, and 357 verst from Zhitomir, on the old road from Kiev to Brest Litovsk. In 1870, Ratno had 458 houses with 2099 residents, 61% of whom were Jewish. It has three Pravoslavic churches, one Catholic church, one synagogue, 20 stores, and 3 fairs. A police division and court solicitor (Inquirant) are headquartered in Ratno. There is a bridge over the Pripyat River behind the town. The Catholic church was built of stone in the year 1784. However, prior to that time, there was already a monastery that had been erected prior to 1504. Today the Catholic community numbers 351 souls."

According to the entry in Guttenberg's Encyclopedia, Ratno belonged to Poland from the year 1366, and became a city in 1440. In 1921, the population of Ratno was 2,410, including 1,554 Jews, for a total of 64.5%.

We find a more significant description of Ratno and its residents in the book of Y. T. L. Lubomirski.

The following is a summary of the material in that work that is relevant to Ratno:

"The city of Ratno is situated between rivers that surround it from all sides. The land is marshy to the point that it is sinking due to the weight of the stone houses upon it. The palace in the region of the city was built during the days of King Zygmunt August of Poland. It is situated on an artificial hill. No trace of the palace remained several decades later. Stefan Czarniecki (A Polish Hetman, the highest commander of the army during the days of King Jan Kazimerz during the 17th century[2]) issued the command to drive many wooden pillars into the bogs in order to build stone houses upon them. However, already in the 18th century, these stone houses sunk into the bogs, from which old wooden houses stuck out. The water reached the thresholds of the houses. A Jewish beggar stands next to the threshold stretching out his fishing rod... On the other hand, a Christian youth, more brave, rolls up his pant legs, dips his thin legs into the water, and fishes for little fishes with his bare hands in the surrounding water." It seems that no special attention is given to the city of Ratno in the historical sources. Despite the efforts of Dr. Philip Friedman to collect whatever is possible, it is difficult to form a complete and reliable image of the town from the 15th century until our time due to the scanty bits of information, which at times even contradict each other.

Translator's Footnotes

1. This statement may be correct in terms of parasangs -- see http://en.wikipedia.org/wiki/Parasang The Hebrew word for mile was in brackets in the original. https://www.jewishgen.org/Yizkor/Ratno/rat012.html - 1r
2. A Hetman is a high ranking Polish army official. See http://en.wikipedia.org/wiki/Stefan_Czarniecki https://www.jewishgen.org/Yizkor/Ratno/rat012.html - 2r

Jews in Ratno[1]

by Fishel Held

In 1938, a booklet entitled "Memories and Impressions from the City of Ratno" was published in Kowel by the M. Weinberg printers. Its author was Fishel Held of Ratno. In the introduction to this booklet by Aharon Yaakov Ginzburg, it says that Fishel Held was the only person in Ratno who remembers events and people. He wrote his memories in Hebrew and translated them into Yiddish. Here we bring sections from this booklet.

Ratno was founded approximately 500 years ago, during the time of the rule of the Polish dukes of the Sangoszko dynasty. The city is located on fields that today belong to the Russian Church, next to the Vizhovka River. During the war between Poland and Sweden in the years 1706-1707, the city was destroyed and its residents were killed. The survivors who succeeded in escaping returned and rebuilt Ratno. At that time, the old cemetery was built, where all of those killed during the war were buried in a mass grave. A small hill on the eastern side of the old cemetery is the only remnant of this mass grave. The few residents of the old city who survived included Reb Yaakov Ratner, who was known as a Tzadik. Nothing remains in writing about him, and we know only what our parents told us about him. The writer of these lines once saw in "Raskin's Table" one line that said, "Reb Yaakov of Ratno died in Krakow in the year...," however, I do not recall the year listed as his year of death.

The leaders of the new city included some residents of the old city who remained alive after the aforementioned war, including the honorable and important Reb Chaim Mechenivker and his son Hirsch. Thanks to their efforts and money, the old synagogue was erected at that time, at the same time as the Catholic monastery in 1784, with the assistance and supervision of the regional governor (wojewodzina) Sosnowska, who then ruled over Ratno and its region through the authority of the government of Poland. After her death, she was buried in the bounds of the monastery, as was later on her daughter. Both of their graves can be found to this day in that monastery.

Reb Leib Sarah's,[2] the mystic, sat and learned in the attic of the Beis Midrash for a long time. Reb Chaim Mechenivker and his son were known for their generosity and dedication to communal affairs. As is told, Reb Tzvi (Hirsch), Chaim's son, had seven sons and one daughter, whereas his younger son, Pinchas Pulmer, had seven daughters and one son. The well-known Avrech family later stemmed from them and spread out throughout many cities in Poland and Russia. They were given the family name "Avrech" during the time of the "First Russian Revision" which was a type of census of all the Jews of Russia and Poland, for before this "Revision," all of the Jews were considered to have disappeared. Then it became the fortune of Yossel the son-in-law of Reb Tzvi Mechenivker to be called by the name Avrech, in accordance with the verse "and they called before him Avrech"[3], which referred to the Righteous Joseph. This name then became the family name of his many descendants, including many Hassidic and Misnagdic Jews, rich and poor, maskilim and Torah scholars, as is found in any family.

Members of the aforementioned Mechenivker family brought as a teacher to their children someone who later became known as the "Maggid of Ratno," Reb Tzvi the son of Reb Dov, who lived in their courtyard in Mechenivka next to the village of Buzaky, 20 kilometers from Ratno. He taught Torah to their children. This teacher was immersed day and night in the service of G-d. The elders of the city tell about a wondrous deed of his that took place during his first years of service. A woman in Mechenivka had difficulty in giving birth. Her situation was very serious and everyone gave up on her life. It was only when this teacher prayed for her with great devotion after immersing in the mikva that she gave birth in peace.

An awesome story is told from the later years of the life of the Maggid of Ratno. It took place in the Beis Midrash on Simchat Torah during the "Atah Hareita" prayer before the Hakafa (Torah circuits). The author does not recall exactly what took place, but this was certainly a wondrous deed, for he became known as a "worker of wonders," and was given the title "The Maggid of Ratno."

The Maggid did not have his own Hassidim, as was the custom of Tzadikim, but this writer of these lines heard from an elder Hassid of Kobrin that Rabbi Moshe of Kobrin would often mention the Maggid of Ratno and even bring down things in his name or tell stories about him. Apparently, both of them belonged to the same group, and used to travel together to the holy Rabbi Shlomo of Ludmir. To this day, various customs of the Maggid are followed in Ratno, such as the recitation of "Barchu" at the end of the Sabbath evening service, and other customs that stemmed from the Hassidim of Karlin. It is known that during his youth, the Maggid saw the Baal Shem Tov himself in the city of Brody, but due to the crowds, he only succeeded in seeing his back but not his face.

The Maggid had no sons. He married off his daughters to Ratno householders. To this day, there are Jews of Ratno who boast of being descendants of the Maggid of Ratno, including: Reb Meir Karsh who was known as Reb Meir Birker, Yisrael-Lipa Bergel, David Greenstein, and others.

The Maggid died on the 9th of Nissan 5578 (1818) and is buried in the old cemetery. Masses of people stream to his grave to this day. The graves of honorable Ratno natives, with fine pedigree and character, can be found next to his burial canopy. Many Jews, both men and women, come to visit his grave during the month of Elul, to pray and to place notes of petition.

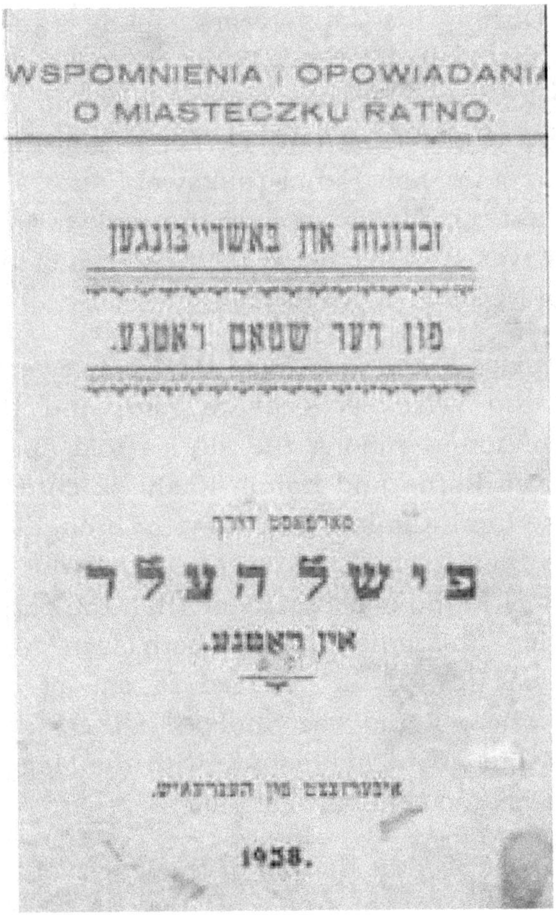
WSPOMNIENIA I OPOWIADANIA
O MIASTECZKU RATNO.
1938.

WSPOMNIENIA I
OPOWIADANIA
O MIASTECZKU RATNO

Memories and Writings
Of the City of Ratno

By
Fishel Held
In Ratno

Translated into Hebrew
1938

The Rabbi of Niskiz

The cover page of the booklet of Ratno by F. Held

After the death of the holy Rabbi Yaakov-Aryeh, who was known as the Kabbalistic Rabbi (Harav Hamekubal), Rabbi Yitzchak of Niskiz ascended the rabbinical seat of Ratno. During the time of his rabbinate, no Jew of Ratno attempted to do anything without receiving the advice or consent of the rabbi, whether in matters of business, marriage matches, or civic affairs. They regarded him as a “seer” who was able to see distant things, and many wondrous deeds were attributed to him. It came to the point that it was accepted within the community that if anyone was so brazen as to do something against the will of Rabbi of Niskiz, he would not live out his year. Let those who believe -- believe.

It is told that he had a pleasant appearance and he became known throughout the Jewish Diaspora. During his later years, many rabbis and Tzadikim from all over Poland came to him. Ratno was his crowning city. He would live in Ratno for several weeks a year. He had a home in Ratno and his own mikva (ritual bath) in the yard of the Trisk Shtibel. For a long time, people believed that this was the mikva of the holy Rabbi Yaakov of Ratno, and barren women from various places would come to immerse in that mikva. Only later did it become known that this was not the place of the mikva of the Maggid of Ratno, and that the Rabbi of Niskiz authorized it.

The rabbi's last trip to Ratno took place in the year 5623 (1863), five years before his death. It seems that Ratno was very dear to him, and the householders received him with great honor. Among the stories told about him, it was said that householders from Ratno and Kamin-Kashirsk entered his court in Niskiz one Sabbath. Those from Kamin-Kashirsk were brought to a table with wine in bottles, whereas those from Ratno were served wine in clay pitchers. The rabbi said, "The war of Ratno is better to me than the peace of Kamin." (The joke being that "krieg" in Yiddish means both "war" and "pitcher," and with the word, "shalom" (peace) he referred to one of the honorable people of Kamin-Kashirsk whose name was Shalom.) Others said that when he was asked from time to time about his dispute with the Maggid of Trisk, he answered that this dispute is an omen for a long life...

The name of the Rabbi of Niskiz is inscribed at the top of the ledger of the Chevra Shas (Talmud Study Organization) of Ratno, for in the year 5609 (1849) peace prevailed between the two organizations that preceded it. This ledger is found in Ratno to this day, and it contains the signature of the Rabbi of Niskiz. In the introduction to the ledger, he wrote in his own handwriting that he is a member of "this and what comes after."

He died in Niskiz on the 20th of Shvat in the year 5628 (1868) at the age of 75, or some say, at the age of 80. After his death, his book "Toldot Yitzchak" was published. It is a Torah commentary in Kabbalistic style.

On the anniversary of his death, many candles are lit in Ratno and a banquet takes place. Some people own small books of Psalms, which people say, were sold by the Rabbi of Niskiz himself. Such a small book of Psalms are hard to find, and the person who owns it would protect it as the apple of his eye, and would not part with it for all the money in the world.

The Jews of Ratno in the Last 70 years

by Yudel Konishter

Translated by Jerrold Landau

Ratno was situated on a large crossroad between Wolhyn, Lithuania and Poland, near the large bogs of Pinsk. Not many relics of Jewish life in Ratno remain. Therefore, we depend primarily on the memoirs of Reb Fishel Held, which appear to us as authentic.

Three hundred years ago, Ratno was very close to the Jazowka River, located south of the Ratno of our day. However, that Ratno was destroyed completely during the war between Poland and Sweden during the 18th century. Only one road remained -- a relic from the old town. It is called "The Old Road". In the large area that spreads out broadly behind the bathhouse, covered with shallow water with reeds, it is possible to see black blocks of wood peeping out from the black soil during dry years -- relics of the houses of the old city that were burnt down during that time.

When the survivors of the war returned, it was natural for them to begin rebuilding their homes not far from the town that was destroyed, on the Prypiat River. It was no wonder that the mud on the streets was plentiful, and never disappeared.

From where does the name Ratno come? There is a theory that it comes from the Russian word "Ratn", which means war, as a sort of hint to the many wars that were fought in the vicinity of Ratno.

The elders of the city relate that during their time, the town was much bigger, and it had many factories, liquor distilleries, tanneries, and horse operated windmills and flour mills. In those days, it was customary to not purchase flour for baking, but rather for each person to grind the wheat or barley in one of the many mills that were located in the town. Only the poor would grind the grains in their own houses with hand grinders.

In those days, the land connections were dangerous due to rain, snow, as well as the danger of robbers if the route was long. Aside from all these dangers, the Jews were afflicted with many tribulations on their way to Kowel or Brisk, the largest neighbors of Ratno. These journeys would take several hours. Connection by water was much easier, for the Prypiat River of Ratno connected with other rivers that led to large urban centers. At times, large ships would bring merchandise and food provisions to Ratno from Pinsk. In addition, daily connections existed with the smaller settlements along the banks of the river, and with villages such as Rechitsa, Sadowice, and others.

Ratno, which was forgotten throughout the years on the side roads, in the midst of bogs and ponds, suddenly found itself on the highway when the road from Kiev to Warsaw, paved between 1840-1850, passed through the town. The ruler also began to pay attention to what was going on in the town, and even to concern himself with its needs. Thus, to the great surprise of the Jews of the town, wooden sidewalks were placed down along the length of the shops in the market square as well as the nearby roads, and it was now possible to walk from house to house with dry shoes, even though the mud continued to exude its odor from the road itself.

The road eased the shipping of merchandise and food provisions from Kowel and Brisk to the town, as well as the shipping of products of the nearby villages that were purchased by Jews of Ratno to the large cities. Of course there were wagon drivers who would import and export. They brought the merchandise from afar in their large, laden wagons to the market square where most of the shops of the town were located. During the summer months when the roads were dry, it was hard for these heavy wagons to reach the market. It was even harder during the rainy season when the ground turned to a dunghill. It was hardest during the season of cold and ice, when the mud hardened and turned into hard clods. It is no wonder, therefore, that the wagon drivers treated their poor horses cruelly, beat them and cursed them severely. When there was no choice, they were finally forced to unload some of the load, and return and reload it later.

The Streets of the Town

The market square was the center and the heart of the town. All of the grain shops, grocery stores, haberdasheries, textile stores and taverns were centered around it. Almost all of the streets of the town extended out from the market square. Zabolottya, or Holijanka as it was called by everyone, extended out from the right, which one would take to go to the train station at Zabolottya. The Street of the Butchers, whose name is indicative of its essence, was opposite the market. The Street of the Synagogues extended out on the left toward all of the synagogues of the town, headed by the Great Synagogue. The Old City Road, leading to the ruins of the old city, winds out from the Synagogue Street. To the left of it extends a long road that reaches the main street. Returning to the side of the Synagogue Street there is a small road that was called Egypt Street for some reason. How did Egypt reach Ratno? Only G-d knows. There was also the Road of the Mill and Slescza Road, which ended at a large square with green grass and a large wooden cross in the middle.

Etrog box (from the 17th century)

It was told in town that a church had once stood in that square. One day, a funeral of a Jewish holy man, who was a fearer of Heaven, laden with commandments, passed by there. Suddenly, the corpse arose and muttered something with his dead lips. Exactly at that moment, the church sunk into the ground, and was as if it never existed. Since the gentiles were afraid of rebuilding the church, they erected the cross in its stead.

The Fairs

The town earned its livelihood from the fairs that took place on Mondays in the large market square and surrounding streets.

On the fair days, the farmers would arrive already at dawn. They would come from the surrounding villages with wagons laden with the village produce. Some of them would be carrying a cow or calf, tied with a rope, behind them. When they gathered in the market square, the farmers would unhitch the horses, put up the shafts, and sit in their wagons to fortify themselves with breakfast. After the farmer sold his animal and his wife sold her dried wild berries, garden vegetables and pig bristles, they would set out to arrange their purchases in the shops of the town. On cold winter days, they would go out in their fur coats and boots to drink in the taverns.

There was no shortage of purchasers of the village products. Purchasers would also come from nearby towns. The fair was bustling. Gentiles and Jews haggled loudly, with curses and swearing, shaking hands or parting in great anger. The horses neighed and the cows mooed. Sometimes, a fist fight would break out over some matter -- over a roll, worth a penny, that a farmer had stolen from the dough trough of a poor Jewess. However, the police would appear immediately, take control of the situation, and haul the gentile to jail.

Reb Nachman Aharon Klein, a wholesaler, would purchase the agricultural products and ship them to Warsaw and Germany. In the autumn, the trade in wild berries was brisk. They were used for making jam, and especially for making dyes. When Reb Aharon Klein died, and his sons, who were large scale merchants in their own right, scattered throughout the world, Reb Zecharia Honik, Reb Levi Yitzchak Bender, Azriel Shlitan and others took their place.

The large fairs took place at the end of the summer, when the cool winds were blowing, and the farmers, who had already gathered in the grain to the silos, began to prepare themselves for the winter by purchasing boots, fur coats for the men, and textiles for warm dresses for the women.

The Merchants of Ratno

There is no merchandisable product in which the Jewish merchants of Ratno did not trade. Here before you are the types of merchants according to their families, starting with the grain merchants.

The farmers of the villages surrounding Ratno were poor for the most part, some because their land was inferior, and others because they did not have land at all. A few months after the harvest, the farmers were already forced to purchase grains of wheat for flour and other food necessities. The Polish residents of the town were also good customers of flour and flour products. Thus, a brisk wheat business developed in the town. Reb Yaakov Lamdan, a Hassid of the Rebbe of Stepan, owned a large grain business. Other honorable householders such as Reb Yehuda Meir Richter, Reb Mottel Klein, Reb Eliahu Janowicz, Reb Itzel Yaakov Izaks, Reb Avraham Fuchs, Reb Yaakov Prosman, Reb Hershel Chamelrir, Reb Chaim Markuza, and Chisia Yankel, the wife of the shoemaker, were all owners of grain businesses, who sold flour wholesale as well as to individuals.

The grain and flour was exported to Kowel, Brisk and Luck, and at times even to cities farther afield. Several of the wheat farmers also traded in salt, which was imported through Zabolottya.

There were dozens of grocery stores in the town. All of them sold on credit, that is -- they inscribed the names in a thick book of debts, and "when they would be able to afford", which for the most part would be after the fair, they would repay.

There were many haberdashery and grocery stores in Ratno, and a general store was not lacking. It was owned by Perel Charna's, a short woman, and accomplished businesswoman. Most of her customers were Jewish. One could purchase from her anything that one wanted, from spools of thread to sheets of silk, from bits of sugar and nuts to chocolate bars. One could even find silver objects for gifts there. She had no children, and her second husband, Berele the Litvak (Lithuanian), was a teacher of children.

Reb Shlomo Michel Avrech, Reb Asher Shapira, and Shaul Perlmutter, or as he was called, "Shoel the Small", sold fine textiles for men and women. A few years prior to the Holocaust, Reb Asher Leker, Reb Shmuel Simcha Olitzky, Malka-Yehudit Richter, and Pesach Marin owned textile stores. There were also stores of iron utensils in Ratno. The largest iron merchant was Avraham Hochman, who was an astute young man who occupied himself greatly in communal affairs. In the later years, he was also a member of the school board. Reb Ben-Zion Steingarten, a great scholar and G-d fearing Jew, was also an important iron merchant. Reb Shlomo Michel Kahn, Yisrael Weinstock, Reb Leibel Waks and his sons, Reb Berl Held and his brother-in-law -- the son of Reb Fishel Held, were also occupied in this business. There was also a brisk cattle trade in the town. The principal cattle traders were from among the important householders and activists of the town, such as Reb Liber Karsh and Reb Moshke Rider. Smaller scale merchants included Reb Berl Larber, or as he was nicknamed, the crier, Motia "Bebnik", Monish Zamel, and his brother Zelik.

Uncaptioned. Houses in the town

They would purchase the cattle in Bessarabia. They would sell the fattest and heaviest cattle in Warsaw. The leaner ones were sent to pasture during the summer, and fattened during the winter with the oats that remained from the beer brewing. They also conducted business at the fairs, selling cattle to the farmers or exchanging them for other animals. Other Jews, including wealthy householders, were horse merchants, such as Felik Chayat whose two daughters settled in Argentina, Berl Leibish's, and others.

The hide trade was in the hands of Reb David Greenstein and his son Yitzchak, who would provide their merchandise on credit to the shoemakers of the town. He and Reb Berl Bergel would purchase the hides of oxen and horses from the local butchers or from Jews who peddled in the villages, and would sell them to outside merchants or give them over to the tanners of the town to work.

Ratno and the surrounding villages, which were situated on large areas of water, were rich in fish. Many villages such as Glukhi, Hirnyky, Tur, Krymne and others raised fish in pools. The largest merchants of pool-raised fish included Reb Mottel Galoz from the village of Tur near the town and his sons Reb Aharon and Reb Chaim, as well as Reb Mottel Klein. They leased pools from the government in the names of gentiles, for according to Russian law, it was forbidden for Jews to lease pools. The large fish were sent to be sold in Warsaw, and the small ones were sold in the local market, so that the Jews would have fish for the Sabbath.

The fishermen who caught the fish from the pools in nets were Jews, including Reb Yaakov Ber from the Synagogue Street, Reb Chaim Maniles, Reb Zisia Marin, Reb Hershel Zopok, and Reb Hershel and Getzel Konishter.

The egg trade was in the hands of women such as Sheindele the miller, Malka Konishter, Rivka Cohen, Rachel Kornblum, and -- in order to be fair to the men, also Velvel Nesis (Glazer) and others. Shipments of eggs were sent to Kowel, Brisk and even Warsaw. They were packed in large crates, with 1,440 eggs per crate. The quality of the eggs was discerned by candlelight. The best ones were exported and the inferior ones were sold to the local marketplace, for the making of challa and the like.

Since the land was poor, the raffia trade also developed, from which hattans were woven. These were a type of sandals that the farmers wore on their feet, which were wrapped in hand-woven cloth. Reb Getzel Konishter and Reb Itzel Cohen were involved in this trade.

Trade was also conducted with earthenware pots. One of the merchants was Avramel, who lived in the unnamed lane next to the Prypiat River. He was a tall man, a Hassid of the Rebbe of Trisk, and the son-in-law of the teacher Menachem.

The peddlers also earned their livelihood in the villages. They would travel from village to village with their wagons, sell various goods to the farmers, and receive agricultural products in return. Merchants such as these who wandered through the villages all week and returned only on Fridays included Shefa Langer and his son Feivel, Avigdor Klonder and his son Asher, Noach Berg, and others.

Local wealthy people were forestry businessmen. Reb Ben-Zion Steingarten, who was a scholar and also expert in worldly affairs, was such a merchant.

Other forestry merchants included Reb Yaakov Shapira, Reb Yitzchak Marsik, Shamai Goldman, and -- from among the early Maskilim -- there was Reb Mottel Tiktiner and Reb Itzel Reichstal.

After the snow would fall during the winter, some people would load up wooden beams that were cut down during the summer upon sleds, and transport them to the banks of the Prypiat River. When the spring arrived and the water broke through the ice cover, they would tie the beams into barges and float them to Danzig. The contractors and officials in the forestry trade included Reb Peisa Grabov, Reb Levi Sobel, Reb Aharon Papir, Reb Leibel Tiktiner, Reb Avraham Droog, and Reb Yehudal Leib Vernik. In Ratno itself, Jews would purchase bundles of firewood for warming the houses in the winter and for fueling the ovens for baking bread. Reb Mottel Reicher, Yoel Wiener and others were in this business.

Reb Yankel Mendelson, or as he was called -- Yankel Rachelkes -- a scholar and a Hassid of the Rebbe of Radzin, and Reb Avraham Fuchs would import foodstuffs and sell them to poor shopkeepers on credit.

Manufacturers and Manufacturing

At the end of the 19th century, there were three horse-driven mills on the Street of the Mill next to the Prypiat River. Of these, only one remained until the later period, that of Reb Nuska Ides and his heir Reb Hershel Ides. There were several windmills owned by Reb Betzalel and his son Nota. An additional windmill belonging to Y. Melniker stood on the main street. Most of the farmers would grind their wheat and barley grains in the wind and water mills in the villages, but there were those who preferred the mills of the town, which were quicker and more organized. In the years following the First World War, a cooperative was formed with Reb Binyamin Kamper, Reb Yaakov Shapira and his sons-in-law, Shamai Goldman, Moshe Eilbaum, Boza Tanis, Reb Yaakov Lieberman and Yaakov Prosman, who set up a steam mill in the town. From that time, most of the farmers would grind their wheat in the town.

There were also factories for edible oils and dyes in the town. One belonged to Reb Nisel Kahn, and prior to that, to Pesia and Rita Chayat, who lived on Krywa Street. The second, which already worked with electric power, belonged to Mottel Klein.

The "Cantonist" Reb Shmuel the son of Reb Pinchas Berg

Reb Aharon-Moshe Melnik

Several bakeries operated in Ratno. Still at the beginning of the 20th century, they would bake bread for the entire week and challa for the Sabbath in every house. However, even at that time, two bakeries already operated in town -- one of Rita the baker and the second Yeshaya Leib Baker. They baked rolls, bagels, and small challas for the needs of the ill, and for the wealthy people who could afford them.

After the world war, when the standard of living rose and people got used to eating white bread even on week days, and the women of the house began to spoil themselves and baked less at home, two more bakeries were added --

that of Reb David Frigel and of Shefa Sofer. They baked fresh bread and challas, and brought a handsome profit to their husbands.

In Ratno, there was a tannery that worked hides for shoes. However, since such a business exuded a foul odor, they located it across the river. Two families, related to each other, owned the tannery: the family of Yossi Akselrad and his sons, and the family of Reb Moshe Melnik and his sons. The two heads of families were great scholars. Whenever they had free time, they would leave their business and study Torah. However, when the season was at its height they would leave their Talmuds as they hastened to work alongside their hired workers. Their children also did not stand at the side. The processed hides were sold in the local marketplace and in the markets of the region.

The "Other Side of the River" gave rise to several eccentric characters. One of them was Meir Akselrad, the son of Reb Yossi. This Meir spent his days as well as nights in the Stolin Shtibel, and his mouth did not take a break from studying Gemara as he plucked hairs from his blond beard. One day, people began to spread rumors that improper, impure books would drop from his bosom. "He peeked and was damaged", people would say. Indeed, after some time, his articles about what was taking place in Ratno began to be published in Hamelitz, and it became clear that he was a Maskil, one of the first in town.

Gitel Melnik who also lived on the other side of the river, was the first president of WIZO (Women's International Zionist Organization) in town. She was a woman of many activities, and worked a great deal for the benefit of the Tarbut School.

Reb Chaim had a wood-engraving workshop on the Street of the Butchers. He would manufacture furniture parts and various utensils for the house and kitchen. However, the majority of his income came from the manufacture of wooden boxes that were used by the farmers to preserve butter and lard during their travels.

The town also had a home-based factory of bone combs. Reb Berl Melamed, nicknamed "Berl the comb maker", and Kotzik the son of Shmuel Kotzik were involved in this. The combs were sold in the local market and at the fairs.

The soda water factory was founded by Reb Chaim-Yosef Chamiliar, who bequeathed it after his death to his son-in-law Reb Shimon Jacobson. The soda water was poured into large brass tanks or small glass tanks, and was marketed both inside and outside the city. In the summer, one could obtain a cup of cold soda, with or without juice, in kiosks set up for that purpose.

There were two factories for wooden tiles in the town. One belonged to Mottel Reicher who was nicknamed Cherkes, and the second to Aharon Katz who was nicknamed Sirochka. Reb Aharon Katz had an exceptional talent in arithmetic, and there is no doubt that under different conditions, Reb Aharon would have become known as a great mathematician. Even though he was not much of a writer, he would solve the most complex calculations by heart and very speedily.

Trades and Tradesmen

Ratno also had many tradesmen of all types. There were at least 15 men's and women's tailors. The best of them were Avraham Tuker, Leibel Chayat, Yisrael-Yankel Chayat[1] -- all for men's clothes; and Moshe Yankel and his brother Yehoshua the Tailor and Abba Fuchs for women's clothes. In addition to these, there were also second class tailors and seamstresses -- all of them proper and upright Jews. The tailors had no work for most days of the year unless a wedding took place in town. On the other hand, the work increased when Passover approached. During that season there were great opportunities both for Jews and gentiles, and the tailors worked day and night in order to prepare the clothing for the festival. It is appropriate to note that during the years 1922/23, Reb Yaakov Shapira and his sons, Reb Eliahu Janowicz and Yudel Konishter opened stores for ready-made clothing, which severely impacted the livelihood of the tailors.

There were also many shoemakers in Ratno. The most expert of them were Reb Yaakov Baion and his sons Yisrael, Itzi and Shmuel, who produced shoes of quality. Chaim the shoemaker (Feldman) and his brothers, and the shoemaker "The American" Sandiok who produced expert shoes. Most of the shoemakers were G-d fearing, upright Jews.

Just as competitors arose for the tailors, they arose for the shoemakers as well. After the world war, Moshe Ginzburg and Yaakov Trajanow opened several shoe stores that impacted their livelihood.

The brothers Zusia and Eliezer Geller, and Yossel the saddle maker who was, if my memory serves me correctly, the son-in-law of Moshe the Shamash, were the saddle makers in the town. They sold their merchandise (saddles, harnesses, straps, and other horse equipment) at fairs.

The hat makers were Reb Berl Feintuch and his sons, Mendel Blatt, Yankel Knaper, Meir Chayat and Feivel Rites. They manufactured hats for any occasion, and they sold them at fairs. On the other hand, there was only one stitcher in the entire town, Janek Apelbaum, who stitched the upper parts of boots for the shoemakers.

Reb Ben-Zion Steingarten, a town notable

The expert furniture makers were Yitzchak Hirsch Berg and his three sons, Pinchas, Avraham and Eli-Ber. Other carpenters were Avraham Weissblatt and Yisrael David and Chaim Sheines who made doors, windows and door lintels. The builders were Kocik from the Old City Street, Eliahu Wiener and his sons, and Rothschild and his sons who lived on the main street. The plasterers were Itzel the Blind, Wolf-Leib Tirenblitt and others, who were unemployed during the winter period.

An ancient Torah crown

There was no shortage of work for those who were able to work in the workshops, such as the manufacturers of wooden tiles, Reb Eliahu Katz, Avraham and his son Moshe Reicher (Cherkes). The tinsmiths of the town were Reb Yitzchak Hirsch Rug and Asher Druk, who manufactured various household utensils in their workshop. They also ritually purged the cauldrons in which the fish were cooked for Passover, and colored the tin roofs during the summer. The wagon crafters were Chaim Weissblatt and Ben-Zion Stelmach.

There were approximately ten butchers in town. The most important of them were Chasia Teitelbaum, Reb Hirsh Chayat and his sons, Reb Wolf, Reb Chaim Yosef, Reb Avraham-Yitzchak ("Wanchek" as they called him), Reb Berl "The meat man" from the Street of the Butchers, Reb Berl Ternblitt, Yosele Reiches, Reb Yosef Marantz, Avraham Geller Koktik and Yankel Chayat. Their livelihood was meager in the summer, especially during the Three Weeks when it was forbidden to eat meat. However, they were busy when Friday came.

The sawyers worked very hard, literally backbreaking work. There were not any sawmills in the town and the region, but people needed planks and boards for building houses. Therefore Reb Matis "Blajaba", Reb Itzel the sawyer and Reb Hirsh-Ber Blaustein would saw the lumber into large planks and prepare wood for building. They would work as follows: They would place the wood to be sawed on scaffolding. One of the sawyers stood on top of the wood and pushed the saw downward. The two standing below would pull it toward themselves. This would then repeat. Despite their hard work, their earnings were meager. On the other hand, the situation of the blacksmiths was better, even though they also earned their livelihoods by the sweat of their brow. These included Reb Binyamin and Reb Chaim-Hirsh Marder of the Smiths' Road, Yosel the Blind in One Eye, his son Nathan, Reb Meir and Reb Leibke Hochman and his son.

The pillars of the economy of Ratno were the wagon drivers, who would make the connections between Ratno and its two largest neighboring cities, Kowel and Brisk. They would transport food and other provisions in their wagons, and at times, they would serve as agents for poor shopkeepers. They would purchase various products with their own cash and sell them on credit to the shopkeepers who were low on money.

There were approximately 15 wagon drivers in the town, who were divided into two groups, depending on the destination to which they traveled. Those who traveled to Brisk included Hodel Kotler, a widow who rented a wagon for her work, her son Reb Eliahu Kotler, Reb Meir Milstein and his son Asher, and Reb Meir Toler. They traveled to Brisk only once a week, for the journey was long and exhausting. Reb Yaakov-Leib Slop and his sons, Meir Mastiszter, Zerach Hochstein, Eliahu Kohn and Yitzchak Hirsh Kotler, a former tailor, traveled to Kowel at least twice a week. Most of the provisions were imported from Kowel due to its proximity to the town. However, of course, there were provisions that were worthwhile to import specifically from Brisk. The two groups had large, covered wagons.

Germans in the Old Cemetery during the First World War

The wagon drivers were G-d fearing Jews. They would worship with the first minyan in the morning, and when they would come to Mincha and Maariv, when they were free from work, in order to hear the words of moral teachings from the preachers or words of Torah from the regular people.

There were four porters in Ratno: Yankel Chodesh who was a former wagon driver, Yosel-Meir Zabichik, Avraham Bezder and Hirsh Bendik. It goes without saying that the work of the porters was difficult, since they would trample in the bogs of Ratno with their loads on their shoulders. Their income was meager, and they did not always have bread for their household.

We will conclude with the musicians of the town, all of whom came from one family. The first and oldest of them was Rabbi Avigdor, who reached a ripe old age and died at the age of 100. He would play the bass with great skill, but could not read musical notes. On the other hand, his son-in-law, Reb Michel Shpilman, who came from the town of Liubsiai, was proficient in musical notes and one of the best musicians. He organized his own band, the members of which included his father-in-law Reb Avigdor, his son Rabbi Hershel and his grandsons Reb Getzel and Reb Yoel. They would play at Jewish weddings and at the parties of Christians. They would play at the parties of Christians with their yarmulkes on their heads, and they would not taste any of the food other than nuts and fruit. They did not look at women at Jewish weddings. After the death of Michel Shpilman, his grandson Itzel headed the band. Its members included the children of the elder musicians, including Aharon Yehoshua Konishter and others.

Translator's Footnote

1. Chayat is a known surname in Ratno, but it also means 'tailor' in Hebrew. So it is unclear in this sentence if the term refers to the surname, to a professional nickname (i.e. Yisrael-Yankel the Tailor), or perhaps even both.

The New Cemetery

Clergy

The Jewish clergy formed their own group in town. These included the rabbis, *shochtim* (ritual slaughterers), *shamashim*, scribes and teachers.

As far back as my memory goes from the end of the 19th century and the beginning of the 20th century, there were two rabbis in Ratno, a father and son, Reb Yankele and Reb Yosef Leibele. The first, who was a great scholar, a man of good traits, and a fearer of Heaven. Along with this, he was also expert in the realities of the world, especially in business matters. His son was also great in Torah, sharp, and an uprooter of mountains[2]. He was a pure, upright person, connected to this world with all the strands of his soul, and considered to be a great Tzadik and a worker of wonders. He died in 5663 (1903). The father and son were buried under the same canopy in the New Cemetery, near the entrance. When people visited the cemetery, they would turn first to the canopy, and leave petitionary notes with requests for health and livelihood.

After the passing of the rabbi, Rabbi Yosef Leibele, a dispute arose in town. Since they could not come to a resolution, two rabbis served in the city. One was sent to us from the Maggid of Trisk, Rabbi Yaakov Leibele of blessed memory. The second, Rabbi Shlomo-Tovia Friedlander of blessed memory was a Lithuanian Jew, who was invited to be the judge of the town. After some time, the Rabbi of Trisk left town and Rabbi Shlomo was left as the only rabbinical teacher. He served his town faithfully until the destruction.

Rabbi Shlomo Tovia was a renowned scholar, expert in rabbinical literature. Along with this, he was a wonderful preacher to his audience -- those who attended the large Beis Midrash. He would toss a plethora of adages and Talmudic discussions into the air, create friction between them, and use Maimonides and other commentators to reconcile them. At the end, he would reconcile all the questions and problems. He did not earn a set salary. Rather he lived from the fees he received for rendering decisions in Torah court cases, payments for the selling of the *chometz,* which the householders would give him generously, payments for conducting wedding ceremonies, and from the sale of yeast. Only in the year 1929 did the community allot an annual salary to him.

There were two *shochtim* (ritual slaughterers) in town, who divided up the *shechita* between themselves, with each having his own week. However, when a dispute broke out between the two rabbinical courts of the Maggid of Trisk and the Rebbe of Niskiz, each one sent out one of their own Hassidim to be a *shochet* in the town. The Rebbe of Niskiz sent out the renowned, G-d fearing scholar Reb Shlomo Yoel Cohen of blessed memory, who had a distinguished appearance and was a fine prayer leader. The Maggid of Trisk chose as his *schochet* a Hassid from Ratno himself, Reb Izak Geller, who was also an expert scholar, a good writer, and exacting in the performance of *mitzvot.* His son Reb Avraham took over the *shechita* duties already in his lifetime. He was a scholar like his father, and also a prayer leader. He took sick on Yom Kippur as he was leading the services, and died from his illness. This took place in 1893, when cholera was afflicting the town. His position was inherited by his brother Yehoshua of blessed memory. After his death, his son-in-law Reb Alter inherited the position, and was a shochet in Ratno until the Holocaust.

From the side of the Rebbe of Niskiz, after the death of Reb Shlomo Yoel, his son Reb Avraham took over. He died a martyr's death on the eve of Rosh Hashanah 5680 (1920) by the Balachowicz murderers. After his death, his position transferred to his son Reb Mordechai Cohen who served in his position until the Holocaust. He perished at the hands of the Nazis along with his family.

The two *shamashim* of the town were upright and G-d fearing: Reb Moshe the Shamash and Chaim Topolowski. Their salary, despite being set by the community, was meager.

There were also two scribes. One was Aharachik Heller, the son of Reb Izak, who was also a prayer leader with a pleasant voice. The second was Reb Hilche, a Hassid of the Rebbe of Trisk. During the later years, Reb Avigdor Hornstein served as a scribe. He was born in Maciejów and married someone from Ratno.

There were approximately 15 teachers. The teachers of young children included Zelig the Straight, Zelig the Limper, Menachem the teacher and Reb Nechemia. The Talmud teachers included Reb Yitzchak Yisrael's (Cohen), Reb Eliezer of Lishnik, Reb Yaakov Prosman, Reb Nachman Hochstein, and others. The greatest of the teachers was Reb Nathan David the Lishniker of blessed memory.

On Krywa Street in the Autumn

Emigrants

Constraints on livelihood were great, and things were especially difficult during the summer months when the farmers would be immersed in their field work, and would not show their faces in the town. All trade ceased during those months. People did not earn a penny. Tradesmen sat idle, shop owners sat on the steps of the shops and yawned, waiting for a customer as if waiting for the Messiah. There was not one branch of commerce that was not affected significantly. Such days of crisis implanted thoughts of emigration overseas in the hearts of everyone. The tradesmen and small scale merchants were afflicted more than others, and it is no wonder that most of them took up the wanderer's staff and set out to seek their fortunes in the golden lands of America, Canada, England and especially the new destination of immigration -- Argentina.

The first immigrants to North America were Reb Shmaya Mordechai Libes who traveled back and forth six or seven times, Berl and Shmulik Konishter, the Knobel and Lurber families, Reb Velvel Heller, Berel Chanche's (Kohn) who was one of the pioneers of the *Haskala* in Ratno, and others. The first to immigrate to London were Shmuelik and Leiba Roitberg -- the brother of Rivka Tuker, Reb David Eilbaum, Yankel Osowski the son of Kalman the butcher, and Meir Leib Wideriec.

The husbands set out abroad first as pioneers going before the camp. There, from afar, despite the lack of knowledge of the language and the local customs, they nevertheless succeeded in finding work and sending some cash to their dear ones on a monthly basis. A new class was formed in the town, the "Amerikaniot". This consisted of the wives of the immigrants. Even if their husbands had traveled to England or Argentina, the Jews of the town lumped them together with America. Every Monday and Thursday, the days of mail distribution in the local post office, the "Amerikaniot" stood on guard at the door of the post office, waiting for a letter from the husband, or perhaps a package with a red wax seal. They never tired of walking to the post office until the fortunate day would come when the ship tickets and money for the journey arrived.

Whenever a family set out for abroad, the entire town would arrange a "living funeral" with a covered wagon that waited for them on the main street. Of course, there was also no shortage of envy by those who remained in the place.

The Great Synagogue

The pride and glory of Ratno was the Great Synagogue, whose fame spread to the entire region, even reaching big cities. The synagogue building, with its two wings, occupied an entire block and, with its four stories, towered above the other synagogues and *shtibels* in its vicinity, as a giant among dwarfs. There were many windows on the top story, and the tin roof was painted green. Everyone who stood before it, felt as if, he was standing before a miniature sanctuary. A long, wide staircase led from the synagogue court to the lane that had two small synagogues on its sides. Early prayer services took place there, and they were therefore nicknamed "Hashkamot" (Arising Early). The Hassidim of the Rebbe of Stobochow worshipped in the first, and the Hassidim of the Rebbe of Liubsiai in the second. Immediately after the main, arched, gate -- adorned with the call of Abraham our Father: "How awesome is this place!" with glittering letters -- was opened, the impressive view of artistic drawing and wooden engravings unfolded, astounding the viewer with their beauty. One would descend to the synagogue via a few steps that led to the *bima* in the center. Atop the *bima* was a huge chandelier with 386 stems in the shape of live flowers. Everything was wonderfully etched in wood. The chandelier was painted blue and white. On the Sabbath of the Torah portion of *Behaalotecha*[3], as well as on the yahrzeit of King David, which was the second day of Shavuot, all of its candles would be lit. The Holy Ark towered high at the eastern wall. It was completely decorated with various wonderful wooden etchings. One would ascend to the Holy Ark by stairs. Above it, literally to the ceiling, three crowns[4] were painted. There was the crown of Torah and the crown of kingship, both decorated with attractive designs. Above them was the crown of priesthood, with the two hands of Aaron the Priest spread out in the priestly blessing. The lovely elliptical ceiling was decked with wood and illustrated through its length and width with wonderful drawings of ancient musical instruments of those mentioned in Psalms[5]: "Praise him with the blast of the *shofar,* praise him with a drum and a harp, praise him with stringed instruments and the pipe. The constellation signs of the twelve months of the year were drawn below them. The walls were made of hard wood and painted white. On one side of the Holy Ark, the wild ox[6] with its large, beautiful horns was depicted, and on the other side, the leviathan with its two fins. Close to the *bima,* there were two large, square boxes filled with sand, in which they would place the large wax candles for Yom Kippur and Rosh Hashanah. The seats of the worshippers were around the sand boxes. A bag of matzo was attached to the southern wall throughout the year.

It was replaced every year before Passover, and served as the *Eruv Chatzerot*[7].

There were two women's galleries in the synagogue. The one above openedinto the main space of the synagogue, and the second one, below, looked upon the men through long, narrow windows. Beneath the steps that were attached to the side of the synagogue and led to the Beis Midrash and women's gallery, there was the *geniza.* This was a collecting area for worn out holy objects and books, which were brought there by all the residents.

The cantor throughout the year in the synagogue was Reb Moshe Labusz. Throughout the year, he would lead the services on the Sabbath of the blessing of the new moon. On festivals, he would lead the *Musaf* service. On the High Holy Days, he would lead all the services, accompanied by a large choir. He knew how to read musical notes, and even composed several of his own melodies that the Hassidim sing to this day. His salary was three rubles a week, which he received from the proceeds of the sale of yeast, allotted by Reb Shmuel Marder who held the monopoly. Several hundred people worshipped in the synagogue on the High Holy Days, but on the cold winter days, they were forced to hire a *minyan* (prayer quorum) so as not to interrupt the tradition of communal prayer. This was because there was no heating oven in the synagogue due to the sanctity of the place, and it was very cold. On the festival of Shavuot, the *bima* would be decorated with many tree branches, so that it looked like a green grove.

All of the *chupas* (wedding canopies) were led to the synagogue with song, and to differentiate, so were the coffins of the deceased. The mourners would make a procession once or twice around the synagogue, and the service would end with the chanting of "Kel Male Rachamim."

Prior to the First World War, at the conclusion of the day of Simchat Torah, when the community would be tarrying at the *kiddush* given by the *gabbai* in his home, and the concerns of livelihood began to gnaw at the hearts from the perspective of "What will we eat?" -- several youths who were still tipsy would gather near the synagogue, and Mottel Mates, Tratz's son-in-law would climb up a ladder that was leaning against the wall of synagogue, and declare cheap prices for all provisions such as potatoes, bread, cabbage, firewood, and animal food. The gathering, standing below, would answer each declaration such as "a kopek for a pod of potatoes" with an enthusiastic "Amen." The synagogue was burnt when the Russian Army was retreating in 1915. The *gabbai* of the synagogue, Reb Yaakov-Leib Kemper, an upright, G-d fearing man whose "*baruch hu ubaruch shemo*"[8] would ring out and fill the space of the synagogue, risked his life to save all 15 Torah scrolls from the fire.

Boating on the Prypiat River

The Great Beis Midrash

The Beis Midrash was a place of prayer for everyone. Even the *Hassidim* would worship there on weekdays, early in the morning and at *Mincha* time. The services would commence before daybreak, to the light of gas lanterns, and would end at noontime[9]. The prayer podium was not empty, even for a moment. When one *Minyan* would conclude "*Aleinu*", the next minyan would commence with a loud and ringing "*Hodu.*" People were never missing, and it was always possible to wait for someone to enter at the last minute. If not, there were always people, old and young, studying at the long tables. At *Mincha* and *Maariv*, the Beis Midrash was full of Jews who came to hear the words of the preacher or the emissary from a Yeshiva -- for if such was in town, he would end up delivering a sermon at the Beis Midrash.

Reb Yechiel Wilkomirski

On Sabbath mornings, people would come there to recite Psalms. The town *shamash* would pass by the houses before dawn, knock on the shutters with his hammer, and wake up the Jews with his enthusiastic melody, "Arise, wake up to the service of the Creator!" In addition to all of his duties in the Beis Midrash itself, the *shamash* would also summon the people to services on Sabbath eves. He would stand at one side of the market square, and then at the other side, and declare in a loud voice: "*Shabbes*!" He also supervised the shopkeepers to ensure that they closed their shops. At times, when the barber was running the scissors and razor after the entrance of the Sabbath. The following week, he would summon the rabbi himself, who would come with his cane in his hand and order him to shut the barbershop on time. The duties of the *shamash* also included overseeing the Sabbath *eruv* [7] that extended the entire length of the town between the two long streets, Krywa and Slescza, until the main road. Every Friday afternoon, the *shamash* would walk the length of the street and examine the pillars that supported the wires of the *eruv*, to ensure that a wire was not torn or a pillar had not fallen. He would repair anything that needed to be repaired, so that the Jews could carry their *selichot*[10] and *siddurs* to the synagogue.

On occasion, when the *eruv* was broken during the Sabbath by one of the gentiles[11], the *shamash* would immediately spread the word. The Jews in their houses who did not have little children would then go to the synagogue wearing their *tallises.* When a Jew was informed that the *eruv* was broken while he was en route to the synagogue, he would stop in his place and wait for a young child to pass by, who would then carry his *tallis* to the synagogue.

Reb Moshe and his heir Reb Chaim were dedicated *shamashim* with their hearts and souls to their Beis Midrash. Jews such as them cannot be found in our day. Reb Moshe would wear a red patch over one eye day and night, but his diligence was not impaired by that. When someone from a larger town or an important person would come to worship in the synagogue on a Monday or Thursday, he would ensure that he be given several long verses in the Torah[12]. After the services, he would approach him, offer him a pinch of tobacco, and exchange a few words with him about the weather. This was a type of "small opening" for the man to understand that he should give him some sort of donation.

The Beis Midrash maintained itself from the donations that were raised from the worshippers on the eve of Yom Kippur and from the donations that were gathered in the plates. However, when these donations were insufficient for lighting the oven on the very cold days, the *shamash* would ascend the *bima* after the reading of the Torah on the Sabbath, and order the worshippers to leave their tallises in the Beis Midrash in order to redeem them for significant sums of money on Sunday morning.

The Shtibel of Niskiz (later of Stepan)

During the early days of the town, the Rebbe of Niskiz ruled over it without bounds.

Nobody attempted to do any small or large act without his explicit permission. After some years, the dispute between the two courts of Niskiz and Trisk grew, and the situation reached the point where each rebbe sent his own *shochtim* and butchers, and each side refrained from eating of meat slaughtered by the other side. After the passing of the Rebbe of Niskiz without leaving behind a son, the court passed to his nephew Reb Meir-Chaimke. Since he lived in the town of Stepan, the Hassidim were called Hassidim of Stepan from that time.

The Hassidim of Stepan were a variegated community of poor and rich, scholars and simple folk. They were "cold" Hassidim for several reasons. First of all, the Hassidim remembered the Rebbe and Tzadik of Niskiz with his many signs, as the Hassidim and men of good deeds testified about him. Second, Reb Meir-Chaim never said any words of Torah at the table, unlike the custom. It is no wonder, therefore, that four Hassidim sinned by speaking bad words about the Rebbe. When this became known, they were expelled from the community of Hassidim. However one of them, Reb Yaakov-Shmuel Rider, who was the *gabbai* and prayer leader in the *shtibel*, regretted his action and returned to his post. This was not before he repented and came before the Rebbe to the light of lit candles in stocking feet, and was chastised strongly. The three others did not repent. Each of them received their punishment during their lifetimes, as is told in town.

Next to the Droog home (the roof is covered with wooden shingles)

A small bridge over the Prypiat

The Shtibel of Trisk

Almost all of the teachers, *shochtim* and scribes of the town were Hassidim of Trisk. They were known for their style of prayer, which was enthusiastic, and full of petitions, emotions, and gestures, and would penetrate the depths of the hearts. The elder Rebbe, Reb Yaakov-Leibele, was himself a wonderful prayer leader. He would conduct the table celebrations as customary in the Shtibel of Trisk, and would expound Torah at the third Sabbath meal (*Shalosh Seudot*).

Thus did things continue in peace and calm until the dispute broke out between the two courts. The story was as follows: The two courts married into each other, as a good omen. Reb Moshele, the son of the Rebbe of Trisk, married Chava, the sister of the Rebbe of Stolin. However, Chava, a beautiful woman who stemmed from the court of her brother that was "democratic" and alert to the goings on of the world, was not satisfied with the court of the Rebbe of Trisk. Before long, she returned to the house of her brother.

Naturally, they began to speak about a divorce. The judges entered into discussions, and they would certainly have reached an agreement. However, while the negotiations were still in progress, the Hassidim of the two courts became involved, and a great tumult broke out. The Hassidim of Trisk in particular raised a great outcry, for it was not for naught that they were known as hot Hassidim. It is no wonder, therefore, that the dispute grew and the entire town was in ferment -- relatives rose up against their kin, and children against their parents -- to the point where fist fights broke out. One positive thing was found among the Hassidim of Trisk, for they were involved with each other both physically and spiritually, and if one of them fell down, Heaven forbid, they would stand by his side with all their might.

The Shtibel of Stolin (Karlin)

The Shtibel of Stolin was close to the Beis Midrash.

The wealthy people of the town worshipped there, including the Shapira, Avrech, Olitzky, Leker families, and those like them. Their mode of prayer was more traditional. Just like their mode of prayer, they were also conservative, and they thought strongly against every new thought and movement. Once one of the Hassidim, a genius and sharp scholar, the son-in-law of Yisrael-Zusia Janowitz heard the poem of Y. Cohen who eulogized Herzl in Hatzefira with the words "Dr. Herzl died, is there a G-d in the Land?!" He then spoke out against Herzl with an outpouring of sharp wrath. G-d performed a great mercy for them by providing them a Hassid, a precious Jew with a refined soul named Leker, who literally sanctified the name of Heaven by proclaiming his faith in Zionism in public. After some time, he was even chosen to be the delegate of the Jewish National Fund in the town.

The Rebbe of Stolin did not speak Torah at the table, as was the custom of the Admorim. When he would come to the town on rare occasion, he would tell his Hassidim about his travels to Switzerland and the Alps, about the landscapes that he saw and other physical things. The Hassidim interpreted everything in a mystical manner, and saw deep devotions in his words.

The Rebbe loved song deeply, and he would sing hymns like no-one else. He even set up a band in his courtyard. He himself and his family members were the chief musicians. The renown of Itzel Shpilman's band reached his ears. Reb Avigdor especially amazed him, who had reached the age of 100 and still played upon his small bass. He was not satisfied until he invited him to his court. Reb Avigdor received him with the honor of an angel. As they were sitting at the table filled with all good things, Reb Avigdor told him that he had purchased the bass from a Russian soldier about 70 years previously. Out of the goodness of his heart, he gave the bass as a present to the Rebbe. The bass was eventually sent to be repaired in Warsaw, and to their great surprise they evaluated it there at a high price.

The Shtibel of Rizhin

The name of these Hassidim came from the city of Rizhin in Austria, whose name was later changed to Sadigor, where the Rebbe lived. The Hassidim of Rizhin were small in number -- approximately only a *minyan* of Jews in total. Their *shtilbel* was at the side, separate from all the rest of the *shtibels*, across the "Nile", which was nothing other than a pond of water during the rainy days. This pond was called the "Nile" on account of the nearby road, which was called Egypt Street (Rechov Mitzraim). On Simchat Torah, when the pond was at its largest, the children would float boards in it, with lit candles atop.

The Hassidim of Rizhin always remind me of two dear Jews and dedicated Hassidim. One of them, Reb Aharon-Shmuel the elder, was a fine Jew, whose milk-white beard flowed down below his collar. He had a pipe in his mouth that he did not extinguish throughout the day. He sat in the puffs of smoke of his pipe, as if he had no interest in this world and its vanities. When he would tell about the *Tzadikim* and their wonders, the listeners would feel that he was floating in the supernal worlds, ascending above the heavens, and seeing 1/60th of the Garden of Eden. Just as he would tell stories with enthusiasm -- such was his way with his studies -- to the point where he divested himself of his physicality

The second was Reb Yisrael-Lipa. He was a merchant, occupied all his days with issues of livelihood, however the Hassidic flame burnt in his heart without darkness. From time to time, he would travel to the Rebbe and return as if he was reborn, refreshed and with the flame of his faith burning in full strength. Immediately upon his return, he would tell everyone with great wonder about the miracles and wonders that he saw there.

The Tashlich service at the Prypiat

Fall scenery

Liber Karsh, a communal leader

The Shtibel of Liubsiai

The Hassidim of Liubsiai and Stobychow were all tradesmen, tailors, shoemakers, and the like. At first they would worship in two early morning *minyans* (*hashkamot*) in the lane of the Great Synagogue. After some time, the tailors, whose livelihood was apparently readily available, built their own *shtibel* beside the Shtibel of Rizhin. In the early years, the tradesmen did not have their own rabbi or shtibel. They would come to any Rebbe that happened to be in town -- the Rebbe of Trisk and the Rebbe of Rizhin. They would offer a donation and bring notes with requests for health, livelihood and children. As time went on, it became clear that the patricians treated them as lower class, and denied them all honors in the synagogue such as *aliyos*and *hakafot* on Simchat Torah. The day was not far off when they understood the full meaning of the words of our sages, "Make for yourself a rabbi." They set up their own *minyan* and were able to be like all other people. They had their own Torah readers and prayer leaders, such as Reb Avraham Tuker the tailor and Reb Yitzchak Hirsch the carpenter who led services with pleasant, enthusiastic voices. On Sabbaths and festivals, the tradesmen would wear their tall, wide brimmed hats, put on their wide belts, and looked no different from the patricians. The tradesmen were generally pleasant, and truly G-d fearing Jews. For example, Chaim the shoemaker looked like a Rebbe, who went out into the streets of the town with his splendid garb and full, black beard. Who merited to receive the first greeting of the Rebbe of Liubsiai after *Havdala* on Saturday night -- if none other than Chaim-Yidl the tailor? He was an upright and proper Jew, who raised fine sons: Yechiel, Avraham, Gezi, and especially Itzi Tuker the hero, who fell along with Trumpeldor in the defense of Tel Hai[13]. The "American" shoemaker, Reb Yehuda-Leib Sandiok, should also be remembered positively. He was meticulous in his observance of commandments, and upright in his manner, who was careful throughout his life to not take an extra coin for his work.

The Beis Midrash on the Main Street

Jews who lived there, on the main street or on Kowel Road, worshipped in the Beis Midrash of the Main Street. This Beis Midrash stood on a hill, and was full of light. There was a *mikva*next to it, so that the people would not need to walk all the way to the *mikva* of the town. The *gabbai*, who was also the teacher, was Reb Yisrael Marantz.

Various Hassidic Groups and Societies

Ratno was a completely Hassidic town The people looked up to the Tzadikim and believed that they had the power to change the works of creation, in accordance with the adage "A Tzadik decrees and G-d fulfills." A constant flame of faith in G-d and the Rebbe burnt in their hearts. The *Beis Midrashes* and *Shtibels* were filled with worshippers and learners all the hours of the day. Elders, youth, and even children sat at the long tables in front of their open *Gemaras* and other holy books. All of them accompanied their studies with the same sweet melody in unison. Anyone looking upon them would have the feeling that their feet were standing in the house of the foundation of the souls of the nation. Even Jews who were busy and occupied with the concerns of a livelihood shook off the mundane dust and entered --

some for a short period of time and others for a longer period -- to unify themselves with a page of *Gemara* or with a book of morality, to ascend to the higher worlds.

Life in the town flowed peacefully, even though at times, the flames of dispute were kindled between the Hassidic courts and other Hassidic groups. There was also no shortage of words of controversy regarding prayer modes. Every dispute was for the sake of Heaven.

As in every Jewish settlement, there were also independent organizations to take care of social and religious matters, called "Chaburot" (Groups).

Chevrat Shas (The Talmud Study Society) distributed the *Gemaras* in its ownership to its members, and at the end of the year, when they had concluded the *Talmud* study sessions, it arranged a celebratory feast for its members, with meat, fish and liquor on the menu. This meal took place in the Trisk Shtibel or the Stepan Shtibel. That day was a festive day in the town. Even the simple Jews, who were not expert in the small letters, paid their membership fees and participated in the meal and the joy, sang Hassidic songs, and listened to the words of Torah, and stories of the Tzadikim and their wondrous deeds. The elderly Menashe, a short, thin Jew, was responsible for the bookcase full of holy books that stood in the corner of the Beis Midrash, as well as on the old ledger book of the organization that had been guarded from the time of the founding of the group.

Chevrat Tehillim (The Psalms Recital Society) was founded by the householders Reb David the shoemaker and Reb Berl Feintuch the furrier.

The **Chevra Kadisha** (Burial Society) concerned itself with the preparation of the deceased for burial and the funeral procession to the cemetery. The gabbai of the organization was Reb David Greenstein. Affiliated to this organization was Bikur Cholim (Society for the tending to the sick), which would send its members to visit poor and isolated ill people, to remain with them for the night, and to tend to all of their needs.

The **Chonen Dal** (Mercy to the Poor Society) was not an organized society. Its members, who were students of the Beis Midrash, concerned themselves with poor Jews who happened to be in the city -- and when were there not such in the city? They would arrange lodging for them with householders who wished to perform a good deed. There were two householders in the town who never rejected a poor person from their tables: Reb David Greenstein, a prominent householder who owned a store for the sale of furs, and who was also the *gabbai* of the Great Synagogue; and Reb Liber Karsh, a cattle salesman who was a Hassid of the Rebbe of Trisk, a proper Jew and a scholar, who later served as the president of the community of Ratno.

The women concerned themselves with the poor of the town. Malka of Ratno especially excelled in this area. Every Friday afternoon, she would go from door to door, wearing an apron, to collect bread, meat and fish for her poor people. On weekdays, the women would go around to the householders with a red kerchief in their hands. The Jews responded and donated, each according to the generosity of his heart.

There were also people who concerned themselves with books. This was the **Tikun Seforim** (Book Repair Society), whose members, attendees of the Beis Midrash, would canvass the householders for the needs of book purchase and the repair of old books.

* * *

The Jews of Ratno were not involved with the outside world. They worked and earned their livelihood with difficulty. They accepted everything with love, and thanked the Master of the World three times a day for the life that He had given them. If they required a marriage match for an older daughter, a child, or health for a sick person, they would travel to the Rebbe or bring a donation to him when he would visit the town. There was no physician or pharmacy in the town. Their places were filled by the medics Shachna and Fishel, whose remedy for all ailments was a bitter powder wrapped in paper, and cups of air. At times, they would also bloodlet. If a wealthy Jew brought a physician from Kowel or Brisk, all of the sick people who could stand on their feet would gather near his house so they could be examined and medication could be prescribed. Only at the beginning of the 20th century was a physician brought for the regional hospital. This was Dr. Lichochovsky and his wife, the midwife. Later, a female Jewish physician, Dr. Krasnopolsky, came to that hospital. During that period, a Christian medic, Doricza, also operated in the city. He was a unique man, the son of farmers who learned his trade during his army service. He would treat poor people for free and give them various items from his small estate. After some years, a pharmacy was also opened in town. The pharmacist was a Pole named Kowelski, who lived in the home of Avraham-Eliezer Rozman on Krywa Street. Civilization slowly marched forward and arrived in Ratno, which was located in the midst of the forests and ponds, far from the happenings of the wide world.

Yehoshua Pogatch, one of the first Maskilim in Ratno, next to his father D. Pogatch

Cheders in Town

The custom was that the teacher of young children would teach their children in his home -- a one-room house that served for all his needs: the room in which the baby's cradle stood, and babies sometimes cry and sometimes sleep; his wife would be busy with household chores, peeling potatoes or plucking feathers, and placing the food into the oven; next to the only window stood the table around which the students sat on hard benches, with the teacher at the head.

There were two teachers of young children during my time, Reb Mottel the Long and Reb Itzi-Zalman. The students were indeed "students of the house of the Rebbe", for every three-year-old child during that era took part in the studies. Since the children were little, the teacher utilized helpers whose task was to bring them to the *cheder* and back, sometimes even by carrying them on their shoulders, especially during the cold and snowy winter evenings. They also helped the teacher in the task of teaching.

Reb Itzi-Zalman was a natural teacher. His soft, pleasant character, his patience and his pedagogic talent endeared him to the parents and students. When a three-year-old child was brought to him, afraid and tense, Reb Itzi would caress and embrace him, seat him on his lap, and ask him his name and his parents' names. When the child calmed down, he showed him the framed Aleph Beit board and pointed to the Aleph with a wooden pointer designed for that purpose -- a pole with two points. As he would do this, candies would begin to fall into the child's lap from the top of the board. The child would be happy, and the Rebbe would explain that the candies were a gift from the good angel. He was promised an abundance of candies if he would be diligent in his studies.

During the winter, the students were in the *cheder* until the evening. During the summer, however, they were dismissed in the afternoon, but not before they recited the *Mincha* service. In the *cheder* of Zelik the Limper, they studied prayer and *chumash*. He was an exacting person who was prone to anger. The strap did not leave his hand as a reminder of punishment, even though he never actually used it other than to hit the table when his anger overcame him. I remember during the days of the summer, when I sat in the stifling cheder with another ten children, who were just as tired and bored as I was. We repeated our Torah verses with Yiddish translation to the Rebbe, to the buzzing of flies. Other teachers such as Reb Zelik the Upright, to differentiate him from Zelik the Limper, who was also the second prayer leader in the Great Synagogue; Reb Nachum, and Reb Yisrael the Teacher, each according to his character and custom, disseminated Torah to the children of Ratno. The students called Reb Yisrael the "swan" on account of his long neck. On Thursdays, the examination day of the *cheder* students, each child who failed the test would be put in a corner with a broom in his hand. His friends would wish him *Mazal Tov* on their way home. He also taught them the craft of writing, at first with a piece of coal on a white board. Later, after they mastered the craft, he had them copy business letters, with a large, curly *B"H*[14] at the top.

Once a year, when we reached the Torah portion of *Tetzaveh*, that deals with the clothing of the High Priest, our serious teacher would soften and perform some tricks. He would cut a breastplate, priestly vest and head plate, fill all of the squares of the breastplate with the signs of the twelve tribes, wear the head plate on his head and the breastplate and vest on his chest, in order to appear to us as the High Priest.

Reb Natan was the greatest and most praiseworthy of the teachers. He taught *Talmud* and commentaries to only three or four students. When he was pleased with the answer of one of his students, he would knock his head with his middle finger. Every student who experienced this felt as if he had been touched by the king's scepter. Every morning, one of his students would come one hour early to the house of the rebbe, set up the urn and spread a few pieces from the heap of sugar in order to sweeten the tea. For this, the student merited to drink a glass of tea with his rebbe and recite the *Shacharit* service in his presence.

There were also several "*cheders*" for girls in the town, where they learned how to recite the prayers from the *Siddur* (prayer book), as well as the craft of writing. One of the teachers in these "*cheders*" was Reb Moshe David, who was known by his nickname "*Shema Koleinu*". He was a straightforward man, quiet as a stone. Perhaps it was for this reason that he was admired by the girls. Completely different from this was Reb Yehoshua-Zalman, who loved mirth and speaking. He served as the live post office of the town. Since he did not teach in his own *cheder*, but rather gave lessons to girls in their own homes, he would spread every piece of news and rumor from house to house. He had another quality -- he loved to sing and dance. He would enter the homes of his students singing the songs of the times, and dancing with all his might.

The Beginnings of Independent Organization in the Town

In Ratno, the mayor was elected at a citizens gathering that took place in the Beis Midrash. Representatives of the local government also came to the meeting, and they kept their hats on out of respect for the sanctity of the place. The elections were public, and the candidate won or lost through shouts of "agree", or "disagree", which were heard from the throats of several drunks who were hired for this purpose from the outset. Nevertheless, there was already a hint to progressiveness in this.

The civic government issued passports and collected the state taxes as well as the special community taxes, such as the tax for kosher meat and Sabbath candles. The rights to kosher slaughter, called "taksa" were issued by lease. Reb Yisrael Bergel was the lessee of the "taksa" for many years. More than once, they would confiscate the bedding or other household implements of a poor Jew who was not able to pay his taxes. Anyone who had a complaint or a request would come to Reb Fishel Held, who served as the secretary of Jewish affairs in the local government. The local government also employed a Jewish policeman. Among his other tasks, the policeman had to bring the tax requisitions and summon those who were delinquent in payment to the government offices. Leizer the Policeman, a tall man who never let his thick stick from his hands, imposed his fear upon all the children of the town. After he died, his place was taken by Feivel, who had pleasant mannerisms, spoke Yiddish spiced with Russian, and rolled his R's like the Russians -- habits that he picked up during his long years in the Russian army. He was one of those who was snatched to the army in his childhood. He withstood all of the physical and spiritual difficulties, was freed after 25 years, and returned to his hometown.

Reb Shmuel Toler, a tall, fat Jew, was elected to the office of mayor several times. At the beginning of the 20th century, Reb Shmuel Marder was elected to this position. In return for his efforts, he was given the yeast monopoly.

The Russian Revolution of 1905 and the Spread of Enlightenment and Nationalism

After the defeat of Russia in the war with Japan, all types of underground Socialist activity proliferated. Large strikes in the manufacturing and communication sectors broke out, and acts of terror increased. The demand for freedom of expression forced the Czar to submit to the demands of parts of the community to convene a "Duma", and it seemed that the Messianic era had arrived -- but not for long. The reactionism increased, a great deal of blood was spilled throughout the breadths of Russia, persecutions and imprisonment became a daily occurrence, and even reached Brisk. We found out about the disturbances in Brisk from the refugees, former Ratno residents, who came to us from there in order to find a temporary refuge. The few members of the Bund who convened meetings in secret places and conducted publicity for their ideas suddenly disappeared from town. The eccentric teacher of girls, Yehoshua-Zalman, went from house to house with his large boots and Hassidic *kapote*, clapping his hands, dancing and singing, "Funia (Russia) Funia the Thief", or "Only today he was a shoemaker and see, today he is already a minister!"

Changes also took place in town. The pioneers who went before the camp were several enthusiastic, intelligent youths such as Yehoshua Pogatch, Zalman Burstein, Avrahamcha Telson, Idel Matis, and especially David Finkelstein who was a great expert in the Hebrew language, and published literary articles and stories in Hatzefira and Hamelitz. Two honorable Jews, a father and son who were crazy about the idea, joined these youths -- Reb Wolf-Leib Kahn and his son Shlomo-Michel. They subscribed to Hebrew newspapers as well as to the Der Freint (The Friend) newspaper that was published at that time in Peterburg. They began to teach Hebrew to the boys and girls, and to preach the love of Zion. During those days, news of the Bilu members who revolted against the way of life of the Diaspora and made *aliya* to the Land of Israel reached the town.

The youths began to found a modern *cheder* in the town. They brought in a Zionist preacher who explained the problems of the Jewish nation within the community. However, all of these attempts met the opposition of the extremist Hassidim, headed by the Hassidim of Stolin, who closed the modern cheder and expelled the lecturer in disgrace.

However, the historical processes did not stop. The times were crazy. The revolution of 1905 was immersed in the blood of Jews. Revolutionaries and their supporters from all strata of the population were imprisoned and sent to exile by the thousands. Young Jews who dedicated themselves with heart and soul to the ideas of the revolution fell into disappointment and despair. Some of them even became involved with nihilistic philosophy. There were also those who returned to their original source -- to Judaism and to the dream of Zionist redemption. Some of these youths reached Ratno and stirred up the town. I will mention here some of the most prominent of them: the Extern Zaslavsky, an eccentric youth, happy and good hearted, whose full beard and disheveled appearance won over converts to vegetarianism; Levin from Brisk whose tongue did not rest even for a moment, and who was an expert chess player; Perlstein from Grodno, who was an expert in the mysteries of the Hebrew Language; Avramcha Telso, who was a superb teacher of literature and the Hebrew Language. Several female gymnasium students, who had interrupted their studies on account of the pressures of the times, joined them: Roza Gurewich, Milrad and Roza Blak of Brisk, Fania Zilberstein, and Mania Aharonson.

These youths, some of them enthusiastic people of action and others endearing eccentrics, shook up the life in the town. They penetrated the homes of the important householders and taught their students Hebrew and Russian. Circles were formed in which the youth of Ratno would gather for discussions, clarifications and parties. They were even so daring as to appear before the Great Synagogue with boxes of the Jewish National Fund, at weddings and circumcisions. Once people became accustomed to seeing them, they donated to these boxes as well.

Reb Meir-Shmuel Marder,
the veteran Jewish "Starosta"

Two pharmacists who settled in the town were an important boost to the *maskilim* of the town. The first was Orimland, a young *maskil* who opened a pharmacy in the house of Velvel Gleizer. The second, Balstichki, opened a pharmacy in the house of Yehoshua Chayat. Balstichki did not belong at all to the Zionist camp when he came to us. He was a Hassid who was involved in Russian culture. He spoke a literary, rich Yiddish. However, he became an enthusiastic Zionist due to the influence of his surroundings. The dentist Goldina, who came from Vilna and married Balstichki, joined them; as did the pharmacist Mogeleinski, who purchased Orimland's pharmacy. The youths of Ratno would gather in these houses, which became centers of serious life of the spirit.

The town also had a sufficiently ample library. The founder of the library was Avraham Ides, a youth of the intelligentsia, who was later murdered by the Poles. During those days, the Shtibel publication began, which assisted the library with easier conditions. Avraham Ides was among the first who ordered published books for his own use. However, with the passage of time, he began to lend his books to everyone who asked, which laid the foundation of the library. The thirst for reading among the youth was unquenchable. They were no longer satisfied with the Hatzefira and Hamelitz newspapers that were disseminated in town. After some years, he sold the library to Itzel Shpilman, who had a store that sold writing implements and textbooks. Shpilman added on and purchased books for his store in Hebrew and Russian, until it became a library fitting of its name. Booksellers would visit even before the founding of the library, as well as after. They would bring holy books for sale, spreading them out on a side table in the large Beis Midrash: *Siddurs*, *chumashes*, Psalm books, *Machzors* (Holiday prayer books), *Kinot* (*Tisha Beav* prayer books), and the like. Among the holy books, hidden from the eyes of the zealots, would also be "impure books" -- story books and novels in Yiddish -- which had many purchasers. Girls and even married women purchased them in order to read them on Sabbaths and festivals, and to walk with their imaginations in the enchanted castles of princes and princesses. Even those who frequented the Beis Midrash demanded such books, hiding them under their *Gemara* and reading them stealthily. Even Moshe-David, the teacher of girls, purchased them and lent them to his students.

Years of Economic Depression, Emigration, and the First World War

The disturbances throughout Russia, the anti-Semitic incitement and pogroms, the economic situation that was becoming progressively more serious, and finally the Beilis case, befouled the atmosphere. An immense wave of emigration overtook Russian Jewry. Thousands of families left the vale of killing and set out for the lands of the west, for the United States and Canada. Echoes of these events also reached us, and many of the best of the Jews of our town packed their few belongings and set out on their journey. The number of residents declined, and with their departure, the economic and spiritual activities in the town were affected.

Then the war which nobody anticipated came. An Austrian duke was murdered in Sarajevo -- and there was war.

War was declared on the Sabbath of Tisha Beav, 1914. Draft signs were posted throughout town, and for the first time in the annals of the town, the Jews were required by government edict to open their stores on the Sabbath. Another edict commanded the Jews to give over all of their copper utensils to the government. Women wept bitterly when they were forced to part from their utensils that were passed down from mother to daughter.

After a few months, after many victims had fallen in the battlefield, an edict was issued to dig pits and erect wire fences.

In the meantime, the Russians poured out their anger over their defeat on the Jews. Wilkomirski and Shimon Shindelmacher were deported to Pinsk as a sort of pledge. Reb Chaim the teacher was snatched in the middle of the street and sent to somewhere in Russia. Only after the war did his family hear from a rabbi in Tashkent, who made it clear to them that their father had died there, alone and in complete want. Nevertheless, these persecutions were only like a mosquito bite in comparison to the tribulations that were awaiting the town with the retreat of the Russians.

The town marketplace

When the Russians retreated, the farmers of the eastern areas set out along with their families and livestock, including geese, cattle and pigs. The sounds of the cackling, mooing and snorting filled the fearful town. As this living stream passed through Ratno, the Russian Army set the town on fire from all four sides. The flames quickly engulfed all of the houses of the Jews. People sought refuge for as long as they could. They did not go far off like the farmers, but rather set up camps in the meadows outside the city. There they lay down sorrowfully, weeping over their lives and their bitter lot. Through the weeping, lamenting, pain and anguish, they dozed off until they were awakened to the sound of terrible screaming. When they calmed down somewhat, it became clear that the German soldiers who had arrived in the interim had attempted to rape women during their sleep, and even confiscated the wagons and horses. Thus, in the darkness of the night, the German saviors turned into thieves and rapists. The disappointment was great and bitter.

During the Time of the German Occupation

In the morning, the Jews returned to the burnt town and shuddered at the sight of terrible destruction. Flames still popped out here and there from the heaps of cinders, and several chimneys sticking out of the ruined houses silently testified to the disaster. The refugees were housed in several houses that remained, with several families in each house. The crowding was great, but the fear of the coming day was even greater. This was on Friday, and the next day, the German "guests" already came and requested with great politeness, with the guns and bayonets cocked in a ready position, that they take their axes and spades and go out to work in fixing the bridges that the Russians destroyed during their retreat.

In general, there was no shortage of work with the Germans: today bridges; the next day, paths and roads. Work materials such as bricks and mortar were found everywhere. There was a great deal of work on the railway line from Ratno to Kamin-Kashirsk. This railway line was laid in haste. The base of earth was not prepared properly, and the ties were shaky. The Jews were therefore called from time to time to fill earth beneath the ties. "Fill! Fill!" shouted the Germans. They were urged on further with a stick over their backs.

From time to time, the Germans would hunt the Jews. Once, on a Sabbath toward evening, a rumor passed through town that the Germans were about to enlist Jews for work in the railway station in Malorita. People began to run through the town as Jews sought hiding places, some in attics, some in cellars, and even some in the tanning building across the river. The Germans chased after them with their weapons, running and shouting "Stop! The thunder should strike you! Stop!" Of course, Jews were taken out from their hiding places and brought to the railway station, where they were forced to load wooden ties on the transport wagons. They did not receive payment or food for their work. The Jews sat in groups after their work and cooked a soup on stoves of twigs. Some of them had never held a pot in their hands before, but they had to eat after the hard work -- especially those who were never engaged in manual labor before.

Another time, the Germans decreed a cleanup action, and dragged the Jews to the bathhouse. The fear of typhus came over them, and they suspected that all the Jews were contaminated. The Jews regarded this as an edict and did whatever they could to get out of it.

However, the necessities of living were stronger than anything, and already several astute and clever Jews, who obtained travel permits and crossed the border to Austria, shuffled about and brought merchandise to the town. The rumor that there was a possibility of crossing the border began to spread, and the number of Jews who received papers from the commanders increased. The Germans did not refuse strongly, especially since there was a reward for their work, for the bribes were effective with them -- fox furs, eggs, butter. They did not reject any gift. The mayor, Eliahu Janowich, even arranged the affairs by giving the commander set percentages of his profits. It seems that all of the Jews in the town tried their hands at the smuggling business. Even the teachers and craftsmen worked in barter and exchange. They did business in horses, cattle and sheep. Some even traveled afar and reached Rostov on the Don, bringing full wagon loads of tobacco and other merchandise. Others came from near and far, and the town was astir.

When the war finished, it became clear that not all of the Jews of Ratno had become accustomed to the conditions of war. Many families who did not have the talents of the smugglers literally starved for bread. The Joint[15] was literally a saving angel for them.

Wagons loaded with sacks of flour and other foodstuff such as oil, sugar, preserved milk and the like, and later also various articles of clothing appeared in the town under the auspices of the Joint. The Joint opened up a kitchen for the needy in the Beis Midrash. At its entrance, one could see destitute Jews standing with their dishes in their hands. The noble, dedicated woman Beila Itzikson concerned herself and took care of the kitchen. The assistance and salvation effort was conducted by Reb Ben-Zion Steingarten, and was assisted by Israel Weinstock, Mottel Ginzburg, Yosef Zisik, Pesach Steinberg, Noach Cohen, Yitzchak Kozak and Leizer Rajsky. Later, they were joined by Binyamin Kamfer, Yitzchak-Hirsch Rog, Reb Yaakov Mendelson and Yoska Bayon.

The Jews who immigrated to America before the war also hastened to help their relatives by means of various delegates. Yaakov Plotzker was such a delegate. He came from America to fetch his son, who remained in the town. He brought with him 6,000 dollars to distribute among the residents of the town by a list that was in his hand. I, who is recording these things, was chosen as a "trustee" for this distribution, but Reb Yaakov Plotzker was unable to come to town because of the battles between the Poles and the Bolsheviks that were taking place at that time in the region, and was held up in Brisk. The situation was salvaged by two woman who volunteered to travel to him. These were my sister, Eltzi-Feiga, and Plata-Leah the tailor. They took the child with them, and when they returned, they brought the monetary donations to the town.

When the battles abated, many orphans were transferred to America and Canada, where they were adopted by wealthy Jewish families. Several orphans set out to those places from Ratno as well. However, many of them remained in the town. A great deal of activity was conducted on their behalf. The committee for the orphans in the district of Kowel, headed by Dr. Czernowicz and Mrs. Reitza Lewin, opened a school for them in the home of Wilkomirski, where Noach Cohen taught. An orphanage was set up not far from the town. Members of the committee in Ratno included Moshe Reicher, Mendel Blatt, Yankel Liberman, Yitzchak-Hirsch Held, and Leibel Baion.

After the Russian Revolution, the government passed to the Social Democratic Party headed by Kransky. This was an era of rebirth in the world, but along with this was also an era of chaos and confusion regarding borders and boundaries. Ratno and its area was captured by bands of Ukrainians headed by Hetman Skoropodsky. His soldiers did not actually enter the town itself, but the atmosphere was full of fear, and everyone felt fear on the horizon.

In the town, a group of youth organized themselves for self-defense. They gathered on Holijanka Street in the field next to Chamiliar's house, and practiced with weapons. After some time, when the government changed and the danger of pogroms increased, the youths went out on guard duty and did their best to protect lives and property.

During that era of blurring of borders between governments, illegal smuggling and business once again spread in town. The Jews hauled any type of merchandise that came to their hands, and gathered heaps of Ukrainian Karbovanets (units of currency), which turned into valueless pieces of colored paper after Pilsudski, at the head of his army, beat the Ukrainians soundly.

A Jew holding up a cup of wine over a dead gentile

Translator's note, this is a reference to the Passover Seder -- In every generation and generation, they arise against us to destroy us, but the Holy One Blessed Be He saves us from their hands

Translator's Footnotes

2. A term for a person who delves very deeply into Torah.
3. The Torah portion of *Behaalotecha* begins with the injunction of the building of the *menora* in the temple.
4. Pirke Avot (Tractate of the Fathers) 4:17.
5. Psalm 150.
6. Mystical animals of the future eschatological era.
7. A Jewish legal device that converts an open area into a private domain, thereby permitting carrying on the Sabbath. See http://en.wikipedia.org/wiki/Eruv.
8. A prayer response.
9. This implies that the morning service was repeated over and over again at different times for different groups of worshippersz.
10. The term '*selichot*' here seems out of place, as it refers to the special prayer books used for the penitential prayers starting a week before Rosh Hashanah and running every weekday morning until the eve of Yom Kippur. They are not used on the Sabbath. I suspect that this is an error here, and the author meant to say '*tallises*'.
11. The term used here is '*shkotzim*', which is a derogatory term for gentiles.
12. I.e. He would be given the choicest *aliya* to the Torah.
13. See http://en.wikipedia.org/wiki/Joseph_Trumpeldor.
14. The acronym for "Blessed is G-d", often placed atop correspondence.
15. The Joint Distribution Committee. See http://en.wikipedia.org/wiki/American_Jewish_Joint_Distribution_Committee.

Municipal and Social Institutions

A bank of commerce was founded in the city already in 1912. One of the founders, in whose house the bank was housed, was Berl Rajsky. The second was Moshe Eilbaum. The bank treasury was composed of shares that were sold to merchants, and from the grants and loans from the national bank. The bank was an important factor in commercial and trade life in the town, and came to the assistance of small-scale merchants. The bank ceased its activities during the war. Only in 1921, under Polish rule, was a new bank founded in Ratno. This time it was called the People's Bank. It was one of 300 cooperative banks centered in Warsaw, with branches throughout Congress Poland.

The first president of the bank was the important citizen Mottel Tiktiner. Later, Moshe Eilbaum served in that role. Yitzchak-Hirsch Held, a young Maskil and true lover of Zion, was appointed as the bank director, a position that he held until the Holocaust. The mathematician Yaakov-Chaim Markuza was the treasurer, and Itzel Karsh and Yisrael Chayat (who survived the Holocaust and arrived in the Land) were the secretaries. The merchants and tradesman, who were members of the bank and who each had to purchase a share of approximately 100 zloty, sent delegates to the committee. These representatives established the size of the loans, and stormy debates broke out among themselves regarding this matter. Here is the place to note the names of several of them: A. Berg, M. Blatt, Y. Kanfer, Abba Fuchs, Yisrael-Yaakov Chayat, M. Shuster, as well as the writer of these lines.

The civilian arm -- the town council -- began to operate in 1924-1925. The mayor was appointed by the government, but the rest of the members of the town council were elected by the Jewish, Ukrainian and Polish citizens; for despite the economic and political persecution, the right of democratic representation was retained in Poland. Since the Jews formed the majority of the population of the town, they were given the vice-mayorship and the right to elect five representatives to the town council. During that time, Mendel Klein served as the vice-mayor, and our representatives were Yisrael-Itzi Baion, Yitzchak Marsik, Yitzchak Grabov and Wolf Brener. Our elected representatives regarded their job as a national mission, and always demonstrated dedication, faithfulness and great skill in protecting the interests of the Jewish citizens of the town.

During the years 1936-1939, when the anti-Semitic agitation was at its peak, the rights of the Jews in Ratno were also restricted. The right of the vice-mayorship was removed from them, and the number of representatives were reduced from five to three. However, the Jews succeeded even then, albeit after a prolonged battle, to maintain representation in the house of representatives of the Kowel district, which numbered 32 members. Our representative, Yitzchak-Hirsch Held, was the only Jew in this house, but his voice was heard loudly, and his speeches in Polish left a great impression and were published in the "Koweler Shtime" and "Glos Kowla" (Voice of Kowel) newspapers.

With the new developments that began in the lives of the Jews, unique Jewish problems came up in the realm of religion, society and livelihood, demanding novel solutions. For this purpose, a communal structure was founded in 1929. The communal leadership was elected for three years and composed of eight members and a president. Ben-Zion Steingarten was elected as president, and the members were Reb Yitzchak Cohen, Liber Karsh, Yitzchak Grabov, and others. The president of the second cadence was Liber Karsh.

The community was recognized by the government and even given the permission to be assisted by the police. Many of the members of the communal council were appointed as members of the Judenrat during the Holocaust period.

For the needs of the community, a special levy was imposed upon all the Jews of the town and its environs, including the town of Wierzba. The secretary of the community, Aharon-Yankel Ginzburg, would make the rounds to all the settlements in order to arrange their affairs and collect the levy.

The Revival of Culture and the Natural Movement in the Town

Despite the political, social and economic persecution, and despite the disparagement and the persecutions, of which the Jews were victims in all places in Poland, it was specifically at that time that the cultural and spiritual life began to flourish throughout the Jewish nation. The Jews felt as if within the stormy era of breaches, deep wells had suddenly been opened that flowed with bounty and overflowed the banks. Youthful, pleasant forces grew within the nation, causing a flow of new blood through the arteries of culture and spiritual creativity. Waves of innovation came to the town as well, and left their imprint on all areas of life.

Bottom row (from right to left): *Reb Fuchs-Shapira (perished), Y. Chayat, P Yunevitz.*
Second row: *unidentified, Nota Roizkes (perished), P. Droog of blessed memory.*
Top row: *A. Y. Ginzburg (perished), P. Marin, L. Shapira.*

The founding pillars of this renaissance were the schools. Even before the war, during the years 1912-1913, the cornerstone of modern education was laid in the town. The teachers would teach their children in the house of one of the students or the teachers. The students sat on benches around a large table and would listen to the teacher's class, which would last an hour or two. The class included the writing of business or personal letters, and Russian at the tip of a fork -- the Russian alphabet, writing of addresses, and the like. On Thursdays, the class was dedicated to arithmetic, focusing on the four operations.

Avraham Telson, one of the first teachers and Maskilim

During those years, a young professional teacher named L. Wahl, arrived in Ratno from Liubsiai, Lithuania. He rented a well-lit room, prepared tables for the students and even hung a board on the wall. According to all opinions, his school was the first of the Hebrew schools. He had few students, but this was a certain beginning. A year later, a true school teaching Hebrew, Yiddish, and Russian opened in the town. The teachers were Avramche Telson, the writer of these lines, and the student Nina Gwirtzman.

In 1916, Noach Kotzker came to us from Minsk. He was an excellent teacher in Hebrew language and literature, and a gifted orator. With him, a new era in teaching and cultural activity began.

After the world war, still during the time of Ukrainian rule, the school of the Hassidim of Trisk that that was housed in the Shtibel moved to its own large house on Holijanka Street. Kotzler would lecture before audiences in that house on Sabbaths and festivals with enthusiastic orations demonstrating wide knowledge on many topics. As a result of his activities, Zionist activities increased, and the idea of the Jewish National Fund penetrated to almost every home. During that era, after the Balfour Declaration, a representative of the Jewish National Fund arrived from Warsaw and called a meeting for the establishment of Keren Hayesod. Even the sworn opponents of Zionism such as Reb Ben-Zion Steingarten, David-Aharon Shapira, Yaakov Pressman and Liber Karsh came to this meeting. Of course, the Zionists were the first to sign on. The meeting took place in the house of Mrs. Doba Cohen.

When the Beis Midrash was rebuilt atop its ruins, the school moved to the balcony of the house. Its number of students grew, and the number of teachers grew to four: Kotzker, Wiskovsky, Hertzman and Cohen. The Poles disrupted the work of the school and almost succeeded in closing it definitively. Only through great efforts, did some of the youths of the region receive a permit to open an integral school named Tarbut, which taught in both Hebrew and Polish. The Tarbut School opened in 1926, and, at the end, had approximately 200 students in seven grades. The teachers Kotzker, Bokser, and Zagorski taught Hebrew, and the principal Riva taught Polish. Eliezer Held served as the secretary of the school, who through her great dedication gave a great deal for the development of the institution.

The Library and Youth Organizations

The library of Shpilman burnt down during the terrifying days of the first year of the war. After the war, a small library for the students was opened. During the 1920s, Noach Cohen, Yaakov Rog and Velvel Rajsky founded the scouting organization in the town. In addition to the ordinary national sporting activities, the scouts began to found their own library. The scouts went from house to house, collecting donations of books from the householders. They also organized various activities, such as the sale of flowers at the fairs, and the like. Eliezer Rajsky, who used to travel to Warsaw for business purposes, would bring several bundles of Yiddish and Hebrew books. Thus, the foundations of the central library was laid with the assistance of many donors. The library was housed in the house of Yaakov Avrech on Krywa Street. The teachers of the town lectured there about various topics to the young readers. After some time, the students' library joined the central library, and the number of readers grew. The library activists, Shlomo

Avrech and Berl Ides, carpenters by profession, obtained boards from various householders and built shelves for the books, and tables and desks for the readers who came to read the books. After some time, the library grew, and Avrech's house was too small to hold it. The library moved to a large room in the house of Eliezer Fuchs on Holijanka Street, not far from the bridge. Debates, discussions and lectures took place there, and were even brought in from the large cities.

Among the piles of straw and hay

A drama club, which performed several interesting performances, existed under the auspices of the library.

During the late 1920s, meeting places for youth already existed under the auspices of the various parties. The youth would gather together in these places during the evenings to listen to lectures and presentations and to participate in debates. The town literally bustled like a hive. At times, debates between the different groups were organized, reaching at times to the point of fist fights. The battle for hegemony between the Beitar and Shomer groups was especially interesting. These two organizations battled with all their might for the soul of the youth. The uniforms, wooden swords and impressive military gait of the Beitar people attracted the hearts of the youth, and their anthem, "With the might of the arm and weapons, we will liberate the homeland!," was on all lips. To the dismay of the Beitar men, the girls turned their backs on them. Their hearts were not attracted by the military ceremonies, and they preferred Hashomer. Therefore, the Shomer attracted the majority and the best of the youth.

I recall the scandal that broke out in the town during the several-day excursion to the areas around the town that organized by Hashomer. The parents, especially the parents of the girls, opposed this and protested against Hashomer and its counselors. Can it really be, they complained, that the girls will spend days and nights together with the boys without adult supervision? A battle between parents and children broke out in every house. Finally, the children won, and they went out on the excursion despite the ban.

The Hashomer youth were especially active during the elections for the Zionist congress, but they were unable to vote due to their age. However, they did everything to ensure that their parents would purchase shekels[16] and vote in accordance to the political leanings of the children.

WIZO (Women's International Zionist Organization) also set up a headquarters and did a great deal to encourage the activities of its members. The first president was the prominent woman Gitel Karsh. Tzvi Kotzker was the secretary and Rachel Eilbaum was the treasurer. The menders of rank were Breindel Gasko, Merida Perlmutter, Suska Zizok, Sheindel Zisok, Rachel Held, and Gitel Konishter. The WIZO organization did a great deal on behalf of the efforts of the Zionist organization and provided important support, including financial, to the Tarbut School. Rozman, Kotzker and Lewin, teachers of the Tarbut School, gave speeches on the role of WIZO. Meetings took place every Sabbath in the large, well-lit hall of the Tarbut School. The activities of the organization were many, and everyone who came into contact with these dear women sensed the strong pulse of nationalism as well as warm humanity that beat within them. Many of the Zionist youth went out to *Hachshara* camps. Fine parties were organized for the youth who set out for the Land of Israel. They were sent off with copious blessings.

The description of life in the town would not be complete if we did not mention the small group of youth who separated from the Zionist organizations. These youths, who went astray in ideological complexity, finally joined the extreme left which opposed the unique existence of the Jewish nation and claimed that the Communist revolution would bring a full solution to the Jewish problem. This group also opened a school that served its ideology; however, due to the Zionist winds that were dominant in Ratno, as well as the opposition of the government, it did not last long.

The Eve of the World War and Destruction of the Town

During the last years, rapid development took place in the town. A new road was paved through the marshes, through which the residents would trample during the autumn and the spring. An important citizen, Mottel Klein, bought in a very powerful electric dynamo that provided electricity for the entire town. Many of the householders lit up their houses with electric light. The town itself installed several electric lamps on the streets.

However, the economic situation in the town became more precarious, and the number of people requiring assistance continually grew. Various agencies were involved with the salvation activities. The People's Bank did a great deal to continue the economic activities. Many donations were distributed amongst the residents, and the charitable fund distributed interest free loans to the poor. However, these conditions not only pervaded in Ratno. The situation of the Jews throughout all of Poland deteriorated rapidly. The government tightened the pressure and aggravated the means of pressure. The Polish hooligans showed their true face in Przytyk, Czestochowa, Brisk, and many other places. The Jews felt as if the earth was burning under their feet.

Tidings of Job also arrived from the world at large, and the news of the agreement that was signed between Russia and Germany literally froze the blood. The Jews saw the thickening clouds and their historical sense told them that they would be the scapegoat.

Reb Fishel Held

One of the interesting personalities was Rev Fishel Held, or as they used to call him, Fishel Sara-Leah's. He was a scholar who was gifted with a phenomenal memory, like the walking encyclopedia of Ratno. During the Czarist era, he served as an assistant to the local government appointed rabbi, whose seat was in Kowel. Birth certificates, marriage certificates and death certificates were all in Reb Fishel's domain. He was expert in everything that took place in Ratno during the eras, and anyone who needed any information about yahrzeits, birthdays, or the like knew that there was an authoritative address for such -- Reb Fishel. He was a lean, weak man, hunchbacked with a small gray beard and dreamy eyes. He wore a long Hassidic *kapote* and a Hassidic hat. He was expert in all the laws during the Czarist rule. After Ratno transferred to the Poles, he purchased a Polish-Russian dictionary and easily became accustomed to the new regime with its rules. In the book on Ratno that was published in Argentina, Y. Konishter wrote that he was an enthusiastic Trisker Hassid; but his son, Eliezer, claims that he was not a Hassid at all, but rather that he revered Reb Yitzchak Ber Levinson (known by the acronym Riba"l), one of the leaders of Haskala literature, quoted him at every opportunity, and even had his picture displayed in an honorable place in his home.

A "mizrach" poster

He related to his official role with full seriousness, and was stringent with the law. However, along with this, he was a sentimental type, who had mercy on every human being. The crying of a baby would bring him to emotionalism. He would verbally attack those youths who did not hesitate to physically maim certain of their limbs in order to get out of army service. When the First World War broke out and many Jews of the town awaited the arrival of the Germans as if literally the Messiah, Reb Fishel was the only Jew in town who hoped for a Russian victory. He fulfilled that which is said, "One should pray for the welfare of the government." During all the debates that took place in the town marketplace of the shtibel, he strongly defended the Russian stance and claimed that the Jews were in for tribulations from the Germans.

Fishel Held and his family

His house was open wide to people who came to take counsel with him on various matters, in particular to those who needed to write requests to the official authorities. One could hear various stories from Reb Fishel about the history of Ratno, and he even wrote a booklet in Hebrew on this topic, which was translated into Yiddish by one of the youths of the town, Ginzburg. (Some sections of that booklet are published in this book.) On Tisha Beav, when the residents of Ratno would visit the old cemetery in accordance with custom, Reb Fishel would go at the head and tell stories about the deceased. His words aroused great interest among the youth, who thereby made some sort of connection with the past of their town.

He had three sons, Berl, Yitzchak Hirsch and Eliezer. The first two perished along with him during the Holocaust. The third, may he live long, made *aliya* to the Land of Israel as a pioneer (*chalutz*) of the General Zionists at the beginning of the 1930s. His son Berl continued the work of his father, also wrote requests to the court, and had a command of the Polish and Russian languages.

Translator's Footnote

16. The token of membership in the Zionist Movement.

A Polish Independence Day celebration

Hebrew Schools on the Eve of the First World War

by Leibel Wahl, New York

Translated by Jerrold Landau

I came to Ratno in 1913 from my small town, Liubsiai, close to the Passover holiday. My aim was to set up a modern cheder in that town, which would teach holy subjects as well as Hebrew and grammar. I got off the train at the closest stop to Ratno, Zabolottya, but I did not find any wagon driver who transported the travelers from the train station to the town. However, I succeeded in finding the train wagon that carried the mail to and from Ratno, and the mailman agreed to take me to the town. He brought me to the home of Necha Ginzburg, who owned the store as well as several rooms that served as guest rooms for Christian visitors who would come in from the region. The son of this Necha, Mottel Ginzburg, was the first to engage me in conversation. He was a happy, pleasant youth. When he found out that I was a teacher and had come in order to open a Hebrew school, he became very enthusiastic, but he saw the need to warn me that difficult work was awaiting me, for the parents were accustomed to sending their children to the melamdim (traditional teachers) throughout the entire day, and that the innovation that I was intending to institute -- a 5-6 hour teaching day -- would not be willingly accepted. Mottel continued to explain to me that, aside from this, a battle was awaiting me with the melamdim and teachers who were already in the town, for I was intending to encroach on their livelihoods. I explained to him that I would need a teacher or two for the school that I was planning, and perhaps even one melamed. In addition to this, I intended to charge no less than 15 rubles per semester for each student, and only the children of the wealthy people would be able to afford such.

Mottel introduced me to a young teacher in the town, Yudel Konishter, who I liked at first sight, for I saw that he had the character of an intelligent Maskil whose roots had been forged in the Beis Midrash, as was usual in those days. I told this teacher about my plans, and immediately offered him to be my partner. This teacher hesitated at first for fear of failure, but after I continued the discussion with the details of the plan and proved to him that this would not harm any person, he accepted my offer of partnership. Later, Mottel brought me to the home of Reb Avraham-Eliezer Rozman, who owned the guesthouse for outside guests. I was put up there. My first step was to produce posters about the intended school and post them in all the synagogues of the town. As expected, these posters aroused many echoes, and the town was in ferment. The melamdim opened up with the first attack, as they declared in public that a "Litvak" has arrived in town who may, Heaven forbid, lead the children to apostasy. To my luck, my host Reb Avraham-Eliezer, himself a Hassid of Stolin was daring enough to testify that he saw with his own eyes that I put on tefillin and ate with a head covering. This testimony softened the attack against me, especially once people saw me worshipping in the Shtibel on the Sabbath.

On Sunday, I went out along with Yudel Konishter to the areas around the town in order to register students for the new school. We registered 40 children within two days, which by all opinions was a great success. We also rented a large, pleasant room, and ordered appropriate furniture for the school from one of the carpenters. Very satisfied with my achievements, I returned to my town for the Passover holiday. I was very surprised, however, when I received a telegram from Mottel Ginzburg just on the eve of Passover, that I must come to Ratno immediately. I began to be suspicious of the fate of my entire enterprise, and I was already in Ratno on the first Intermediate Day of Passover. It quickly became apparent to me that the melamdim in town had succeeded in convincing Yudel Konishter to break his partnership with me. They even made him understand that they were preparing to "deal with" that "Litvak" (i.e. me) in a way that would knock sense into me and warn others against attempting to open a modern school in Ratno. I took into account the "refined" situation of my partner and advised him to stand at the side and not become involved in the matter at all, while I would conduct the battle myself.

Mottel Ginzburg and one of the important householders in the town, Reb Binyamin Kamfer, were enlisted to assist me. Along with them, I visited once again the parents of the children who had been registered for the school and spoke sincerely to them, telling them that they would not be disappointed. Our joint efforts succeeded. I opened the school, I also hired the melamed Reb Nota Shapira, I brought a Russian Language teacher from Brisk, and we began to teach.

Results were not long in coming. Within a brief time, many other parents came to register their children, and I prepared to rent two additional rooms for the needs of the school. I also held negotiations with two melamdim who accepted for themselves the duties of teaching the holy subjects. However, due to technical reasons, I was forced to abandon the expansion plans, and had to satisfy myself with accepting only 25 additional students. I added the veteran teacher of the town Avraham Telson to the teaching staff, as well as his son-in-law, the melamed from Brisk. I exchanged the teacher of Russian, replacing her with Nina Gwirtzman, who later married M. Ginzburg.

The town was small in those days, but there were already youths with nationalist feelings who were active for the funds, in the dissemination of the Zionist idea, in the organization of youth groups and book debates, etc. In the home of the pharmacist Mogilensky, a Zionist and a man of intelligence, as well as in my home, these youths would gather for discussions on current events, sport topics, and the like. We also founded a band. There was no shortage of fiddle and mandolin players in Ratno, and the girls would sing the popular songs of those day.

I recall the names of many of these youths: Henich Karsh, Leibel Shapira, Avraham and Mordechai Ides, Mottel Ginzburg, Berl Held, Baruch Hindich, Yehuda Finkelstein, the sisters Breindel and Reizel Cohen, Gittel Hindich, Perl Kaminsky, and others. I began to feel at home in the town that became dear to me, especially after luck shined its face toward me, and I got to know Gittel, the daughter of Shalom the shochet, with whom I fell in love and married. A life of happiness was awaiting me were it not for the outbreak of the First World War a short time after my marriage.

The first day of that war is etched very well in my memory. It was the Sabbath, the eve of Tisha Beav. The draft edict that was published aroused fear and terror. Husbands were separated from their wives, brides from the bridegrooms, and children from their fathers who were sent to the front. The situation in the town became very grim, and people lost their mutual trust. My first loss was the private lessons that I gave. A short time later, the number of students in the school started to decline. The situation continued to deteriorate as the front approached the town. One could hear the thunder of the cannons, and the Russian soldiers began to dig pits around the town -- a clear sign that the Germans were approaching. The school was closed, and the fear about what was awaiting the next day swept over all the residents of the town. I purchased a horse and small wagon, loaded up my wife and young child, and we traveled back to my town of Liubsiai. From that point, our period of wandering began. Here is not the place to describe this tiring period. All of the paths were blocked by war refugees. We were not able to rest in Liubsiai once we arrived there, for the Germans arrived and issued an order to evacuate the residents because the battles in the region were about to break out. I once again picked up my walking staff, and we began to wander in the direction of the town of Maciejów, where the family of my brother-in-law Yehoshua Hindich lived. There I found out that my beloved town Ratno had been destroyed completely, with only one road remaining. People from Ratno arrived in Maciejów in order to purchase flour and food provisions for the starving population. Since I had nothing to do, and I wanted to see Ratno again, I also hauled food provisions there. I was shocked when I arrived there. There were heaps of ruins, and the pillars of smoke were still rising and covering the sky. The house of my good friends Reb Avraham the shochet and his wife Doba was not burned down, and I went there. A pleasant experience awaited me in their home. At lunchtime, a young man entered and asked the head of the house if he could get some food in exchange for payment. I looked at his face, and immediately two shouts were heard, "Kotzker!", "Wahl!" as we recognized each other. We had been friends already when we were studying together in Pinsk. Kotzker remained in Ratno until the Holocaust, whereas my family and I immigrated to the United States.

Between the Two World Wars

In the Days of Bulak Balachowicz

Translated by Jerrold Landau

The years 1916-1922 form a very gloomy period in the annals of Jewish martyrology -- a period drenched in the blood of many Jews who were murdered in many villages in the vicinity of Ratno. When the Russian soldiers began to retreat from the area in 1915 in the wake of the German attack, many Russian soldiers hid in the dense forests and towns. They would often emerge from their hiding places in order to pillage the Jews who passed by on the paths, set the houses of the Jews on fire, and perpetrate acts of murder and violence to the extent that their hearts desired. The Germans and Austrians attempted to capture these hooligans and even imprisoned the farmers who gave them refuge in their houses, but they were not able to uproot these bands that benefited from the protection of the townsfolk. Another wave of disturbances and murders passed through during the years

1920-1921. These were carried out by the Balachowiczes, who were a unique unit in the Polish Army. The wave did not pass over towns like Kamin-Kashirsk, Ratno, and others such towns, as well as larger cities such as Pinsk. However, the worst came in the small villages of the regions. With this, the hooligans succeeded in completely uprooting the Jews and Jewish life.

No exact details exist about the beginnings of Jewish settlement in these villages in Wolhyn and Pulsia. However, according to testimony from various eras, one can establish that this began more than 200 years ago. The Jews arrived in these villages from the nearby towns such as Ratno, Lywona, Wierzba, and others. The factor that caused the Jews to wander to the villages was the relative poverty in the towns. In order to save themselves from the disgrace of hunger, they agreed to live in remote villages, where the majority of the residents were Christian farmers. During the early years, many Jews earned their livelihood from the taverns that they leased from the poretzes (landowners), where they sold liquor to the farmers, and where the wayfarers stopped to rest a bit and to feed their horses. There were also many Jews who opened small stores or purchased the produce of the farmers' fields to sell in the marketplace of the nearby town. Slowly, the Jews laid down roots in these villages and earned their livelihood with relative comfort, but they never severed their connections with their towns of origin. These connections were economic and cultural. They had to be present in the town for all family events, such as at weddings, circumcisions, Bar Mitzvas or funerals. Even more so, they would come for the Jewish festivals. Even though they had a minyan in the village, they preferred to be in the town for the festival along with a large multitude of Jews. Thus, they would come with their entire family before Rosh Hashanah, and remain until after Yom Kippur, as they would for other festivals.

In the latter half of the 19th century, after the liquor trade had been given over to a monopoly, many Jewish tavern keepers remained without livelihoods, but they quickly found other sources of livelihood. They were not attracted to farming. Aside from this, it was forbidden for Jews to own farmland according to Russian law. Nevertheless, Jews succeeded in circumventing the law and working at farming. However, their numbers were few. They set up a windmill and milled the grain and wheat of the farmers. They were involved with the threshing of grain for food for cattle and horses. There were some Jews who formed partnerships to purchase machines for the cleaning of wool, or to set up an oil press. With the passage of time, they broadened their business, and rented ponds for fishing from the government (in the name of a Christian). They exported the fish to Brisk[1] or Warsaw. They leased forests to utilize the cut trees for building materials. There were also Jewish craftsmen in the towns, which made things easier for the farmers who would no longer have to depend on the craftsmen in the towns. It was natural that neighborly relationships formed between the village Jews and the gentile population. Mutual contact strengthened, but the feelings of jealousy toward the Jews did not disappear. They could not understand why the status of living of the Jews was higher than theirs, despite the fact, that they toiled from morning to night in the fields with all types of hard work. The authorities also knew how to fan these feelings and how to turn the wrath of the villagers over their difficult conditions toward the Jews who "sucked their blood", "killed the messiah", etc. -- these matters are known.

The anti-Semitism of the villagers increased during the times of emergency. This was the situation during the time of war with Japan and the defeat of Russia, the 1905 revolution, the time of the Beilis trial[2] and especially the First World War when all the foundations of life and society were shaken up. The villagers repeated morning and night that the source of all their troubles and tribulations was the Jew, and it is justified to kill him.

It is therefore not surprising that the villagers granted refuge to the Russian soldiers whose hands were dirty with the blood of the Jews. They also served as guides for the Balachowiczes and collaborated with them, just as some 20 years later they collaborated with the Nazis during the Second World War.

I will note here, for testimony and remembrance, the villages around Ratno in which Jews were murdered without any intervention.

Wydranica -- a village four kilometers from the town. Approximately ten Jewish families lived in the village and worked in the cattle trade and peddling. Three Jews were murdered in this village by the Balachowiczes, including a young person from Ratno.

Glukhi (Jews used to call this village Luch) is located at the side of the road that leads to Maciejow, a distance of 5 kilometers from Ratno. The Jews worked in the raising of fish, and provided fish for the Sabbath to the Jews of Ratno. The Balachowiczes murdered two Jews in the village.

Zamshany, a village about ten kilometers from Ratno, had a population of 15-18 Jewish families. Seven or eight Jews were murdered in the villages by the Balachowiczes. It is appropriate to note that when a relative of one of the murdered people came from Ratno to bring the deceased to a Jewish burial -- they murdered him as well.

Luchich. Only two or three Jewish families lived in this village. The Balachowiczes murdered the son of one of the residents.

Birky, along the route to Kamin-Kashirsk, was populated by 10 Jewish families. The Balachowiczes murdered eight Jews of the village.

Krymne was a village 25 kilometers from Ratno. However, from the perspective of Jewish life, this was not a village but rather a town. There were approximately 70 Jewish families in Krymne, and there was a Beis Midrash, a bathhouse with a mikva, and other Jewish institutions that served not only the Jews of Krymne, but also the Jews of the surrounding villages who would go there to hear words of Torah from a preacher who happened to be there. There was also a Jewish school in the village as well as a chapter of Hechalutz. The Jews did everything in their power to maintain a Jewish way of life in the full sense of the term. Particularly strong ties existed between the Jews of Ratno and the Jews of Krymne. Often, Jews of Ratno who had difficulty with their livelihood would move to Krymne in order to find their livelihood. On the eve of Rosh Hashanah 5680 (1920), when the Balachowiczes were retreating, they murdered 60 Jews in that town. It was many years before the wounded people recovered. Many of the Jews of the town who survived the terrible slaughter left the town. Some of them moved to other cities and towns, and others emigrated from the country that considered their blood to be worthless. With the passage of time, Jewish life was reconstituted there. The youths set up a cultural center, a library, and a drama club. Youths from the nearby villages participated in all these activities.

Lubochin was a village three kilometers from Krymne. Very strong ties existed between the Jews of this village and the Jews of nearby Krymne, particularly between the Jewish young people of these two settlements. Approximately 50 Jews of this village were murdered by the Balachowicz hooligans.

Jorowicz -- this village was also close to Krymne, and nine Jewish families lived there. The village was well-known for its hosting of guests, and it was known that a Jew who would find himself there would immediately find good hosts. A 12-year-old girl was among those murdered in the village.

Dubechno. Twenty Jewish families lived in this village, which had a train station on the Kowel-Brisk line. The Jews were primarily occupied in the lumber trade. Among them there were scholars such as Reb Chaim Dubczaner and Reb Pinchas Goldman. The Balachowiczes murdered Jewish families in this village, as well as in the nearby village of Rakita.

The hooligans also indiscriminately murdered many Jews in all of the rest of the villages in the vicinity of Ratno. These villages include: Zdomyshel, Tur, Zalissia, Zabolottya, Zhyryche, Khotivel, Wielimcze, Rechitsa, Kortelesy, Sidroviche, Zalukhov, Shchityn, Hirnyky, and Szack.

This scroll of tribulation imprinted its stamp on the lives of the Jews in the region for many years. The stories of the murderous deeds and the miraculous deliverances that took place with the Jews who escaped the wrath of the hooligans never ceased, for there was barely any Jewish family who was not affected. The word "Balachowiczes" frightened not only the older people who remember well all that took place during that bloody year (1920), but also the younger children who heard about the atrocities from their parents.

The most frightening act of murder was carried out by the hooligans in Kamin-Kashirsk. Their cruelty knew no bounds. According to reliable testimony, approximately 120 people were murdered, and 220 children were left as orphans. In one piece of testimony, it is stated that when they were reckoning the number of victims to "Batka"[3], he said, "It is a bit too high, but we will arrange matters with the government somehow on this matter."

Translator's Footnotes

1. Brisk is equivalent with Brest Litovsk. https://www.jewishgen.org/Yizkor/Ratno/rat059.html - 1r
2. For information on the famous Beilis Trial, see http://en.wikipedia.org/wiki/Menahem_Mendel_Beilis. https://www.jewishgen.org/Yizkor/Ratno/rat059.html - 2r
3. "Daddy", a nickname for Bulak Balachowicz. https://www.jewishgen.org/Yizkor/Ratno/rat059.html - 3r

The teacher and students in the School in Krymne

The Scroll of Tribulations

(A Gloomy Chronology from the year 1920)

Translated by Jerrold Landau

In 1933, through the initiative of the Jewish community of Ratno, a special committee was formed, consisting of Moshe Droog, Nota Roizkes, and A. Y. Ginzburg. The purpose of the meeting was to collect detailed information of the pogroms perpetrated by the Balachowiczes against the Jews in the villages and towns of Wolhyn and Pulsia, and to publish this in a special booklet. The members of the committee began to write to the other communities and Jewish institutions in all of the villages and towns in which the Balachowiczes left their bloody tracks. They even went out to visit these settlements, and held meetings on this topic with Jewish representatives. The central committee of the Zionist Organization in Warsaw also supported this effort. However, the initiators quickly had to abandon this project, for they and the supporting

Jewish authorities received hints that the Polish government would not look kindly upon the publication of a book on the pogroms perpetrated by the Balachowiczes. Such a "hint" under the conditions of the Polish police during that era was sufficient to dissuade the members of this committee from carrying out their plan. Much information, yellowed with the passage of years, remained in the hands of Moshe Droog, one of the members of the committee. This information contains descriptions of eyewitnesses who survived the terrible campaign of murder perpetrated by the Balachowiczes. The hair stands on end even today when reading these descriptions. Even though the hooligans were satisfied with murdering only a few Jews in Ratno itself, veritable slaughters were perpetrated in the villages, and the Jewish residents of these villages drank from the poison cup until it was emptied. Y. Konishter also gathered a great deal of material about what took place during that time in various villages in the vicinity of Ratno, and collected testimony from David Golden, Moshe Feigels, and Naftali Gloz. Here we publish a summary of his words.

Untitled Section[1]

by Sh. Goldman

Translated by Jerrold Landau

I had already endured traumatic experiences when I was a seven-year-old child, witnessing the terrors of the pogroms against the Jews with my own eyes. This took place in 1920. The government of the District of Wolhyn had passed from hand to hand. The Germans were in power, then the Balachowiczes, and after them, the Poles. Each retreating regime caused trouble for the Jews. Each arriving regime caused trouble for the Jews, blaming them for collaborating with the preceding regime. Members of the subsequent regime did the same thing. It is no surprise that the Jews were afraid of every change of government, for they knew what such was liable to bring. When the Balachowiczes retreated, one of the captains warned the Jews that a great danger was approaching. However, no person was able to imagine the essence and extent of this danger.

The few Jews, who had gathered together from the area, gathered in the home of the Grabov family in the neighboring village of Rakita to worship on Rosh Hashanah. We saw the retreating Bolsheviks through the windows of the house. Some time later, the Balachowiczes arrived. They removed the Jews from the house and stood them in two rows -- men separately, and women and children separately. A commander came and delivered a short speech that was full of blame against the Jews for helping the Bolsheviks. They were sentenced to death unless they paid ransom. Every family brought its gold and silver that was hidden in their homes, so that they could save their lives. Those who did not bring any, because their Ukrainian neighbors had succeeded in stealing it, were shot on the spot. With my own eyes I saw how they shot the father of Eliahu Yitzchak Reif after he returned empty-handed, without ransom. I also saw how Reb Burech, who succeeded in bringing ransom (by chance his family was not with us) was able to save the Reif family from this fate by informing the captain that Mrs. Reif was his wife, and that her children were his children. The captain asked the woman, "How many children do you have?" In her state of emotion and confusion, she told him a number that was one less than the correct answer. Then they shot her son, despite all of her pleading.

After paying ransom, we returned to our house that had been ransacked. The Ukrainians had emptied it of everything. Before we began to organize, one of the Satondists (a small Ukrainian sect of Sabbath observers) arrived and ordered us to escape immediately because the hooligans were returning a second time to attack us. We escaped to the nearby forest, and hid in a dense area of trees and shrubs in a bog. We waited there until the wrath subsided. Our objective was to arrive in Ratno by walking during the night. We were hungry for bread. I remember that I searched through Father's pocket, and found some bread crumbs. In the forest, we met other Jewish families from the nearby village of Krymne, where the Balachowiczes had also perpetrated a great slaughter. We arrived in the town of Ratno after about ten days. For a long time, I could not free myself from this terrible nightmare of the Balachowiczes. Like me, many other youths witnessed the acts of the Balachowiczes in the villages, where the Jewish residents were treated like sheep for the slaughter. The lesson of these pogroms had more impact on the basis of Zionism than anything that I learned later regarding Jewish history.

Translator's Footnote

1. In the table of contents, this is called "In the Eyes of a Child", which from the context, is accurate. https://www.jewishgen.org/Yizkor/Ratno/rat059.html - 63-1r

The "Balachowiczes" Come to Town

by L. Baion

Translated by Jerrold Landau

The entire town was enveloped with fear and darkness that Rosh Hashanah eve. A deathly silence pervaded, a frightful silence. The last lights coming forth from the blinds also went out and not even a small sound was heard, but everyone was awake nevertheless. A Jew who was late for Selichot crossed the dark marketplace. He hastened his steps, as if someone was following after him. The town was literally convulsing. Changes in government were impending, and nobody knew what would come in their wake. After midnight, flames were seen ascending from some building near the Rycz-Sponczyk mill. The building was burning, and nobody was attempting to extinguish or control the fire. People waited impatiently for morning. This was a sleepless night for all the residents. Nobody was able to sleep. At daybreak, the rumor spread that the Bolsheviks disappeared from town. Other rumors spread from mouth to mouth in the town marketplace. Some said that large battles had taken place during the nights, and the Bolsheviks suffered a serious defeat. Others said that strange characters were seen in the nearby villages, and one can surmise that these were spies from the Polish army.

The unease increased during the afternoon hours. Twelve hours had already passed since the Bolsheviks had retreated, and no sight of a new Polish regime had appeared. An atmosphere of panic pervaded the town. Rumor had it that the farmers of the region were preparing to come to town and perpetrate a pogrom. The nervousness and unease increased from minute to minute. The fact that the town remained without any government confounded and froze the senses. Rosh Hashanah was at the threshold. The marketplace was empty. All of the shops were closed. The Jews were preparing themselves for the Day of Judgment.

The sounds of galloping and wagons approaching the town were heard in the silence of the evening. This was Arjon, the water-drawer, who also served as the Sabbath Gentile[1] of the town. This time, Arjon brought tidings of Job: "In the name of Chona from Prochod I have come to inform you that the Balachowiczes are marching in the direction of town. Save yourselves while there is still time!"

This news caused veritable panic. Many people remembered the slaughter that was perpetrated by these Balachowiczes six weeks earlier, when they retreated along with the Polish Army. Everyone was afraid for his skin. Who would be among the victims now? Not long passed before dust rising up could be seen. “They are traveling!” Jews began to flee from the houses and the streets in the center of town to the dark alleys populated by the poor population, with the hope that perhaps they would not reach there. The house of Yaakov-Shlomo, by the Pripyat a distance from the town, filled up with people: merchants, shopkeepers, wealthy people, and even the wealthiest person in town, Reb David-Aharon Shapira, came to find refuge in that house. Everyone sat perplexed and looked out the window. The riders had already approached the “Yentl” Bridge that joined the two sides of the town. Echoes of the galloping of horses and the first shots that the Balachowiczes shot in the air for their own pleasure were heard. The sun set and the evening shadows burst forth. Leibele, the son of Yankel-Shlomo, was sent outside by the perplexed Jews to see if the riders had left the town. The lad attempted to reach the marketplace through side alleyways; however the voice of a rider stopped him: “Stand, Jew, and give over your money!” Leibele attempted to explain to the rider that he had no money, and that he never had any, but a strong slap on the cheek quieted him. “Where can I get boots?” asked and demanded the rider. Leibele, directed by his sense of responsibility, decided that it was better to lead this Balachowicz to his own home rather than have him kill other people, Heaven forbid. His mother, Meita, stood at the entrance to the house. “Give me boots!” thundered the Balachowicz loudly. Meita enticed him with a pleading voice, “Why are you standing outside, Poritzl[2], you are tired and sweaty. Come into the house, wash up, and rest.” The Balachowicz acceded to her request, entered the house, washed up, received a clean towel, and it seemed that the motherly pleasantness of the woman had its influence upon him. He put down his gun, removed the bullet magazine, and asked in a lower voice, “And where are the boots?” Meita answered him calmly, “New boots, Mr. Poretz, are not found now, for we have been living in wartime conditions for three months. However, if my husband's or my son's boots fit your feet, they are yours.” The “Poretz” liked Yankel-Shlomo's leather boots, and they were given to him. Meita asked the Balahowicz to sleep over in their home, for the members of the household are afraid to remain alone at night. However, he did not agree, and calmed her, “Do not worry, my old woman, no harm will befall you. Our youths will only play a bit in your town...”

When the horseman left the house, the city notables came out of their hiding places in the attic and in the barn. They breathed calmly when they found out that the entire “matter” only cost Yankel-Shlomo's leather boots.

Reb David-Aharon enwrapped himself in his tallis, turned his face eastward, and began the Maariv service with the festive melody. The women and men who were present could not hold back, and the Rosh Hashanah service was conducted with tears and sighing. The next morning, the townsfolk who were hiding in Yankel-Shlomo's house found out that indeed “A few of the youths played.” Two Jews were killed because of this “game,” including Avraham the shochet [ritual slaughterer] who had been nicknamed “The Jewish Rabbi” by the hooligan horsemen. It was also discovered that in accordance with a command of the deputy of the Hetman (the leader of the Balachowiczes), 30 hostages were taken. If the Jews would be unable to furnish the imposed fine of 10,000 rubles by nightfall, the hostages would be taken out to be killed.

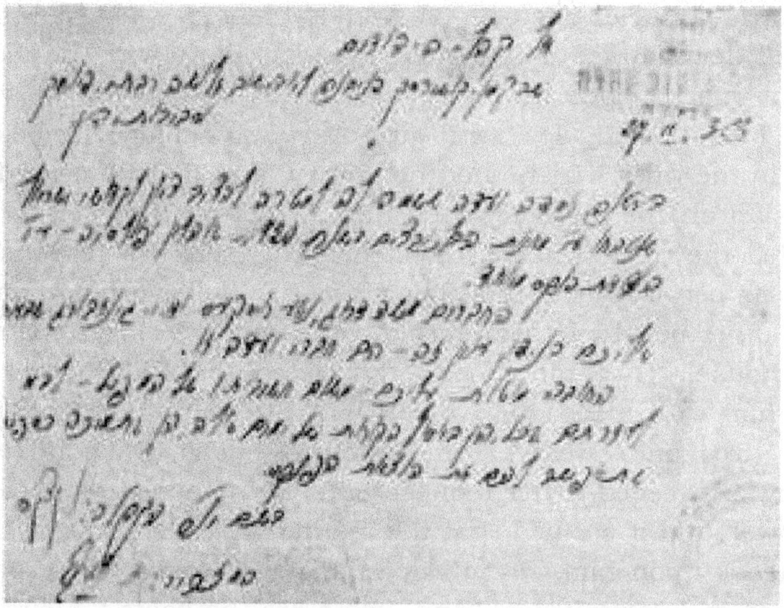

A letter from the community of Ratno regarding the collection of material for the book on the Balachowiczes

Translator's Footnotes

1. “Shabbos Goy”, the gentile who performs various necessary work for the Jews on the Sabbath. https://www.jewishgen.org/Yizkor/Ratno/rat059.html - f65_1r
2. A diminutive for a gentile landowner “Poretz” https://www.jewishgen.org/Yizkor/Ratno/rat059.html - f65_2r

In the Days of Bulak Balachowicz

by Binyamin Fuchs

Translated by Jerrold Landau

It took place on Sunday morning, the eve of Rosh Hashanah. My father Avraham-Yona woke me up for the Selichot service, and I heard my mother Reizel pleading tearfully in his ears that we must leave the village and go to Ratno, to be among the Jews, and whatever would happen with the Jewish people would happen to us too. She was perplexed. She did not wish to remain in the village. She was afraid that the farmers and Balachowiczes were about to pass through. On the other hand, Father claimed, "Where can we go with all the children? Who will host us and feed us? The journey is also fraught with danger due to the many acts of plunder on the roads. And what would happen with our house and property here? Everything might be plundered and pillaged." Mother retorted that if we did not go to Ratno, she suggested that we hide in the forest until the fury passed.

I went with Father to Selichot. Approximately a minyan (prayer quorum of ten) of Jews gathered; all of them, of course, discussing one topic: What to do? Where to flee and how to flee? Cannon shots were heard from time to time, from which we could realize that the front was very close, perhaps eight kilometers away, in the vicinity of Krymne. One Jew said that he heard from a gentile that the Soviet Army had placed canons in Krinski, where the fairs took place, in order to transfer to the front. The discussions took place until Itzel from Rakita issued a decision, "Jews, in any case we cannot travel anywhere, for all of the routes are closed off. The Kovel-Brisk Road is sealed off by the army, and the route to Zdomyshel is also closed off, for the Bolsheviks are preparing for a counterattack there. The only place left for us is to go to the forest."

The elderly Leib Rabin then shouted, "How can this be? Tomorrow is Rosh Hashanah? How can we worship in the forest? To read the Torah?" After discussions back and forth, it was decided that the services would take place in the home of Itzel of Rakita, which was close to the forest and surrounded by a grove. During that discussion, several people noted that the Balachowiczes only killed and pillaged while they were retreating, but they would not harm anyone now that they were advancing. To counter those who were confident, Chaim-Ber's wife, Dova, reminded everyone what the Balachowiczes perpetrated six weeks earlier.

My mother continued to claim that she saw dark things, and that in her opinion we should escape to the forest and hide there. However, since most of the Jews thought otherwise, she accepted their decision. The night of Rosh Hashanah passed with deathly fear, literally. All the Jews of the village gathered in the home of Yitzchak Grabov. They only dispersed to go to sleep late at night, the men in the barns and the women and children in the houses. As I lay down with my father in the barn, he hugged me strongly and held me close, as if he was having a premonition about what was to happen. That is how we spent that night. The next morning, I heard Father and Mother whispering between themselves. Then Father sent me to Dubechno to take a glance at our house there. He instructed me not to go on the main road, but rather through the fields. If I were to meet anyone along the way, or anyone were to recognize me, I was to return home immediately.

When I returned from my tour, the Jews were already reciting the Shmone Esrei of Shacharit. I noticed that Father was weeping, completely covered by his tallis. I cannot even speak of Mother, for she never stopped weeping from the day that they murdered her eldest son Shmuel-Betzalel. The services continued, but in the midst of the Musaf Shmone Esrei, we already saw through the window that horsemen were entering. They shot several shots, and commanded that the services stop and that all the money be turned over to them immediately. If not, they would kill everyone on the spot. They conducted a careful search of everyone, and even ordered those people whose clothes they liked to strip and hand over their clothes. They took everyone outside and organized them in rows of four, women separately and men separately.

Adamka, a gentile from Lubochin who was known as a murderer and was their leader, constantly issued new orders and beat the Jews. During the tumult, Yitzchak Grabov snuck out of the line, entered the grove and began to escape. Adamka chased after him but did not succeed in catching up to him. Everyone standing in the lines, men and women, were brought to Dubechno, accompanied by a guard. They organized us in a military formation behind the church, not far from Chaim-Ber's house. One of their leaders, a bald man, approached us, and Adamka discussed the situation with him. After the discussion, this leader took out some sort of Communist proclamation from his pocket and began to read it to us. He frequently mentioned Trotsky in his speech, and added that all of the Jews were Communists and Bolsheviks, and that they were guilty for everything that was taking place, and therefore must all be killed. After he concluded his words, they brought their machine guns close and began to maneuver them in order to instill fear into us. The head of the group said that he would only free us if we were to provide them with a sum of 2,000,000 rubles.

Chaim-Ber and my father, Yona Fuchs, approached the head of the group and explained to him that such a sum cannot be found even among the entire village population, Christians included. However, they expressed their agreement that all the Jews would give them whatever money and jewelry were in their possession. Two soldiers were sent with each Jew in order to hand over the money from their houses, while the women and children remained hostages. Chaim-Ber Reif was the first to return. He explained to the head of the group that he did not succeed in finding his jewelry. He was then commanded to take several steps back, and he was immediately killed. My father and other Jews returned later, and handed over their property. The head of the group informed us that we were permitted to return to our houses, and there was no reason to fear further, for the regular army was about to enter and they would not harm anyone. As this was taking place, some gentile arrived and informed him that the pit was already ready. Without taking into account whether all the Jews had paid the ransom money, the head of the group issued a command to remove the youths and young men from the rows and kill them, for otherwise they would join the Bolsheviks. One of the youths, Yaakov the son of Moshe Krasker, retorted, "Take us with you. We are prepared to fight against the Bolsheviks." The bald commander responded, "We do not trust Jews." Nine youths were taken from the rows and taken out to be killed: Yaakov Krasker, Shmuel Fuchs, Hershel Kagan, Manes Biber, Leibush Reif, Yidel of Kraska, Velvel Wirda, a teacher from Sedliska whose name I no longer recall, as well as an adult Jew who was in the village at that time by chance. The survivors were ordered to return to their homes. We then found out that the neighbors had pillaged our property, and only returned it to us when they saw us coming back.

The Balachowicz soldiers arrived in the village at nightfall. Some of them entered our house, demanded money, and beat all the members of the household. Our pleas and explanations that all of our money had already been taken were to no avail. They wanted to kill Father, and only let up when we began to weep and beg that they have mercy on us. However, they beat him with deathly blows, and we were only able to revive him with great effort.

We left the house with the intention of going to the forest, but it was impossible to get there, for the army surrounded the town from all sides. We arrived in the house of a farmer, but he would not agree under any circumstance to let us into his house. We entered an abandoned house, went up to the attic, and remained there for the night. In the morning, we realized that Father's wounds were serious. There was no place uninjured, and he was swollen all over. We left the abandoned house and began to run through the fields, for a farmer that we met along the way told Father that the army had left the town, and if we wanted to save ourselves, we must flee to the forest. One of the Balachowiczes recognized us and began to shout for us to stop. My Father thought that this was the voice of his brother Eliezer, despite the fact that we had called upon him to flee, for the Balachowicz was the one who called upon him to remain. We, Mother and the children, hid in some barn, while Father was caught by the Balachowicz, who tortured him, and tied him to a plow. My father tottered and the Balachowiczes killed him.

We hid in the forest for a few days. We were unable to light a fire in a way that would not disclose our hiding place. We continued to wander, and we only arrived in Ratno on the eve of Sukkot. That day, all of the martyrs who were murdered by the hooligans in the village were brought to a Jewish burial.

The Balachowiczes

by Sh. Goldman

Translated by Jerrold Landau

(In memory of the days of the Balachowicz Pogrom in 1920 in the village Dubechno, where I am now located on January 1, 1932.)

– – – Lashing of the whip, great fear intermixed with black colors, weakness and personal feebleness. Chains on the hands, and lack of vision to break them. Weakness of the knees from lack of faith in their health. – – They packed up the moveable possessions, loaded them onto wagons hitched to two cows – to travel and arrive at a “Jewish settlement” a distance of three parsangs, so that they can be afraid along with everybody – – – and wait until the last moment, that perhaps will be delayed and might not even come. Flight. The Jews – men, women, and children – made haste. They broadened their steps in order to “shorten the way,” pass over abyss of destruction and arrive at “a safe place,” even though it was clear that the “safe” place was not so, and the fetters of destruction were stretched over the entire earth: east, west, north, and south. A sure sign of destruction – flying feathers. Large, empty houses remained as a memorial to the destruction. The wind broke through strongly to sweep away the remnants that were left behind due to the great haste. The eternal secret was exposed: a volcano to which one would return. The volcano quiets – and the settlement continues with its existence. When it erupts – which could happen due to any small factor – in its anger, rocks are scattered all over. All important things are broken: the water – a place of life for the fish, the forest – for the animals, the land – for the people. Every nation and its land, every people and its homeland, its source – to where it returns and in which it lives. We can state clearly: whoever is the Jew that wishes to live – he will return to his source, to his land, to his homeland. Whichever Jew does not understand this important thing – his end will be destruction and ruin.

"A stiff-necked people." Stiff-neckedness that is only a soft platform, a saddle prepared for every rider. It will be pleasant for the rider. On account of the great joy, it will hug him to the point of strangulation, until the bones break, until the soul shrinks. Then it will let him go so that the process of dying will be prolonged, so that the body and soul will convulse from pain, so that he will recognize that his fate is the fate of all of his brethren, weak as he is, and so that he cannot shout out his final shout – a call to change the situation, to assuage the fate, to heal.

(Yehoshua! Keep this for this is from a private diary!)

I Hate you, Ukraine

by Sh. Goldman

Translated by Aaron Goldman

I Hate you, Ukraine.
If only I had the strength, I would break apart your skies and your land.
And turn everything to chaos,
If only I had the power to break it into pieces
To destroy and annihilate what I cannot tolerate, and what I hate,
To exhaust my wrath and anger on them,
I cast my arrows and ploughed to pieces your land
Soaked with the blood of my slaughtered brothers.

("Expressions" Booklet 4, 5689 / 1929.)

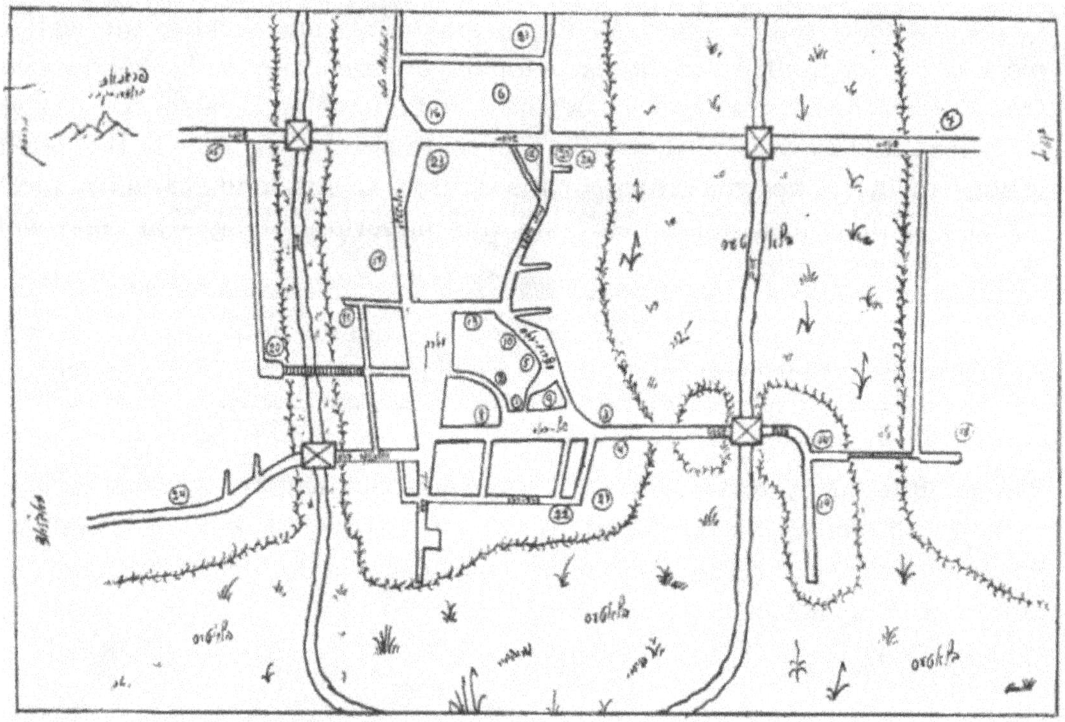

Map Key

1. Beis Midrash
2. The Shtibel of the Hassidim of Stolin-Karlin
3. The Shtibel of the Hassidim of Stepan
4. The Shtibel of the Hassidim of Trisk
5. The Shtibel of the Hassidim of Rizhin
6. The old cemetery
7. The new cemetery
8. The Tarbut School
9. The ruins of the Great Synagogue
10. Leibishe's Shtibel
11. The Workers' Union
12. Beis Midrash
13. The People's Bank
14. Church
15. Windmill

16. Church
17. Windmill
18. Windmill
19 Church
20. The Hide Workshop
21. The Polish cemetery
22. The bathhouse
23. The hospital
24. The Pravoslavic cemetery
25. Town hall
26 The steam station
27. Bridges
28. Small bridges

{Map of Ratno: Some street names are noted on the map. Many cannot be made out clearly due to the cramped script.
"Shul Gasse" is below 9.
"River" is noted in the two between the bridges
"Marshes" are noted in the areas
"Highway" is noted in the main road running along 15, 16, 23, 12, 25, 26
"Bath Street" is noted along 22
"Brisk" is noted at the top left exit from the map
"Zabolad" is noted at the bottom left exit from the map (probably a reference to the town now known as Zabolottja, which is indeed in that direction.)}

The First Zionists

by Yudel Malkus

Translated by Jerrold Landau

Yudel Konishter

In the town both, the father and son, were known as meshugoim (crazies): the father – Wolf-Leib the Crazy, and the son – Shlomo-Michel the Crazy. If an outsider came to the city and asked about Wolf-Leib Cohen with out adding the description "meshuga" – it is doubtful people would realize to whom they were referring. This nickname stuck with both the father and the son.

The father, an elderly Jew with a small, grey beard and dreamy eyes, would often sit on the steps of his store in the center of the market, completely immersed in a book. At times, he would lift his eyes from the book and call to his son, "Shlomo Michel, come and see what the Holy Zohar[1] says about the Land of Israel."

Like his father, the son was nearsighted. He was tall, heavy-boned, with a black beard scattered with grey hairs. He was always looking into "Hatzefira", the Hebrew daily newspaper that had arrived directly from Warsaw to the maskil of the town, who derived a double measure of enjoyment from the feuilliton of Nachum Sokolow or the his weekly article "From Eve of Sabbath to Eve of Sabbath," which to him was very sweet and tasty. Both of them, the father and the son, were expert in the small letters[2]. They knew how to study Gemara, and even set daily times for study. Both were enthusiastic Zionists by the end of the 19th century, when Zionism was still not widespread among the Jews. During those days, when Dr. Herzl used to travel around in order to convince the governments of that time to recognize the justice of the Zionist idea, our "crazies" followed after him, and did not miss even one iota of anything going on regarding that topic. Furthermore, when the Zionist Congresses started to convene, their enthusiasm for the Zionist ideal grew. They regarded Dr. Herzl as the Messiah the son of Joseph who would precede the Messiah the son of David[3]. They began to win Ratno Jews over to the Zionist idea. Since they were the only adults in Ratno who regarded themselves as Zionists in all aspects, they were known by the nickname "Meshugoim," which stuck to them for the rest of their lives.

Ratno was a Hassidic city, whereas the father and son were Misnagdim[4]. Nevertheless, their stance as opponents of Hassidism was not particularly sharp, for there was a true danger in that during those days. However, they did not hold back from denigrating the Hassidim and Tzadikim in the ears of the few Maskilim that lived in the town.

When new winds began to blow in the area, winds of progress and Zionism, there was no stopping them, and they also arrived in Ratno. David Finkelstein, an intelligent young man, knowledgeable in Hebrew and a talented writer, came to town as a Hebrew teacher. He would send articles from Ratno to "Hamelitz" and "Hatzefira". At times, these newspapers would also publish a story or article from him. He was one of the first to bring an omen of spring – the words of Zionism and love of Zion, to the Jewish youth. Also during his Bible and history lessons, he would succeed in weaving the ideas of the revival of the nation and its Land. A group of youths gathered around him, including

Yehoshua Pogach, Zalman Burstein, Itzel Mates's (Itzel the Litvak as he was called in town), Avraham Telson, and others. This group would read new books and newspapers in Hebrew, hold discussions on current events, especially those connected with Zionism and the Land of Israel. The only thing they were lacking was a meeting place, for everyone considered them to be heretics and was concerned about their influence over the youth. They had no choice other than to choose the waiting room of the post office, which was almost outside the bounds of the city, on the road. This was their headquarters. They met in the post office several times a week, under the pretext that they were going to get the mail for their parents (at that time, there was no individual mail distribution in Ratno). Under this camouflage, they conducted their cultural activity among the youths of the town.

At a certain point, these youths decided to open a type of modern cheder in the town for the poor of the town. They took the teaching role in this school upon themselves for free, with no salary. Since nobody could be found who could rent them a room for this purpose, they went further afield and opened their cheder in the house of Sarah the smith on the road, with a small number of students from among the common folk. However, the zealots of the town did not sit around with folded arms. They cried out against these heretics who were liable to turn the youth of Ratno away from the straight path and lead them to a bad crowd. Things reached the point where they threatened the woman who owned the house that housed the cheder with excommunication. She was unable to withstand this danger, and she forbade the students from coming to her home for their lessons. Thereby, this first educational effort of the Zionist group failed.

However, this failure did not discourage them. They were taken by the Zionist idea, and determined to impart the Zionist consciousness to the youth of Ratno, and to lead them from darkness to great light. They decided to bring in a special, Kabbalistic preacher to lecture on matters of Zionism in the Beis Midrash on the Sabbath between Mincha and Maariv. The youth posted notices of this lecture with sufficient lead time, and there were many Jews in the Beis Midrash at the set time. As he was still standing at the lectern, dressed as a regular preacher, lecturing about Herzl, Nordau, and all the efforts to redeem the soil of the Land of Israel, etc., the zealots began to shout loudly, "Get out of here, you shegetz![5]" They were not satisfied until they picked him up and removed him forcibly from the Beis Midrash.

The Beis Midrash turned into a battlefield. The few Zionists among the worshippers, including the two aforementioned "meshugoim" and the youths who initiated this gathering, came to the aid of the lecturer and defended him and the ideas about which he had preached to them. However, they were the minority, whereas most of the crowd was among the zealots who believed that the Land of Israel would be redeemed only through "the Messiah riding on a donkey," and to whom every Zionist idea was nonsense and an evil spirit.

However, the two "meshugoim" and the youths who supported them did not despair, and this failure did not break their spirit. They continued to win over people to the Zionist idea, and paved its way in our town. To them, Zionism was the content of their lives. Reb Yosef-Leib the elder always kept under his kapote booklets and pamphlets that proved that Dr. Herzl was none other than a messenger form on high, a form of the Messiah the son of Joseph; and, like Moses in his time, was sent by Divine providence to redeem the Jews from the present day "Egypt." In his conversations with householders such as Reb Eizik the Shochet [ritual slaughterer], Shlomo-Yoel the Shochet, and others, he never missed an opportunity to demonstrate his proofs that Dr. Herzl "stands before the angels" to bring redemption to the nation. The son was like the father. He too did not refrain from action. He conducted his publicity among younger people, among the young adults, and was assisted primarily by the "Arguments," "Hatzefira," and the Haskalah literature. Slowly but surely, the ice melted. The seeds planted by these "crazies" sprouted. The justice of the Zionist idea paved its way. Among the charity plates placed in the synagogues on the eve of Yom Kippur, there was an additional plate for the Jewish National Fund, and the people took note of it. The redemption of the Land earned de jure recognition also in Ratno. New pamphlets were sent from the Jewish National Fund headquarters in Warsaw to register the names of those who donated at least 20 kopecks. A collection was taken up for the Jewish National Fund at every festive occasion, wedding, circumcision, or engagement party. After some time, a Zionist organization was set up in Ratno, and regular Zionist activity began to be conducted in Ratno.

Our "meshugoim," the pioneers of Zionism in Ratno, were now literally proud of their craziness, and they bore their nickname with honor and pride. It is interesting that the elderly Reb Yosef Leib, who had a great deal of difficulty with his wife, foresaw the day of his death. Not only this, but he also knew from the outset that on the day of his death, she would also die, for her mission would be finished with his death, since she would not longer have anyone upon whom to pour out her wrath. This indeed took place in 1916, when Reb Yosef Leib died at the age of 90 exactly on the day that he foresaw, and his wife died that same evening.

Translator's Footnotes

1. The primary work of the Kabbalah. https://www.jewishgen.org/Yizkor/Ratno/rat070.html - f1r
2. Referring to the commentaries on the Talmud, printed in a smaller font. https://www.jewishgen.org/Yizkor/Ratno/rat070.html - f2r
3. See http://en.wikipedia.org/wiki/Messiah_ben_Joseph https://www.jewishgen.org/Yizkor/Ratno/rat070.html - f3r
4. Opponents of Hassidism. https://www.jewishgen.org/Yizkor/Ratno/rat070.html - f4r
5. "Shegetz" (literally "disgusting thing") is a derogatory term used for a gentile. https://www.jewishgen.org/Yizkor/Ratno/rat070.html - f5r

Political Parties and Organizations in our Shtetl

by Moshe Honik

Translated by Jerrold Landau

Our small shtetl of Ratno was situated on the main route between the two important Jewish centers of Kowel and Brisk. The Jewish population did not have any feelings of inferiority, for Ratno was also a type of center for the smaller towns and many villages in its area. The Jews in these small settlements would come to Ratno for material reasons (the fairs) as well as for spiritual reasons (on Sabbaths and festivals), just as the Jews of Ratno would go to Brisk and Kowel. In any case, for the 2,500 Jews who lived in Ratno (there is no exact statistic, but this is the accepted estimate) always had the sense of living in an important Jewish city. To a large degree, this was due to the fact that the Jews were concentrated on several streets, and wherever you went, you would see Jews.

Like in all Jewish towns, the economic center was the marketplace. The massive Jewish population was concentrated on the Synagogues Street, the Butcher Street, Holianka Street, Egypt Street, Krywa Street, the street that led to the main road, as well as in all the alleyways that spread out from those streets.

The Jewish Community

The central Jewish institution was the community structure, whose activities grew and became more widespread in the latter years. This was the supervisory institution of religious life (ritual slaughter, the rabbinate, the two cemeteries). It also was involved with helping the needy and in other social activities. All strata of the Jewish population were represented in the communal organization: Zionist, non-factional, religious, tradesmen, and merchants. The prestige of the community increased when it was given the opportunity, through a government law, to collect a special tax from the Jews. This raised its stature in the eyes of the Jewish population and enabled the community to pay the salaries of all the clergy: the rabbi, rabbinical judge, shochtim, etc. The minimal payment was five gold coins (zloty). The Jews of the surrounding villages were obligated to pay this tax, for they also made use of the services in Ratno. The communal council was required to present a monthly accounting of its activities to the Starosta (district leader) of Kowel.

Elections of the community took place once every two years, which included debates, election publicity, disputes between the various factions, etc. Each list augmented its publicity through speakers that were brought in from outside (Kowel, Warsaw), and the shtetlof Ratno rejoiced. Throughout the period of two months, the approaching elections served as the topic for deliberations and debates in every house. The factional urges that were generally under control during normal times would break forth in all their strength during election periods. After the elections, all the disputes were forgotten, and Jews from all streams and factions would sit at one table without schisms and shouting, as if the disputes and conflict had never existed. The concern for communal matters and for the social and cultural needs of the Jewish population united them once again. Indeed, it can be said that the communal administrators of Ratno excelled in their dedication and faithfulness to issues of public interest for which they were responsible, and demonstrated great responsibility in their tasks. On the eve of the Holocaust and during the Holocaust itself, these elected officials demonstrated that they were worthy of their positions, and their positions were worthy of them. They rose to great heights of selfless dedication and sanctification of the Divine Name, as many Holocaust survivors can testify.

During the final era, the following people stood at the helm of the community: Liber Karsh (president), D. A. Shapira. Ben-Zion Steingarten, A.

Berg, M. Blatt, Y. Grabov, Asher Leker, A. Shedrowiski, A. Skop, and M. Y. Chayat. The technical secretary of the community was Eliezer Held, who lives today in Israel. A. Y. Ginzburg filled this role on the eve of the Holocaust.

Ratno also had a city council with a mayor who was almost always anti-Semitic. An additional proof of the anti-Semitism of the Polish government was that the mayor was always a Christian even though the majority of the population of Ratno was Jewish. Representatives of the Jewish population in the city council included Mendel Klein, who served as the vice mayor, Yisrael-Yitzchak Baion, and others. However, their influence and ability to act on behalf of the citizens who elected them were significantly restricted.

The People's Bank

From among the various communal institutions that were active in the shtetl, it is worthwhile to especially note the people's bank, which attained renown throughout the entire region. This bank stood at the right hand of the merchants, shopkeepers, tradesmen and ordinary Jews, and helped them during times of difficulty. This was the most important public institution in Ratno that succeeded in striking roots in the shtetl. It had inroads with all strata of the population. This achievement was, to a large degree, a result of the dynamic activity of the director Yitzchak Hirsch Held of blessed memory and his assistants Yitzchak Karsh of blessed memory and Yisrael Chayat, who lives today in Israel. During the final years before the Second World War, when the economic depression reached its peak, the bank was the sole support for the majority of the Jewish population. The main activists in the bank directorship of that era were Zecharia Honik, Moshe Ryder, Yaakov Kanfer, Yehoshua Bekerman, Yehuda Konishter, and Yaakov Chayat.

As in every Jewish shtetl, Ratno had a charitable fund that had been set up with the assistance of the JOINT. Its activities were focused primarily on the poorer members of the community, who were helped with loans from the fund, thereby enabling them to obtain the equipment necessary for their work (sewing machines, etc.) and to sustain their families. The following people stood at the help of this fund: M. Blatt, Y. Kanfer, W. Brener, M. Cherkes, M. Klein, A. Berg, Y. Grabov, and Y. Steingarten.

Yitzchak-Hersch Held

Many communal activists who were active in these institutions spent entire days volunteering fully on behalf of these institutions. In Ratno of those days, working for the community in a non-voluntary fashion was unheard of. Helping one's fellow was one of the most important commandments. We can see how far things went by an adage that was common among the community prior to Passover, when the communal workers conducted the Maos Chittin[1] campaign dedicated to providing Passover matzos for the poor of the city, "Give or take" - that is: there is no intermediate state. Either you give to the poor, or you receive from this campaign. It is worthwhile to note that these volunteer workers toiled very hard for their own livelihoods. They earned their own bread through the sweat of their brow. However, their first thought was to do good to one's fellowman, to act benevolently with Jews who were experiencing difficulties with their livelihood. Some of these campaign workers were continuing the traditions of their ancestors in setting up public banks, charitable funds, mutual assistance funds, etc.

The directors of the People's Bank (1925)

The members of the older generation - our fathers and grandfathers, toiled greatly for their livelihood, and earned their bread with the sweat of their brow, as is stated in the ancient verse[2]. The tradesman in his workshop, the shopkeeper in his shop, and the peddler wandering around the villages were all in the same situation. They did not eat or sleep sufficiently. During the late afternoon, one could find dozens of Jews on the Street of the Synagogues going to attend a mincha and maariv service. This street was holy to the Jews from previous generations, and especially during the time that the Great Synagogue stood there. Everybody spoke about the beauty and praise of that synagogue, which eventually went up in flames. All of the shtibels and the city Beis Midrash that was not affiliated with any specific rebbe were also located on that street.

The deep faith of the Jews in the Creator of the World and the eternity of the Jewish people was expressed on that street. All of the tragedies, disturbances and evil decrees that befell the Jews in that small shtetl were unable to tear the Jews away from that faith forged in fire and blood. I pondered this matter at times. Even after I cast off the faith, went out to a "bad crowd," joined Hashomer Hatzair, and went on hachshara; I still valued and revered these Jews for the strength of their faith. It is no surprise that the stamp of the Street of the Synagogues was recognizable throughout the entire shtetl. Only after many years, when the youth in Ratno took their fate into their own hands and the ranks of the Zionist and pioneering movement captured their hearts - did the Jewish street free itself from the imprint of the Street of the Synagogues, and its stamp was not felt as much. The person who played the decisive role in this mater was undoubtedly the teacher from Pinsk, Noach Kotzker, who arrived in our shtetl and filled the role of a guide to the Jews by founding the Tarbut School, which turned into the spiritual center of the shtetl and educated the youth toward Zionism and pioneering.

The volunteer firefighters

I recall the public battle that was conducted in shtetl with respect to establishing this school. The Hassidim and Orthodox Jews regarded the establishment of Tarbut as a form of revolt against the rule of religion and their own hegemony. I especially recall those who put their efforts toward this task and did not retreat: Yehoshua (Shea) Bekerman, Yosef Zesak, Noach Kotzker, Yitzchak-Hirsch Held, Asher Leker (all of whom perished in the Holocaust), and Yudel Konishter who died in Argentina. Only now, with a retrospective view, it is perhaps possible to evaluate the important task that they filled at that time, as well as the many obstacles that stood in their path. What today seems natural and something that the times demanded was at that time an unrealizable objective. In the later years, people such as Bokser, Zagorski, Lewin, Roizen and Amalia Droog of blessed memory had great influence on the Tarbut School. The latter was the daughter of a Ratno family, who graduated the Teachers' Seminary in Vilna and later became a teacher in the Tarbut School.

The various youth movements were first set up in Ratno in the years 1924-1926. Without doubt, they were a result of the tireless efforts of the teacher Kotzker. As far as I remember, the first of them was Hanoar, founded by Leibel Avrech. Later, other movements arose: Hashomer Hatzair, Hechalutz, Freiheit, and Beitar.

Without doubt, the largest and most firmly based movement was Hashomer Hatzair, which conducted serious educational activities and had great influence upon the youth. It is fitting to note that, during those years, it was a nationalist scouting movement that had not yet crystallized ideologically. The majority of the youths in the shtetl passed through this movement, including those who later set up other movements.

It is appropriate to elaborate on the historical role that Hashomer Hatzair filled in Ratno. Hundreds of youth in our shtetl passed through the melting pot and the educational endeavors of that movement. Anyone who wishes to see the praiseworthy fruit of that movement need only survey the list of Ratno natives scattered throughout Israel and the Diaspora, to see what types of roles the former Hashomer Hatzair members have filled and continue to fill. It is a fact that in every place, they form a vibrant and active kernel. This is no coincidence, but rather the fruit of the education that they received in their time. To a large degree, we can attribute this fruit to the merit of Moshe Droog, who lives today in Israel. The chapter was founded in the home of Moshe Goldstein (today in the United States). The first members, who were called

"Kfirim" include: A. Chayat (today in the United States), Chaim Ides, Zelig Bander, Yisrael Honik (today in Argentina), Zelda Feintuch, Dvora and Chaya Grabov (today in Israel), and Yosef Steinberg (today in Canada). I own a photograph of the leadership of the Hashomer chapter in a later period, which includes: Zelda Feintuch (in Israel), Moshe Pogatsh of blessed memory, Henia Karsh, Moshe Konishter of blessed memory, M. Ch. Fuchs (in Argentina), Berel Honik of blessed memory, Baya Vernik of blessed memory, Zeev Grabov (in Israel), Chaya Prusman (in Israel), Golda Droog of blessed memory, Baya Vernik of blessed memory[3], Beila Leker of blessed memory, Eliahu Zesak (in Israel), and the writer of these lines.

The WIZO women's organization (July 8, 1932)

Aside from Hechalutz Hatzair (Young Hechalutz) about which I will write specially in this article, there were other movements in the shtetl that did not last long and did not gather many youths into their ranks, but nevertheless filled an important role in the education of the Jewish youth. Among these was Freiheit, under the leadership of Yisrael Honik and D. Frigel. This organization was composed primarily of working youths, who also comprised the youth of the left leaning Poale Tzion. Brit Trumpeldor (Beitar) existed in Ratno and was founded by Meir Ryder of blessed memory. As time went on, when the

Revisionists left the Zionist organization, great ferment began and Beitar caused a storm within the spirits of the Jewish youth. Meetings and demonstrations were frequently arranged. The ideological chasm between the camp of Working Land of Israel and the Revisionists deepened, and a battle broke out over the soul of each youth. The following were the most active members of the Revisionist camp in those days: Mogilenski, Zisa Marin, Eliezer Marin, Motel Ternblit, Velka Chayạt (all of whom perished in the Holocaust), and others.

There were also members of the left leaning Poale Zion in our shtetl, but one can count them on the fingers of one hand. I recall two of them: Nota Roiskes and Levi Shapira. Nevertheless, the dearth of members did not hinder them from conducting recognizable activity, especially in the realm of Jewish culture. They would bring to the shtetl speakers such as Zerubavel, Yoel Mastbaum and others, and they spared no effort to increase the cultural activities in the shtetl. Later, the members of the left leaning Poale Zion found an arena for their activities in the ranks of the League for Working Land of Israel, which encompassed all of the Socialist Zionist groups as well as many supporters who did not belong to any party. This league conducted many activities during the time of the Zionist Congress, conducted a special campaign (KPE'Y), and even helped other youth movements from an economic perspective. Later, Haoved was founded with the help of the league, under the leadership of Blatt. Its ranks included tradesmen who were preparing to make aliya to the Land of Israel. I own a photograph of the committee of the league. The photograph includes: Yisrael Chayat, Riva Shapira, A. Y. Ginzburg, Yisrael Kanfer, Dvora Karsh, Mendel Blatt, A. Feintuch, Chava Ryder, Yitzchak-Hirsch Fuchs, Yisrael Bander, Moshe Konishter, Yona Stern, Nota Roiskes, Moshe Pogatsh, Eli-Yitzchak Reif, and the writer of these lines.

I will write a few lines about the General Zionists in Ratno, who mainly belonged to the Al Hamishmar radical group under the leadership of Yitzchak Greenbaum. The main activists in this part in the shtetl included Yosef Zesak and Yehoshua Bekerman of blessed memory.

These people neglected their own businesses and livelihoods, and spent nights and days involved in Zionist activity. Adult Jews with Zionist consciousness gathered around them, and devoted most of their energies to the Tarbut School in the shtetl. Many supporters, lovers of Zion and ordinary Zionists who did not want to belong to a specific party, but did want to express their appreciation of the Land of Israel and Zionism, were involved in these activities. Among the General Zionists, there were experienced and responsible communal activists who were greatly admired by the youth of Ratno. They put their best efforts in helping the Zionist youth. These include Y. H. Held, L. Grabov, Yaakov Liberman, and others.

During the final years before the war, the Mizrachi organization was also founded in our shtetl. Its spiritual leader was the dedicated Zionist Asher Leker of blessed memory. Their circle of members was quite restricted, but they had influence upon the religions circles who at first opposed the revival of Hebrew, and were only drawn close to Zionism through Mizrachi. As was told to me, the influence of Mizrachi grew before the Second World War, and the number of members increased significantly.

A rally in the yard of the shtetl hall in honor of May 3. (1936)

From among the anti-Zionist organizations, which were a minority in the shtetl, it is appropriate to first note the Bund. The moving force behind the Bundist organization and its living spirit was Efraim Kotler of blessed memory. Despite the fact that he was handicapped, he gathered the working youth of the shtetl around him, and dedicated all of his time to the movement. Even his opponents appreciated his personal integrity. In that manner, he was a symbol. There is no doubt that he helped greatly in imparting education and meaning in life to many youths. Of course, the Bundist organization did not have great influence in the city, but its activists functioned to the best of their ability within their narrow circles, and served their party faithfully. During the final years before the war, Efraim Kotler began to show signs of drawing close to the Socialist Zionist circles.

The "Leftists" had more serious influence in Jewish Ratno. Youths from the intelligentsia circles belonged to that faction, such as: Leibel Baion (today in Mexico), A. Shapira (today in Cuba), Chona Tyktiner, and Niska Shapira, Chaim Grabov (today in Argentina) and others. The group bore the banner of Communist outlook, and those who were involved excelled in their idealism and great dedication to their party. This group also attempted to set up a school in Ratno according to their ideals, but the Polish authorities closed it down after some time. The circle of tradesmen was also under their influence. They were not shaken by the persecution of the Polish government and imprisonments. No small number of them were sentenced to extensive periods in jail. Those who succeeded in emigrating overseas are numbered among the "progressive circles," as they call themselves in those countries.

A most important cross-factional institution that brought representatives of all the organizations and factions together was the Jewish National fund. Asher Leker of blessed memory, who served for many years as the chairman of the Jewish National Fund, dedicated a great deal of time and tireless efforts to his activities for the fund. Zalman Kamfer, the treasurer, was an example of a soldier who constantly stood on his guard. Both of them encouraged the youth toward activities for the benefit of the fund, and there was a constant competition between the various organizations for first place in bringing in income toward the Jewish National Fund.

Translator's Footnotes

1. Literally, "Money for wheat" - the pre-Passover charitable campaign to enable the poor to be able to provide for the needs of the holiday. https://www.jewishgen.org/Yizkor/Ratno/rat070.html - f75-1r
2. Genesis 3:19. https://www.jewishgen.org/Yizkor/Ratno/rat070.html - f75-2r
3. Mentioned twice in this list, likely in error. https://www.jewishgen.org/Yizkor/Ratno/rat070.html - f75-3r

Activists of the League for the Working Land of Israel
Among them: Y. Chayat (of Israel), Moshe and Yisrael Honik (of Argentina), A. Y. Reif.
The rest of them perished

In the shade of the thick tree in the Old Cemetery

The first group of scouts

The First Scouts

by Yaakov Rog

Translated by Jerrold Landau

When I came to the city of Luck in 1921, I was in the Great Synagogue on the Festival of Shavuot, and I heard speeches by various people about Keren Hayesod. The women were greatly influenced by the words of the speakers, and it was as if they removed their jewelry and gave it over to the fund. Suddenly, a group of scouts entered the synagogue. When I saw their fine parade, I decided that we should set up such an organization in Ratno. I began to work toward that objective when I returned to Ratno.

My plan seemed appropriate to my friend Noach Cohen, and the first group convened on the Sabbath after Shavuot. The group included Velvel Rajsky, Noach Cohen, Nota and Niska Shapira, Leibel Grabov, Asher-Leizer Kolodner,

Leizer Rajsky, Yisrael Zesak, Leibel Blostein, Eliezer Held and me. We gathered on the road near the mill of Binyamin Kamfer and began to deliberate over our plan of action. Among other things, we decided to send one of our members, Zeev (Velvel) Rajsky, to Kowel to obtain information and guidance from the scouts there. We waited for him with baited breath. When he returned to Ratno, he shared with us the information that he had obtained in Kowel, and I recall that he said, among other things that the greeting of the scouts is: “Be prepared,” and the response to the greeting is, “always prepared.”

We began our activities and the signing up of boys and girls as members. The leadership was composed of the members: Velvel Rajsky, who was given the title of “minister of order,” Noach Cohen as secretary, Yaakov Rog as head of Group Aleph, and Asher Leizer Kolodner as head of Group Bet. Every Sabbath, we would arrange a parade near the windmill in the old city, and at times near the tannery. Since we did not have a permit, all of our activities were conducted clandestinely. As time went on, we founded a library and used our meager funds that we collected from the monthly membership dues to purchase books. We asked Mordechai Fuchs of Malrita, who was with us at that time, to prepare a list of books appropriate for purchase, and Leizer Rajsky traveled to Warsaw to purchase the books. Thus was the foundation laid for our large library. The adults, who had their own library, were jealous of our library and proposed to us that we unite the two libraries, but we did not agree to this proposal.

After some time, we began to perform theater. Our first play was the “Get” (Divorce) by Shalom Aleichem, a four scene performance. Our plays were performed in the Women's Gallery of the Beis Midrash, and the income from the two performances reached 70 dollars. This money enabled us to send one of our members to Argentina. Our other performances included “Samka the Clown,” “Broken Hearts,” and “The Loafer.”

We rented our first premises in the home of Yaakov Avrech. When we moved from there, Niska Shapira wanted to give us several pictures, and he ordered a set of portraits of Nachum Sokolov, Chaim Weizmann, and Bialik. When the pictures arrived, David Aharon Shapira took the picture of Bialik and tore it. We were then forced to stick the picture together from the torn pieces. A picture of Dr. Herzl was added to our headquarters, and various newspapers were also ordered.

Our activities were varied: we collected money for the Jewish National Fund, donated money to plant trees in the Land of Israel, sold flowers at various fairs that took place in the shtetl, etc. We also participated in political activities prior to elections to the Polish Sejm, and we conducted publicity for National List Number 16.

There was no foundation for a secure future in Ratno. The situation in Poland became more serious. We could not travel to the Land of Israel at that time, so we decided to prepare for immigration to Argentina. One of our members was first to travel, and then others followed. Four people rented a common room, and we prepared ourselves for immigration and for the absorption of new members.

The First Buds
(Sections of memories)

by L. Baion

Translated by Jerrold Landau

Tomorrow was still covered in a cloud and the future was not secure at all. Battles still took place in the vicinity between the Ukrainian nationalists, the Red Army and volunteers of the Polish Army over rule of our district. For several weeks, there was no reliable government in the shtetl. There was an atmosphere of wantonness, and everyone did as they pleased. Gangs of Ukrainians roamed around the forests and the villages of the region, attacking passers-by, killing and pillaging. Wagons carrying dead Jews from the villages appeared daily in the shtetl. No ray of light was on the horizon, and the footsteps of redemption were delayed in coming.

It was specifically during those cold, serious days that the dawn of social and ideological awakening began among the younger generation. Evening meetings in the dark Beis Midrash where people analyzed various problems were not sufficient. The need for the youth to have their own place was felt, as well as the need for social-organizational activities. A hall for social gatherings was opened up for the first time in the shtetl. A house stood at the edge of Holianka Street that had served as the civic prison. It is symbolic that specifically that house turned into a meeting place for the youths. It was renovated, a small stage was built inside atop which a blue and white flag fluttered.

I recall one of the first meetings dedicated to defining the ideology of the group. We, 12 and 13-year-old youths, were then scouts from the side. The chief speaker was Noach Kotzker, the teacher of the shtetl. His words centered on the Zionist ideal, the vision of the prophets, Dr. Herzl, and the Balfour Declaration. He called upon the youth of the shtetl to gather around the blue and white flag of Zionism and to struggle for the realization of the dream of a Hebrew State. Some of those gathered came from the "wide world," and were imbued with class consciousness and ideas of social revolution and a class war. They attempted to oppose the idea of Zionism blended with Socialism. They were also stubborn in expressing their outlook, and it was clear that they were more sensitive than they were able to express. It was finally agreed that the new organization, Bnei Zion, would also include the Socialist idea in its program.

The activities of the Bnei Zion group included weekly meetings with lectures on various social and Zionist topics, recreation evenings, and literary evenings. A list of topics was also issued so that the members of the organization, who were people of understanding, would be able to prepare and hear the words of introduction. It quickly became clear that nobody aside from the teacher Kotzker would be able to carry out this task. The purpose of appearing before the community was to restrain people from going on the stage and stating their words, thereby imposing fear on the community.

Going to the Bnei Zion hall had a festive aspect to it. The festivity was especially felt during the literary celebrations, for which the members of the dramatic club of Bnei Zion prepared for a long time. Thanks to the activities of this group, specific artistic talents were revealed among the youth, which earned communal recognition. We will mention only a few of them here: M. Merkazi, Maya Shapira, Chaya Itzikson, Hershel Shapira, and others. Activists were trained in the arena of social activities of Bnei Zion, who later ran various institutions in the shtetl such as the public kitchen, the Jewish National fund, the school, and other institutions.

When the desire to take part in sporting activities, scouting, hiking, and sailing was aroused among the older youths, the Hatzofeh organization was set up in the pattern of a similar organization in nearby Kowel. This was a nationalist organization by nature. It celebrated all the national holidays with parades in the streets, it conducted activities for the Jewish National Fund, but it did not conduct cultural activities worthy of the name.

The "Tarbut" School at its inception

Among the students: Moshe Gutman of blessed memory, Aryeh Avrech of blessed memory, Moshe Stern, Moshe Droog, Ruth Greenstein, Pnina Droog of blessed memory, Pesl Miryo of blessed memory, Sara Papir-Goldman, Sara Ginzburg-Schwartz, Mordechai Gefen

When the activities of the older youths weakened and they entered into the yoke of family life and the struggle for existence - a new cadre of youth who had passed through all the nightmares and frights of the First World War ascended the stage of communal activity in the shtetl. They began to act with great momentum, raised heads, and natural optimism, as if they were making up for what was lacking in the preceding years. The first objective was a civic library. This was during the time of flourishing book publishers such as "Shtibel" (in Hebrew), "Kultur League: (in Yiddish), and the publication of other books that flooded the marketplace with a great bounty of books, and aroused a great thirst among the local youth for reading. What did they not do then to quench this thirst? They saved their last coins, presented literary critiques and held celebrations, organized flower days, etc. in order to bring the best of literature to the library. The first meetings of this youth group were held in the home of Nachum and Velvel Rajsky. Many youths went there to play chess or checkers, and especially to exchange books. Every new monthly shipment of books was received with literal trembling and awe. When the youths discovered that the exchange of books lacking hard covers caused damage to the books, many learned the bookbinding of craft, and bound the books with their own hands. Our member Leibel Blostein especially excelled in this work.

The influence of the Hebrew and Yiddish books on these youths was beyond estimation. Their eyes were opened to see what they had not previously seen, to become familiar with issues and problems that had been far from them. They would debate out loud on the intentions of various authors, and tell each other about the content of new books or articles and essays that were published in "Hatekufa", "Miklat", "Chaliastra", "Ringen", "Bicher Velt", "Literarishe Bleter" and various other publications. They would also read these publications during parties.

I will mention positively here our good, heartwarming friend Binyamin Ponach, who in the evening served as a resource for youths who were experiencing difficulty in reading. He would tell them the content of various books, such as "Ba'aish Ubacherev" (With Fire and Sword) by Sienkiewicz that was published in Hebrew translation at that time by Shtibel publishers. He lovingly fulfilled this role that he had taken upon himself. At that time, there was nobody to direct the youths in reading and to show them what comes first and what comes last in reading. However, after some time, several of them excelled and served as librarians and guides for their friends in reading. I recall that when the library obtained the first works of Peretz Markish, Melech Ravitsh, Uri Tzvi Grynberg and others who were pioneers of futurism in poetry and literature. In the same manner that earlier youths would sit over a page of Gemara, delving into the commentaries of Rashi, Tosafos, and others; young people would sit together and attempt to uncover the various expressions in these works, so that they could understand the personalities of the authors. Some of them learned entire works by heart, and some took bets as to how much of a certain work they knew by heart.

During the years 1924 and 1925, a group of about 30 youths sprouted from this group and founded Hechalutz. Thus began the physical and spiritual preparation for aliya to the Land of Israel. However, this path of Hechalutz appeared overly revolutionary for the more conservative of the youths, who were not ready for this revolution that included leaving the home, traveling to a Hachshara kibbutz, proletariatization, etc. There were also those who regarded the Hechalutz movement as a nationalist movement that contradicting Socialism, world revolution, and human emancipation. However, there is no doubt that the Hechalutz organization was the most significant factor in developing noticeable communal and cultural activity in the shtetl. In the Hechalutz hall, there were clubs that were involved with the study of the doctrines of Borochov, A. D. Gordon, and classical Socialism. Lectures on various topics were frequently arranged, with debates and discussions continuing until late at night. The members of the central and district leadership who visited us gave very positive reports on the Ratno chapter after their visits.

In 1926, the first three members of Hechalutz in Ratno went on hachshara: Shlomo Pogatsh, Yitzchak Kozak and the writer of these lines. When we returned to the shtetl after a year of hachshara, we strengthened the chapter significantly, and encouraged other members of Hechalutz to follow in their footsteps. At that time, and with the influence of the first pioneers, many members ended their lives of boredom and idleness, and went out to work in the paving of roads, quarrying of stones, and other jobs; changing their petite bourgeois attitudes toward manual labor.

A serious crisis affected Zionism and the pioneering movement during the years 1927 and 1928. The Mandate restricted aliya to the land, and the members that were authorized for aliya sat in their homes without anything to do as they awaited their certificates. The pioneering movement weakened. The Jewish youth could not relate calmly to what was taking place around them, to the increasing anti-Semitism, to the oppression of the national minorities in Poland, and to the strong hand raised by the government against the progressive movements. The economic situation also worsened at that time, due to the taxes that worked against the poorer classes and the workers. In the wake of all this, many of the younger generation came to the conclusion that the ideals of Zionism and pioneering were also a form of escape from the front and of evading the problems that were afflicting the masses of the Jewish people. “Let us turn toward the work of the present!”, “Let us turn toward the shtetl, toward the working fathers and their worries!” - These were the mottoes that were heard from the maturing youth. The intelligentsia in the shtetl turned its hearts toward the working youth, and attempted to direct their paths of lives and educate them. There was also a change in attitude toward the Yiddish language and the potential held within it. In the wake of this, a chapter of O.Y.Sh. (Organization of Jewish Schools) was founded in Ratno, as well as an analogous cultural club that organized lectures, discussions, and debates on the issues of culture and literature. This cultural activity eased the melancholy in which they youths found themselves, scattered the heavy clouds, and slightly assuaged the pressure and tribulations of the Jews under the semi-Fascist Polish government of that time. The activists of the Yiddishist movement girded themselves for a heavy task - the establishment of a Yiddishist school in the spirit of their ideological principles. They succeeded in reaching this goal that they had taken upon themselves, but the school only lasted for four months, for the Polish government closed it with the pretext that the building was not appropriate for a school.

In the Old City

The local government authorities began to "take interest" in the activities of the progressive circles. They followed after O. Y.Sh. and its members, and did not hold back from engaging outside provocateurs and local agents to spy on the circles that appeared to them as leftists. As a result of these espionage activities, almost all of the members of the workers movement were arrested.

This was in the autumn of 1929, when mass imprisonments took place in the cities and towns of Pulsia Wolhyn, and dozens of members of the youth circles of Ratno were arrested and hauled to Kowel. They were tortured and interrogated through many brutal methods. There was no concrete evidence against most of the prisoners, and they were forced to free them after several days of imprisonment. Only two of the prisoners, Chona Tyktiner and Aharon Shapira, remained in prison and were later sentenced to five years of imprisonment.

From that time, the youth circles began to disband. The pursuing and slander discouraged many youths from continuing their activities. Some of them got married, remained in the shtetl or traveled to other places, and entered the yoke of livelihood. Others reached the point of complete despair over everything that was taking place in Poland, and immigrated to the United States, Argentina, and other places. A new guard entered into social activities in the shtetl. They too faced many problems that had no easy solution with the realities of those days. The years 1922-1936 were years of spiritual activity, ideological battles and aspirations for a better and more beautiful life.

Letter to a Friend

by A.Y. Ginzburg

Translated by Jerrold Landau

Aharon Yankel Ginzburg of Ratno Writes to his Friend L. Baion in Mexico about his Ideological Struggles

Ratno, July 5, 1937.

It was a summer Sabbath eve. I was busy with my work and other matters all day. You recall that I always had many jobs and few blessings. And you see, just as there was a form of competition between my various jobs (a painter, a secretary of the community, and a secretary of Y.Sh.A), there is also some sort of conflict in my spiritual life. I am a Yiddishist, and I simultaneously love the Hebrew language. The Land of Israel is close to my heart, but I also love Birobidzhan. I like the Communist idea, but I still remain a nationalist idealist. I have searched for a bridge that could bridge these various poles, and it seems that I have found it. I have read your letter, and before that, I read your articles in various newspapers in Mexico, and several things surprise me. First of all, I see that you participate in nationalist Zionist publications. Second, you are already writing in a different spirit, almost in the national spirit - far from the class war and closer to the people of Israel. Third, your articles are printed alongside greetings and announcements of Bar Mitzvas, circumcisions, and other Jewish happy occasions.

I do not imagine that you are not true to what you are writing and publishing. I attempted to resolve the various contradictions in that, while you were still stuck in the confines of Jewish life along with masses of Jews, you felt choked in that life and wanted to spread your wings and anchor yourself in other realms; but now, when you have gone out to the wide, strange world (Mexico), you have choice: to assimilate along with everyone or to return to our roots. This is all through the principle of responsibility toward the upcoming generation whom you, as a teacher, must educate.

Therefore Leibel, we must stand on guard, and protect the existence of the nation. Whoever wishes to be responsible for the maintenance of the Jews as a people must give preference to the national problem over the social problem, at least until we reach the level that other nations have reached. It was specifically from the Soviet Union that I have learned that we must restrain somewhat the rhythm of our "revolution." Whereas this was the path that led to national and social liberation for the Russian people, for us the path of revolution is liable to lead to disappearance... I cannot come to terms with the command to wander tens of thousand of kilometers to the banks of the Amur River in order to clear the Taigas there - something that Ivan himself did not do[1] - to wipe out with one stroke of the hand our history from "In the beginning G-d created," and to begin our existence from the year of the great revolution of 1917.

On the other hand, if we do not go to Birobidzhan, a second great danger awaits us - to assimilate and disappear from the stage of nations. What would we attain? We would help establish a beautiful world for others, and we would commit national suicide ourselves. This is indeed the situation. The Russian revolution is liable to cause 3.5 million Jews to disappear, not from great tribulations, but rather from too much comfort, so to speak. Woe to us for such good fortune!

And with respect to the Land of Israel. It is true that this is a small land that cannot absorb many Jews, but it can become the force that assists the existence of Jews in the Diaspora. Therefore, we must nurture and study the Hebrew Language, not only because this is our living language, but also because this language added a great deal of charm to our Yiddish Language. If we are truly interested in the existence of the Yiddish Language, it is our duty to also nurture Hebrew.

My conclusions are as follows: Our nation is forging a way to the family of nations. The solution is not assimilation, nor is it Socialism. It is forbidden for us to commit national suicide. Just as we overcame the dangers in the time of lack of culture, we will also spiritually overcome the dangers lurking in the times of culture and flourishing civilization.

Enough of these matters. I wish to add something of my own: I await the possibility of emigration, but in the meantime, all of the lands are sealed. Aside from my work hours, the days generally pass in idleness. The evenings are spent in discussions with friends. My friend Levi Shapira is about to leave today for his new home in the State of Cuba. Where will my home be?

Indeed, in the last few weeks, various events took place in the city of your brother. (This is referring to the pogrom against the Jews of Brisk). The conclusions from all this are clear: With regard to the outside, in relation to the outside world, we are all Jews - -the rich, the poor, the middle class, the workers - the dangers await us all.

With warm regards,

Aharon Yankel

Translator's Footnote

1. The Amur is a river in Birobidzhan, the Russian area in the Far East, bordering China, designated as a Jewish national republic within the Soviet Union. The use of the name "Ivan" here is meant to symbolize a typical Russian. https://www.jewishgen.org/Yizkor/Ratno/rat086.html - f86a-1r

The New Era in Ratno

by Simcha Lavie

Translated by Jerrold Landau

At the end of First World War, when the refugees who had fled to other places and the young people who had fought in the battles began to return, new winds began to blow in the shtetl. There were those who hoped that the new Polish government would fulfill its obligations toward equal rights for all citizens without discrimination between religion and nation, as was formulated in the international agreements. However, this rosy dream began to fade very quickly. The various decrees of the Polish government proved that this was nothing other than a pipe dream. The turn for the worse of the situation of the Jews was noticeable in all areas. This fact increased the social ferment and the inroads of various parties whose mottoes also began to penetrate little Ratno.

Changes in the way of life began to be clearly noticeable. These were not drastic changes, but were changes nevertheless. In addition to the youths who returned from the battlefields, youths from larger cities arrived in Ratno after they married Ratno girls. These people also were a factor in the change of values, which was expressed in modes of dress, hiding the tzitzis, secular books that took the place of holy books, social gatherings, etc. There is no doubt that these changes worried the Orthodox communal administrators, who regarded them as a form of revolt against the accepted modes of behavior and was liable to weaken their decisive hegemony in the Jewish community. This was further exacerbated when the Zionist activities began to increase in the shtetl. The establishment of the Tarbut School was apparently one of the signs foretelling the beginning of the new era, and it is no surprise that the efforts of various householders to establish this modern school was a thorn not only in the eyes of the cheder teachers who were afraid that their livelihoods would dwindle, but also in the eyes of the members of the various shtibels who were particular about exacting religious education for their sons and daughters. The shtetl, or more precisely the Jewish community of the shtetl, was divided into two camps. One camp consisted of those who preserved the embers of the old traditions in its full essence for the education of the children, way of life, etc. The second camp was composed of the more liberal or progressive folk who began to circulate around the doors of the parents in order to register the children for the Tarbut School. The latter group included Moshe Eilbaum, Yehoshua Bekerman, Leibel Grabov, Mottel Ginzburg, Amalia Droog, Yitzchak-Hirsch Held, Berl Held, Avraham Hochman, Yisrael Weinstock, Yosef Zesak, Baruch Tanis, Asher Leker, Berka Mogilensky, Asher Perlmutter, Noach Kotzker, and others.

At around that time, Bundist and Communist groups also began to operate in the shtetl. These activities were very restricted, and were assisted primarily through "injections" from the headquarters of these parties. However, one could not ignore them. The Bund directed its activities primarily toward the circles of the tradesmen, whereas the Communists directed their publicity primarily toward the circles of the workers. Despite the ideological opposition between the Bund and the Communists regarding all things related to the actual problems of Poland, they had a common front with respect to anything relating to Zionism. The common denominator was the hatred of Zion.

It can be said that this era, until 1927, was characterized by an increasing controversy between the Zionists and non-Zionists. The youth movements were still absent from this battle or controversy. The dispute was primarily between the adults. As time went on, separate lists for the civic elections of the Zionists and non-Zionists arose, and the division left is mark on all areas of communal life. The library was divided into two, and a separate Yiddishist library was set up. A Yiddishist school was founded. It was weaker than the Tarbut School, but it was supported by the Bundists and the circles close to them. People were certainly talking in the shtibels about the controversy and the opposition between the different camps, but it seems to me that the majority of the Jewish community did not stick its head into the thick of it, and stood at the side. The economic situation grew more serious and the Jews felt that their salvation would not come from the factions that were fighting among themselves. Many began to search for various means to immigrate overseas. Some arrived in the State of Colorado in the United States, and were followed by relatives and friends who heard about the land of gold. Others went to Argentina and Canada. The disappointment in the new Polish regime apparently penetrated the community, and anyone who could escape did so.

A noticeable change took place in 1927. The pioneering movement gained recognizable momentum in Poland, and our shtetl was also taken over by that movement.

Mendel and Gittel Klein, Yitzchak-Hirsch and Riva Fuchs, Dvora Choker, Feiga and Shachna Steinberg, Maya Steingarten, Pearl and Yitzchak Shapira

The one to come first was without doubt the Hashomer Hatzair movement, which forged a path to many youths who began to see their way in life as tied to this movement. Our friend Moshe Droog, who joined this movement while he was studying in Kowel, was the person who laid the foundation of the Hashomer Hatzair chapter in Ratno. Almost all of the students of the Tarbut School of all ages and classes, quickly found their way to this chapter. The central activists of the chapter included Chaim Ides, Chaya Droog, Dvora and Chaya Grabov, Yehudit Sandiuk, Zelda Feintuch, and others.

At almost the same time, a group of members organized themselves in the shtetl and set up Hechalutz Hatzair. This organization primarily catered to the working youth, including tradesmen and others, for whom the ideological path of Hashomer Hatzair was not acceptable. The prominent members of this group included Charna Greenstein, Maya Weinstock, Batya Chayat, Avraham Grabov, Mordechai Yanover, Shmuel Goldman, Yisrael Honik, and the writer of these lines. This group was helped by the leadership of Aryeh Avrech, who was already among the central motivators of the Hechalutz movement, and visited the various chapters from the Hechalutz headquarters. It is worthwhile to note that despite the difference in ideology and educational methodology between these movements, both functioned with the idea of honorable mutual coexistence. The competition between them was based on constructive foundations: in activities for the Zionist funds, in common events, activities of Hechalutz, and the like.

At the beginning of 1929, the first group of Ratno natives went out to hachshara. At the end of that year, in the midst of the disturbances of 5689 in the Land of Israel, our member, Mordechai Gefen, was authorized for aliya, and he set out on aliya. From that time, the path to actualization and aliya was open to many youths of Ratno - each person in the context of his movement. Many Ratno natives made aliya in this manner. The following are the names of the first ten people to make aliya, in the order of their aliya: Mordechai Gefen, Moshe Stern, Shmuel Marder, Isser Kwashnyk, Moshe Gutman, Simcha Lavie, Moshe Droog, Shmuel and Sara Goldman[1], Eliahu Feintuch, Ch. Givoni...

A group of activists

Bottom: Amalia Droog, Sheina Itzikson, Feicha Honik

Sitting: A. Ginzburg, Pogatsh, Esther Eilbaum, Chaim Steinberg, Sara Yunevitz

Standing: M. Eilbaum, B. Cohen, A. Held, Ch. Rider, Shapir

Translator's Footnote

1. Sara's maiden name is Papir. https://www.jewishgen.org/Yizkor/Ratno/rat086.html - f91-1r

On the Borders

by Aryeh Avrech

Translated by Jerrold Landau

Our mothers hardened their hearts to their sons and said: If you have a grocery store, you will ensure your livelihood. You were not created for greatness, and you must not set out overseas. Your house stands here at the coast, where your cradle was located, and where you will find comfort for your souls. A foolish spirit has entered into you. You speak of high and lofty things. Better than that would be for you to bear the yoke, live as a family with a mother of children, just as your father and I raised and nurtured you. You will be merchants. Do no disparage the small things. Earn coin after coin, and see a purpose in life. Climb the ladder higher and higher and merit to conduct business with the large cities of the country and amass a fortune. Your name will become known. - No dear mother! I cannot remain in your house - for it is destroyed. Idleness is consuming me like a moth and boredom is like mildew to me. There, outside, movement is beginning, calling toward life, work, and creativity.

The hidden gate is opened before us from there. It is like the gate of the Garden of Eden has opened before us, and a new light, the light of life, is sown for us. Let us arise, brothers and sisters, and go light the eternal candle in our home, which is the kibbutz.

Mother, you light the candles on Sabbath eves. We also light the candles on the eve of our great Sabbath, the eve of our aliya to the Land. We will prepare ourselves in great holiness to greet the queen that is waiting by the gate. We will wait with a trembling soul for the great moment when the voice will be heard, “And the children have returned to their borders!”[1].

Dear mother, will you prevent us from returning to the motherland? Will you prevent us from greeting the great Sabbath that comes at the end of the six days of work and creation? Will you withhold life from us?

The day will yet come when you too, Mother, will be called to join us and dwell in security in our home.

5689 (1929) (Lehavot, booklet 2)

Translator's Footnote

1. Jeremiah 31:16. https://www.jewishgen.org/Yizkor/Ratno/rat086.html - f91a-1r

Young Chalutz [Hechalutz Hatzair] in Ratno, Passover 5688

The Era of Ideological Excitement

by L. Baion

Translated by Jerrold Landau

Even though Ratno was dependent on larger cities from an economic perspective, this was not the case from a social and cultural perspective. The larger cities were not dependent on Ratno, and apparently Ratno was not dependent on them. Jewish life in the town was forged through the generations, and had set patterns and norms. The way of life was based on tradition and religion, and there were no factors that deviated from that path. Sabbaths and festivals, weddings and circumcisions, Bar Mitzvah and Shalom Zachar celebrations and the like were based on the traditions of many years, and they formed the transcendental connection of Jewish settlements.

The town had its own clergy: a rabbi, rabbinical judge, scribe, teachers of children, beadles, teachers, etc. who forged the spiritual life, and never felt any need for any trusteeship or assistance from the Jewish communities of the large cities. Even honorable matters such as the writing of a Torah scroll, the acceptance of a new rabbi, the choosing of a gabbai and the like never deviated from the narrow confines of the small Jewish community. The Hassidic movement did not function in this manner. The movement forged connections and relationships between Jews in various cities, including Ratno. All of the Hassidic shtibels that were centered on the Street of the Synagogue (Shul Gasse) developed and nurtured social activities and mutual connections on the way to or from the court of the Rebbe, and through various meetings with the Rebbe himself. This led to economic and business connections that strengthened throughout time. This way of life continued until the outbreak of the First World War in 1914.

The world order was shaken up in the wake of the world war, and cracks began to form in the set Jewish way of life. New winds began to blow in the world, which reached the narrow alleyways of tiny Ratno. The war sowed destruction around. There were frequent changes of regime which brought destruction and ruin in their wake. It was primarily the Jews that suffered. The retreating and advancing armies first took out all their wrath upon the Jews. Each side accused them with spying for the opposing side, and the Jews paid the full price for every defeat and every victory, even if they had no connection to either.

Hechalutz in Ratno Sept. 27, 1930

The Beginnings of Political Organization

At the end of the war, signs of small changes in the way of life began to show. The most significant was that the connection between Ratno and the regional city of Kowel was strengthened. The Zionist movement began to organize, the Hatzofeh scouting organization arose, dramatic clubs were founded, and various groups for social activity for orphans and other social needs were formed. In all such activities, there was influence as well as direct assistance from external institutions, the center in Warsaw, and the large neighboring city of Kowel. At around that time, the Jewish public bank was set up, which offered assistance to the merchants, tradesmen, and small-scale merchants. Various political movements sprouted and rose, including the General Zionists, Poale Zion, Young Zion, Hitachdut, Bund, and the

Communists. All of these movements developed cultural activities. The debate between those faithful to the Hebrew Language and the Yiddishists was particularly felt in the town. Each side maintained its own school. At that time, the tradesmen's union, the professional union and the civic library were also established. Emissaries and speakers came from Kowel to lecture or organize party activities. The motion was bi-directional, however, since delegates from Ratno also went to the various conventions and gatherings.

I wish to rescue from oblivion several episodes related to the beginning of the pioneering movement in our town.

The years 1924-1926 were the golden era of this movement. Chapters of Hechalutz sprouted up throughout Wolhyn in an almost spontaneous manner, gathering in thousands of youths who had reached the decision that they must move over to a more productive life and bind their fate to the kibbutz movement of the Land of Israel. At that time, hachshara also developed - that is, dozens of places in Wolhyn in which the chalutzim [Zionist pioneers] would have to prove their level of fitness for physical labor, their readiness for personal actualization, and their ability to accustom themselves to a collective life. In the hachsharah points in the city, the members worked at road construction, wood chopping, various building efforts, and any other job that came up. Their salary went to the kibbutz kitty.

One of the largest hachshara kibbutzim in Wolhyn was in Klesowa [Klesov], not far from the city of Sarny, where the members worked primarily in rock quarrying. Aharon Werba of Kowel, one of the leaders of Hechalutz in Wolhyn, would visit the chapters, help organize the work, choose the members who were to go to hachshara, and organization various events in the cities of Wolhyn for the benefit of hachshara and aliya. He interrupted his studies in the Diaspora due to economic reasons, but did not want to continue in the petite bourgeois lifestyle of his parents. Therefore, he immersed himself, with his full enthusiasm and energy, into the activities of Hechalutz, which he regarded as his primary objective. He arrived in Ratno as an emissary of Hechalutz, in order to strengthen our activities, to lecture, and to solicit for some campaign of Hechalutz. He impressed us greatly with his interesting lectures and his personality. It was immediately recognizable that this youth was blessed with talents. Indeed, the days that he dwelled in our town were like festival days to our youth.

Elka Papir on Hachshara in Kosow (1935)

I also went out to hachshara in Klesowa, and remained there for 11 months. My connections with several members in Kowel were strengthened - especially my connection with Yisrael Wachsman. These connections finally led to a specific ideological crisis. We both were troubled, and we both had doubts about the path of the movement. We both regarded the idea of the kibbutz as promoting social isolation and distance from the social struggle. We decided to view the kibbutz as a specific group enclosed in the bounds of the collective, and not involving itself in the general struggles that break out within the group. Many questions began to go through our minds: Does this not smack of egoism toward the chosen group? What is our role in the struggle against enslavement and toward salvation that was being conducted by Socialists throughout the entire world? Are we able or permitted to remain neutral in that struggle? We infected other members in Klesowa with our concerns and our doubts, and the debates regarding these matters were very vibrant, ending with our victory. In a general meeting of all the members who were certified for aliya, a decision was made to accept our ideological principles. The following is the text of the decision: "The kibbutz must be a small-scale social laboratory, which must prepare the spiritual leaders of the collective to take their appropriate place at the time of the social revolution, and to direct the world economy." This was more or less the version that was accepted with the most votes. From then on, the doubts and concerns deepened. New reasons arose in addition to the aforementioned reasons: the chalutz and kibbutz movement separate themselves from the world Socialist movement, do not identify with the workers striking for an increase in salary and better working conditions, and at times become strikebreakers by acting as scabs in workplaces that are in the midst of a strike. An additional complaint was that the chalutz movement directs its revolutionary fervor only toward the Land of Israel, and thereby distances parents from their children, instills a lack of faith in the youth toward their parents and their way of live, disparages Jewish culture and the language of the masses of the Jews by negating the Diaspora, etc. etc. We began to sense the need for a certain ideological sanitization that would bridge the gap between us and the masses of Jews in the Diaspora and their culture. The motto was: to return to the masses, to strengthen their class and situation, and to forge a strong permanent connection with their language and culture. The members who were attracted by these ideas gave up on aliya to the Land of Israel, and, from that point, invested all of their energy in completely different activities: setting up Jewish schools and libraries, bringing culture to the masses, promoting enlightenment, conducting lectures, founding Yiddish newspapers, and other such activities. I recall that Peretz Markish[1], Yaakov Zerubavel[2] and others were among the lecturers brought to Ratno and Kowel.

(From the "Pinkas Kowel" book.)

Translator's Footnotes

1. See http://en.wikipedia.org/wiki/Peretz_Markish https://www.jewishgen.org/Yizkor/Ratno/rat086.html - f94-1r

2. A Labor Zionist leader (1886-1967). https://www.jewishgen.org/Yizkor/Ratno/rat086.html - f94-2r

Hechalutz Hatzair [The Young Pioneer]

by Shmuel Goldman

Translated by Jerrold Landau

We were young. The realm of our lives was narrow, and the desire to organize began to foment in our hearts. The feeling of "young pioneers" began to enchant us like a legend. Our knowledge of the various issues of the movement was cloudy and unclear. The opportunities for organization were also meager. Idle, without work experience and financial means, but with energy and zeal, we continued without interruption with the idea to which we aspired, but did not exist. Day by day, we gathered in the fields and engaged in discussions. We knew one thing: our actions would succeed if we learned how to raise our restricted group to a high level with diligent effort.

The cultural work relating to pioneering issues was successful. Slowly but surely, we became a significant factor. Our knowledge broadened, and new members were added. One of our primary goals was to infiltrate the ranks of the populist working youth. We worked with the challenge of a meager location (a narrow room without sufficient light or room to sit). Nevertheless, our numbers grew with time, and approached 30 members. "Bituyim," our publication, of which five issues had already been released, helped significantly in gaining members. In particular, our influence increased in the Polish school, which most of the children of meager means attended.

The chapter grew and various questions floated about. We sent two members to the convention of directors in Beresteczko. The convention had a positive effect on the work of our members. They learned about the problems of the movement and better connected to its values. When they returned to the organization, they dedicated themselves to the work with their full energy. It was particularly difficult to organize the youths of the movement. We were lacking the appropriate mindset for this. It was only after frequent requests from their side that we organized them into a regiment called Tz'Yzyk. Today this group has 25 members, most of them students of the Tarbut School. They are dedicated to the organization, are concerned with it, are active in the Jewish National Fund, etc. There are two groups in this regiment: Dror and Amal. A member of the Bachurot section directed the group. The regiment committee is composed of directors of the groups and members chosen by the entire regiment. Through joint effort with Hashomer Hatzair, Hechalutz was organized into a group that numbers 60 members today. Our comrades are active in it and concerned for it. A female member of our chapter participated in the convention of leaders in Zelena (near Kowel) during the summer. Two others participated in the Hechalutz seminar in Warsaw. Today the chapter has 80 members who are organized into three different strata: Bachurot, Neorim, and Tzeirim. Each stratum has its own unique plan of activities.

Hechalutz Hatzair, issue 7, 1931

To Escape from the Valley of the Shadow of Death

by Batya Chayat

Translated by Jerrold Landau

It was a summer day. I sat alone at that time next to my house, while the wings of imagination bore me far away from the world of reality. I saw wonderful and amazing visions. Images passed before my eyes. I try now to remember, but I cannot bring them back to life. Yes, I do recall something. -- - - -- It was a summer morning. The sun had risen to make its path in the bright blue skies, and I was in the expanse of the fields. Everything around me was pleasant. The drops of dew winked in the heavy light from the grass, and the pleasant aroma that wafted up to my nose made me completely drunk. Mountains covered with grey could be seen in the horizon through the clear air. The thick grey and the peaks reached the heavens. -- -- --

Everything alive within me roared, and I was pinched. I woke up, but the echo of vague things arose within me. Wake up, leave the wasteland, flee, save your soul from the valley of the shadow of death, lest destruction overtake you.

I became sober, but my spirit did not quiet.

From the booklet “Bituyim” (Expressions), a publication of Young Hechalutz in Ratno. 10 Tevet, 5689 (1929).

Six that were Designated

by Avraham Grabov[1]

Translated by Jerrold Landau

We were six with innocent childhood whims. When the glances of the eyes could interpret the matter - the face blushed... We, two girls and four boys, gathered together in the sand dunes, near the coniferous trees. Friendship flowed from their words, and the truth was clarified: From today, we are members of Hechalutz Hatzair. When we returned to the city, the six of us had different faces. The field served as the place for the discussions. We were sustained by the newspapers of previous days. We spoke about connections with the headquarters, about "ourselves" and "them," about difficulties. It was still too early to speak about attracting the youths, even though we had the desire to impart our ideas to others. We had already received several letters from the headquarters, which imparted hope to us. We also read an article in Hechalutz Hatzair about such matters.

The town was in ferment, and the work of the secretary was beyond compare. The duty was accepted with love. There was internal organization, heartfelt love, and mutual responsibility.

We rented a room before the end of the summer. The windows were broken, and it did not even have a bench or a table - just four unplastered walls. We were careful to pay the monthly rent. Everything was in order.

If the candles burnt out, a member would run home, a distance of a kilometer or more, without anyone asking him to do so. He would return with a red face, breathing heavily, with a candle in his hand. The group sat on the floor. One person held the candle and a second one read. After deliberations, they would disperse with fear of the next day. From time to time, everyone would be enthusiastic over new programs. Doubts would be intermixed with dedication and worry.

With the passage of time, the small group took on an entirely different form. The self-interest grew. The childhood caprices gave way to conflict, and there was a desire to expose the bad in other people. There were conversations that were not for a positive reason.

From within the ranks sprouted the individual, the one who bore the load: it could not go on like this. He saw the need for changes, and would not abandon it. At night, during long evenings, in the morning, masses of demanding children stood before his eyes.

Months passed, half years went by and the youths grew up. Intelligence exuded from their eyes.

Traditional notions, concepts from the parents that had been collected in the minds of the youths, fell away in heaps within one evening.

The youths knew about freedom of thought and democracy, and became skillful at critical inquiry. The bounty of life beckoned to them, and they came to the group willingly to take hold, to take hold. He, the member of the ranks from that time, was like an overflowing well that gave of its bounty. He snatched a glance of pity upon himself at every appropriate moment. Before him were dusty souls, eyes thick with beauty, demanding and complaining.

... And the town - its Sabbaths continued on like the slumber of a cat. The light in the houses gave evidence of people sitting by the table playing cards. An extended yawn. In his heart - desires, aspirations, and pining for the expanses.

5681 (1921) - Hechalutz Hatzair, booklet 7.

Translator's Footnote

1. The style of this article is awkward, and was difficult to translate. There was a mixture of first person and third person - and I changed it to first person for
clarity. https://www.jewishgen.org/Yizkor/Ratno/rat086.html - f98-1r

by Shmulik Goldman[1]

Translated by Jerrold Landau

The pioneering movement was the central point of my life. I differentiate between two periods of my life: the first period was before I came to pioneering, and the second period was when I was within the pioneering organization and movement. Very few impressions remain with me from the first period, but I do remember the following: My father was fleeing and a Polish Hallerczyk was chasing after him, a man chasing after a man: a man fleeing and hiding from another man. A second moment was during the pogroms when they were murdering Jews. A feeling of revenge was awakened within me, and this came to fruition during my day to day activities.

I got to know Hechalutz for the first time through my work in digging trenches in the field. I enjoyed this, and thoughts about the kibbutz began with desires for pioneering "harmony." I was among the organizers of Hechalutz Hatzair (before this, I was a member of Hashomer Hatzair) in my Shtetl. After I joined the chapter and began to work, the feeling of revenge passed. I understood the immorality of this. There were teachers in the Polish school who insulted the honor of the nation. There were altercations between us, and I was removed from the school more than once. I transferred to a Hebrew school. I did not find myself properly there either. They did not educate in the pioneering spirit.

I said that a Hebrew school of this nature had no rights of existence. At home, they did not permit me to work in the chapter.

I wished to actualize. I was 16-years-old, not yet fit for physical labor, but my will was strong. I was certain that the kibbutz would accept me. How could they not accept me when I wished to actualize? I escaped to the moshava. I met other young pioneers. Klesowa became my objective. Many legends floated around about it. There was a story of a group of members who stubbornly tied their fate to the place until the gates of the Land would open. It was told about a march on foot to Warsaw, to the Office of the Land of Israel, in order to demand the opening of the gates of the Land.

I struggled with "connections." I befriended everyone. This angered my parents. As time went on, they also got used to this reality in the house, but they did not yet get accustomed to the idea of hachshara. We worked at chopping trees. After work, we did not go home, but rather to the hall. We danced a great deal until we fell to the ground in exhaustion. This was a moment of enthusiasm. We already began to feel this in the chapter. I was very dedicated to the chapter. I always dreamed about agricultural work.

When I returned from the moshava, I began to work in the district. I thought: I must not remain in the chapter, I must actualize. I was the first one of our Hechalutz Hatzair chapter to go on hachshara, and this was without authorization. The separation was very difficult. I had a feeling of regret, but I overcame it and restrained myself.

From Klesowa I went to the pioneering seminary. I wished to obtain a scientific grounding (even now, I want to learn very much). The conversations on "friendship" left a strong impression on me. "To love a person even if he is bad." The farewell party at the seminary, the words of Tabenkin and Grinbaum, were words filled with flames. I got sick and traveled home. Even at home I took no interest in the business of my father. I could not tolerate myself for living under the support of my father, so I traveled to a kibbutz. The natural setting in Neman influenced me greatly and established my relationship to nature.

(From a discussion about my path to the movement, and my way in it.) At the conference of directors in Lachowice, 5691 - 1931.

Translator's Footnote

1. Untitled in the text. In the table of contents listed as "My Path to the Movement." https://www.jewishgen.org/Yizkor/Ratno/rat086.html - f98a-1r

Mornings in my Town

by Avraham Grabov

Translated by Jerrold Landau

As I was walking in the marketplace, rays of sunlight sparkled in my eyes.
A cool wind caressed me, and various feelings went through my insides.
I saw the shops before me.
The shops, upon which the merchandise was arrayed on the shelves: lies and falsehood!
They are still closed tight. They also seek rest and fragments of dreams.
There is no movement. Only silence sings and rings.
And I am standing here as if in a circle, it is dancing around me, it is closing me in,
To where? Where should you go? Stand here!...
My heart wonders, and my hands spread asking questions:
Should I indeed remain here, and not go out to the field at sunrise?

The Second World Seminar of Hechalutz Hatzair in Grochow (1931)
At the rightmost edge of the top row: Avraham Grabov of blessed memory
At the left most edge of the third row: Shmuel Goldman

Moments

by Avraham Grabov

Translated by Jerrold Landau

He[1] derived a special type of enjoyment in my home as he sat next to the oven having sad thoughts, unintentionally making a line with the finger on the dew-covered window panes with everything that comes to mind: his name, and the names of the family members. After all this - words in the vernacular lacking any meaning, that entered the system during the school parties from long ago, wrote themselves.

He would stand and look, think and ponder, weave his own and borrowed threads, about the complexities of life and the riddles of the universe. Atop this - was the clock with its deathly ticking, as the death of a person. These were indeed unpleasant moments, frightening as the sparks of madness that removed all self-control from a person and left him open to blind fate, where anything could happen. However, they also had a unique charm, some sort of comfort for the soul and satisfaction: who are the human insects, crawling in such an absurd manner to earn their bread - can you understand it? Enjoyment sprouts up in the depths of agony. And when he would go out to stroll - he would bear upon himself a burden of thoughts that cast dust throughout all the cells of his brain, about the difficulties of life and personal preparations, about internal calm and certainty in the face of death. He would continue to go, kneading the mud with his shoes, as the rays of sunlight beat down upon him, penetrating him - without sensing the tears on his eyes.

Why did the tears come? Perhaps over the 15 years of his young life? It was not that. Strange hidden forces pulled him in both directions, with him in the middle.

Many attempted to interpret these goals. Dreams fluttered by: perhaps to abandon this "nonsense" and come to the status of Father, who sits every Saturday night surrounded by merchants like the spider from which many threads spread out.

No! No! Not this, not this. A life of understanding and human feeling.

Hints beckon. The heart is pulled after "great men." Wholeheartedly, he swallowed biographies of poets, writers and people of renown. Books of memoirs, and learning parables from them, were pleasant to him. A feeling of a mission welled up inside of him. How? In what way? To where? It was not clear.

5693 (1933) Hechalutz Hatzair, booklet 15.

Translator's Footnote

1. As in other articles by this author, the story mixes the first and third persons. https://www.jewishgen.org/Yizkor/Ratno/rat086.html - f100a-1r

by Shmulik Goldman[1]

Translated by Jerrold Landau

"How pale is your face! How strange is your gaze. Are you ill?"
My gaze is strange and my face is pale when I look upon you who are immersed in the Diaspora.
I am not ill. It is only you who are ill!
My gaze is strange as I peer into the depths of your conscience and see:
It is empty of anything new, it is full of old withered stuff!
You have only one concern - to fill your stomachs.
The fleshpots, the onions and garlic, will always stand before your eyes.
You are the generation of the desert, you will not feel the desolation;
Dead corpses do not want to know and understand the transition to life!
Your feeling has dimmed. Your flesh will be ploughed over and your skin will be flayed.
Then the old refrain will emanate from your mouths:
"We are sanctifying the Divine Name!"
-- You know that G-d commanded you to be killed over a commandment,
But to attempt to build over the destruction and to change your situation -
This too will not enter your spirit!

(Bituyim [Expressions] booklet, Ratno.)

Translator's Footnote

1. This poem is untitled https://www.jewishgen.org/Yizkor/Ratno/rat086.html - f101-1r

The Cyzyk Group in Ratno. September 27, 1930

I Will Not Allow!

By Shmulik Goldman[1]

Translated by Jerrold Landau

It seems that Mother and Father tried to plant gall and wormwood in me,
The weeds that grow on a desolate field.
And intend to bind me in chains,
Also the redeeming hands for the abandoned soul.
I will not allow -
You believe!
And what if my back is not used to being bent under a heavy load?
It will become accustomed!
And what if my feet are not used to walking on scorching stones?
They will get used to it!
And I will not allow Mother and Father to bind me in chains.

(Published in the Massada publication in Kowel, 5689 - 1929)

Translator's Footnote

1. This poem is untitled https://www.jewishgen.org/Yizkor/Ratno/rat086.html - f102-1r

Sara Ginzburg, Ruth Greenstein and Shmuel Goldman of Ratno on Hachsharah in Klosow

Spring on the Roads

by Shaul Greenstein

Translated by Jerrold Landau

The fields and meadows clear out. Paths overflow between the colorful carpets. Trails intersect in the blue horizon, and a pleasant silence whispers a secret all around. Wayfarers go along the way in wagons and on foot, and many Jews go to the fair in the nearby city. They go in grey groups, one like the next. The same groans, the same conversations, the same sunken eyes and faces wrinkled with tribulations. Footpaths lead to the different chapters. Lone people go through the paths in the fields alongside the spring sun. It is like a colorful kerchief spread out before the fields. The wind plays with my coat. I walk with a joyous heart and sense the pulse of spring in my veins. Jewish towns. Lowly houses, poverty and lack. Worries of livelihood darken the faces "like the underside of a pot." There is sadness, sadness. Even in the spring. Only in the chapter, in the meeting hall, is there a bright, encouraging corner. The eyes sparkle and the hearts are bound together and alert: what will we do on hachshara? What is with the movement? What is the news from the Land? More than once when I came to the chapter that I had been attending for several months, I see: the context widened, the membership grew, it strengthened. You are filled with an internal joy when you witness the joy of a gardener watching the growth of his saplings, woven with strands of love.

There is a faithful splendor to our pioneering movement. It is spring. A pleasant, bountiful spring. Far off, the thunder roars, but the heart swells with joy. What type of deep faith and encouraging hope fill you as you see the trees budding, the fields growing with pleasant greenery, and the young pioneers who are growing up and making aliya to the towns of Israel.

Booklet 3-4, Hechalutz Hatzair, 1939.

In the Workshops of the Early Pioneers

by Sh. Goldman

Translated by Jerrold Landau

{Translator's note: the following marginal text does not form an article of its own, but rather serves as editorial background to the article.}

We find a brief expression of what was transpiring in the souls of the Ratno youth during the early 1930s, with the background of the boredom and the lack of prospects in the town, in this chapter from the diary of Shmuel Goldman, who is well-known from the Book of Klesowa. We should note that he was a 17-year-old lad at the time he wrote this material in his diary. This was written in February, 1930. The words speak for themselves and require no commentary. Even if we strip away the cloak of rhetoric which was natural for a youth of that era in those towns, we see a realistic picture of the reality. Shmulik Goldman, a 17-year-old lad, expresses his personal revolution. He left his parental home, did not even bid farewell to his father, and set out for a place that to him symbolized the epitome of pioneering that was both harsh and wonderful, which was the motto of Klesowa during that time.

***

... My town Ratno. Sabbath. Heaviness of the heart, and there is no air to breathe. It is constricted around. I have no more place here. Tomorrow I will be leaving the town to the place to which my heart entices me to go. There I will sense the taste of freedom. There I will not have to lean on the shoulders of Father and Mother. I will be a productive man – a worker – sustaining myself through the toil of my hands. I packed my clothes and other personal effects in a suitcase. On Sunday, I will be traveling from here to Klesowa.

It was Sunday morning. I got up – and I found that sadness pervaded in our house. Father was groaning. Mother was weeping. The hope of Father and Mother was that I would not be able to live on the Kibbutz, for one must work hard there and I am so weak in body. Aside from this, the conditions of life there cannot be compared at all to those which I am accustomed to from home. I would certainly escape from there in a brief period and return here. I parted from my parents. Mother hugged me and embraced me, but Father refused to part from me. It was silent around. There were tears on all faces. There was silent wailing. Everyone was weeping – and me too... Next to the bus there were dozens of people who came to bid me farewell. Their eyes were fixed upon me – some with indifference and some with jealousy.

The bus moved. The trip was quick, and I was already in Sarny. In another half an hour I would be in Klesowa, the place I so desired, the place which led to the rift between me and my parents and made me cause them so much suffering.

I arrived in Klesowa on a rainy day. There was a sharp contrast between nature and my golden dreams... The first person to greet me at the train station was a lad who was not a member of the Kibbutz. I asked him, "How do we get to the Kibbutz?" He looked at me and said, "How nice are your shoes, but in another hour they will no longer be in your possession. In their place you will receive a pair of 'rubbers.' It is also too bad about the nice coat that you are wearing. Arise, lad, and travel immediately back to your home!" "Don't worry," I answered him, and continued on my way. Then I was met by a lad who had a sort of old hat on his head, torn pants, and "rubbers" on his feet. I asked him the way to the Kibbutz, and he showed me the way there.

I came to the house of the Kibbutz. The windows were broken. There were wooden planks in place of glass window panes. It was filthy and damp. Drops of water dripped from the ceiling incessantly. There were loaves of bread upon the long tables. On one of the walls, there were dusty red bands covering the pictures of Borochov and Trumpeldor. My eyes fixed upon the inscription on one of the pictures, and I stared at it for a long time. Suddenly, one of the girls who worked in the kitchen ran in and asked me, "You are new, from where are you? Perhaps you will eat something?" She ran into the kitchen and returned with a small dish of porridge for me.

The girls who worked in the clothing warehouse took my suitcase from me and left in my hands only work clothes. One of them brought me a pair of "rubbers."

I met a girl whom I knew from our mutual participation in the "Hechalutz Hatzair" (Young Pioneers) counselors' camp. There, her face and white hands were suffused with such delicacy, whereas here, her face exuded somberness and worry... There was only a simple greeting, "So you are here too? All the roads lead to here"...

The next day, I went out to work in the quarry. I dug up rocks to load on the wagons at a quick pace. Someone turned to me and said, "During the first days, until you get used to the work, you should not dig up large rocks. Leave me the heavy ones, and you take the light ones." At first I was embarrassed, but the pleasant words of the lad were friendly, simple, and convincing.

In the evening, a meeting took place to celebrate the five years of the existence of the kibbutz at that place. More than 200 hearts beat together in the narrow room. It was as if the walls and the ceiling were breathing heavily and sweating. Life was difficult; issues were difficult, but true... One of them said, "We have known failures, but we have overcome them. Through suffering and stubbornness, we will forge here a workshop for Hebrew pioneering." A second one continued on by telling about "a difficult winter, lack of work, desertion... but we grew and we are now a large group." Every word that was spoken hit its mark, was etched upon the heart, created enthusiasm, and demanded. Will I also be able to persevere as they did? All the strands of my soul whisper, "Yes!" After the meeting, there was dancing until midnight.

We set out for work early in the morning. Despite the pains of acclimatizing, I entered into my work, which became natural for me.

The Hechalutz Carpentry Workshop in the town

The Uniqueness of our Chapter

by Devora and Yehudit, Mesilot

Translated by Jerrold Landau

We both joined the Hashomer Hatzair movement when we were about ten years old. This was at the time when organized activities began among the youth of Ratno. The Hashomer Hatzair in Ratno excelled in its dynamic activities over and above all the other chapters in the Wolhyn district. We now realize that this accomplishment was only due to the leadership of the chapter head Moshe Droog. He succeeded in organizing the activities of the chapter in such a manner that we would be able to continue the appropriate activities even when he was absent from the chapter. Indeed, Moshe Droog was forced to remain in Kovel throughout most of the days of the week since he was studying in the gymnasium there. Only now can we begin to appropriately appreciate his unique way of action, for, as we know, many youth movement chapters in Wolhyn weakened greatly or even disbanded when the chapter head left or made aliya. Such a thing did not take place in Ratno. The chapter occupied all of our free time. The Hebrew language was used primarily in the chapter, but there were also echoes of Yiddish. The students of Noach Kotzker and the excellent teacher Brodsky had no difficulty with their free expressions of Hebrew; however, there were also those in the chapter who did not study in the Hebrew school or who stopped their studies too soon.

Our household quickly made peace with our membership in the movement, even though this membership meant parting from the home, i.e. our aliya. The Zionistic pioneering spirit that had brought us to the youth movements, primarily Hashomer Hatzair and Hechalutz, slowly penetrated many of the Jewish homes in the town. As we got older and entered the older levels of the movement, aliya to the Land was no longer considered something unusual, as it was when the first ones, Mordechai Weinstock and Stern, made aliya. Life in the town was supported upon nothingness. The youth saw no chance that the dark skies would brighten. The clouds over our heads in the town did not clear, and there was no chance that they would clear. We bound ourselves firmly with the Land of Israel, and the realities there interested us much more than the realities in Poland.

We joined the nucleus of the Tel Chai Kibbutz that was organized in Wolhyn. We went to Hachsharah, and made aliya to the Land. After some time, our Tel Chaim Kibbutz merged with the Mesilot Kibbutz of the Beit Shean Valley. We are located there to this day.

There is no doubt that Hashomer Hatzair in Ratno was the prime factor that forged the spirits of the hundreds of youth who passed through this chapter. It strengthened their spirits, placed challenges before them, and taught them how to deal with the many difficulties and stumbling blocks in their path. This was perhaps true with every chapter of Hashomer Hatzair, but it seems to us that this was proved most clearly with the Ratno chapter. There was something unique about this chapter, and only someone who has passed through all the educational chapters and groups in this chapter can understand the essence and reasons for this uniqueness.

Dvora and Yehudit, Mesilot

The Chapter of Hashomer Hatzair in Ratno

by Zeev Grabov

Translated by Jerrold Landau

The impetus to found the chapter came from Amalia Droog. She was a student of the Hebrew Gymnasium in Kovel and belonged to the "Galei Aviv" brigade of the Hashomer Hatzair Chapter in that city. When Amalia came to Ratno for summer vacation, she advised her brother Moshe to establish a chapter of Hashomer Hatzair in Ratno. Moshe agreed, and was assisted in his first steps by Motka (Mordechai) Melamed of the Kovel chapter. This took place in the summer of 1928.

The first members of the movement were the grade six students of the Tarbut school, including Zelda Feintuch, Dvora and Chaya Grabov, Yehudit Sandiuk, Chaya Weintraub, Pnina Ternblit, Feiga Marin, Berl Honyk, Zelig Bander, Chaim Ides, Moshe-Chaim Fuchs, Simcha Leker, Eliahu Feintuch, Yosef Steinberg, and others. Most of these youths left the chapter after a brief period. Only Chaim Ides, Berl Honyk, and Moshe Chaim Fuchs remained.

Connections were quickly forged with the central leadership in Warsaw as well as the leadership of the Wolhyn District in Rowno. Sections, brigades and groups began to form, in accordance with the organizational structure of the movement of that time. The living force behind the chapter was Moshe Droog. The leadership of the chapter included: Zelda Feintuch, Chaim Ides, Berl Honyk, Moshe-Chaim Fuchs, Chaya Grabov, Henia Karsh, and others. The chapter grew for a period of two to three years, and it already had four groups of "Kfirim" (ages 10-12), two groups of young scouts (Tzofim), two groups of older scouts, and a group of graduates who formed the kernel of the chapter.

Every group had a counselor. The activities and programs were conducted in accordance with the plans received from Warsaw and Rowno, and were carried out primarily through the counselors themselves.

The "maon" (as the location of the chapter was called) was located first in the house of Shefe Langer, then in the house of Chmiler, and then in the house of Zelda-Leah's, until finally it settled in a spacious hall that was designated for that purpose as a meeting hall, replete with a stage for performances and public gatherings. This house belonged to Itzel Baal-Chotem (literally With the Nose) and was a beehive of activity on all the days of the week. It was decorated with all types of drawings and insignias, the work of Goldale Droog. Every group had its own corner in the hall, and set activity days. The counselors of the "Kfirim" came from the "Hatzofim" group, and the counselors of "Hatzofim" came from the graduates. The names of the "Kfirim" groups were "Zrizim", "Zivoniot", "Charutzim", and "Dganiot". The names of the "Hatzofim" groups were: "Snuniot", "Yarden", "Nesher", and the like. Each group had its own flag that bore the insignia of the group. The groups formed the brigades, which also had their own flags. In one word – the organization was exemplary. The group often had visits from the central and district leadership. These visits inspired a renewed wave of pleasant activities, with new songs with which the group became familiar. They also firmed up the connection between the chapter in Ratno and the entire movement. For the most part, the visitors would be hosted in the homes of Chaya and Devora Grabov or Moshe Droog. A wall newspaper, in which many members of the chapter participated, appeared monthly. Many Zionist activists would come to look at it and enjoy the fine Hebrew of the articles of the Ratno youth, who gave expression to their thoughts and aspirations in this publication.

An important event in the life of the chapter was the public examination that was organized by the "Kfirim" with the participation of the parents and teachers. People would only be accepted into the movement after they passed this test. Then, the head of the chapter would give them the blue band and affix the "colors" to their shoulder, and they would be considered "Shomrim" in all respects. This was an impressive event, and served as a topic of discussion for the members of the chapter, the students of Tarbut, and in the homes of the members.

After the ceremony, the inductees would repeat the ten commandments of Hashomer, They would be especially careful with the "Shomer word." The meaning of the "Shomer word" was truth and firmness, and woe unto anyone's use of the Shomer honor word for a matter of falsehood...

Older members of Hashomer Hatzair

Nine of them made aliya to the Land of Israel. The rest perished in the Holocaust

With the crystallization of the ideological path that began in the Hashomer Hatzair movement, a deeper delving into the education activities began to take place. This was helped significantly by the publications of the movement: "Hamitzpeh" – the publication of the Hatzofim, and "Hashomer Hatzair" – the publication of the graduates. Tens of copies of these two publications were distributed in Ratno, not only among the members of the movement. During the early 1930s, the personal soul

was already accentuated. That means: going out to Hachsharah and aliya to the Land. Although the Socialist idea was the founding idea of the movement, scouting as not pushed aside, for the Ratno chapter nurtured it from its inception.

{Summer Moshava of Hashomer Hatzair in the village of Vydranitsa.}

The following fact testifies to the level of success of the chapter in scouting and parades: In 1935, the Hashomer Hatzair chapter organized a festive parade to celebrate Lag Baomer. The Jews of Ratno, and not only Jews, watched the parade that brought joy to their hearts, for we rehearsed it properly and were attentive to each and every detail. The next day, I met Aharon-Shia Konishter, Moshe's father, who transmitted the following announcement to us: "The chief of police asked me to transmit the request to you and Golda Droog that the Hashomer Hatzair chapter appear in the parade in honor of the Polish Independence Day on May 3, which will take place in a few days." He repeated himself and stressed that we were to appear in the same fashion as we did on Lag Baomer, "with full arms", meaning with full splendor and glory, for the "who's who" of the district of Ratno would be present, and the police chief desires that the parade leave a deep impression. To add strength to the request, Konishter added that the chief felt the need to point out that if we do not appear in the parade – we will have nothing more to do in Ratno.

Things moved along, and nobody imagined that we would respond anything, but positively, to the police chief. We appeared appropriately, and I recall that Golda Droog even recited a poem in Polish, which also left a deep impression. In return for our participation in this parade of the Third of May, we were later able to carry on our activities in the chapter without any government interference.

Literary judgments were often organized in the chapter on various topics, such as: Shakespeare's Shylock, Bialik's "Lion without a Body", Shabtai Tzvi, and others. These "judgments" attracted large audiences, and those who participated in them in an objective manner prepared seriously for their appearance as witnesses of either the prosecution or defense.

There was great preparation in the chapter in 1933 in anticipation of the celebration of five years of its existence. The movement in general spoke about intensification, enrolling new members, deepening the educational activities, etc. The Ratno chapter took part appropriately in all of this. Within a few months, the girls wove the flag of the chapter with colorful threads. A splendid parade through the streets of the city took place to dedicate the flag. The play of Yitzchak Lamdan, "Massada", was performed at the party celebrating five years of the existence of the chapter. A great deal of preparation took place for this play. The chapter was decorated with many mottoes and symbols, and this was the first time that the electric lighting operated. The hall was filled to the brim with adults and youth who purchased tickets for this festive occasion. The celebration was opened by a choir conducted by Meir Rider, singing the song Lehava, Alay Lehava" (A Flame, A Flame is Upon Me). This was followed by an athletic display in the form of a pyramid. The conductor of all of this was Moshe Droog. At the end of the celebration, the members of the leadership of the chapter as well as those graduates who excelled in their activities were granted the "Third Level", as a sign of "be strong and powerful." Those who received this symbol affixed it permanently on their Hashomer shirt and were very proud of it.

Golda Droog (standing) and her friends Bilha and Zahava

The chapter also utilized outside people for its educational activities. For example, Mordechai Janower, a member of "Young Hechalutz", would give lessons in Hebrew literature; the teacher Kotzker would lecture on various topics; Avraham Grabov, a member of "Young Hechalutz", would lead various discussions with the graduates of the movement whenever he would be in Ratno. During the long vacation, Amalia Droog would give lessons on the knowledge of the Land.

A leadership change took place in the chapter starting from the years 1933-1934. Moshe Droog began to prepare for aliya, and he transferred the leadership of the chapter to Chaim Ides. After he went on hachshara, Zelda Feintuch became the head of the chapter. The next one, after Zelda went on hachshara, was Moshe Konishter. When he too went on hachshara along with all the members of the "Nesher" group, the leadership of the chapter was given over to Goldale Droog and the writer of these lines.

The new leadership of the chapter was not shy about its advancement. Serious activity took place in all areas. It is especially worthwhile to make note of the Chanukah and Purim parties that were conducted with great fanfare. The meetings of the chapter served as a forum for an accounting of the activities for the funds, including the fund for the workers of the Land of Israel (Kapa"i); for noting the names of the groups that excelled; and for laying the plans for future activities. Chaim Ides served as the librarian of the Y. Ch. Brener Library. The librarians and their advisors regarding the purchase of books held an annual meeting in the home of the teacher Kotzker. They would update the catalog of the library and identify those books that were "forbidden" to those of a young age.

The chapter fulfilled a special role in its activity on behalf of the Jewish National Fund. Among other things, the income from the selling of bottles and various rags in the summer, horseradish harvested from the frozen ground for Passover, work in the baking of matzos, chopping trees in the winter, and other such activities of this sort was donated to this fund. A portion of the funds was donated to the Hashomer Fund and to purchase sports equipment for the chapter.

During the 1931-1932 school year, new teachers were hired for the school, including the teacher Rozen, who was a member of Beitar. It is obvious that the Hashomer Hatzair chapter was a thorn in his eyes, and it was difficult for him to witness its constant growth. He used all sorts of means to turn the students toward Beitar. Despite his great success in teaching Polish literature in the upper grades, he did not succeed in transferring students from Hashomer Hatzair to Beitar. After some time, young teachers who were graduates of the Tarbut Seminary in Vilna, were hired as teachers. Some of them had been members of Hashomer Hatzair. Of course, we found common ground with them, and they participated with us in everything related to the activities of the chapter. The teacher Shlomo Karlin, young, handsome, and musically inclined, is to be especially noted. He organized a mandolin band in the school, and also helped establish a unique band whose instruments were bottles filled with water in varying amounts. After Amalia Droog returned to Ratno as a graduate of the teachers' seminary and began teaching in the school, additional growth of the chapter began, and the Hashomer education deepened. This continued until the Soviet invasion of the city.

The cooks at the Summer Moshava: M. Droog. Ch. Grabov, H. Karsh, Y. Sandiuk, D. Grabov, Z. Feintuch (all in Israel), and Y. Frigel (perished)

The Summer Moshava

As is known, these Moshavas (summer settlements or camps) were the daily bread of the Hashomer members. The primary leadership of the movement, as well as the leadership of the Wolhyn region, organized many summer Moshavas, both central and in outlying areas. However, the members of the Ratno chapter were unable to participate in these Moshavas, for the cost was beyond the means of the parents, most of whom were lacking in means and to whom such an expense seemed superfluous. The leadership of the Ratno chapter decided to organize a local summer Moshava. The plans and preparations for this began after Passover. One of the activities designated to provide means for the summer Moshava was the collection of sugar. Every member of the chapter was required to bring one cube of sugar when he came to the chapter. Thus, 2-3 kilograms of sugar were collected each month. We would sell the sugar at a low price to one of the shopkeepers who was numbered among our friends. The income would be divided into two: one half would be dedicated to the fund for the Moshava, and the other half would be kept for an emergency. What type of emergency? It means that, if heaven forbid, a danger existed of losing the flag of the Jewish National Fund, which the movement had received since it dedicated most of its income for that fund. Throughout three months, we collected sufficient money to rent a barn and a house next to the village of Vydranitsa, a distance of approximately 7 kilometers from Ratno, where we intended to conduct the Moshava.

However, sugar itself was insufficient. When the time came to go out to the Moshava, we began to collect "other vegetables"[1]: potatoes, cucumbers, groats, noodles, and other such provisions which were to serve as our daily fare in our summer Moshava. The campers were expected to bring eating utensils, pots for cooking, firewood, and the like. Many of them had to bring these from their own homes.

Two or three days before we went out to the Moshava, a group of older people went there to prepare the area, and especially to dig tables from the sandy soil, in accordance with all the scouting principles of Boyden-Paul upon which we depended.

The Moshava itself lasted for two weeks. We slept on straw and hay in the barn. The flag of the chapter fluttered high, and an honor guard stood next to it day and night. Attempts were made to steal the flag, but they failed, for the eyes of the scouts were alert, and the members of the guard fulfilled their role faithfully. Aside from various study sessions, the summer Moshava made trips in the region to acquaint themselves from close up with the landscape, the plants, etc. At the end of the Moshava, we arranged a large parade with torches through the streets of the town.

The Hechalutz Hatzair organization also learned from our attempts, and they too arranged a Moshava in that same village, not far from the Hashomer Hatzair camp. It is fitting to note that friendly relations generally pervaded between them and us. I recall only one case of a battle between us. This took place when it became clear that Hechalutz Hatzair was about to receive the guardianship of the flag of the Jewish National Fund, as it succeeded in bringing in a larger sum that year than did the Hashomer Hatzair chapter. Everything was arranged for the flag to be given over to them. However, when the deputy, Mr. Asher Leker, and the secretary, Mr. Kamper, were making the final preparations, Berl Honyk, who was responsible for Jewish National Fund activities in our chapter, suddenly appeared. He brought with him two young scouts with a large sum of money that had been collected from the sale of sugar, and gave it over to the fund. Thereby, he tipped the scales and averted the danger that the flag would not be left to us. The movement breathed a sign of relief...

The Final Years

After the graduates of the "Nesher" group went out to Hachshara in the Shomria farm in Czestochowa, the leadership of the chapter was transferred to a younger group, as had been said.

Reb Asher Leker, delegate of the Jewish National Fund. One of the town's notables

Members of Hashomer Hatzair of Ratno in the Hachshara Camp of Czestochowa

Hashomer Hatzair of Ratno, Lag Baomer 5692 (1932)

From that time, the central kernel was the "Tel Chai" brigade, and Goldale Droog demonstrated that she could be depended upon as she held the scepter of the head of the chapter appropriately. Moshe Ponetz, from among the graduates, helped her and me significantly with the organizational and educational activities. In 1938, 20 of the graduates went out to hachshara in Rowno. They returned to Ratno with aliya permits, but the gates of the land were virtually closed and certificates were not available. This situation caused a negative feeling among the graduates, which got worse as the economic situation in the town became more serious. Signs of the worsening depression could be seen everywhere. The Tarbut School was also struggling hard for its existence. The chapter was a sort of drop of comfort in the increasing sea of tribulations. At that time, the activities of the choir were renewed under the conductorship of Aharon Roizman, who replaced Meir Rider after he transferred to Beitar. Performances were put on, the income of which was dedicated to the purchase of books for the library, which already had more than 1,000 books from the choicest of literature.

The final performance put on by the chapter was "The Yeshiva Student". It enjoyed success.

When the Soviets invaded Western Ukraine in September 1939, a dark, heavy cloud descended over all the activities of the Zionist institutions and organizations. All of the movements which served as the "Additional Soul" of the Jewish community of Ratno were forced to liquidate their activities. Thus came the end of the spirit of Jewry during the Soviet era even before the Jews themselves were physically liquidated by the Nazis.

Translator's Footnote

1. A play on words of "shear yerakot" from the four questions of the Passover Seder. https://www.jewishgen.org/Yizkor/Ratno/rat103.html - f1r

Right to left: Moshe Droog (in Israel), Aryeh Avrech and Mordechai Yanover of blessed memory

The Pact of Trumpeldor (Beitar) and the Revisionists

by Dov Marin

Translated by Jerrold Landau

Right to left: Group of Hachsharat Beitar in Zelba on Simchat Torah, 5694 (1933). Marin and Steingarten, members of Beitar in Ratno, on a hachshara group

Even before the Beitar youth movement was officially organized, there were several Revisionists in Ratno who followed the path of Jabotinsky and were educated with his statements that were published in the Jewish daily newspapers in Poland. They were waiting for an appropriate time to found the movement. The events of Av[1] 1929 in the Land of Israel formed a fitting occasion for such. As far as I recall, Beitar was founded in the town at the end of that year. Janusz Jundorf of Kovel came to us to organize the first members of Beitar and instruct them in the ways of the movement. After some time, a second counselor from Kovel, Vernik, arrived. He also helped crystallize the ideological path of the movement in a significant fashion.

The founding of Beitar in Ratno aroused excitement among the ranks of the youth. Ideological debates began in the upper grades of Tarbut and on the Jewish streets. The majority of the youth had already been "taken" by Hashomer Hatzair and Hechalutz Hatzair, especially those youths who studied in Tarbut. Therefore Beitar attempted to gain a foothold in the Polish school, and indeed, several students of that school joined us. These students learned Hebrew at Beitar (which they did not learn at school), Hebrew History, knowledge of the Land, and the like. My brother Zusia Marin of blessed memory was one of the first commanders of Beitar. He also went through Beitar hachshara in Zelba. Later, the Steingarten brothers became active in the movement (their father was also an active Revisionist), as did the pharmacist Mogilenski and others.

Our family moved away from Ratno in 1932, and therefore I cannot describe the activities of Beitar in Ratno during the 1930s. However, from time to time, I would come to Ratno and would find out that the activities of the early ones were not in vain. A headquarters was set up through the dues of the members, and the youth of all ages and strata kept faith with their movement. The activities of the Revisionists increased in the wake of the establishment of Beitar, and Brit Chail was set up in Ratno. I recall that more than thirty people traveled from Ratno to Kovel to hear the speech of Zeev Jabotinsky, who was visiting Kovel. Incidentally, the teacher Rozen accompanied Jabotinsky on his speeches through Poland.

It is appropriate to give more details about the teacher Boris Rozen who advanced the Tarbut School in Ratno in a significant fashion, and served as its principal with respect to the certified authorities. According to everybody, he was a gifted teacher, as well as an enthusiastic Beitar member. He attempted to win over people to Beitar, but he did not have great success in that realm in the Tarbut School. He had come to Ratno from Rowno, and he served as the commander of Brit Hechail in the region of Wolhyn. There are contradictory reports regarding what took place with him during the war, but I will not deal with them since they are not verified.

My uncle Leizer Marin was also one of the key figures of Beitar for some time. He even served as the commander of Beitar despite the fact that he was already older than the customary age in the movement for a role of that sort. It is appropriate to especially note Meir Rider, who also served as one of the commanders of Beitar. He was endowed with talents, and excelled especially in conducting choirs, organizing dramatic clubs, and the like. He had been a member of Hashomer Hatzair for some time and also conducted the choir of that movement. Through the influence of the teacher Rozen, who was also his relative, he joined Beitar.

Other Beitar activists who I remember include Moshe Kamfer and his sister Toibale, Leibel Wohl, Itka Zaks, Nuska Shuster, Leibel Liberman, and others. I must point out that it was not easy to be a member of Beitar, for the other movements directed all of their arrows against us. Spirits became stormy and the incitement against us became especially harsh in the year 1933, after the murder of Arlozoroff. At that time, the unbridled incitement against the Revisionists and Beitar took place in the large and small cities of Poland, and our town was no exception. Beitar stood up against this attack with pride and honor. It conducted the battle as appropriate, but never preached hatred against Jews who were political opponents. I recall that when I made aliya to the Land of Israel in 1938, it was hard for me to make peace with the great hatred that pervaded between the members of the various factions at that time.

Zeev Grabov tells that when he made aliya from Argentina in 1950, he went to visit his fellow native Yisrael Steingarten of blessed memory, who was working at the Ramet building company at that time. He wanted to obtain details from him about his brother Leibel, who was among the first 30 killed in Ratno when the Germans entered the town. At the end of their conversation, Yisrael told him that he had been among the most active Beitar members in Ratno: "You should know, Velvel[2] that despite the fact that I am an Etzel[3] man and made aliya on the Altalena, and you were one of the heads of Hashomer Hatzair, I regard you first and foremost as a native of Ratno and the former counselor of my brother Leibel. My door is always open to you. Your political inclinations do not prevent me from helping you to the extent that I am able, were you ever to need any type of assistance."

I have included this story because it is very typical of the education that we had received at that time within the Beitar movement of Ratno.

Activists of the Orphanage in 1928

Among them: Moshe Reicher, Mendel Blatt, Yaakov-Hirsch Held and Label Baion

The Workers Union

by Dov Marin

Translated by Chaim Grabov

Workers in Ratno (1930)

When the normalization of public life began in the town after the First World War, the various social movements began to crystallize. The establishment of a secular Hebrew school hastened this process significantly, but this also began to signify the social differentiation between the various strata in Jewish society. The students of the Hebrew school were mainly children of the well-to-do, merchants and shopkeepers. However, there was no small number of children from proletariat origins in town – the children of workers and tradesmen whose economic situation forced them toward the yoke of livelihoods during their early youth. These children did not go to school at all, or sufficed themselves with the basics of knowledge, including the study of reading, writing, the basics of arithmetic, and the like. They triumphed, and turned into carpenters, shoemakers, tailors, blacksmiths, tinsmiths, seamstresses, and other such tradespeople. The chasm between them and the studying youth continually increased. One factor for the deepening chasm was the issue of "pedigree" which was very important in the town, and the unwillingness of the youth to violate it. Another factor was the long, 14-15 hour workday that did not permit them to form their own framework and express their potential. These working youths were educated on the street. Competition and struggles were their daily bread. They would spend their Sabbath afternoons on the bridges of the town cracking seeds and planning various pranks. With the passage of time, a primitive "class awareness" developed among these youths.

It was expressed through feelings of hatred toward the children of the well-to-do people for causing them to be socially isolated to some degree, spending time only amongst themselves and not intermixing in the circles of the well-to-do youths.

A significant change of situation took place with the passage of time. These youths got older, and began to regard the bitter situation in the town from a different viewpoint. They saw the empty space, the true problems awaiting them that apparently had no answers, and the lack of prospective for a better future. The answers that were given by the teachers in the cheders or the Hebrew school were insufficient to settle the mind. A rebellion against the existing order and way of life began to brew. Then the motto began to grow: Yiddishism and secularism. During the years 1922-1928, these thoughts were given organizational and social expression by Wolf Brener in the first phase, and then by Leibel Baion. Yiddishist social-cultural activities began. The first activities were the setting up of a library, and the organization of a literary club in the home of the brothers Aharon and Levi Shapira through the initiatives of Leibel Baion, Niska Shapira and the Pogatch brothers. The most intelligent of the youth would gather together in the literary club, read modern Jewish literature, and dissect the national and social problems that were presented in this literature. In this club, the foundations were laid for the indoctrination of the Jewish youth with the principles of Marxism. The activists of this group obtained the books from the fathers of scientific socialism, and disseminated them among their members, thereby increasing their knowledge of the problems of social and national inequality.

When the activities of this literary circle ceased due to persecution of the Polish police, many of the youth separated themselves from all the activities and became indifferent to the problems that reality thrust before them. However, there were those who continued to progress in the direction that reality dictated: toward an organized workers camp. The following were included among the latter: Chuna Tyktiner, Aharon Shapira, and Ch. Warszawer. The aims that they set for themselves were to organize the workers, to free them from social backwardness, and to instill a class consciousness into those whose employment and way of life decreed that they would be an inseparable part of the working class. The watchword of the establishment of the workers' union had a great reverberation. The professional organization of the workers in the town was helped by this and served as an example for the workers, and brought them to a situation of organizational-social creativity. From their inception, the organizational activities ran into difficulties due to the government opposition of any organization of workers, causing a portion of the youth to be afraid of supporting such a professional workers' organization. On the other hand, there also were idealists who did not shrink from persecution by the police and continued on with the activities. These included David Langer, Akiva Druker, the brothers Moshe and Aharon-Shmuel, the seamstress Bracha Feiga, and others. With their last pennies, they succeeded in renting a room in the residence of Itzel Blostein. Thanks to a certain amount of help from Niska Shapira, the son of David-Aharon Shapiro, an intelligent youth who related to the progressive movement with admiration and understanding, an organization was established which very quickly turned into the home of the working youth. The large room was filled with various professional workers and seamstresses (the sewing trade was the only trade in which the girls of the town were employed). On Sabbath eves and afternoons, the former street youths gathered in the premises of the organization, listened to lectures and discussions on issues of the day, programs of questions and answers, and the like. After some time, a choir was founded whose repertoire include the workers' songs of Reisen, Edelshtat and Bobshover. Public singing encouraged and strengthened the class consciousness. Fear of the police inhibited even those who regarded themselves as members or supporters from visiting the premises. Everyone knew that the organization was not considered legal by the authorities, and any act of slander could cause the members to be sent to prison in Kovel or Luck for several good years. However, it is appropriate to note that even our harshest of opponents from among the Jews were not prone to slander. Even in the midst of the fiercest of debates, the only weapons on the Jewish street were – reasons, ideas, and mutual convincing.

Jewish unity overcame ideological divisions. There were cases where the opposing side, the pioneering Zionists, warned the members of the organization about a sleuth who was making the rounds in the area. However, the need for some legal approval of cover for the organization grew from day to day. We turned to the district center for professional organizations in Luck to use its influence upon the Polish Workers' Party (P.P.S.). We informed them about the existence of the professional organization in Ratno in which workers from various trades were organized, and we requested that they allow us to join their umbrella. They responded positively, but the conditions of our acceptance were that all official work and correspondence must be conducted in Polish, and the secretary of the organization must be a worker and member of the organization or a paid official. Since it was impossible to find a worker who would be able to conduct the secretariat in Polish, the members of the organization decided that Ch. Warszawer, who was unable to join the organization, would serve in the role of official secretary – a task that he had previously fulfilled in a voluntary organization – for the salary of 20 Polish zloty a month. Then we had to also obtain official recognition from the police authorities of Luck, which was a very difficult task. The secretary had to travel to Kovel and stand before a cross examination by the police who had difficulty understanding why a workers' union was needed in a town such as Ratno. We finally obtained official recognition thanks to the intervention of Y. Shochet, a member of Hashomer Hatzair from Kovel, with someone who was known in government circles. The union was legalized at the beginning of November, 1928. News of this spread through the town and aroused great joy among the supporters. I recall that on the first Sabbath eve following the legalization, when a question and answer evening (Kestel Avent) was arranged, there were many new faces in the hall. We also rented the hall from Itzel Lorber in order to arrange a festive opening. All of our friends and supporters did their best so that the opening would indeed be festive: they baked cookies, organized drinks, raised contributions, and on one evening in the latter half of the month of December, the sound of Aharon-Shaya's trumpet and musical instruments heralded the onset of the festive event. At first, they gathered in the hall of the organization, sang the International, raised glasses, and enjoyed refreshments. Then they all marched to the large hall where the celebration was to take place, accompanied by a band. The parade was headed by Aharon Shaya with his trumpet, followed by his father with a flute, and the drummer. Invited guests from Kovel and Malorita honored us with their presence. This was the first time that a celebration of this sort took place in Ratno. The proletariat youth began to feel that they were also a factor in the town. The activities of the organization increased. Speakers were invited from outside, public debates were organized, and large-scale publicity activities took place. We did not have official permits for conducting lectures, but our members stood in alleyways surrounding the premises, checking out any suspicious movement. Thus, they were able to issue a warning in the event that an "unwanted" guest appeared in the area.

In February 1929, Pilsudski's police began a process of persecution against revolutionary workers' movements in the district of Wolhyn, and a wave of arrests and persecutions began, not passing over Ratno. The secretary of the union emigrated abroad, and the central activists, David Langer, Chona Tyktiner, Aharon Shapira, and Leib Baion were imprisoned in Luck. Many people avoided activities under the auspices of the union. The activities of the union ceased; however, during its time of existence, it was a type of unique flower in the "garden" of various organizations that operated in town.

Translator's Footnotes

1. August https://www.jewishgen.org/Yizkor/Ratno/rat113.html - f1r
2. Velvel is a Yiddish diminutive for Zeev. https://www.jewishgen.org/Yizkor/Ratno/rat113.html - f2r
3. See http://en.wikipedia.org/wiki/Irgun https://www.jewishgen.org/Yizkor/Ratno/rat113.html - f3r

With the first snow

The Tradesmen and the Unions

by A. Berg

Translated by Jerrold Landau

The movements in social life that came in the wake of the great Russian revolution did not pass over the small towns of Poland. Various social and economic organizations were founded throughout Poland at that time, including the Union of Tradesmen that was set up in Warsaw, which took on the aim of raising the status and position of the Jewish tradesman and placing him on the political stage. Movement in this direction began only in 1924 in Ratno. Three tradesmen - Mendel Blatt, Yisrael and Yaakov Chayat -- responded to the call that came from the center in Warsaw, and took it upon themselves to organize the tradesmen in Ratno. The headquarters sent us Mr. Goldberg who assisted us in our first steps. The first publicity meeting took place in the large Beis Midrash, and Mr. Goldberg impressed the Jewish craftsmen with his descriptions of the deprivation of the tradesmen in all places. Thirty members registered for the union, and the organizational activity began immediately. A council and leadership committee were chosen. The chief activists were: Mendel Blatt, chairman; Yisrael-Yaakov Chayat, vice chairman; Yitzchak Feldman; Chaim Weisblau; Abba Fuchs; Moshe-Yaakov Chayat, and the writer of these lines.

We encountered many difficulties. The Jewish craftsman was always of a lower class in the town. The merchants and shopkeepers looked him over from top to bottom, and never displayed any inclination to draw him close to communal activity. Many mocked the possibility that the tradesmen had any possibility of organizing themselves and beginning to address their problems. The tradesmen themselves even began to hesitate regarding the possibility of organizing themselves. Throughout the generations, they had become accustomed to being treated as doormats, and would say "yes" to everything that was said or decided by the honorable householders. It is no wonder that after several months of activities, the heads of the new organization stood on the threshold of despair and helplessness. The right of existence of the organization could find its justification through the reduction of the burden of taxes for the tradesmen, and prevention of all sorts of other bad events. However, in those years (1924-1925), Ratno had an appointed rather than elected city council, and the tradesmen had no representation in it. How could a new organization justify its right of existence? Two events assisted this.

On a cloudless morning, when Meir Chayat, a hat maker by profession, prepared to travel to a fair in a nearby town, government representatives came and confiscated the entire stock of hats that he had with him due to old debts that had not been paid. He requested the help of the organization, and Mendel Blatt and I went to his assistance. We went to the mayor, presented his complaint in the name of the organization and even showed him our authorized charter. We demanded that the confiscated merchandise be returned to Meir Chayat, for it was in fact not his, and if it was not returned, he would be left literally with only a morsel of bread. The mayor acceded to our demand, the merchandise was returned to its owners, and our esteem rose. The second event that also raised our status was our success in bringing in four representatives of the tradesmen to the leadership of the Jewish National Bank. We succeeded in this after serious publicity efforts by the tradesmen who had joined the bank as members. Now, they discovered that they were able to be a meaningful force in communal life. The chairman of the council of the bank was always a representative of the tradesmen.

Not infrequently, disputes broke out between our representatives and the representatives of the small-scale merchants and shopkeepers. However, the bank director Heller was a wise, intelligent man, always successful in removing the obstacles and mediating between the sides.

In 1926, elections for the town council took place. After many debates, a national block was set up that included the Zionists, merchants and tradesmen, who joined together in a single block for the elections. The second list was the progressives, and the third consisted of the Ukrainian population. Eight Jews and four Ukrainians were elected to the council; and one Pole, one Ukrainian, and two Jews were elected to the leadership. The representatives of the tradesmen on the council were Yisrael Yitzchak Baion (on the leadership) and Avraham Berg, Mordechai Reicher, and Yosef Marantz (on the council). This was already a significant representation from our young organization.

As time went on, through dedicated work in communal affairs, our representatives succeeded in earning the appreciation of the Jews in town. They fought against any difficulty, they demanded their rights and stood on guard for the just demands of the various Jewish organizations. Our representative on the leadership committee ("Levnik"), Yisrael Yitzchak Baion, was especially successful. He used to say, "I am supposed to be chummy with the landowners at the various meetings and gatherings, but no more than necessary, for they will take advantage of it for their personal benefit."

In 1929, we founded the loan fund for the tradesmen. The first 15,000 zloty were given to us by the Polish national bank. This was the first and also the last grant from the Polish government, which hoped that this type of credit assistance would be able to strengthen the manufacturing in the town. The tradesmen themselves paid membership dues. According to the charter, only tradesmen would be able to receive loans from the bank, and under no conditions other than any other businessmen. A problem arose: what would be the situation with the wagon drivers whose situation was very tight? After many deliberations, we decided to issue loans from the fund to them as well. This cost us dearly, for the majority of the loans given to the wagon drivers were not paid back at all, and we were forced to cover them from our own pockets. Despite this, the capital of the fund grew. However, eventually we were forced to liquidate it, for it hindered the development of the Cooperative National Bank, whose progress was of interest to us.

Elections took place in 1928 for the Jewish community councils in the border districts of Poland. We decided to enter on a special list and prove to ourselves and others that we are were an influential element in the town. We won a great victory: four of our members were elected to the communal council - Mendel Blatt, Aharon Shderovitzki, Chaim Weisblau and the writer of these lines. During the first meetings of the communal council, a just battle was conducted for recognition of Rabbi Shlomo Tovia Friedlander as the rabbi of the community. He had served as the rabbi in our town for more than 25 years, and always lived under meager conditions. Not everyone appreciated his poverty and purity. "We, the tradesmen, loved and appreciated this man, and fought for his rights. Among other things, our delegates fought for progressive taxation, for the inclusion of Jews from the surrounding villages under the rubric of taxation, for rights of communal membership for those who could not afford to pay taxes, etc."

We are proud of our representatives and of our achievements in the Jewish community of Ratno.

"The Yeshiva Bachur" play by the group of amateurs. All of the participants in the play perished, with the exception of A. Liberman

Chapters of Memories and Experiences

Memories of the Distant Past[1]

by Isser Kamintzky

Translated by Jerrold Landau

Many memories of my childhood in Ratno remain with me today, and I will try to put some of them in writing. I remember very well the Shtibel of the Stepan Hassidim, which was very large and had many windows on all sides. Along the length of the shtibel were ovens that were lit in the winter. Several young men who had completed their studies in the cheders would sit and study in the shtibel.

I remember very well the house in which the Stepan Rebbe stayed whenever he used to visit Ratno. On winter Sabbaths, the house would turn into the women's gallery in which our mothers would worship. Behind the house was the yard that separated the New Shtibel from the Old Shtibel of the Hassidim of Stepan. A flask of water stood there for washing the hands after attending to the call of nature. The jokers of the town would light candles on the small wooden planks on the eve of Simchat Torah and sing heartily "Kol Mevaser Mevaser Veomer"[2]. I did not know then nor do I know now the meaning and purpose of this joke. To us children, the Old Shtibel of the Hassidim of Stepan seemed as if it was shrouded in mystery. Many legends were told about the place where the bed, table and chair of the Reb Yitzchak, the Tzadik of Nischiz of blessed memory, stood. Our grandfathers and grandmothers would tell about the great works of wonder of this Tzadik, and also about the great dispute between the Nischiz dynasty and the court of the Rebbe of Trisk. During our youth, we were very curious to know what took place in the four ells[3] of this Shtibel. We would peek through the cracks in the broken shutters, or follow Reb Chaim, the shamash of both the Great Synagogue and the Stepan Shtibel. He was very diligent about maintaining the cleanliness of the two houses of worship for which he was responsible. He was among those who "delayed taking leave of the Sabbath and hastened entering it," as is said in the Sabbath hymns. I recall that when gas lamps were installed in these two houses of worship, Reb Chaim would carefully climb the ladder and light the lamps with awe and trepidation. He enjoyed the sight of the Jews coming to the Welcoming of the Sabbath service attired in their Sabbath finery, with their finely groomed beards. He was especially happy when he succeeded in finding hosts for all of the guests that had come to town for the Sabbath.

Behold, with the eyes of my spirit I see Reb Ben-Tzion Steingarten of blessed memory as he walks with measured steps from his place at the eastern wall behind the bima. Several important people, enwrapped with their tallises, with the silver tallis adornment (atara) covering their heads stand next to him. He recites the "Yehi Ratzon" prayer on the Sabbath preceding the New Moon (Shabbat Mevorchim) with a trembling voice.

Reb Ben-Tzion, the pleasant and scholarly Jew, had the constant rights[4] to lead the congregation in this Rosh Chodesh prayer. He recited the prayers with sweetness, and with such a melody that it seemed as if he intended to "forcibly" extract a good month for his Jewish brethren from the Holy One Blessed Be He. His prayer "A long life, a life of livelihood, a life of fear of Heaven and fear of sin", was splendid in my ears. When he reached the words "and all those who faithfully occupy themselves with the needs of the community", it was impossible not to feel that he was attempting to convince the Holy One Blessed Be He that his brethren of his people were all precious and proper Jews. When the Days of Awe approached with the prayers of Rosh Chodesh Elul, Reb Ben-Tzion would instill upon the worshippers the fear of the approaching Day of Judgment. The next day, a larger number of Jews attended the services. Even those who would customarily recite the Shacharit service privately preferred communal worship during Elul. The sounds of the shofar blasted forth from all of the Beis Midrashes, and we, the jokers of the town, would take the shofar into our hands when nobody was looking so we could try our skill at blowing. The special melodies of the prayers of the High Holy Days could be heard from the homes of the prayer leaders as well as the Beis Midrashes. The elderly and youths would recite their daily Psalms with extra devotion during the month of Elul. Even Mottel the deaf mute, who was always an enigma in my eyes, seemed to become more observant. This Mottel had a great knowledge of arithmetic, and at times, when we would ask, he would demonstrate his prowess at mental calculations. During Elul, Mottel would get angry if we would ask him something in the middle of the services. He would put a finger to his mouth as if to say, "it is forbidden to speak."

The trepidation of the approaching Days of Awe was also felt in the cheder of Nechemia the teacher.

Group of members of Hechalutz in 1929

Sitting (from right to left): P. Honik, Sh. Itzikson (perished), B. Cohen (Argentina), Sh. Pogatch and G. Karsh (perished)

Standing: A. Droog (perished), A. Held (Israel), L. Baion (Mexico), M. Shapir, G. Shapira, R. Ponetz, Ch. Marsuk, and L. Aharonson (perished)

All of the students studied with extra meticulousness, and we worshiped with devotion. Reb Nechemia would tell us, "Remember that you young people can attain much more than we adults are able to attain through prayer from the depths of the heart." It is no wonder then that during Elul, we would engage in soul searching and attempt to atone for the sins that we had transgressed...

Reb Avrahamche Telizon also taught in Reb Nechemia's cheder. He was a pleasant and precious Jew, who dressed splendidly. He would also give lessons ("Urok") in the homes of the children. My father of blessed memory forged a special friendship with this teacher. He would bring him various gifts from his trips to Danzig: a pocket knife, a watch, a purse, etc. Later Reb Avrahamche, along with his friend Reb Yudel Konishter, founded the first school in the house of Reb Mendel Stoler. He was a teacher of Hebrew and Yiddish, while Yudel, who was nicknamed Yudel Malka's in the name of his mother, taught Russian. Yudel became known as an intelligent and erudite young man, who forged paths toward Haskala in the town and was a subscriber to the Hebrew "Hatzefira" newspaper. I remember well how our teachers would educate us toward the land of Israel, and the enthusiasm with which they taught us to sing the national hymn "Hatikva"[5]. Thus did the love of the homeland, the Hebrew Language and Zionism become instilled in our hearts already in our early youth. There is no doubt that as a result of this education, the majority of the youths of Ratno later joined the Zionist organizations.

The days of Selichot[6] are etched in my memory. We would arise at 3:00 a.m., when the entire town was still enveloped in sleep. Father would go in front, followed by the elder sons. Other Jews would come out from the various lanes, walking in the direction of the shtibelsand the Beis Midrash. Some held a lantern in their hands, while others lit the way with a candle. When we arrived at the Shtibel, there were already several Jews there sitting next to the tables and lecterns. The main task of Selichot was of course filled by the cantor, who had prepared himself for this prayer beforehand. The Selichot lasted until the Shacharit service. Then we would make haste to the bathhouse to immerse ourselves prior to the onset of the festival. Reb Gedalia the bath attendant was in charge there. He would give the broom and pail of water to every important householder, and would run from the mikva to the oven in order to maintain the temperature of the water. There was great preparation and bustle in the bathhouse. The screams of the children reached the heavens... One child lost his underpants, while another was searching for his lost pants or coat in his friend's sack. New faces were seen on the streets of the town. These were the village Jews who lived an isolated life in their villages throughout the year and satisfied themselves with a bare minyan [prayer quorum] on Sabbaths. On the High Holy Days they would stream into the nearby town to celebrate the festival along with the other Jews. Such was the custom from days of yore, and they would generally stay with relatives and acquaintances. The village Jews would bring delicacies with them to town: fowl, eggs, dried fruit, and the like. The Jews of Ratno would welcome the villagers pleasantly. If any of them did not have a place to stay, they would accept the situation and sleep in the attic of the Beis Midrash. In town, they would joke a bit about these village Jews who were not knowledgeable in the customs of the festival and the various prayers. We, the children of the town, would dandy ourselves before them in our new clothes, shoes and hats.

I recall the home of my uncle Reb Avraham the shochet [ritual slaughterer], who would take on a new role prior to Yom Kippur, when all the Jews prepared their Kaparot and hastened to the house of the shochet with their chickens. My uncle would spend many hours sharpening his chalafs [slaughtering knives], so that no mishap should take place with the shechita, Heaven forbid. It was crowded all around as everyone shouted to the shochet, "Reb Avraham, please slaughter mine already." My uncle conducted his holy task with great patience, as if the voices were not directed to him. He would carefully examine each bird, and then sharpen his knife very well again. Toward the evening, Reb Avraham would sit in his salon ("Stolowa") with an open Gemara, completely immersed in the tractate, with a unique, sweet tune emanating from his mouth. He only stopped this melody for a moment when his wife Dova entered.

I see the Sabbath afternoons in our town before my eyes. After the ample Sabbath meal, Jews would go out to stroll on the sidewalks. Men were going to drink cold soda water to help the kugel or the chulent, the main courses of the Sabbath meal, "go down in peace." After that, they would observe the commandment of "sleeping on the Sabbath." After their nap, the tea flasks prepared specially for the Sabbath would be removed from the stoves, and several glasses of tea would be enjoyed with or without spices. Then people would go once again to the Beis Midrash, to recite "Pirke Avot"[7], attend a lecture, or study "Ein Yaakov"[8]. This was also the time for visits of guests, and for the children to stroll on the streets. It goes without saying that on these walks, "rumors" would be spread about a certain boy who apparently loves a certain girl "over the ears," or a certain girl who has her eye on a certain boy... On these Sabbath afternoons, the more serious youths would engage in debates on issues of the day or on books that they had read during the week. We would borrow the books from the library of Itzel Spilman, who was nicknamed Itzel Kli Zemer [the musician], since he played the violin at all of the Jewish weddings that took place in the town. More than one bride shed tears during the "seating" ceremony at the sound of his sad melodies. The image of this Itzel stood before my eyes when I later read Sholom Aleichem's

"Stempenyu." His was the only private library in town before the First World War, and one could also find there the various monthlies and weeklies to which Itzel subscribed.

In the Old City in the winter

Dust was raised in the city toward evening, when the gentile Winka brought back the flocks from the meadows. The housewives would sit on the sidewalks next to the houses, examine each animal well, and express their opinions about the "Jewish animals." The gentile Nesczia, who spoke Yiddish as if she were a proper Jewish woman, ran from one Jewish house to the next to milk the cows[9]. She had pieces of challa in her purse that were given to her by the women in honor of the Sabbath. I see myself entering some Shtibel for the Mincha service. The characteristic melancholy of the departure of the Sabbath was already felt in the Beis Midrash, as the extra soul exits and the weekdays, filled with their worries and tribulations, stand at the threshold. Several dozen Jews sit along the table, including Yehuda Meir Richter with his long neck, reciting the Aramic prayer "Askinu Seudasa." The custom was that on each Sabbath late afternoon, people would take turns in bringing the challa, more precisely "Kviltz," and salted fish for the Seuda Shelishit (third Sabbath meal). Each one of those at the meal received the "kezayit"[10] that would be sufficient to recite the Hamozieblessing. The time came for the hymns, which poured out as the pinnacle of lofty, sweet tunes. They began with "Baruch Kel Elyon," and moved on to "Yetzave Tzur Chasdo," etc. Reb Moshe, the cantor, would often teach a new melody to the congregation that he himself had composed, and the enthusiasm overflowed. The Jews did not want to part from the holy Sabbath, and they would be ready to sit a long time and continue with these sweet melodies. However, Reb Chaim the shamash lit the candles next to the Holy Ark and someone began the Maariv (evening) service with the gloomy chant of "Vehu Rachum Yechaper Avon"[11]. This was a clear sign that the Sabbath had departed. Several shopkeepers hastened to leave the Shtibel so that they could open their stores, with the hope that some income would be realized to greet the upcoming week.

Agricultural Hachsharah, in a manner of speaking, in front of the camera...

Jews and Ukrainians at the Third of May Celebrations

A Wedding of the Honik family. The grandmother is in the center

Translator's Footnotes

1. In the table of contents at the front of the book, this chapter is called "Memories of the Recent Past." https://www.jewishgen.org/Yizkor/Ratno/rat123.html - f1r

2. A refrain from one of the prayers of Hoshana Rabba, which occurs two days before Simchat Torah. The refrain means, "The voice of the herald heralds and proclaims," a reference to the bearer of the tidings of the coming of the Messiah. https://www.jewishgen.org/Yizkor/Ratno/rat123.html - f2r

3. An ell is an archaic unit of measure, often considered as an alternate form of a cubit. The expression 'four ells' generally refers to a restricted space, not just in area but also in mindset and outlook. https://www.jewishgen.org/Yizkor/Ratno/rat123.html - f3r

4. The Hebrew term here is 'chazaka' which implies an established right to a specific ritual synagogue honor. https://www.jewishgen.org/Yizkor/Ratno/rat123.html - f4r

5. Today the national anthem of Israel. https://www.jewishgen.org/Yizkor/Ratno/rat123.html - f5r

6. The period of recitation of penitential prayers prior to Rosh Hashanah and Yom Kippur. The elongated Selichot service described in the lines below, followed by immersion, is likely the Selichot of the eve of Rosh Hashanah. https://www.jewishgen.org/Yizkor/Ratno/rat123.html - f6r

7. The mishnaic tractate “Chapters of the Fathers”, customarily studied during summer Sabbath afternoons. https://www.jewishgen.org/Yizkor/Ratno/rat123.html - f7r

8. An anthology of the aggadaic (lore) sections of the Talmud. https://www.jewishgen.org/Yizkor/Ratno/rat123.html - f8r

9. An act forbidden on the Sabbath to Jews. https://www.jewishgen.org/Yizkor/Ratno/rat123.html - f9r

10. A halachic volume (of debatable size) that defines the required amount for any obligatory eating. It is the required amount for the matzo and maror on Passover eve, as well as the required amount of bread that would result in an obligation to recite the Grace after Meals. (There is a halachic error in this sentence, as the Hamotzieblessing can be recited on any amount of bread, whereas the Grace after Meals requires a “kezayit”.) https://www.jewishgen.org/Yizkor/Ratno/rat123.html - f10r

11. “And He, being all merciful, forgives sins” -- the opening phrase of the weekday Maariv service. https://www.jewishgen.org/Yizkor/Ratno/rat123.html - f11r

My First Attempt at Agriculture

by Simcha Lavie

Translated by Jerrold Landau

The built up portion of the town had already been located on the north branch of the Pripyat River for some time. We had a plot of land at the bend in the main road, which my father had received from his father-in-law as a dowry after he married my mother. This plot of land had been passed down for many generations as an inheritance within our family. At first, my father used it as a vegetable garden for the family that had grown with the passage of time. I recall that preparing the plot for planting was accompanied by worry and concern. We planted with worry and harvested with joy. Pavel Zhuk and his family dragged away the harvest. This Pavel Zhuk was a Ukrainian, not necessarily from the highest classes of his people. His name was often involved with acts of crime, and not without basis. When he did not stop pillaging the vegetables from our garden, my father girded himself with strength, entered his house, and spoke to him at length. This Ukrainian did not attempt to deny his acts, and told my father with a cunning smile, "You are an intelligent and learned Jew, and you see with your eyes that I am unable to suffice myself within the bounds of my plot of land. Come and let us make a business deal and remain friendly. You will transfer your plot, which is next to mine, into my name, and I will transfer a larger plot to you in the region of Ricz-Spunczyk on the way to the village of Ukuszy." My father did not immediately reject the proposition. He deliberated, took advice from his friends, and finally decided to agree to the proposed business arrangement. Thus did my family begin to grow grain and potatoes. Several years later, when I grew up, I took upon myself the responsibility for cultivating this plot of land. I supervised the plowing and planting, but the wheat harvest was performed by Anatoly, one of the finest of the Ukrainians who lived in Ratno. We had an agreement with him that he would keep 2/3 of the harvest, and the owner of the plot would keep 1/3.

From that time, I was the constant overseer of that plot of land, and thus my first relationship with "mother earth" was formed. My frequent visits to the plot of land were surprising to the farmers, who had trouble understanding why a young Jew would be involved in working the land, for they were accustomed to seeing Jews in their roles as merchants and shopkeepers. To the merit of Anatoly it should be noted that he did his best to respond to this "misunderstanding", and even explained to the farmers who could not "comprehend" the situation that I was planning to travel to the Holy Land and earn my livelihood from working the land.

I myself derived great satisfaction from my closeness to the earth and working the land. I always remembered the enchanting stanzas of Bialik's poem "In the Field":

"Tell me, mother earth, broad, full, and large

Why does your field not deliver a lowly and yearning soul also to me?"

I went out to our field, not as a stranger. I attempted to listen and understand in accordance with the words of the poet, "That which G-d is speaking from the stalks of standing grain, how slowly the wind is causing the bent stalks to rustle, what the Ziz-sadai[1] is secretly embroidering." Even if my ideal of becoming a tiller of the land was not realized during those days -- I still recall those days in Ratno with satisfaction, when I was so close to nature and the work of the land, to the merit of Pavel Zhuk.

Translator's Footnote

1. A mythical bird. https://www.jewishgen.org/Yizkor/Ratno/rat123.html - f1ar

The Terror of Fires

by Chaya Frusman

Translated by Jerrold Landau

Memories of recurring fires from my early childhood accompany me. Our street bordered on the alleys of the anti-Semitic Ukrainians, who schemed against their Jewish neighbors in various ways. Even members of the citizens' guard, who made the rounds at night with kerosene lanterns to protect the Jewish houses, did not succeed in protecting us from fires and arson. I recall that we children went to sleep without getting undressed, and prepared to exit the house in haste in the event of a fire. At times, we would go out half naked in the middle of the night. We were afraid to go to sleep, and nightmares afflicted us even after we fell asleep. I would often awaken at night screaming. It seemed to me that I heard voices saying, "David, David, get up, there is a fire!"

I recall one night, when I jumped outside and saw light as if the middle of the day -- light from the large tongues of fire ascending to the heavens along with rising pillars of smoke. People screamed and wept, and ran hastily to the well and river to fetch water. We children were also involved with extinguishing the fire. We ran with pails full of water, and when we reached the place of the fire, we would give the pails to older people. Our house burned down that night, and we were left without a roof over our heads. We sat on the bundle of belongings that we succeeded in salvaging and wept. Do not forget that all of the houses of the city were made of wood, and one spark would be sufficient to cause the fire to spread. I saw one woman lamenting over her burnt dough-trough since she would have nothing in which to prepare her dough for the baking of the Sabbath challas. We sat next to the embers and burnt houses until morning, guarding our remaining household objects lest they be pillaged by the gentiles. Jews gathered around us in the morning, offering assistance. All of those afflicted by the fire spread out among neighbors. My family and I lived in the house of my father's wagon driver. We lived there until we rebuilt our house.

Many years have passed since then, but even now, every time that I see a fire or hear the word "fire" -- I remember that night when our house went up in flames along with many other houses.

How do you Teach?

by Berel Kahan

Translated by Jerrold Landau

One of the most important melamdim [teachers of young children] who had his own cheder in town, was Menachem the Melamed. I recall him as a man in his early fifties, tall and thin, with a very straight gait. White hairs could already be found in his black beard, and his yarmulke under his hat was full of sweat.

Menachem the Melamed lived close to the Pripyat River that cut our town in two. There were three rooms in his house: a large room, a bedroom, and a small kitchen with an oven for cooking and baking bread. In the large room that served as the study room, a long table stood with two long benches next to it for his 10 - 12 students. A footstool stood at the head of the table that served as the seat of the melamed himself. Aside from this furniture, there was a chest of drawers, a closet and a bookshelf in the room.

Menachem's wife, or, as she was called, the rebbetzin, was a very young woman of approximately 30 years old. She was his second wife. She always had a year or two- year-old baby in her arms. The wicker cradle in the room belonged to that baby.

Menachem was known in town as a good teacher of Chumash and Rashi, but not everyone wished to send their children to his cheder, for he was known as someone who was prone to anger and who did not spare the strap from his students. He would whip them on their buttocks, and he would even tie them with chains. On the other hand, on "Nitl" night[1] when it was the custom to refrain from teaching, Menachem would entertain his students. He would teach them to play dominoes and make good plays in the game. He would derive a great deal of pleasure when he realized that we caught on.

During the days of Chanuka, we would bring two or three kopecks for preparing latkes. During the evenings, the Rebbetzin would fry very tasty latkes for us. We would eat the latkes, play dreidel and cards, and we would all wish that these festive days would continue on and not be followed by the regular grey days of studies and whippings by our teacher.

After we already knew the trop[2] and the Torah portions, Menachem would begin to teach us Chumash and Rashi, and then the Early Prophets. Every two students shared one bible. The teaching methodology was that the Rebbe would read outline, and we would repeat after him "Vayedaber-Hot Geret, Adoshem-Got, El Moshe, Tzu Moshen, Leemor-Azoi tzu zugn", etc.[3] Friday was designated for tests. Every one of the students had to recite two verses from the first section of the weekly Torah portion, in turn. I recall that on one of those Fridays, when Matas, one of the students who was the son of Nisi the Shoemaker, did not know the explanation of a certain word in the weekly Torah portion, Menachem slapped him soundly on his cheeks, and the boy burst out in bitter crying. "You will cry more," shouted Menachem, "You are a veritable gentile, and I need to hit you more. Lie down immediately!"

Menachem's way of doing things was that if a child was to be whipped, he would have to pull down his underwear with his own hands, lie on the bench, and, without saying anything, present his back for the whip of the melamed. However, this Matas felt that the Rebbe was too stringent this time, and that slapping him on the cheeks was a sufficient punishment for not knowing the explanation of a certain word, therefore he decided to not present his back for the beatings, not pull down his underwear, and not lie on the bench in accordance with the Rebbe's command. He remained sitting on the bench and did not move from his place. This rebellion set the Rebbe off. He attacked the student and tried to force him to lie down so that he would be able to whip him. However, the student began to kick the Rebbe with his feet, and hit him on his heart and his face. The Rebbe gave in. This was the first and perhaps the only time that his verdict was not carried out...

It seems to me that the primary skill of our Rebbe was in teaching the first section of every Torah portion, as well as in the first chapters in the Book of Joshua. That far, and no more. If we had finished studying the Book of Joshua and the term had not ended, for some reason, he would begin to teach us the Book of Daniel. He would manage somehow with the Hebrew portion of that book, but when he reached the Aramaic chapters, it would be like the "wagon began to grate," as if the wheels were broken...

This Rebbe's methodology in teaching Yiddish writing was very interesting. Before I began to study with Menachem, I had learned writing from the teacher Zelig the Hunched, as we would call him on account of his way of walking. Zelig's methodology was straightforward: We would purchase a piece of paper for a small coin and bring it to the Rebbe. He would fold it into four sections, and draw straight lines on it. These would be the writing lines, and it was forbidden to go outside them. The Rebbe would write the entire aleph beit on the first line in pen or a duck quill dipped in ink. On the rest of the lines, we would have to write the entire aleph beit with our own hand in accordance with the Rebbe's writing style. After we already knew how to write all the letters, we had an additional exercise - to write the aleph beit backwards, starting from the last letter and in groups: Tashrak, Tzafes, Nimlach, Yatchaz, Vehadgba...

When I began to study with Menachem, I already knew how to form words from the letters. I remember that I would often write the sentence that is commonly written in the cover of books, in this form: "This book belongs. To whom does it belong? To he who bought it. Who bought it? He who paid. Who paid?" Etc. Etc.

With Menachem, we began with a veritable steel pen. Once a month, Menachem would prepare a form of a letter for writing ("Firgris"), and we would copy it throughout the month. I recall the text:

"Baruch Hashem, Day... In our community"

"To the honor of the sage and leader, Mr. ..."

First I wish to inform you that I am feeling well and living in peace. May G-d let me hear the same from you, Amen Selah. Second, I wish to inform you that I am sending fifty oxen with the person bearing this letter, and the Blessed G-d will help, and everything should be with blessing and success. Amen. From me, the undersigned."

Menachem would change the form of his letter each month. He would exchange the oxen for grain or boards, and instead of Warsaw, he would send them to Danzig or Leipzig...

It is worthwhile to note that Menachem the teacher became well-known in Ratno for his methodology of teaching writing, and his exercises. Other teachers did not involve themselves at all with teaching writing, perhaps because they themselves did not know how to write...

Teachers and Writers

Jewish education was not only in the hands of the melamdim. As time went on, other educators who were called morim (teachers) or sofrim (writers or scribes) arrived on the scene. I will mention a few of them here. The first is Hershel Shachne's. Before he arrived here, he tried his luck in the United States. Apparently, he did not succeed there. He was known as a great scholar, for he was one of the few in town who was able to write a letter of request ("Frashenia") to the district judge. This Hershel would teach us Yiddish, Russian, and also a bit of English, so that we would be able to write the address of a letter to the United States when necessary. He lived in the home of his father Shachne, who was known as Shache the Doctor, in a tiny room that was designated for the entire family. The larger room in this house served as the teaching room. I only studied Russian with him. He had one textbook that he had purchased from a Russian peddler during one of the fairs. I recall that, aside from the Russian alphabet, this book had a story for children called "Golden Fish." Teaching did not provide enough income for Hershel to support his family, so his wife knitted socks. She was born in Brisk, from where she had brought a sewing machine, the first of its type in Ratno. Since she was always busy with the machine, Hershel had to fill in for her in various household tasks, especially in caring for the children. Since the couple had many children, one could often see and hear Hershel busy with his children in the small room, while his students were sitting and reading the story of the golden fish in Russian out loud in the large room. Hershel would correct the mistakes while he was caring for one of his babies... The meager tuition fee (60 kopecks per month for two hours of lessons a day) was not enough to keep Hershel in teaching. Hershel did not last long in Ratno. He returned to the United States, where he was employed in preparing Jewish children for their Bar Mitzvahs.

The Teachers David Finkelstein and Avraham Telison

After Passover in 1899, a young Jew named David Finkelstein came to Ratno from the town of Liwona.

In town, they said that he had to leave his hometown because he did not have good relations with his grandfather, who was the rabbinical judge of the town. He was divorced, and he brought with him his tallis and tefillin, but not one piece of clothing worthy of the name. He lived with the Frishberg family as well as in the home of Getzel Konishter. Instead of paying rent, he taught their two daughters. Two members of the intelligentsia of the town, Yehoshua Pogach and Zalman Burstein, felt it necessary to order a suit for him from Eliahu-Pesia the tailor, who also served as the jester at weddings. I do not know what David Finkelstein did for a living in his hometown, but in Ratno he set up a four grade school scattered in different places: one class with the Gemara teacher Yaakov Prossman, a second in the home of Berl Vernik, a third, only for girls, in the home of Reizel Kuperberg, and a fourth, also for girls, in the home of Asher Shapira. The tuition fee in those days was one ruble per month. There were two hours of lessons per day. This was a reasonably high rate in comparison with the tuition fees receive by other melamdim. David Finkelstein taught us Hebrew and Yiddish. His teaching style was literal translation. He used the textbook of M. M. Dolitzki during his Hebrew lessons. He made us transcribe a chapter of the book, and then corrected our mistakes. Once a week, he taught us the Book of Proverbs, and I also recall that he taught us the Book of Ben Sirah[4]. I also recall that he once wrote out for us a large Hebrew article in the religious nationalist spirit. He read us the article and we wrote it in our notebooks as he was reading. One of the students of the class showed the article to the Lithuanian teacher in our town, who enjoyed the juicy expressions and noted that he had never before seen anything in that style. There were rumors in town that he taught the Song of Songs in the style of the heretics - that is: in accordance with the literal content as a romance between a young man and woman, and not in accordance with the commentary of Rashi, who interpreted it as love between the Holy One Blessed Be He and the community of Israel. This resulted in him losing his rights to teach girls in the home of Asher Shapira. Sometimes, he would read us an article from the Hamelitz newspaper, to which he was the only subscriber in Ratno. (Aside from Hamelitz, two copies of Hatzefira would be sent to Ratno. One was for a group of young people who read it together, and the second was for Yitzchak Marsik, the son-in-law of Chona Tyktiner, who had a fine Hebrew library in his home). I do not remember for how long David Finkelstein remained in our town, but I do know that he was finally forced to leave the town because he was in dire straits, literally to the point of hunger. I myself was a witness to the fact that my friend Getzel, the son of Chaim-Yudel, brought him a package of food without anyone seeing in the evening. My heart was literally pained at the dire straits of our teacher. I do not know where David Finkelstein went after Ratno, but he once came to visit the town, and I went to see him. I saw an edition of Hamelitz on the table in the room where he was staying, and the address on the wrapper said, "The Correspondent David Finkelstein."

Translator's Footnotes

1. Christmas Eve, or possibly the eve of the Eastern Christmas, when, by Jewish tradition, one is not supposed to study Torah. https://www.jewishgen.org/Yizkor/Ratno/rat123.html - f132-1r

2. The cantillation notes of the scriptures. https://www.jewishgen.org/Yizkor/Ratno/rat123.html - f132-2r

3. Each word or phrase of the verse was read in Hebrew and then translated into Yiddish. This verse is "And G-d spoke to Moses saying." https://www.jewishgen.org/Yizkor/Ratno/rat123.html - f132-3r

4. A book of the Apocrypha. https://www.jewishgen.org/Yizkor/Ratno/rat123.html - f132-4r

5. The photocopies are of poor quality, especially on the right side. The top right article is only the last part of a longer article, apparently, and was written by David Finkelstein. The lower right article is under a headline called "Telegrams", dated Saturday, August 19 (13 Elul). Top left is the bottom portion of an article written by Ch. Shakhabenson. The lower left article is written by David Finkelstein, and states that it is from Ratno. It discusses the visit of the "holy grandson" (evidently a Hassidic leader) to our town. The right side of this article is partially obscured.

The text of the top right article and the lower left article appears on the side articles of page 134 and 135. https://www.jewishgen.org/Yizkor/Ratno/rat123.html - f132-5r

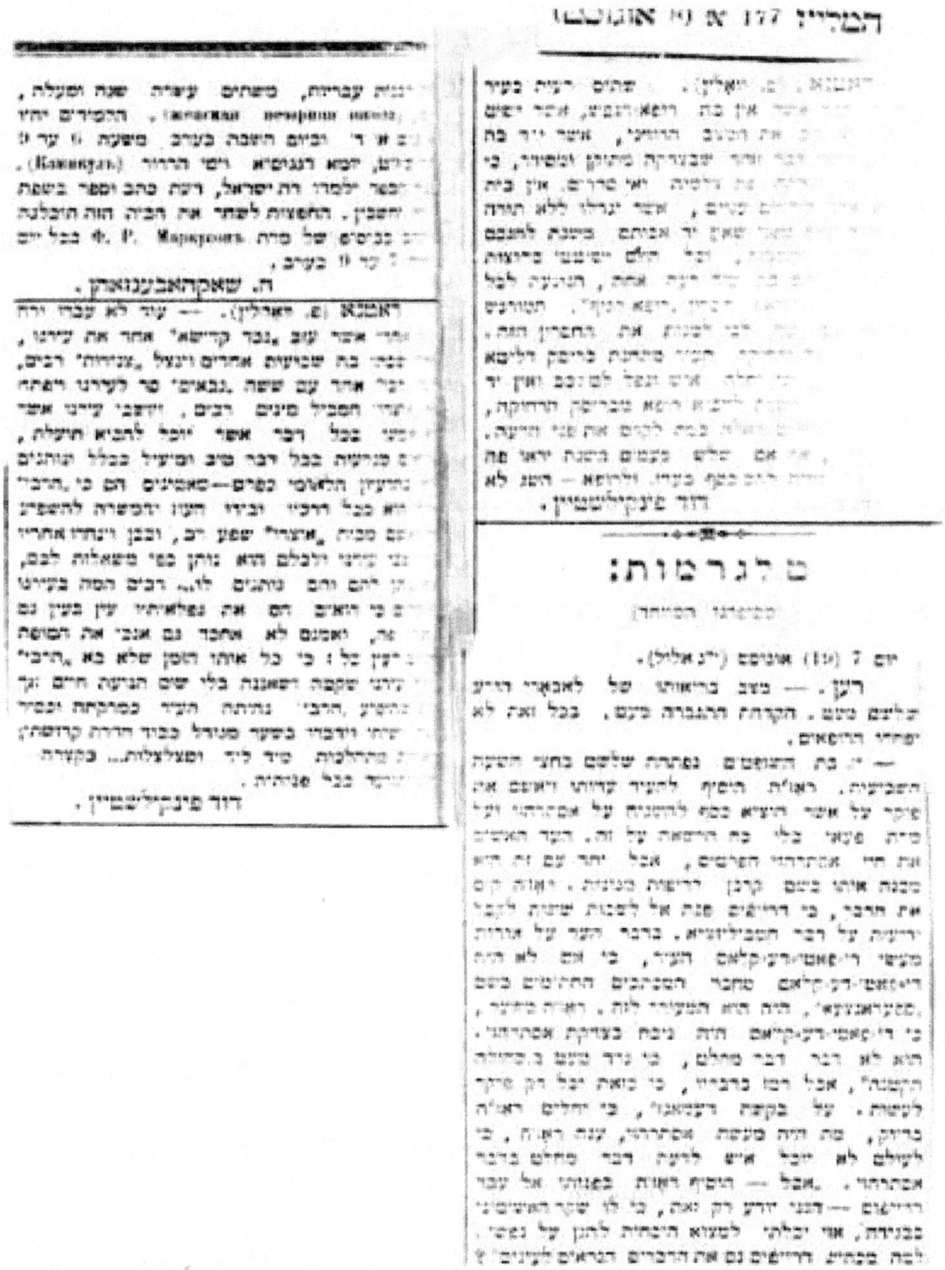

Pages from "Hamelitz" with an article about Ratno by Y. Finkelstein[5]

With the Stain of Poverty

by Berel Kahan

Translated by Jerrold Landau

Just like many other small, remote towns in Poland, our town was also very poor from an economic perspective. It had no factories or industrial enterprises, and it was also far from the railway station. In my time, Ratno had no bank or loan fund that could provide economic assistance to small scale merchants or forestry dealers. Therefore, it was natural that the town was enveloped in poverty and hardship, and there was almost no difference between the poor and the rich.

The forestry traders floated lumber to Germany via the Pripyat River. The cattle merchants would pass through the villages in the region, purchase the cattle from the farmers, and export them to the capital city of Warsaw. This was the occupation of Itzikl, the cattle drover. He would gather the cattle together to take them to Brisk, and from there on to Warsaw.

Approximately half of the livelihood of the town came from the village population. The many shopkeepers in the town were primarily dependent on this source of livelihood. During the fair days, the farmers from the village would stream to Ratno to sell their produce. With the money they received, they purchased all of their needs for their farms and households in the village. On the other hand, the livelihoods of the Jewish tradesmen were dependent on the city population.

The condition of life of the farmers was very primitive, and they got by on very little. On the other hand, the standard of living of the Jews in the town was significantly higher than that of the villagers. The Jews depended on the carpenter to fix their table or bed, the tinsmith, the watchmaker, the bookbinder, etc. Indeed, there were tradesmen in town who were needed by both the city Jew and the village gentile, such as the shoemakers, tailors, furriers, blacksmiths, hat makers, etc. Even they did not earn any more than "water for porridge," as we used to say, and a single worry always pressed at them: how to obtain the provisions for the Sabbath?

I recall many episodes that highlight the great poverty in the town. I will relate one of them that relates to me personally. My father was employed in a lumber business. He spent all the days of the week in the forests, and only returned to town on Fridays. He returned to the forests early Sunday morning.

Despite his backbreaking work, his income was barely sufficient to sustain the family. I was the only son of my parents, and I often walked through the alleyways of the town with torn pants. One day, when I was innocently walking in the direction of the market, I passed by Shapira's textile shop. By chance, Shapira's son, who assisted his father, was sanding next to the door of their store. He noticed me and my torn pants, and called out, "Child, go tell your mother that I have a piece of cloth in my store that can be bought cheaply, and then she can sew new pants for you"...

I recall that these words made me feel embarrassed, despite the fact that I was then a young child. I did not tell anything to Mother, for I knew that she did not have money to buy me new pants. However, from that time, I made efforts to avoid going by Shapira's store...

Berl Kahn (Chanche's)

Articles from "Hamelitz" Newspaper

by David Finkelstein

Translated by Jerrold Landau

"Hamelitz" edition 37, 1901

Ratno (Wolhyn District) - It has not even been a month since one "Holy Grandson" left our town after spending a few weeks here, rescuing many "channels." Already another Rebbe with six gabbaim [assistants] has come to our city and opened up his treasury consisting of many different types. The residents of our city who believe in everything that may bring a benefit without detracting from any good and effective thing in general, and who place their opinions with the nationalist idea in specific - believe that such a Rebbe is righteous in all his ways, and has the strength and ability to bestow influence upon their heads from his bountiful "treasury." Therefore, all the residents of our town stream to him, and he gives to them everything they ask for. He gives to them, and they give to him... There are many in our city who claim that they see the wonders with their own eyes while he is residing here. I myself will not contradict his wonders in public: for throughout the entire time that the Rebbe did not come, our city was quiet and peaceful without any movement of life. However, from the day that the Rebbe appeared, the city became like a seething pot. People would speak in the gateways about the greatness of his honor and splendor of his holiness. Coins would clang from hand to hand... In short, there was bustle and movement in all directions.

"Hamelitz" edition 177. August 8, 1899.

Ratno (Wolhyn District). There are two evils in this city, aside from the fact that it has no spiritual physician who would set his heart to improve the spiritual status that has fallen greatly, and found an orderly charitable methodology, since all charitable endeavors here are disorderly; there is also no school for poor children, who grow up without Torah and without worldly knowledge, for their parents cannot afford to educate them in the ways of Torah and commandments, and they wander through the streets every day. There is one more evil that affects every individual: that is, the lack of a physician. This is felt strongly, but there is nobody who makes any effort to rectify this lack. There is no railway line here, and the city is approximately eight miles from the Brest Litovsk railway station[1]. If a person gets sick, and the relatives of the sick person cannot afford to bring in a physician from far-off Brest, these unfortunate souls have no means to fend off the evil. It is wondrous that despite the fact that the face of the Rebbe appears here three times a year, and they have money for him, but they cannot afford a physician.

David Finkelstein

Translator's Footnote

1. (From the editor): As the crow flies, the distance between Ratno and Brest Litovsk is approximately 80 kilometers, not eight miles as the text suggests. https://www.jewishgen.org/Yizkor/Ratno/rat123.html - f134a-1r

Teachers and Educators at Tarbut

by Zeev Grabov

Translated by Jerrold Landau

The directors of the "Tarbut" School

From right to left: Noach Kotzker, Mrs. Katz, M. Gamarnik (all perished), and the secretary A. Held (Israel)

Amalia Droog of blessed memory, one of the founders of Hashomer Hatzair

The foundations of the Tarbut School in Ratno were laid at the end of 1926. However, it is worthwhile to note that even before that, some attempts were made to found a more modern school alongside the old-fashioned cheders that had not progressed with the spirit of the times. These attempts, however, were not crowned with success. Some said that a certain event that shook up the Jewish residents of the town was the factor that moved them to establish Tarbut. They were referring to the time when the teachers of the Polish public school took also the Jewish students to the Polish cemetery to have them participate in the planting of trees around it. Whether or not this was the case, the conditions for the establishment of the school had already existed for some time. What was missing was the primary moving force and the living spirit, but this problem was solved with the arrival of the teacher Kotzker to Ratno.

There is no doubt that the locals, especially the committee that was established for this purpose (Reb Asher Leker, Yeshaya Bekerman, Yehuda

Konishter, Yosef Zesak, Leibel Grabov, Yitzchak Hirsch Held, Berl and Eliezer Held, Yaakov Liberman, Moshe Eilbaum, and Gittel Karsh) played a major role in the establishment of this important educational institution. However, we must not ignore the assistance from outside that was given by the Zionist activist Moshe Perl of Kovel, who greatly assisted with the obtaining of the government permit; the supervisor of the Tarbut schools of Wolhyn, Shmuel Rozenhak; and the Tarbut headquarters in Warsaw.

Pairs of volunteers who went from home to home carried out the task of registering the students, and more than 100 students were registered in the first phase. This was an impressive accomplishment, and the school year opened with that number of students and a teaching staff that included, aside from the principal Kotzker, also the teachers Bokser and Klonitzky who had come from outside of Ratno, and the Ratno teacher Nechemia Hochstein ("The sweet toothed"). They taught the following subjects: Kotzker – Hebrew; Bokser – arithmetic and geography; Klonitzky – the early grades and kindergarten. At the beginning of its existence, the school was located in the home of Hodel Kamiler, but the local activists concerned themselves with a more fitting location, which was in the residence of Azriel and Chaya Shlitan on the Synagogue Street. The new premises were also not ideal for a school, but the rooms in the new premises were more spacious, filled with light and air. They engaged the Polish language teacher Lirenfeld to replace the teacher Klonitzky who had left. The daughter of Trebichinsky of Ratno taught Polish in the lower grades. When the great fire broke out in 1929, the Tarbut School went up in flames – and it went back to its first premises in the home of Hodel on Holinka Street. When they finished the building of the home of Bracha Shlomo-Michel's in the center of the city, the school moved to that home. It was given three large rooms, a secretary, a waiting room, and a large playground. There was a change in teaching staff, which now included the principal Noach Kotzker, the teacher Gavriel Zagorsky, and the teacher Klara Ryba. This took place in the 1929-1930 school year. The number of students reached 200. Zagorsky introduced new teaching methodologies, and his Bible classes enthralled the students, for he knew how to bring the chapters of the Bible to life in a dramatic fashion. Even the teacher Ryba who taught us Polish succeeded in endearing Polish poetry and literature to us, which to this point had been like a closed book to us.

We must attribute the two plays "Jephtah's Daughter" and "The Snatchers" to the teacher Zagorsky. These were performed by the students of the school, and brought a great deal of satisfaction for the Tarbut activists, the students, and indeed the entire Jewish population. Everyone was sorry that this teacher had to leave Ratno in the following school year (1930). He went to complete his studies in the Rabbinical Seminary of Frankfurt am Main in Germany. He then studied medicine in Switzerland, made aliya to Israel, and worked as a gynecologist. Several teachers who came from outside to take his place did not acclimatize to Ratno and left after a very short period of teaching. At the end of the 1930-1931 school year, the teacher Klara Ryba also left her work in the school. Fifty years later, her former students met her in Israel. She was very happy at this meeting, just as she was happy to participate in various events organized by the organization of Ratno natives in Israel.

Students of the "Tarbut" School with the teachers Kotzker, Klonitzky and Bokser

At the beginning of the 1931-1932 school year, the Tarbut headquarters sent us two excellent teachers. One of them, Elchanan Levin, taught Hebrew and mathematics. The second, Boris Rozen, a teacher for all subjects taught in Polish, had previously completed his studies at the Stefan Batory University in Vilna. From that time, the Polish ministry of education stopped persecuting the Tarbut School, which it had done previously because the level of its students in Polish had been below the minimum requirements according to its estimation. It also waived its demand that the principal of the Polish school also be the principal of Tarbut. The two aforementioned teachers succeeded in advancing their students in the subjects that they taught. At times, contests took place between the students of the upper grades of Tarbut and those of the Polish school with respect to their knowledge of Polish literature. The students of Tarbut always had the upper hand. Without a doubt, this was due to the teacher Rozen, who excelled in his didactic teaching style, and succeeded in raising the level of interest of the students in the subject material.

The 5691/2 (1931/2) school year

"Pan Tadeusz" of Mickiewicz, "With Fire and Sword" of Sienkiewicz, the poems of Slowacki and others became a source of interest for the students thanks to his methodologies. The teacher Rozen also developed the physical education curriculum, and gymnastic exercises became an honorable part of every school celebration. He was a Beitar follower by his outlook and political leanings, and also tried to influence the students to leave Hashomer Hatzair and Hechalutz Hatzair and transfer to the ranks of Beitar. However, he did not have any success in that realm. The students remained faithful to those movements, which had hegemonic status in Jewish Ratno.

These two teachers left Ratno at the end of the 1933-1934 school year. New faces again appeared in the school: Shlomo Karlin, a graduate of the Tarbut teachers' seminary of Vilna; and Amalia Droog, who was a native of Ratno. At first, she did not want to serve as a teacher in her native town, but after much urging and after she married the teacher Gamarnik of Kovel, she accepted the job of teaching in the school. The teacher Karlin organized a mandolin band in the school, and settled in the town after he married Golda Droog, a Ratno native.

During the final years, the school struggled for its existence. The paltry support and tuition fees were insufficient to ensure that the salary of the teachers be paid on time. The teachers who regarded teaching not only as a job, but rather as a mission, did not have it in them to arrange strikes, like today, and became accustomed to their bitter fate. During the later years, two Ratno natives joined the teaching staff -- Binyamin Pogatz and Yenta Teitelbaum – after they graduated from the Tarbut teachers' seminary of Vilna. Noach Kotzker continued to serve as principal. I am not mentioning his praise specifically, for I know that many already have praised him, and whoever adds, detracts.

By Zeev Grabov

The committee and the teachers of the "Tarbut" School in Ratno, July 3, 1932

First row, sitting from right to left: Y. Hochman, B. Held, Y. Zesak, Y. Bekerman, Y Steingarten, N. Klein

Second row, standing from right to left: A. Held, L. Grabov, the teachers Levin, Kotzker, Rozen, unidentified, Y. Karsh, M. Droog, Sh. Perlmutter, and A. Y. Held

Noach Kotzker - Teacher and Educator

by Noah Cohen

Translated by Jerrold Landau

One of the interesting characters for close to thirty years, plowing in the furrows of Jewish education in Ratno, was without doubt the teacher Kotzker, who was honored and beloved by the Jewish youth. If the Jewish youth of Ratno, of whatever party affiliation, earned a good name throughout the Jewish Diaspora in any realm of activity, this was thanks to a large degree to the education of Kotzker and the values that he instilled.

Kotzker was a native of Pinsk, and was a graduate of the famous courses for teachers in Grodno. He was a friend of the renowned pedagogue M. A. Beigel and of Tzemach, one of the founders of Habima. When the First World War broke out and the Germans conquered the city areas, Kotzker wandered to the village of Zabulote and served as a teacher of the children of the few Jews who lived in that village, which also had a small railway station. Of course, this work did not satisfy Kotzker's spirit, for it restricted his horizons and he saw no satisfaction from it. He began to take interest in the nearby region, and thereby arrived in Ratno, which was 20 kilometers away from the village of Zabulote. One of the residents of Zabulote, Chaim, assisted him in this by informing Yudel Konishter, a teacher and educator in Ratno, about Kotzker, and his talents and abilities. Konishter conferred with Eliahu Janowicz, who served as the mayor at that point, who in turn conferred with the German commander, who agreed to bring Kotzker to Ratno and open a school that would dedicate an appropriate amount of time to the German Language. He also agreed to provide a certain amount of support from the German authorities.

One clear morning during the summer of 1916, a wagon stopped at the home of my father Reb Avraham the Shochet on Holinka Street. Reb Chaim Zabuloter and Noach Kotzker got off the wagon. A day or two after he had arrived in Ratno, after he had become acquainted with the difficult economic situation in the city, Noach Kotzker offered himself to me and my sister Rachel of blessed memory as a free teacher. After some time, he succeeded in setting up a Jewish school with the support given to him by Janowicz.

The Jewish educational situation in Ratno at that time was particularly poor. The Jewish-Hebrew-Russian school under the leadership of Avraham Telzon and Yudel Konishter was no longer in existence at that time. Only a few cheders remained in town. There were a few teachers, including Itzel the melamed who was known as a good Gemara teacher, who had left teaching and turned to business. The difficult economic conditions directed the thoughts of the parents away from problems of education. Many of them were satisfied if their children would know a portion of Chumash, provided that they would be able to assist their parents with their livelihood. The appearance of Kotzker under such conditions was literally a salvation, and an obstacle to the increasing ignorance.

Among his first steps was arranging mixed classes with boys and girls. This step was revolutionary with respect to the concepts of those days, and there were people who opposed it. However, with the passage of time, this ensured that among the girls of Ratno, there would be some who were conversant in Bible and even Mishna no less than the boys.

Since most of the houses in the town were set on fire by the Russians as they were retreating from the town, and there was no building appropriate for housing the school, the Shtibel of the Hassidim of Trisk served as a temporary premise for the new school. The Jews of Ratno quickly realized the benefits of this new educational institution and the new principal. This was the beginning of a new path in Jewish education, the likes of which was not known in the town to that point. The classes of the teacher Kotzker were very different than those of the teachers who "ground through" the chapter of Chumash and Bible with their students in a rote fashion, repeating word for word after the teacher. It was impossible for the students to not sense the new winds that were blowing. The educational attainments were recognized immediately, and the students connected to their teacher with bonds of love and appreciation. Kotzker also arranged various performances and celebrations for the students, which provided a good opportunity for the parents to appreciate the achievements of their children, as they watched them successfully filling their roles on the stage under the guidance and direction of the new teacher.

The teacher Kotzker was the first in town to tie education with day to day life. Thanks to him, the anniversary of the death of Dr. Herzl, 20th of Tammuz, was recognized publicly for the first time with an assembly. Other events connected to Zionism and the Land of Israel were similarly recognized. Noach Kotzker became the moving force behind public and Zionist activities in our town. He began to give presentations on Bible and other topics. Things reached the point where the first public assembly hall was established in Kamiler's house, leading to the establishment of various Zionist youth movements at a later stage. Kotzker possessed a great deal of knowledge, and was also a talented orator. It is no surprise that many Jews flocked to all of his lectures. In those days during the time of the German occupation, when the Jews found themselves in dire straits, and the sole cultural institution that had existed, the public library, also went up in flames, Kotzker's lectures were the only spiritual treasure in the town. They encouraged the youth in the struggle for a better future, and instilled faith in such a future. When the private houses became too small to accommodate everyone who would come to the lectures, Kotzker advised that a multi-room location be rented which would serve as the center of all cultural activities in the town. Indeed, opposite the house of Privrov at the edge of Holinka Street, there was a house that was suitable for this purpose. This house, which belonged to Hershel Kamiler, a wealthy resident of Ratno, served as a prison before the war. With the help of several friends, Kotzker turned this place into a community center, similar to those that existed in larger cities in the region during that era. The day of the dedication of the community center was a holiday in the town. Young and old streamed to Holinka Street, although there were some zealots who regarded this innovation with an unpleasant eye. Kotzker was of course the host of the celebration, for he spent his days and nights ensuring that everything would be arranged appropriately, and that the townsfolk would support this new spiritual center.

In praise of Kotzker, we should note that he never attempted to take the stage for himself. On the contrary, he attempted to educate and prepare his students for public performances, especially the older ones, and to include them in every communal event that he initiated and planned.

It is no exaggeration to say that a new era of social life in Jewish Ratno commenced with the opening of the community center, especially for the Jewish youth. During the years 1918-1919, dozens of performances and cultural events took place in the community center, which turned into a veritable cultural center.

The many activities that took place in the community center were thorns in the eyes of the gentile neighbors. It was possible to sense their evil glances, as they were unable to come to terms with a radiant community center. They were unable to cause any damage, however, since a guard of young Jews was set up to prevent any difficulty. Nothing bad occurred as long as the Ukrainians were in power. This was not the case after the Polish conquest, and the tidings of Job of the slaughter perpetrated by the Poles in Pinsk on the 5th of Nissan 5680 (1920) arrived, where they attacked the Jewish community center under the pretext of "arresting spies" and took 35 of the finest Jewish activists to be killed. The heart prophesied bad tidings, and one day the news spread in town that Kotzker had been imprisoned. Later arriving information indicated that the Poles demanded that he, as the chairman of the Jewish meeting place, turn over the illegal weapons in the possession of the meeting place to them. When he refused to comply with their request, they ordered that he be given 25 lashes on his naked body – a form of punishment that was in vogue with the Poles at that time. This event left its mark upon the Jewish community.

A class of the "Tarbut" Schoolmwith the teachers Rozen, Lewin, Kotzker and the secretary A. Held

Around that time, Kotzker got married to Ginzburg, and thereby became a Ratno resident. Under his leadership, the school flourished and developed, and the number of students progressively grew. At that time, the school was housed in a story built for it above the BeisMidrash. The name of Kotzker as a prominent educator and good organizer spread to the largest cities in Wolhyn. The educational activists in Kovel even succeeded in bringing Kotzker to them for a period of time, but his connections with Ratno and its Jewish youth were apparently sufficiently strong, and he returned to the town. In 1926, the school joined the Tarbut network of Hebrew schools of Poland.

The golden age of that educational institution began at that time, for it gained renown in the near and distant regions as an institution with an excellent teaching staff and a choice principal. The students of Tarbut in Ratno left their impressions in their roles as members of youth movement delegates to the regional conventions and summer camps of the various organizations. This too was apparently a result of the education at Kotzker' school. It is fitting to note another fact: most of the graduates gravitated to the left camp of the workers' movement. It seems that Kotzker, being a Socialist himself, succeeded in instilling in his students the values of the workers' movement, social justice, and love of one's fellowman.

Around the time of the Second World War, when the economic situation in the town became more serious and the school suffered from a significant deficit, Kotzker began to think about leaving Ratno and emigrating. In a letter to Yehuda Konishter and his wife in Argentina dated March 5, 1935, he writes among other things: "Ratno is declining significantly from day to day, and all of its residents are jealous of those fortunate people who have left or can still leave – as I do in my dreams!" That is to say, he too was dreaming about this. He was unable to obtain a certificate for aliya to the Land of Israel due to his advanced age, so he prepared to travel to Argentina. However, it was difficult to obtain a permit. He remained in Ratno, and went on his final journey to Mount Prochod along with hundreds of his students.

The summer Moshava of the Tarbut School in Ratno, Vydranitsa,

July 25, 1932

The Kamiler House -- the headquarters of the activities of the youth movements

Young Zionists in the town

Top row right to left: A. Marsik (perished), M. Gutman (Israel), D. Fuchs (Argentina), G Weinstock (perished), M. Stern (Israel), Y. Shapira (killed in the Soviet army), B. Eilbaum, Sh. Cohen (Argentina), A. Avrech (died)

Second row: M. Kamper (died in Canada) M. Gefen (Israel), Ch. Ginzburg (perished), M. Droog, Sh. Ginzburg (United States), P. Vernik (Israel), M. Grabov (Argentina), M. Rider (killed in an accident in Ratno)

Bottom (kneeling): Y. Karsh, R. Kaminer (perished), D. Marin (Israel)

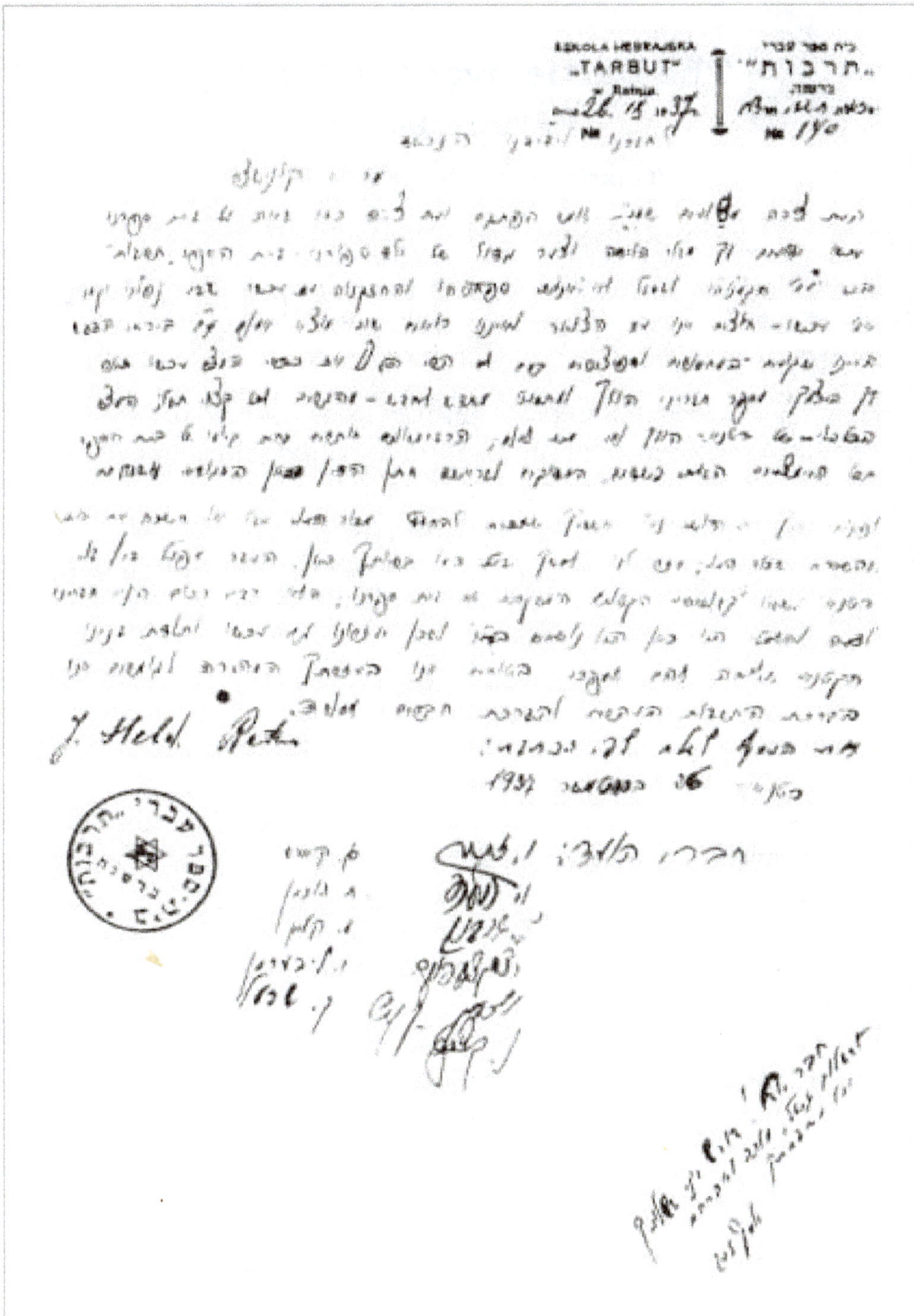
SZKOLA HEBRAJSKA
„TARBUT"
w Ratnie

בית ספר עברי
„תרבות"
ברטנה

Letter from the directors of "Tarbut" to Y. Konishter in Argentina, September 26, 1937

The Battle over the Library

by Yisrael Honik

Translated by Jerrold Landau

I wish to dredge up from the abyss of forgetfulness an event from the time when we belonged to the youth movements, which today would perhaps seem ridiculous or meaningless, but in those days was treated by us with excessive seriousness.

In those days, it was customary that if one or a group of activists of a certain youth movement had a dispute with the other members of the movement, they would not only leave the movement, but would also immediately join a different movement or perhaps establish a new movement in order to anger the opposing side, and also so that they would have a place to discharge their youthful energy. In general, Ratno had no shortage of movements and organizations for the local youth. There were also ephemeral organizations that arose and disappeared quickly. However, the Hashomer Hatzair movement maintained its stand at all times and under all conditions. In this manner, it was perhaps different from other youth organizations. However, one day after a dispute that was not of an ideological-conceptual character, a serious group of Hashomer Hatzair members decided to separate from the movement. At that time, I was part of that group. Since we were unable to remain without an organization, Heaven forbid, we decided to reestablish Hechalutz Hatzair that had existed in the past and had disbanded. I recall that the headquarters of the original Hechalutz Hatzair had been on Holianka Street in the home of Leizer Dibczner, near the bridge. Its leaders at that time were L. Avrech (who died in an accident in Israel), L. Ginzburg (currently in the United States) and Shlomo Cohen. These members had developed intensive activity in the chapter. During the time of their activity, Mottle Weinstock, Moshe Stern and others had made aliya to the Land of Israel. When the chapter disbanded for various reasons, its library of several hundred important Hebrew books remained orphaned. Therefore, the members of Hashomer Hatzair jumped upon the find and took possession of the books. I was the librarian, and I am able to assert that Hashomer Hatzair supervised the library well, but after I left the chapter with a group of members, they fired me from my task of librarian. This pained us, and since we began to reestablish Hechalutz Hatzair, we searched for means and ways to "conquer" the leadership of the library, for we felt ourselves fitting for this, given that the library had been established by Hechalutz Hatzair and I had served as the librarian for a long period. We raised the issue in a semi-conspirational meeting and hatched a plan to conquer the library from Hashomer Hatzair. We saw no reason to conduct negotiations on this matter, given that we were aware of the stubborn attitude of Hashomer Hatzair with respect to the library. Three members were given the responsibility for taking the necessary steps to return the prestige and the books to us: Maya Weinstock, Avraham Grabov of blessed memories, and the writer of these lines. The plan was straightforward: to enter the room by force in which the bookcases stand, to remove several hundred books, to hide them in a secret place, and then to send a notice of such to the Tarbut committee and the school principal Noach Kotzker, who was held in wide esteem, about our actions so that they would negotiate with us and arrange for our participation in the leadership of the library. The day that was set for this effort was the eve of Yom Kippur. It seemed to us that this time frame was appropriate from a strategic perspective, for the hall would be closed and everyone would be busy in their houses with kapores[1] and other preparations for the holy day.

On the set evening, we went to Chamilar house, where the meeting place was located, with sacks and crowbars to open the door of the hall and the doors of the bookcases. The people in the house did not suspect anything when they heard the banging, for they were sure that the members of Hashomer Hatzair had come as they did every evening for activities in the chapter. We conducted our work calmly, removed the most important books (including the new books that had been obtained) as well as the library catalog, packed them very well into the sacks that we had brought, and snuck away secretly through the darkened Holianka Street until we reached the house of Eliezer the stableman, who was a Stoliner Hassid. We went through the gentile alleyways until we reached our warehouse. We had to cross several fences, calm the dogs that attacked us, and overcome other obstacles. Next to our warehouse there was a small house filled with cloth and rags. We hid our cultural treasure there. We had reason to suspect that my brother Berl of blessed memory, who was faithful to Hashomer Hatzair, would certainly search that house. Therefore, we hid the books very well so that nobody could find them. Maya brought the catalog and other important papers to the home of Gittel Karsh of blessed memory and hid them in the oven. The next day, we convened an urgent meeting of our members. We informed them that we carried out our mission, and we sent a letter to Kotzker, as was agreed. The news of the theft of the books spread through the entire shtetl, and things were in ferment. The shtetl was like a seething pot. Members of Hashomer

Hatzair went around and searched for the books. My brother Berl ran to the warehouse and surrounded it, but did not succeed in finding the hidden items. The teacher Kotzker convened a special meeting after he received our notice, and made efforts to arrange matters. After deliberations that lasted for several hours it was decided: a) to set two positions in the library leadership for representatives of Hechalutz Hatzair; b) that those who perpetrated the theft will not serve as members of the leadership. We gave our agreement to this decision and signed the agreement along with representatives from all sides. Our group designated Shmuel Goldman (today in Israel) and Batya Chayat of blessed memory as our delegates to the leadership of the library.

Translator's Footnote

1. A symbolic ceremony of expiation of sins carried out on the eve of Yom Kippur with a chicken or rooster. See http://www.chabad.org/library/article_cdo/aid/407513/jewish/Kapparot-The-Chicken-Thing.htm https://www.jewishgen.org/Yizkor/Ratno/rat137.html - f141a-1r

Thou Shalt not Make Graven Images (About the character of Reb Shlomo-Aharon Olitzky)

by Leib Olitzky

Translated by Jerrold Landau

Reb Shlomo-Aharon was a descendent of Reb Aharon of Karlin. This fact alone was sufficient to place him among the finest of the Hassidim of Karlin even beyond Ratno. However, aside from this, he also had fine personal traits, for he was an educated Jew, very pious, spending day and night with Torah and Divine service. All of the Jews of the town, not only the Hassidim of Karlin, treated him with honor and respect as if was the rabbi of the city, a veritable rabbi. Many asked him to take upon himself the rabbinate of the city, for why was he looking afar when the town itself was such a fitting place for the crown of the rabbinate. However, Reb Shlomo-Aharon was a modest and discrete man, and he told those who urged him:

"Who am I and what am I that I should put my head toward the crown of the rabbinate and become pastor of a holy community such as Ratno? I am wary of the level of responsibility that such a role would impose."

He was not involved at all in the burden of livelihood, despite the fact that the family was blessed with six children and it was no easy matter to feed such a family. He relied upon his wife to take care of the household affairs and members of the household.

His wife was a simple woman; a village native with a healthy and straightforward intellect. She was strong, and a veritable woman of valor, as is said, "A helpmate for him."[1] With her straightforward intellect, she realized immediately that the prayers and Torah study of her husband would not feed their children. Therefore, she hitched herself fully to the burden of livelihood, and talked well of both herself and Shlomo-Aharon, saying, "He occupies himself with sublime matters and everyone honors him, with crumbs coming to me too, and after 120 years, he will rise to a fine portion of the Garden of Eden on account of his prayers and studies - and this too is for the good..." She, Fruma, had a store in which one could find everything from "a thread to a shoelace,"[2] including colorful textiles from the farmers who would come to Ratno, dyes, meat on a spit, eggs, pig hair, various leather products, dried mushrooms, dried fruit and the like, and all types of haberdashery. Merchants from Brisk or Kowel who would come to Ratno would come to Fruma's store and not leave empty handed. She was more than busy throughout the six workdays in running the store and the household. She bore the burden as best she could. Only on the Sabbath did she rest a bit from this great burden, breathe a bit, and prepare herself for the great burden that awaited her during the coming week. It is unclear if Reb Shlomo-Aharon himself understood how she managed with the double taskof housewife and shopkeeper. She never even attempted to involve her husband in her mundane affairs and her shop. However, on rare occasions, in order to fulfill her obligation toward the community and the family, she would ask for his advice in some matter or another.

Reb Shlomo-Aharon did not withhold his advice from her, which was one and the same in all cases: "Fruma, do according to what you feel is right, and the good G-d will send his good angel before you..." This was the division of labor between them. She involved herself with the affairs of this world and materialism, and he concerned himself with spirituality and matters of the World To Come.

Years passed. The children grew up and the worries increased. Fruma's health declined. She ignored her problems, saying, "Who has time for such things?" However, when her illness worsened, she was forced to leave her work in the store and take to her sick bed. Nevertheless, she never stopped worrying about the store that she abandoned and the well-being of the children. She worried particularly about her Shlomo-Aharon, while he himself awaited the mercies of G-d and would utter incessantly: "Master of the Universe, do not place such a serious test before me, for who am I and what am I without her..."

She was granted a reprieve for some time, whether due to his prayers or her own strength, and she returned to direct the household and the shop. However, it was not long before Fruma's health took a turn for the worse. They summoned the oldest son Nachman from Trisk, and Reb Shlomo-Aharon sat with his three sons while they recited chapters of Psalms incessantly with devotion and feeling. At times the eyes of the sick woman would open, and she would look at the children and their father immersed in the recitation of Psalms and say, "You are reciting Psalms for the elevation of my soul? After my death, I permit you to support the gate of the cemetery with my body, but as long as I am alive, I beg you: save me, take me to the best doctors." Then Shlomo-Aharon straightened up, lifted his eyes heavenward and said, "One must fulfill the will of a seriously ill person!"

Reb Shlomo-Aharon Olitzky

The two oldest sons Nachman and Shlomo-Simcha set out for Kiev with their mother in order to solicit the advice of the doctors, but they returned from Kiev without her; with a bit of red sand from her grave in their shoes.

After the Shiva [seven day mourning period], all matters of the household and the shop were conducted by the daughters and the youngest son Asherke. Shlomo-Aharon continued to study Torah as was his custom, but the absence of his wife was felt at every footstep. The home was like a ship that lost it captain.

Shlomo-Aharon never thought about remarrying, for he could not forget Fruma of blessed memory. Even though he did not speak much about her, one could see that he never stopped thinking about her. Only on Sabbath eves when he returned from the synagogue and began the prayer "A woman of valor who can find" did the children feel, through his tune and words, that the soul of their mother was floating around the Sabbath candles, and Father's sad melody was sung in her memory.

Thus did years pass. The three daughters married, as did the youngest son. The house emptied and the bustle ceased. Now, Reb Shlomo-Aharon could sit in his house without any disturbances. The household and the shop were now run by Shmuel Simcha and his wise and well-bred wife Chavale of the Shapira family. They took it upon themselves to care for the comfort and well-being of Father. Indeed, Chavale worried about him and related to him as a faithful and dedicated daughter.

Everything went on as usual until the First World War broke out. When the Russian Army retreated from the town, the Cossacks burnt down many houses, including the house of Shlomo-Aharon. Nobody had time to rescue even the bedding. Shlomo-Aharon, his son, his daughter-in-law and grandson were forced to move to the home of another Jew and to live in cramped conditions. His energy dwindled, his senses of hearing and sight declined, but his splendid appearance remained as in days of yore.

One winter Sabbath morning, as Shlomo-Aharon was walking to the shtibel of the Hassidim of Stolin, shuffling along in his usual manner every Sabbath, wearing his Sabbath kapote and his tallis upon his shoulders with its silver adornment, wearing his streimel upon his head all the way to his neck, with only his long curly peyos showing out from the sides, his eyes closed and teary from the blinding light of the sun and snow - the city police chief

of the German occupation army came to him. It seemed that the captain was astonished at the splendid appearance and demeanor of the elderly Jew, to the extent that he cleared the way for him as if to give him appropriate honor. The next day, a Jewish policeman with two armed gendarmes came to Shlomo-Aharon's house with a command for him to appear before the civic police chief dressed exactly as he was dressed on the Sabbath morning when they crossed paths.

All the members of the household were surprised. Only the devil knows what this German was plotting? Some people recommended trying to bribe the chief, but Shlomo-Aharon said, "The law of the Land is the law." In the middle of a weekday, he donned his Sabbath clothes and walked upright to the office of the German police chief, accompanied by the Jewish policeman and the German gendarmes.

News of the summoning of Shlomo-Aharon to the police chief spread throughout the town and inflamed all the spirits. Who knows what awaited the holy community of Ratno from this strange summons? Many Jews, including Shlomo-Aharon's two sons hastened to the house of the Rabbi to ask for advice. Some advised that a delegation of the Jewish community, headed by the rabbi himself, set out to appear before the police chief. Of course, even the Jewish mayor Yeshaya Shapira was summoned, and was prepared to go to the police headquarters. The rabbi calmed his flock by saying that no evil will befall Shlomo-Aharon, for the police officer asked that this holy man with whom he had crossed paths the previous day appear before him; Shlomo-Aharon is indeed a holy man, and with the help of Heaven, the German will not harm him. The entire town was in ferment, and who knows how far things would have gone had not Reb Shaya Shapira returned quickly from the police headquarters and calmed everyone down by stating that Reb Shlomo-Aharon was summoned by the German for one purpose only: to be photographed. Apparently, the police chief had sensed the extent of the patriarchal image of this holy Jew and decided to photograph this unique character, whether for his private album or whether for other purposes.

The tension in Ratno abated with these words. Some people laughed and others wept, but all of them were surprised that this German chief wished to perpetuate the image of this sublime, honored Jew. However the "protagonist" himself, Shlomo-Aharon, left the police headquarters in mourning. He was sorrowful over the photographing of his image, for there is a taint of "do not make for yourself a graven image" in this, as is written in the Torah[3].

About a week later, the granddaughter of Shlomo-Aharon came from Rudka with a copy of the photograph in her hands. He had requested it from the city police chief and had received it. Shlomo-Aharon acceded to the request of his beloved granddaughter, and agreed to hold the photograph in his hands and take a glance of it. However, he did this as if he was compelled to do so, and as if he was holding an abominable object in his hands. Was this a small matter? It is an image! After he cast an astonished look at his picture, he was overtaken by shuddering. The photograph appeared to him like a sort of solar eclipse, and his eyes in the photograph appeared to him like the eyes of a bird in the hands of the shochet [ritual slaughterer] just before he cut it with a knife. He mumbled to his granddaughter "Miredelke, quickly bring me a pitcher of water so that I can wash my hands and place me upon my bed. This German has slaughtered me." ...

That year, Reb Shlomo-Aharon returned his soul to his creator while he was lying on his bed in the home of his son Reb Shmuel-Simcha.

(Translated from Yiddish by Simcha Lavie, the grandson of Reb Shlomo-Aharon, the son of his daughter Chasia of blessed memory.)

Translator's Footnotes

1. Genesis 2:20. https://www.jewishgen.org/Yizkor/Ratno/rat137.html - f147-1r
2. Genesis 14:23 https://www.jewishgen.org/Yizkor/Ratno/rat137.html - f147-2r
3. The second of the Ten Commandments. To this day, some Hassidic Jews frown upon photographing a human face. https://www.jewishgen.org/Yizkor/Ratno/rat137.html - f147-3r

Tidbits

by Zeev Grabov

Translated by Jerrold Landau

Itche-Mordechai the shoemaker was paralyzed in half his body. When they would bring him shoes to fix, his wife would utter, "Why are you bringing him shoes to fix. Do you not know that he has two left hands?" If they would tell her, "In any case, he has eight children," she would retort, "If they would make children with hands - I would have remained a virgin to this day."

*

Sheina-Beila prepared dough for the Sabbath challos, and as was her custom, she always put it into bed beside her husband so that it would rise appropriately. She got up at dawn and lit the oven, approached the bread to take a handful of dough as per the law of tithes, but was not in any way able to break off a piece of the dough. She began to curse, as was her custom, and her husband lay in bed full of laughter. "Let your soul be ground up," she said to him, "What is this laughter about?" The dough did not rise, and what will be with the challos for the Sabbath. Her husband responded, "Sheina-Beila, you are touching my hernia and trying to take a piece of it. The dough has risen appropriately".

*Gedalia Schneider the shoemaker was a unique character in the town. He used to dress in the latest fashion that arrived in Ratno, and he tried to look and sound very intelligent and spiced his words with words from the Haftara[1]. When he went out in the morning, the teacher Kotzker, who was known as a man of culture and someone who was current in social and political affairs, appeared. Gedalia said to him, "Good morning Mr. Kotzker! What is new, Mr. Kotzker? Perhaps you can pay me a check of five zloty? Many think honorable Mr. Kotzker, and much peace upon you."

After such a conversation, he boasted to everyone, "I had a very interesting conversation with the teacher Kotzker regarding very important matters."

*

Berele Sara Leah's[2] had been a widower for many years. Whenever he saw two women conversing, he would set his path so that he would pass between them and lightly touch them. When people noted his custom of directing his path between women, he would respond, "What can I do? One must not forgo even small pleasures during these difficult times..."

*

After many years of bachelorhood, Inyuman[3] the water drawer had finally succeeded in marrying a woman from Kowel. When he was asked about how he was succeeding in his affairs, he responded, "Great success. I will always only get married to women from Kowel..." Incidentally, this Inyuman was among the 30 Jews selected by the Germans to stand by a pit to be shot. As the Germans were busy preparing for the murder, he was heard to mutter, "What am I doing here? I have not yet had a chance to give my horse a drink." As he muttered, he left the line and disappeared without anyone noticing. Thus was he saved, and he survived until the final aktion.

*

Yancha, one of the twins, accompanied his wife to her eternal rest. He was lamenting over her grave and saying, "She appeared, without the evil eye, so good and lovely during the latter period, and now, may we be protected, she is being brought to burial"...

*

Beni, the son of Hershel Benddek the porter and the drummer in Avraham-Yankel the musician's band, used to say, "All night long the moon goes around and around my house, but when it reaches my window, the sun is already shining at full strength..."

Translator's Footnotes

1. The section from the Prophets read after the Torah reading on Sabbaths, festivals and fast days. https://www.jewishgen.org/Yizkor/Ratno/rat137.html - f149-1r
2. This type of nickname means "Berlele the son of Sara Leah." https://www.jewishgen.org/Yizkor/Ratno/rat137.html - f149-2r
3. Likely a nickname for Binyamin (Binyuman). https://www.jewishgen.org/Yizkor/Ratno/rat137.html - f149-3r

About the Town

by Chaim Hazaz

Translated by Jerrold Landau

"... In any manner that you judge the Diaspora and a Jewish town, perforce you will measure the great values therein, such as: fear of Heaven, study of Torah, love of one's fellow Jew, longing for the Land of Israel, faith in the redemption and the coming of the Messiah, and many other such things. Translate these values into the language of modern man and compare them to the values of Today. A Jewish person in the Diaspora, in a Jewish town, would be found by a book for the entire day. Every man, including an ordinary person, was involved with Mishna, Midrash, Ein Yaakov, and Psalms. It goes without saying that this was the same case with a scholar, whose mouth never desisted from Torah day and night, and who was not seeking any reward. A person who is interested in the book, whose entire scope of interest is with the book, is of course a sublime person. How much more so is an entire nation. Therefore, we have been nicknamed: The People of the Book.

It is no wonder that a Jewish town was filled with great spiritual powers. Great rabbis, heads and leaders of the people would come forth from the town. The first Maskilim, various types of Socialists who dedicated themselves to the redemption and freedom, and all sorts of dreamers and visionaries of the redemption of Israel sprung forth from the town."

Impressions from a Visit to Ratno in 1937

by Mordechai Gefen

Translated by Jerrold Landau

It was the time of the British Mandate in the land of Israel. The aliya restrictions imposed by the Mandatory Government were at their height, and the national institutions in the land attempted all types of means and tactics to circumvent the decrees and bring Jews to the Land. One tactic was arranging fictitious weddings between citizens of Palestine and girls from the Diaspora. In brief, we referred to these as "fictions." I was also obligated to fulfill the commandment of a "fiction." I received money for the trip and was supposed to bring a girl from Maciejów after I would "get married" to her. This was a golden opportunity to visit my family and the town that I had left in

1929. I do not feel obliged to describe my feelings about this upcoming trip, especially as I approached Ratno.

When I arrived in Kowel, I met two girls from Ratno who were studying in Kowel. I asked them to inform people in Ratno about my arrival, for I knew that the entire town, that is -- the Jews of the town, would come to meet me at the bus station. I deliberately got off next to Marsyk's house and walked to my home in a roundabout fashion. However, Shachna, the owner of the bus upon which I was traveling, did not keep a secret, and told people that I had got off the bus near Marsyk's house. This caused crowds of Jews to congregate at the house. I was not able to have time alone with my sister and family, for many Jews streamed to the house. The joy and emotions overflowed. The meetings in various houses, in the chapters of "Hechalutz" and "Hashomer Hatzair" and the many parties in my honor began the next day. I did not tire of speaking, and they did not tire of listening. They wanted to know everything that happened to me in the Land, with details and minutiae. I had the feeling of being on a mission. I was one of the pioneers who had traveled to the Land of Israel from Ratno. I was bound to the townsfolk with thousands of strands, and I felt like an emissary. What did I not tell them about? I did not hide any thing, even small matters. I told about my first three years in Givat Hashelosha, about my work in the Dead Sea Brigade, and about our valuable work on the Kalia-Jericho Road, about our hikes from Givat Hashelosha to Kfar Giladi, about my visit to the Western Wall in Jerusalem, about the notes that I removed with great curiosity from the walls of the Western Wall to find out what Jews were requesting from the Creator of the World, about my work in digging wells, about the building of a new settlement -- Kfar Sirkin, about my roles in defending the settlement during the disturbances of 1936, about my work with defective buildings, etc., etc. I saw that my listeners were drinking up my words with thirst. I saw tears in the eyes of some of them, and if my memory does not mislead me, my eyes were also not dry as I was telling and telling. I remember that many people asked to see my hands -- the hands of an Israeli worker -- to see if there were any calluses on them or perhaps just to see what the hands of a worker in the Land look like. Even the Ukrainian residents of Ratno who remembered me well did not take their eyes off of me. They looked with awe upon the grandson of the merchant Liber Kirsch who had become a farmer in the Holy Land. I told them as well about my work in the orchards, about my various attempts at agriculture, and about the differences between the work from here and there. They would wink their eyes and express astonishment. (Who could imagine that within a few years, many of them would become involved in the murder of Jews?)

Chanuka party with the participation of a guest from the Land of Israel -- M. Gefen. 1936

My visit to the home of David-Aharon Shapiro is etched in my mind. As is appropriate for an honorable guest such as myself, refreshments were offered, and, among other things, oranges were served. They was not, Heaven forbid, whole oranges, but rather orange slices. Only a wealthy Jew such as Shapiro would have allowed himself to purchase oranges. When the orange slices were served, I took the opportunity to tell them how we grow oranges in the Land, and how we eat oranges (entire ones, not slices). Among other things I told them that I worked as a harvester in an orchard during my first years in the Land, and my job was to transport the fruit on a plank that contained four crates of freshly harvested fruit. Along the way to the packing plant, my friend who was my partner with the plank and I would take oranges from the crates, cut them into four pieces with a pocketknife, squeeze the juice directly into our mouths, and bury the peel in the ground. Once, the orchard keeper noticed that we were delayed in arriving at the packing plant. He came out to meet us and caught us in the act of burying the peel of the fruit that we ate. He shouted in Hebrew, “Gefen, don't bury the peels. This wastes time. Leave them as is.” I told them that after this event, we continued to squeeze the juice directly into our mouths, but we did not bury the peel because it would be a waste of time... Everyone laughed at this story.

Despite the fact that my task for this visit was the "fiction," that is, to marry the girl from Maciejów, I felt the need to explain to the youth and adults, anywhere that I found myself, what was taking place in the Land, what was the purpose of the struggle that we were undertaking, what was the character of the youth who grew up in the Land. In one word: I saw myself as an official emissary for all matters.

The three months that I remained in Ratno were like a "seminar" for me. I learned about the realities and conditions of the Jews in Poland, as was revealed to me. The economic situation had declined since the time I left Poland due to the taxes of Grabski that sucked the marrow from the bones of the Jews, decrees and oppressions that renewed themselves each morning, and worst of all -- the lack of prospects of a better life in the future. The pioneering movement was also in the straits. The lack of certificates lead to a situation where many youths had already gone on hachsharah or were still on hachsharah kibbutzim, but had given up hope completely and did not believe in the possibility of aliya to the Land. It was therefore natural that many of them immigrated to America, Canada, Argentina, and other countries with the help of their relatives who had previously immigrated to those countries. For all the time that I was there, I had the thought that it was all sitting on nothing, that there was no foundation or purpose for Jewish life there, and who knew what would happen there. I was particularly troubled about the youths who were fluent in the Hebrew Language, had received a Zionist education at the Tarbut School or through the youth groups, and who now found themselves in a downtrodden and oppressive situation without any possibility at all of actualizing their hopes and dreams.

In the eyes of my spirit, I can see my farewell to the Jews of Ratno. Their eyes said everything, as if they were pleading with me to take them to the Land. How different was this departure from my departure when I made aliya in 1929. At that time, many of them expressed their surprise at such a radical step: to travel to the Land during the time of pogroms (the disturbances of Av 5689 / 1929). It appeared as if they were nodding their heads in astonishment regarding Mottel Weinstock[1], who was leaving a family and a stable economic situation to endanger himself with this journey.

At this time -- tears flowed from the eyes of many; but those were tears of jealousy because I had merited what I had merited.

I could not have realized that this would be the final farewell.

Translator's Footnote

1. Mordechai Gefen is the Hebraised version of Mottel Weinstock. https://www.jewishgen.org/Yizkor/Ratno/rat152.html - f1r

The Mission

by Zeev Grabov

Translated by Jerrold Landau

(A story based on experiences from the time of the First World War)

Mother said, "Father is going to the war."

"And where is this war?" I asked mother, "And when will he return? So many days have passed, and father has not yet returned. The High Holidays are approaching, I want Father."

Tears flowed from Mother's eyes. She felt sorry for me. "Don't cry, Mother," I pleaded with her. Mother caressed the hair of my head, and gave me a peace of bread smeared with oil.

Every Friday, I went with my two younger brothers to the bathhouse. My brothers did not even know that Father had gone to war. Even Yosele the orphan was going to the bathhouse himself, without his father. "Yosele's father had died," said all the children. All summer, his father had coughed and expectorated, with green phlegm. They brought him on a wagon to Kowel, and many Jews accompanied him. He did not return, for he died. Yosele was left as an orphan. He recited Kaddish, and he went to the bathhouse himself.

Every morning, we heard the sound of the shofar. The month of Elul had arrived. The water in the river was cooling off, and it was impossible to bathe. Everyone was preparing to greet the Day of Judgment. My father was going to return before the holiday. I would stand beside him in the synagogue and pray from the large Machzor[1]. After the services, we would go home. Father would recite Kiddush over wine, and give everyone a taste of the sweet, red wine. The house would be happy and pleasant.

I waited for Father to return, but he did not return. One day, I returned home, and saw many people in the house. Mother was sitting a low stool, with a light cloth around her head. Her eyes were red from weeping. What had happened? Perhaps father had already returned from the war? No, this is not how one greets a returning father. I fell at Mother's feet and asked, “Mother, where is Father?” Mother said, “My orphan, Father will never be returning.” This was the first time that I had heard the word “orphan.” After that, I heard the word many times. Now it was clear to me: I was an orphan. I was not a lad like the other lads, but an orphan who must bear the yoke of the house, and assist with the livelihood of the household: three brothers, my mother, and I, the eldest.

It was winter. The marshes were frozen, and a thin, white frost covered the windows. The days became very short, and we went to bed early, for we had to conserve the kerosene in the lamp. At times, we went to sleep hungry. The cries and pleas of Mother reached my ears: “Oh, Dweller on high, please help a widow and four orphans!” My heart ached. I wanted to cry; I closed my eyes and saw Father. -- -- --

Neighbors came to help out Mother. Acquaintances even came from the nearby village of Wydranica to advice Mother to move to the village until the wrath of the accursed war would pass. They said that in the village, the orphans would have what to eat, they would not freeze from the cold, and they would even have a teacher.

One morning, we got up, loaded our baggage on a wagon hitched to a gaunt horse, and set out for the village of Wydranica. In the evening, we arrived at a small house whose roof was covered with straw that had darkened with age. Gittel (we called her the Good Gittel) stood in the doorway. She took some sweets out of her apron and treated us: “Eat children, so you will be healthy.”

Good Gittel hugged and kissed Mother. They both wept. Gittel helped Mother take off our clothes. The aroma of boiled potatoes reached our nose. A grey, earthenware plate of potatoes stood on the table. There was also cheese, and a great deal of bread.

Things got easier for us. We had some space in the house. The days passed very quickly, for we were not hungry. A year passed. During our second winter in the village, difficult days came once again. We again tasted the taste of hunger. The war was dragging on. It was hard to obtain bread. My two younger brothers and my sister cried when they were hungry. I tried not to cry. From time to time, Good Gittel came to our house and took out a piece of bread or some potatoes from her apron. The Good G-d should repay Gittel for the goodness of hear heart.

One day, Gittel came with news: "Tomorrow, they will be distributing grain kernels in Ratno. Perhaps Velvele[2] will get up early and go to Ratno?" Velvele was I - the eldest. Mother asked, "Will you go, Velvele?" I answered, "Yes mother, I will go."

I set out on the journey at dawn. The sky was still full of stars, which for some reason looked to me like the eyes of the dogs of the shkotzim[3]. They were threatening. I held the fringes of my Tallis Katan[4] as a portent against fear. I went to do a good deed, to bring grain kernels to my widowed mother and all the orphans. G-d will help me. I passed through the grove and went up to the road that led to Ratno.

I stood in line to receive the grain kernels. The cold was literally penetrating the bones. The sun was shining, but the winter sun only warms those who are wearing a good fur and leather boots. A person wearing torn clothes and worn out shoes is not warmed by the winter sun. I learned this from experience, just as I learned that the day drags on and on if you are hungry. That day, I was very hungry. I went out early in the morning, and I had not even tasted a drop of water. I advanced in the line. I found myself standing beside a large pile of grain kernels. The evil inclination incited me to sin. I quickly tied my pants below my waist, and took a handful of kernels and placed them in my torn pant pocket when nobody was looking. The Good G-d should forgive me - I thought to myself, and took another handful and another handful. There will be some bread for Zeldele, for Shabtaile... Mother will not weep.

My turn finally came. A man wearing an official hat and wearing a coat with shiny buttons asked me, "Child, how many are you?" I answered, "A mother, four children, and my father did not return from the war." The man filled up the sack in my hand with kernels. I loaded the sack on my shoulder and began to walk toward home. A good feeling accompanied me throughout the way. A sack filled with kernels that I was bringing to Mother, and there was also an abundance of kernels in my pants tied at the pockets. Mother would certainly be very happy when she sees everything that I have brought. My brothers and sister would also be waiting for me with baited breath. Now they will not starve. We will have bread to satiety.

The strong wind was liable to blow away the sack on my shoulders, but I held it firmly with my right hand, as I held my left hand next to my body to warm up a bit. The wind whistled, and snowflakes blew about. The trees at the side of the road were bare. They too were cold. I continued on with my remaining strength, but I felt my energy depleting. My feet became so heavy, and the sack on my shoulders was so heavy. My eyes closed. Mother was far away. Father was no more. They are waiting there for me and for the kernels. I must arrive. I must. I put a few kernels in my mouth and chewed. I prayed to the Good G-d to help me. Perhaps he was angry about the kernels that I stole? Thoughts of regret afflicted me. I sat down on a cut off stump, only to rest a bit, not to fall asleep. To rest a bit, and then to continue along the way - I must not fall asleep. Mother is waiting -- -- Here she is grinding the kernels that I brought, white flour was piled on the table. Mother kneaded dough, put it in the oven, and white cakes came out of the oven. Father was also there. He returned from the synagogue completely covered in white snow. I suddenly felt pricks in my hands and feet. I opened my eyes with great difficulty. Where am I? Where is Mother? Someone is massaging my hands and feet. Now I recognized an elderly farmer woman standing next to me, as well as the picture of an icon - a picture that I am forbidden to look at, as I learned. I felt for my Arba Kanfot [3] with my frozen hands. Mother! Where is Mother? A sob broke forth from my throat. The farmer woman massaging my frozen hands calmed me, "Don't cry. My husband went to call your mother. He was returning from the forest toward evening with a wagon laden with twigs of wood, and found you frozen and sleeping. We made great efforts to revive you. Thank G-d, you are alive and well, and we even have the kernels." The good farmer woman offered me warm milk to drink.

Then I realized what had happened to me. I was lying oven in the house of the farmer who saved me. Then the door opened and my mother entered in a huff. She came up to me on the oven, hugged and kissed me, and wet me with her tears. I also cried, and our tears blended. The tears were warm and salty. Then I breathed calmly. I had fulfilled the mission that I had been given. I brought bread to the mouths of my brothers and sister, and the mouth of my widowed mother.

Translator's Footnotes

1. Festival prayer book. https://www.jewishgen.org/Yizkor/Ratno/rat152.html - f155-1r
2. Velvel (diminutive Velvele) is the Yiddish form of the Hebrew name Zeev. https://www.jewishgen.org/Yizkor/Ratno/rat152.html - f155-2r

3. A derogatory term for gentiles. https://www.jewishgen.org/Yizkor/Ratno/rat152.html - f155-3r

4. The tallis (fringed garment) worn as an undergarment at all times. Also known as Arba Kanfot. https://www.jewishgen.org/Yizkor/Ratno/rat152.html - f155-4r

A gathering of town mayors of the region of Ratno with the participation of the rabbinical judge Shlomo-Tovya Friedlander and the teacher Noach Kotzker

The "Tel Chai" troupe of Hashomer Hatzair with the counselors Golda Droog (standing) and Zeev Grabov (seated)

The Holocaust Era

In In the Days of Soviet Rule
About the first days under the control of the Soviet regime

by Pearl Vernik

Translated by Jerrold Landau

We were afraid to leave the house during the first days after the Poles left the town. Nobody knew what would transpire during the day, and how the new regime would behave. The new regime began to impose order in the town after a few days. Our feeling was that we were sentenced to a "prolonged death" under Soviet rule. First, they removed us from our spacious, beautiful house, and housed us in the same house as the Fuchs family. All of the businesses of the Shapira family were expropriated and nationalized, since the regime considered them to be a bourgeois family. The right to work was taken away from the family. We were given identity papers with a special sign (a black page) that identified us negatively to all the citizens and made us eligible for deportation to forced labor camps in Siberia. I benefited from a unique status. Since I was fluent in the Russian Languages, I was granted the right to work. I directed a branch of the government sick fund. This gave me the possibility of helping the Shapira family to a significant degree.

My father's family had an easier situation. Apparently, the new regime did not consider them to be a bourgeois family, and two of the sons were permitted to work since they were considered to be a "proletariat element". Therefore, they were able to manage. Thus did life continue until 1941.

Sh. Vernik relates:

The great fear of what was liable to come already began in July 1939. During those days, a draft of adults to the Polish Army was proclaimed, which was a clear sign of approaching war. After the Molotov Ribbentrop agreement on the partition of Poland between Germany and the Soviet Union, we already knew that Soviet rule was awaiting us.

Chaos pervaded in the town for several days. There was no government, since the Poles had left and the Russians had not yet arrived. Many Jews preferred to leave the city and seek refuge in the nearby villages, for they were wary of the disturbances that were usual during the time of a change of regime. My father of blessed memory did not want to leave the house, and asked me to remain with him. Our relatives, the Shapira family and my sister Pearl traveled to some village with the intention of remaining there until the wrath would pass and the situation would become clarified.

Our house was located at the end of the main road leading to Kowel, and we were therefore able to see the Polish army men and installations in their retreat. I recall that a day before the entry of the Soviets, a caravan of the Polish Army passed through that street. They took out a farmer, who placed a red flag on his house to welcome the Soviets to the city, to be killed. To the best of my memory, this was the only casualty during the time of the change of regime. My father of blessed memory and I welcomed the Soviet soldiers with joy and a small meal. We knew that this was a miniature evil. Despite the fact that Father referred to the Soviet soldiers as "Yachfanim"[1], he knew that one must follow the law of the land, and therefore one must welcome the new regime in an appropriate fashion.

After some time, when the first news came of the Nazi atrocities in the region under their occupation, we began to understand that our situation was better, and that we must utter a blessing over the evil, for there is a greater evil...

The first steps of the new regime failed to instill a sense of security in us. Everything in the stores in Ratno was quickly transferred to the Soviet Union. The Soviets purchased and took everything that came to hand, from shoelaces to eggs. It did not take long for all of the shops to be emptied. Anyone who hid merchandise was liable to a serious punishment. They indeed paid, but the money was non negotiable and it was impossible to purchase with that money new merchandise to replace what had disappeared. Father was correct: "Yachfanim"...

The following is written on the back of the photo: "I take leave of my friends, saying to them: my brothers, be in peace, and let us be together in the fields of our mutual homeland." Written by A. Papir (Nir)

The residents accepted the situation, for they knew that any complaints against the government might lead to deportation to the far-off plains of Siberia. The only thing that could be done was to complain within the confines of the family, with nobody to see or hear. Even the youths of the town, who were mainly Socialists, realized that all of the talk of equality without discrimination between nations and races appears good on paper; but things appear entirely different in the day-to-day reality. We had no choice other than to accept everything "with love", to stifle criticism, and to not arouse the wrath of the Socialists in our Ratno. The disappointment was bitter. The disappointment deepened after the new regime began to bare its fangs. The new institutions (including a court, prosecutor, and secretariat of the Communist party) began to prepare the Jewish youth for new ways of life and ideals. Of course, from that time, one had to be silent about the Land of Israel, for Zionism and other such concepts were fundamentally invalid. News reached us about deportations of "Capitalist elements" to work camps, but there were apparently not too many Capitalists in Ratno... and in any case, nobody was deported. On the other hand, my uncle Shlomo-Tzvi, his daughter, and son-in-law who lived in Luck experienced this deportation, for they were considered to be property owners. The daughter Dvora returned from the work camp after three years (today she lives in Israel). It is possible that several Jews of Ratno might have experienced these camps in Siberia, but the Soviets did not have the chance to "impose order" in smaller settlements such as Ratno within the two years. They only had the chance to nationalize businesses, expropriate houses, etc. Apparently, nobody attempted to refuse their requests, and when the general prosecutor came to our house and said that he wanted half the house as well as the sofa and the bicycle, his request was fulfilled. With time, my father was able to find out that this prosecutor was a reasonably good neighbor, and it was even possible to conduct some sort of business with him.

After some time, they began to draft young Jews to the Soviet Army. This situation improved the situation, for it was known that if one of the sons of the family was serving in the Red Army, the family would be in a good situation with respect to the government, and would have all the rights that the authorities granted to citizens.

I was drafted to the Red Army along with eight other youths from Ratno in the latter part of 1940. Our camp was near the city of Kolomyja. Until the outbreak of the war between Germany and the Soviet Union, we worked at building an airport. We were located in a work camp that served as a corridor to the main hall, that is - to prepare youths before their actual draft to the Red Army. We were under Soviet rule for the duration of a year and a half, and we felt the Soviet boot "in all its glory."

A group of youths in Ratno (1935)

Tanya Bokser (Gandelsman) tells:

The war, with all the tribulations and suffering related to it, already began in September 1, 1939 for the Jews of Ratno. The road that divided the city into two was a main road in Poland at that time, and it was natural for it to serve as a target of bombardment. Most of the residents of the city escaped to villages at the time of the outbreak of the war, and our neighbors, Ukrainians who were known for disgrace, knew how to extort the maximum from the Jews who came to seek refuge under their roofs. Despite the fact that they were accustomed to making agreements on the price at the time that the Jews entered their village homes, they would set new terms and demands each morning, until the situation became loathsome to the Jews, and they returned home to Ratno.

When we returned to the town, we already knew about the partition of Poland into two, with the eastern sector of the country, including Ratno, being transferred to the Russians. The leftists in Ratno, or those who were known as such, displayed great excitement at the impeding changes, and tried with their enthusiasm to excite the rest of the residents who were very wary about what was awaiting them. The city council prepared a splendid welcome for the Red Army. A gate of honor decorated with many flowers was set up. Red flags fluttered for show atop all the houses. The residents tore off the white section of the red-white flags of Poland that they owned, and the entire city was decked in red... Representatives of the city hall waited on the road to greet the Soviet soldiers. The vigil lasted for two days, for they did not know the exact time that the army would arrive. In the meantime, an entire division of Polish soldiers passed through the town on their way to Zabolottya. On the route of their retreat, they passed the place where the enthusiastic devotees of the Soviet regime were waiting, waving their red flags and hurrying to settle scores with them.

In our house, we were interested to know the whereabouts of our neighbor Pesia Sheines. The family was gathered into one house, and soldiers with weapons stood around us. A few of them went through the closets to search for red flags that would prove the anti-Polish sentiments of the residents. To our good fortune, they did not succeed in finding the red flag in our house, and they satisfied themselves with confiscating the fresh bread that had been baked during the night. Of course, during the retreat, they did not forget to shoot in all directions, and many bullets fell upon beds under which the frightened residents were sleeping.

When the soldiers of the Red Army entered the town, the enthusiasm began to dwindle. Various shopkeepers and merchants succeeded in hiding the merchandise that was in their possession, but they had to sell anything that remained in the shops. Business died down after several days. The tradesmen also went around without anything to do, with the exception of the shoemakers who had plenty of work, for they had to patch the old shoes since there were no new shoes to be found. Almost all sources of livelihood were closed off. A significant portion of the workers became government officials if no taint was found in their "pedigree." The economic situation grew more serious from day to day. The Jews were very bothered that they would no longer be able to prepare a proper Sabbath, for what would the Sabbath be like without challas, fish, and meat, as the Jews of Ratno were accustomed to from time immemorial. The bread line increased from day to day. Many people stood in line at the cooperative for long hours in order to purchase what was available. People learned that they must buy everything that was available for purchase, whether or not they required the merchandise...

In contrast to the serious economic situation, there was great pride in the cultural activities. The local elementary school turned into a ten grade school. Many people who had interrupted their studies under the former regime returned to the school bench. Various educational courses were organized. There were special courses for illiterate people, choirs, meeting halls, clubs, etc.

Cultural energy directed toward the instilling of Communist ideology to the broad community was felt.

The Tarbut School turned into a Yiddish school. Most of the teachers got accustomed to the regime and the new conditions. Many clubs were organized under the auspices of the school.

For me, the Soviet regime was literally a golden era. Despite the serious economic situation in the home, I returned to my studies. I studied Slavic languages (Russian and Ukrainian), I was active in various cubs, and I was also one of the three first members accepted to the Komsomol[2]. The two others were Ukrainians. In the Komsomol elections, I was also elected to the committee of the entire district and to other committees. My activities gave me a true feeling of happiness. My happiness especially grew after I was sent to study in Lvov on the recommendation of the party institutions, as was the custom in the Soviet Union. I continued with my activities in the Komsomol and was elected as second secretary of the school even when I was studying in the Teknikom.

During the era of Soviet rule, the school in Ratno organized a large choir that quickly learned the Soviet songs. Its appearances during national holidays earned them great acclaim. My brothers and sisters studied in the Yiddish school.

I wish to note in particular a young, nice and very talented teacher, Moshe Karlin, who married Golda Droog. Golda worked together with me in the office. She managed the tickets and accounts of the cooperatives and displayed great skill in her work. She was known as a charming personality, and earned great approval. It is fitting to specifically mention this lovely couple, Golda and the teacher Karlin, as well as their tragic end.

The chief accountant of the cooperatives was Yitzchak Held, and his assistant was Yisrael Chayat. In addition, the following individuals also worked as government officials: Hershel Schneider, Yisraelik Weisblat, Dvora Held, Motel Kacyn, Mordechai Langer, Susia Frigel, and others.

Translator's Footnotes

1. Hooligans https://www.jewishgen.org/Yizkor/Ratno/rat159.html - f161-1r
2. See http://en.wikipedia.org/wiki/Komsomol https://www.jewishgen.org/Yizkor/Ratno/rat159.html - f161-2r

Embers of a Broomwood Fire

by Shlomo Perlmutter

Translated by Jerrold Landau

Already on September 1, 1939, giant Polish signs were displayed in the town, giving notice from the Polish president Mościcki that "The eternal enemy of Poland invaded our country, and we will return with war to its gate." Many people crowded around these signs, as if this was some sort of surprise. People spoke of the impending war for many weeks before this time, and from the depressed eyes of my parents and family members, I too realized that something unusual was about to happen. Now, that the matter of the war had become a fact, I comforted myself with the knowledge that school would not recommence, that the long vacation would continue, and that I would not have to travel to Kowel where I had been studying in the gymnasium...

The next day, the noise of the German Messerschmitt[1] bombers disturbed our calm as they dropped their loads on the roads upon which rows of Polish army vehicles and the first caravans of refugees had been moving since the early morning hours. I recall that my grandfather Shmuel Simcha of blessed memory attempted to calm us sitting with the entire family around the table: "We do not need to be afraid of the bombs, and there is not reason to escape from them, for each one falls in the place preordained by Divine providence."

Many refugees passed through the town, and one day, a Jewish family that had escaped from Warsaw ate at our table. From this family, we heard details of the behavior of the Nazis in the areas that they had conquered. I internalized the true reality of this war when I saw that the father of this family gathered the crumbs of bread that were left on the table and hid them in his pocket...

On September 17, we saw airplanes flying low over the town dispensing proclamations. Many people, myself included, ran to collect them. The proclamations informed us that the Polish state had collapsed, and the Russian army was about to enter the town and liberate us. In truth, I did not understand the meaning of this liberation, but there was a feeling of relief. This meant that it was not the Germans who were coming to us, but rather the Russians, and this was also a positive thing.

It was not long before a caravan of Soviet tanks arrived in Ratno from Kowel. Along with all the children of Ratno, I ran to welcome the soldiers of the Red Army who displayed great politeness, permitted us to sit on the tanks, distributed boxes of Russian matches to us, and told us a great deal about the wealth and plenty in the great expanse of Russia, from which we would shortly be able to benefit ...

It was not long before delegates of the Soviet regime, along with several local Ukrainian collaborators and several Jews who were known for their Communist inclinations, came to us and began to impose order in the town. The shopkeepers were commanded to open their shops, and tradesmen were ordered to return to their workshops. The new rulers stated that the lines of communication between Brisk and Kowel would be reopened, so it would be possible to stock up on new merchandise and renew the inventory in their shops.

The owner of the textile shop began to suspect that the sources of his livelihood had been closed off.

*

I returned to my studies in the Hebrew Gymnasium of Kowel, but to my great surprise, it was no longer a Hebrew gymnasium. Instead of Hebrew and Bible, the Russian, Ukrainian and Yiddish languages were taught. The change was extreme. It was particularly difficult for me to come to terms with the fact that the teachers who had formerly taught Hebrew had begun to teach Yiddish. I could not bear to see the anguish of my beloved teacher Yosef Avrech, left handed, who later became well known for his acts of bravery during the actions in Kowel. I recall that he invited me to his home one day and gave me a private lesson in Bible. We studied the 11th and 12th chapters of Jeremiah, and my beloved teacher explained to me the interpretation of the war of the prophet against the people of Anatot. I will never forget the dual meaning of the verses "What business has my beloved in my house, seeing that she has practiced lewdness"[2], and "You would be right, Oh G-d, if I dispute with You, I will reason with You, why does the path of the wicked prosper? Why are those that deal treacherously secure?"[3]. He repeated the end of this verse several times, and I understood his intention very well, even though he sufficed himself with innuendoes, for these were very obvious innuendoes...

In contrast to specific teachers who demonstrated the ability to become accustomed to the new regime, there were many students who did not easily get used to the new spirit with its fundamental changes. The spirit of Zionism and our love and desire for the Land of Israel was hard to uproot. We organized groups, and continued to secretly study Hebrew and Bible in parallel with our courses in school. Several teachers came to these groups and gave us clandestine lessons in Bible and Hebrew, despite the danger involved in this... In a postcard that I sent to my friend Avraham Papir (Nir) in Ayelet Hashachar on January 17, 1940, I gave expression to our feelings during those days. (The content of the postcard was later published in the Davar newspaper in the Land of Israel.)

I would travel from Kowel to Ratno once every two weeks. The great change was also felt in Ratno. My friends who had graduated from the Tarbut Hebrew School with Noach Kotzker as the principal began to study in the public school. The Tarbut School became a nine grade school with the language of instruction being Yiddish. Kotzker was not allowed to set foot therein. The Hebrew library was closed and there were tattlers in the town who transmitted details of all the Zionist activities to the security services (N.K.V.D.) One day, I invited approximately ten good friends to my house, and we established a group for the study of Hebrew, despite the danger involved in this. I gave this group the name "Gechalei Retamim"[4] [Coals of Broomwood]. All the members of this group swore before the Holy Ark of the Synagogue of the Stepan Hassidim to refrain from saying anything about the existence of this group and its aims. Whenever I came to Ratno from Kowel, the members of this group would gather in our house, close themselves off in one of the rooms, study Bible, read the poems of Bialik and Tchernikovsky, and even sing Israeli songs in a whisper. To the best of my memory, the following people belonged to this group: Avraham Cohen, Davidl Sheftel, Chayale Hochman, Merida

Liberman, Chaya Kotzker, Golda Karsh, my brother Shikale and his friend Henich Droog, Avraham Mogilensky, and others.

*

It is appropriate to mention something about one of our activities - bringing back the confiscated Hebrew books. It happened as follows. We found out that the banned Hebrew books were housed in the wall closets in the Papir house, where dances were arranged by the local authorities every Saturday night for the youth. On one of those evenings, all the members of our group came and spread themselves out among the dancers. When the tumult reached its peak, Mogilensky and Davidl Sheftel pulled out the electric plugs. Our members began to carry out the action in the darkness that ensued. We emptied the shelves of Hebrew books into sacks that had been prepared from the outset. By the time the electric "disruption" was repaired, all the Hebrew books were already in the secret place designated for them. The operation succeeded without any of the adults knowing about it. Davidl Sheftel and I traveled to the gymnasium in Kowel the next day, as if nothing had happened. However, the N.K.V.D. men quickly followed after us, and opened a detailed investigation with the goal of revealing the books and the perpetrators of the "iniquity." Dozens of adults were brought to the investigation, but they never thought that the "sinners" were 12 to 14-year-old children. It did not take long before my grandfather unintentionally almost placed us in the trap. One day when he was working in the barn, he discovered some of the books that had been hidden there. He brought the books out into the garden and hid them in the snow. "Heaven" helped us, for that night, a heavy snow fell, that better covered the books. When the snow began to melt in the spring, it was necessary to take the books to another hiding place. We consulted about what to do with them, and after obtaining advice from my uncle Reb Asher Leker, a wise, scholarly Jew who was dedicated to the Zionist idea with heart and soul, we transferred the books to the Shtibel of the Karlin Hassidim, and hid them in one of the geniza[5] closets. Despite the ban and the danger involved, we continued to read Hebrew books, and the members of "Gechalei Retamim" distributed them amongst the youths of the town.

Translator's Footnotes

1. See http://en.wikipedia.org/wiki/Messerschmitt https://www.jewishgen.org/Yizkor/Ratno/rat159.html - f161a-1r

2. Jeremiah 11: 15. https://www.jewishgen.org/Yizkor/Ratno/rat159.html - f161a-2r
3. Jeremiah 12:1. https://www.jewishgen.org/Yizkor/Ratno/rat159.html - f161a-3r
4. There is a footnote in the text here as follows: I proposed this name based on the explanation of my teacher Y. Avrech, may G-d avenge his blood, that "coals of broomwood" (Psalms 120:4) have a unique characteristic: The fire remains therein when they are already dim, and any wind can fan the flames anew. Of course, the meaning was that we young people will guard the flames (the national-Zionist spirit) until the propitious time. https://www.jewishgen.org/Yizkor/Ratno/rat159.html - f161a-4r
5. The place where worn out books and holy writings are placed. https://www.jewishgen.org/Yizkor/Ratno/rat159.html - f161a-5r

A Chapter from my Diary

by Avraham Berg

Translated by Jerrold Landau

Ratno was conquered by the Nazis on June 23, 1941. During the first days, German soldiers were not seen in Ratno, and the occupation was merely strategic. Not far from where we were, the conquering Nazi soldiers divided into two branches. The right branch marched across Ukraine and the left branch marched through White Russia. Our town was left in complete disarray, and no trace of the occupiers was seen for two weeks. At that time, it was possible to escape to Soviet territory via Kamin Kashirsk and the surrounding forests in the direction of Sarny and Kiev, but who thought about escape? During those two weeks, small units of the Soviet Army passed through Ratno on their way to the Soviet Union. Some of them were armed, and others were already wearing civilian clothing, and sought hiding places in the homes of the farmers as workers or shepherds. Jews from the Soviet Union were among the retreating Red Army soldiers. They were equipped with machine guns and wanted to break through to the depths of Soviet territory. They convened a meeting in the middle of the market, and called the local youth to join them. Were we to have listened to them and joined them, or were we to have created partisan units - and there was more than enough weapons at that time - the destruction would not have been so great. However, who could have imagined in those days that the Germans would perpetrate their satanic plans upon us? Therefore, the local youth did not join the retreating Jewish Russian soldiers who were passing through the town.

In the meantime, the tribulations and poverty in the town increased from day to day. Tidings of Job arrived from the cities and towns of the area, instilling melancholy in all the residents. Local activists and leaders attempted to calm and support people. According to them, the German anti-Semitic incitement was nothing more than a means to win the war. However, as the Germans advanced and gained strength - what need would they have to kill Jews? Even after we heard the confounding news of the murder of Jews in various places in the region, it was hard to believe that such was the case. We heard with our own ears the blood curdling provocations of Goebbels on the radio, but everyone still tried to convince themselves that the evil will not come upon themselves, and that they themselves would somehow succeed in escaping.

This illusion did not last long. The great tragedy began through our close neighbors, the anti-Semitic Ukrainians, in the town and in the surrounding villages. On Saturday, July 5 (10 Tammuz) 1941, at 5:00 p.m., we found out that the Ukrainian intelligentsia, that is to say the sons of the landowners and the priests, visited the villages and demanded that the farmers come to town to perpetrate pogroms against the Jews, rather than wait until the Nazis would arrive. The despair and fear that overtook the Jews cannot be described. Everyone went about perplexed and downcast.

It took place the next day. On Sunday July 6, at 5:00 p.m., armed shkotzim entered town, and immediately began shooting in all directions. They broke into the shops and private houses, and pillaged and robbed anything that came to hand. The first victim fell at the beginning of the pogrom - Binyamin Framan, the son-in-law of Leiber Karsh. Before he fell, he succeeded in killing one of the hooligans with an axe. The pogrom perpetrators were surprised when they realized that the Jews knew how to respond to war, and they fled back to their villages, taking their victim with them.

The next day, the pogrom perpetrators continued the work of pillaging on a larger scale, but this time, they satisfied themselves with merely pillaging and shooting in the air. No victims fell. That evening, when the Nazis in Kowel found out that the Ukrainians were pillaging in Ratno and anarchy prevailed in the city, they sent a unit of soldiers armed with machine guns to Ratno. The soldiers opened fire upon the pogrom perpetrators, whom they thought were young Jews who had come to aid of the Jews of Ratno, and therefore were returning the fire. The Nazis killed ten of the village pogrom perpetrators during this exchange of fire.

On Tuesday, July 8, the Nazis ordered all the Jews out of their homes and concentrated them on the road next to the house of Izik Steinberg. Among those gathered were some elderly people who were only able to walk with difficulty, as well as women with babies in their arms. After a few hours, the elderly and the wives with children up to the age of 13 were freed. They interrogated and tortured the Jews for ten full hours. They did not pay attention to the fact that it was the villagers who shot at them, and they placed the entire blame on us. One of the group, a Nazi captain, cursed and disparaged the Jewish nation, saying that it was the cause of all the difficulties. A loud voice calling out, "No!" was heard from the crowd of Jews gathered on the street. This shout emanated from the mouth of Yitzchak Hirsch Held of blessed memory, a lad with national consciousness. Nobody turned him in despite the demands of the Nazi captain who wanted to know who was responsible for the brazen shout.

The Nazis did not hesitate, and they immediately issued their verdict. Since they were greeted with shots when they came to town, they must immediately kill 70 people. They would grant us mercy by including the number of pogrom perpetrators who were killed in the number. Sixty people, 30 Jews and 30 local Ukrainians, were to be killed. They agreed that instead of killing the 30 Ukrainians, they would kill 30 Russian prisoners of war. These were hauled from the Kowel Road and killed by shooting. They chose 20 strong Jewish men to bury the dead. Then the Nazi captains passed through the Jews who were gathered in the square, examined each one and chose 30 people who were placed separately. Two of the 30 succeeded in disappearing and escaping (one of them was Binyamin the water carrier, and the second one was not a native of Ratno). The 28 Jews were hauled to the same spot where the 30 Russian prisoners of war had previously been taken, and were killed there. Among the 20 strong men who were given the task of buried the victims were the fathers of two sons who dug graves for their children with their own hands: my brother-in-law Nathan Marder and Yaakov Steingarten (the latter was later saved, and succeeded in arriving in the Land of Israel via Italy). When the son of Nathan Marder, who had already been wounded badly, saw his father, he called out, "Father, I am still alive, bring me a bit of water, my insides are burning." Nathan was very perplexed and did not know what to do, for the

Nazi murderers stood close by. When they left, he attempted to save his son, but it was already too late. One of the 28 Jews was saved - Yaakov Klodner from the old city, the son of Asher who was nicknamed "Der Geier."

It was quiet in town for several weeks, however the echoes reached us of the pogroms and slaughter that was taking place in other cities and towns were sufficient to embitter our lives. It was clear to us that this was the calm before the storm.

A flood of decrees was issued against us. The first was the decree that every Jew was required to wear a yellow patch. This was a moral degradation for each of us. Later, a Judenrat was imposed upon us, and the situation worsened throughout the following months. In all the towns of the region, Kowel in particular, Ghettos were established for the Jewish population. Murderous aktions began, including the murder of 18,000 Jews of Rovno[1]. We felt that the ground was burning under our feet, and the noose was tightening around our necks.

The economic situation deteriorated. There was a complete paralysis in all areas of work. The pillage of Jewish property continued. The Jews were forbidden from leaving town. All of their cows and horses that they owned were stolen. It was even forbidden for a dog or a cat to be found in a Jewish home.

To the extent that our situation worsened, the situation of our Ukrainian neighbors and the village farmers improved. The anti-Semitic venom permeated their bones, and they were interested in exploiting the Jewish tradesmen, and they attempted to obtain permits for such from the Nazi rulers. To a certain degree, this was to the benefit of the Jews, for the Jewish tradesmen who worked in the villages received their payment in the form of food products, which saved the town from starvation. There was another benefit to working in the villages: the hand of the Nazi occupier did not rule there, and it was somehow possible to breathe and even to hope for better days.

Our town Ratno was fortunate. A ghetto was not set up for the Jewish population, as was the case in many other cities. They did not hunger for bread, and life was more comfortable than in the settlements of the area. However, it was not long before various decrees were issued. Endless taxes were imposed. Furniture, high quality clothing and all valuables were confiscated. The Nazis took everything that they wanted, packed it up, and sent it to Germany. Every sign of opposition was liable to cost one's life. The harshest thing was the demands placed on the Judenrat to supply Jews for "work". At first, the Judenrat decided to send only bachelors to the "workplaces". A period of weddings then began in the town. Anyone who was able to got married, without investigating whether or not the girl was appropriate for him. These were weddings of sadness and not weddings of joy. Everyone knew what "work" meant, and therefore they did not investigate carefully, but rather did all that they could to avoid being on the list of those sent to work. It very quickly became clear that the number of bachelors was small, and it was necessary to include married people on the lists of those to be sent.

In December 1491, the Nazi authorities set up a union (Artel) of workers in the paradigm of the Soviet Union. All tradesmen were unified in a single cooperative that had all types of professional sections. The profits of the sections were tallied up, and 20% of the profits were designated to carry out the Nazi propaganda.

Translator's Footnote

1. The translator of this article wishes to note that two of his great aunts, along with their families, were murdered in the large einstatzgruppen aktion in the Sosenki forest of Rovno around November 6, 1941. https://www.jewishgen.org/Yizkor/Ratno/rat159.html - f166-1r

These I Remember

by Shlomo Vernik

Translated by Jerrold Landau

I was among the 50 youths who were drafted in Ratno to go to work in Kowel. It seems to me that the aim of the Nazis was to reduce the number of young men in town to the extent possible, and thereby to make it easier for them to carry out their designs without disturbance. My brother Aharon was also one of those who was to be sent to forced labor in Kowel, but my father volunteered to go in his place. He claimed: I do not want to be bereaved of both of my sons, and if someone of our family is destined to survive, let it be my son. Mother wept bitterly. The agony was felt in all corners of the house. The sadness was felt especially on the Festival of Shavuot, the first holiday without Father in the house, for all holidays had been celebrated with all the family together.

After some time, the youths who were sent to work in Kowel were taken out to be murdered. Father succeeded in hiding in a chimney, and began to return to Ratno a few days later. When he came close to the town, several Ukrainians met him and told him that there are Germans in the town, and it would be best to disappear. Father refused and said, "What will happen to my family will happen also to me."

I worked in the sawmill in Zabolotya together with 80 other people of Ratno. We were allowed to return home on the Sabbath eve, and return to the camp on Sunday. It was a distance of 25 kilometers, but this did not bother us, for we were happy to get together with our family and friends even once a week. One Sabbath when I came home, I was surprised to see Father sitting with the family and telling them of all the tribulations that afflicted him in Kowel. We sat down all together, and not just for one evening, and listened to Father's stories as the fear in our hearts increased.

We looked out the windows the next morning, and saw Ukrainian vehicles on the street. It was obvious that something was about to take place. I recall that Father approached me, gave me my tefillin and a pot of cooked food, and said to me, "I am very suspicious that the verse 14 in the Book of Jeremiah, 'one from a city and two from a family'[1] will happen to us. Guard the tefillin and perhaps they will also protect you. Go quickly to your workplace in Zabolotya, for you have a work permit, and you are better protected than we are. Perhaps you are destined for life, and you will continue our large family." He broke out in bitter weeping, as if his heart predicted that we would not see each other again. That day, Father, Mother, my young sister Breindel, and two children: the son of my sister Perl who now lives in Israel, and the son of my sister Batya were all taken out to be killed.

* * *

Who did not know Mendel the glassmaker of Ratno? Who did not use him for the summer or winter windows after a fire or on another opportunity? This Mendel was a quiet, modest Jew. He conducted his work faithfully, and raised four children who helped him in his work. In the town, everyone knew that Mendel and his sons would even clean the windows in the houses of people who could not afford to pay. When they would get money – they would pay.

I recall that when I was seven years old, a large fire broke out in Ratno and the home Mendel the glassmaker was also burned. My father Yehuda Leib Vernik of blessed memory housed the family of Mendel in our old house. He had a large family: Mendel Plotzker, his wife, four sons and two daughters.

However, Father was very happy to have the opportunity to perform this commandment, even though this lasted for a year and a half.

I met four of the sons of this Mendel in the work camp of Zabolotya. I was working in carpentry and they worked in glassmaking and smithing. We had a work permit from the Germans, which in those days was like a life insurance policy.

All 80 of the people who worked in the camp lived in very cramped conditions in several dismal bunks. Each morning, we spread out through the area, each person to his own work in the large sawmill. In the evening, we returned to the bunks. During this period, I learned to appreciate the Plotzker brothers, the sons of Mendel the glassmaker, for their fine deportment. The eldest Simcha was the leader who held authority, and he was indeed worthy of such. He was a strong lad with broad shoulders. He had formerly served in the Polish army. He was wise and decisive in all his actions. The other two brothers, Moshe Yankel and Yehuda Leib, were also positive characters. When the aktions began in Ratno and the tidings of Job regarding the deeds of the Germans began to arrive in quick succession, Simcha and his brother convened a secret meeting with those people that they believed they could trust. We decided unanimously to not wait any longer, and to escape at the first opportunity. The decision to escape with fraught with many difficulties, especially due to the fact that we had wives and children. It was not easy to escape with them, and it was even more difficult to escape without them. We took council together and decided that we would escape no matter what, and that the sign would be given in a few days. The next day, I worked as usual in the carpentry shop, but I sensed unusual preparations. I looked out the window and saw that they had taken Simcha out. They brought him to the threshold of the carpentry workshop, shot him, and he fell. A veteran Ukrainian technician who was responsible for the machines approached the dead Simcha, moved him by his legs, and said, "I wish that I could see the last of the Jews in this situation." That day, they also took Simcha's brother out to be killed. Apparently, the Germans found out about the plans of escape. They gathered the rest of the workers in the camp and told us that it was to our luck that they found out about the plans for escape in time, and therefore we could continue to work. If we would remain orderly, we would live. Thus, I continued to work in the camp for eight more months, until I escaped and joined the ranks of the partisans. This image of the murder of Simcha stood before my eyes throughout the entire time that I was in the camp. A shudder passed through my body as I passed by that hated Ukrainian technician, but would could I do under those conditions? On day I heard that the technician had fallen ill. Indeed, we saw that he was weakening from day to day, until one day we merited to see him fall down not far from the place where Simcha had been killed – and he never got up again. We regarded this as a miracle from heaven. This strengthened and encouraged us. We began to believe that there is justice and there is a judge, and perhaps we would yet see a better world.

* * *

I recall Moshe Kagan still from my childhood. He came to our house often from Zabolotya, where I now was, and father would host him. He was a strong, healthy Jew, but his speech was somewhat strange, as he only uttered short, cut-off sentences. Father explained to me that this Moshe was my second cousin, that he was strong and brave, and that all the gentiles were afraid of him. As was told, Moshe had a strong rib frame on his belly, and that he could choke any person on this "frame." During the First World War, Moshe fought against various marauding groups, and showed them his power. Hearing of his deeds of bravery was an unforgettable experience for me. I met Moshe when I was working in the carpentry shop of Zabolotya, and we made plans about how to escape to the forests.

One morning, as I was working in the carpentry shop, a German and two Ukrainians burst into the carpentry shop, and gave a package to the German director of the workshop, that included broken guns that were brought to be fixed at the workshop. A Polish woman who worked in the carpentry shop, Juza Plock, who also was busy with the Germans at night, disclosed who had brought the guns to be repaired. They hauled Moshe outside the village, gave him a spade, and ordered him to dig a pit. Moshe understood their intentions. As he was digging the pit, he attacked the two Germans who were standing at the side with his spade. They were seriously injured from the severity of the blow. Their two guns were broken, and we were ordered to repair them quickly and in utter secrecy. Dozens of bullets sliced through the body of Moshe, may G-d avenge his blood, after this deed. The stories of his past were proven to be true. He fell as a hero.

Translator's Footnote

1. Jeremiah 3:14 https://www.jewishgen.org/Yizkor/Ratno/rat159.html - f166a-1r

Sorrowful Memories

by Ben-Zion Kamintzky

Translated by Jerrold Landau

I was about 13-years-old when the Second World War broke out. Everything that took place to me then is etched strongly in my memory. I see the home of my parents standing near the main street leading from Ratno to Brisk (Hornyk). My father was a tradesman, and he also owned agricultural land, a barn, a stable, and a fruit orchard. He was considered as "one of the people." He nurtured good relations with the Ukrainians, and it seems that due to these relations, he and our entire family were saved from the Holocaust, as will be told later. Mother took care of the home, and especially of the education of the children: the sisters Beilcha and Udel, and me, the only son.

Father supported and maintained a private teacher in our home who taught me Hebrew as well as general subjects. I also studied with a Rebbe in the cheder, and later in the Tachkemoni School in Brest Litovsk. After that, I studied in the Tarbut School in Ratno. I became a member of Hashomer Hatzair, and became fluent in Hebrew. The teacher Kotzker was the one who taught me Zionism, and love of the people and the Land of Israel.

I remember well the years prior to the war, especially the many pogroms that were perpetrated in the cities of Poland during the years 1936-1939, as well as the anti-Semitic propaganda under the influence of Nazi Germany. More than once, my sister Beilcha escaped from Brisk to Ratno due to these pogroms and the Jew-hatred that was well-rooted in the Poles during those days.

In the eyes of my spirit, I see the first days of the war, when the Russians beat a hasty retreat from the town, and our Ukrainian neighbors began to pillage. I stood on the road next to our house along with several other Ukrainian "shkotzim"[1] of my age. Suddenly, an army car with Germans appeared. The S.S. captain exited the car and requested in German that we bring eggs. When he saw that his German was not understood by the youths, he utilized various hand gestures to explain his request. When we brought him the eggs, the captain gave the Ukrainian youths some German money (Reichsmarks) and emphasized, "Do not give this money to the Jews!" I understood very well the meaning of this statement. I saw myself degraded. I fled home, lay down upon my bed, and wept. Perhaps that was when I first felt that I was of a lower class, a person of no value, a Jew...

When the command that every Jew must wear a yellow 12 centimeter Star of David upon the back and the chest, my feelings of embarrassment and degradation deepened. I recall that I went out one day without the Star of David. An infamous Ukrainian policeman named Ivan ran into me, grabbed me, and beat me until I was bleeding. He kicked me with his boots and threatened me with his gun.

He finally demanded ransom money from my father and my father was forced to give him a gold bracelet.

One autumn day in 1942, two days before the High Holy Days, Breitza Frumka (who died in the United States) came to us, knocked on the shutter, and shouted to my father in a choked voice, "Herzl, escape, save yourselves, the shtetl is burning, the Germans have surrounded it from all sides, and the great slaughter is approaching!" There was no room for thoughts. We escaped. My parents, my sister Udel and her two children, my brother-in-law Yaakov Hochman of blessed memory, and I found refuge in the home of a Ukrainian farmer at the edge of the city, two kilometers from the Prochod Mountains. The next morning, the farmer brought us bitter news: the Germans and the Ukrainian police were drafting residents to dig pits in the Prochod Mountains. That was that. The time of the final aktion had arrived. Throughout that entire day (13 Elul), we heard shots. The gentile who had given us refuge ascended a tall tree and looked across the Prochod Mountains. At times, he came to our hiding place and told us what he had seen. He wept, and we all wept with him. We knew that the end had come to the lives of our dear ones, our relatives, and all the Jews of Ratno. The shouts of "Shema Yisrael" echoed across the entire length of the Prochod Mountains. They were taken out as sheep to the slaughter. There was no, and there was no possibility of any, attempt of resistance. The thought that we were alive and all the rest of Jews had been killed and murdered was frightening and oppressive.

The Vow of the Anti-Semitic Ukrainian

That evening, the Ukrainian farmer asked us to leave his house. He was afraid of slander. Having no choice, we moved to a grove in the region and hid there. At midnight, we saw some sort of moving image in the grove. We identified it by the light of the moon. This was a Ukrainian who was known as a Jew-hater, an avowed anti-Semite. We did not know whether he intended to kill us or turn us in to the Germans. In any case, we did not have any delusions, and we surmised that our end was coming as well. We were all surprised when this Ukrainian suddenly fell upon my father's neck, burst out crying and began to tell his frightful story: “In the evening after the slaughter, I went to the Prochod Mountains to search for silver, gold, and clothes that had been left behind by the murdered Jews. When I approached the place, I heard groans bursting forth from the ground that was still quaking. There were still living, breathing souls in the bowels of the earth... Blood was still flowing from the channels that came from the layers of sand... I was not able to stand there, and I fled... I swear to you, Herzl, that I did not take anything. I fled while I still had my soul, and as I fled I made a vow that if I find a Jewish family, I would try with the best of my ability to save them. I swear to you, Herzl, in the name of everything holy, that I will bring you food every day. I will protect you. You must live.”

That is what the anti-Semitic farmer said through his weeping and sobs. In order to prove that he was telling the truth, he told us to remain where we were, and he would go to his house to bring us food. My father and brother-in-law apparently could not believe that he really meant it. Perhaps he went to bring reinforcements to turn us into the hands of the Germans in return for the monetary reward that the Germans used to give to everyone who turned in a Jew? When he left us, we escaped to a different place...

We met him again after some time. He searched for us. He was not angry at us for escaping. He understood our concern. He told us that he brought food and milk for the children, but when he came to our hiding place and did not find us, he realized that we did not believe him. This Ukrainian farmer remained faithful to us and always helped us. We found support and encouragement in his house. He fulfilled his vow, and the fact that we remained alive is due to him.

We Were Saved On Account of Thieves

It was a very cold winter, and snow fell without stop. We trembled from cold and fear. We dwelt in some structure filled with straw and fodder. We attempted to dig very deep into the pile of fodder to warm up a bit. We were dirty, and the lice ate us voraciously. We were oppressed and desperate. We were certain that we were the only Jews who had survived. The murderers conducted thorough searches, and any Jew who was found was immediately killed. We thought that the Nazi motto of “Judenrein” had been realized.

At that time, our hiding place was in the house of some gentile widow. She pleaded with us to leave her house. She was afraid that they would kill her and us together. We returned to our house that stood on the noisy street through roundabout paths. We had one and only hope: that the Germans and their Ukrainian collaborators had already conducted searches in that house, and perhaps we would be able to stay there for a day or two until we find another hiding place. My family members remained in the house, whereas my brother-in-law and I went out in the darkness of the night to the small settlement of Siltse in order to search for a hiding place for the entire family. After remaining in our house for two days, the Ukrainians entered at night in order to pillage what was left. They moved from room to room, and when they reached the room at the edge where my family was sitting, and they saw people, the robbers became frightened and fled. Of course, my family members were also frightened. They fled from the house and found refuge in the barn of a farmer - and thus we were saved again. The next day, the Germans arrived and set up a police station in our home.

The Death of Yaakov Hochman

We continued to wander from one hiding place to the next. Ukrainian farmers assisted us, supported us, and advised us where to hide. All types of gentiles gave us food. In the evening, I would go with my brother-in-law to the houses of the farmers, from where we received bread, milk, potatoes, and the like. During summer nights, we gathered potatoes in the fields and cut fruit from the trees. One summer evening in 1943, a year before our liberation, I went with my brother-in-law to search for food. We decided to not go together. Rather, we each went to a different farmer. After I furnished myself with several loaves of bread, I decided to walk among the bushes in the direction of the hiding place of the entire family. Shots rang through the air, and I lay down in the bushes, trembling in fear. This was the first time that my brother-in-law was not with me. I was afraid of his fate and the fate of my family. Who knew which of them were hit by the bullets? I saw dark things in my imagination.

I lay silently for a long time, and then decided to crawl along. I reached the barn in which my family was hiding. They also heard the shots and were concerned about our fate. They were happy of course that I had returned in peace, but who knew what happened to Yaakov? He was a brave, optimistic man, and the pillar of strength within the family circle. He had served in the Polish Army, and knew how to overcome all fears. I had become very close to him during the long nights that we would wander together in the fields, groves, and the houses of the farmers. I attempted to calm my family members, and told them that Yaakov would certainly return early in the morning. Instead, the gentile came to us in the morning, and told us the bitter news. He found Yaakov lying on the crossroads, with a bottle of milk and a loaf of bread in his hands. The gentile covered him with a blanket, and at night, according to our request, he buried him atop a hill in the area. However, the family, including my widowed sister, her two orphaned children, and all of us were grief stricken. After some time, we found out that he had been murdered by a young Ukrainian who wished to take revenge for his father who had been killed by the partisans, who according to him were Jewish.

In the Hands of the Ukrainian Nationalists

... Good news began to arrive. The Germans were defeated in Stalingrad as well as on the eastern fronts. The German Army retreated and the Russians advanced. There was a ray of hope. We continued to move from hiding place to hiding place, but now we were no longer as oppressed as previously. At that time, we found refuge with a farmer named Vokolka, who helped us greatly. A change took place with the Ukrainians who had collaborated with the Germans. They decided to sever their covenant with the Germans and begin to struggle to establish an independent Ukrainian state. These people were headed by a Ukrainian general named Bulba[2], and they were called "Bulbovchi" after his name. They fought against the retreating Germans as well as the advancing Russians. We were caught between the hammer and the anvil. Our situation became more serious and required us to take extra precautions, for the Ukrainians were organizing in the forests and the groves in which we found refuge. The discussions amongst ourselves were conducted in sign language. We were afraid to utter a sound. My sister's young children who had lost their father talked in a similar fashion. One day two representatives of the Ukrainian organization suddenly appeared accompanied by the farmer who had saved us. They had a unanimous announcement: since my father had a trade and knew how to fix weapons, our entire family had to move to their camp near Khoteshov, where they would protect us. My father would work at fixing weapons, I would help him, and my mother and sister would weave scarves and socks for their fighters. We could not refuse, and we moved to their base, where a small house was put at our disposal. They treated us well in accordance with the explicit directive of their commander.

I had been accustomed to night living during the two years of wandering. I loved the dark that protected me, and I recognized all paths in the dark. I was afraid of the sunlight, for the light was liable to turn us in to the murderers. It therefore seemed strange to me to walk in the light of day, to absorb the sun rays, to breathe the clear air, to be free, and to see people outside and not be afraid of them...

Everything had now changed with our way of life. We slept on a bench rather than a pile of straw and fodder. We ate at a table rather than in a barn or sheep pen. We felt that the "Bulbovchi" Camp was like a royal palace... We lived with them and enjoyed our freedom for seven months. Indeed, this was a very forced freedom, for we knew very well what these Ukrainians had perpetrated against the Jews in the past. We also knew that they did not maintain us out of love, and if they reached the conclusion that we were no longer of benefit to them, they would not spare our lives. However, as long as we were of benefit to them, they provided all our needs. We thought on occasion: what will these murderers do with us? We searched for means of escape, but the nationalist Ukrainians were stationed throughout the area. Our attempts to make contact with the partisans who were some tens of miles away also came to naught. My father became friendly with one of the captains, a member of the staff that was responsible for us. He greatly valued our work at repairing the weapons and weaving the scarves. His nickname was "Stochka" and he had been a policeman in his time. He revealed a secret to my father: they had decided in their group that in the event that the partisans were to advance to us and attempt to conquer the area, they would kill us. He swore that he would save us if such a time came.

One evening, I visited the house of one of the farmers along with the friendly captain. The host brought refreshments and liquor. Our friend became drunk, and "when wine enters, secrets come out." He said that the situation had become serious, the partisans were pressing from all sides, there would be a need to retreat, and they would be forced to carry out the plan that he had told my father secretly.

Before we returned home, the captain tapped my shoulders and said, "Do not worry, as long as I am alive, no harm will befall you."

Despite his promise I was very depressed. When I returned home, I told the members of my family what was about to happen. Sadness descended upon all of us. We did not sleep that entire night. What could we do? Now more than ever we wished to live, to witness the final defeat of the Nazis, and to taste the taste of true freedom. However, we knew that they were following after all of our footsteps day and night.

Toward the next evening, the Ukrainians retreated from the area due to the pressure of the partisans who had begun to clear the area to prepare for the advancing Russian Army. We remained alone among ten families of farmers. We had been warned that we were forbidden to leave the house in which we lived. We were awake all night, tense and uptight over any sound from outside. Our friend Stochka returned to us toward morning. He was tired and unshaven. He told us that they wanted to come at night to kill us, but he convinced his friends to refrain from carrying out their plan, and promised them to turn us over to them. He advised us to flee in the direction of the partisans, and asked that we remember him positively. Tears flowed from his eyes, and, from the appearance of his face, we sensed that he was speaking the truth. We felt sorry for him, and we advised him to escape together with us, but he did not want to betray his friends. We parted from him in great agony.

At that time, Frumka was with us. She was the girl who had warned us before the extermination that we should flee from our home. She and my mother went out as scouts to search for the partisans in the direction that the friendly captain had mentioned. However, in the interim, the partisans arrived to the place we were, riding on horses. They were surprised to meet Jews and young children. There were Jewish partisans among them. It was difficult for us to believe what our eyes saw: Jews fighting with weapons in their hands. The partisans burned all the houses, took all the weapons and sacks of wheat, and left the place. We joined them. We arrived in Khoteshov and from there to Kamin Kashirsk, where we met other Jewish Holocaust survivors. After years of wandering, affliction and terrible tribulations, we began to breathe the breath of freedom. The Russian Army took control of the area, and we were able to walk through the streets without fear.

Translator's Footnotes

1. A derogatory term for gentiles. www.jewishgen.org/Yizkor/Ratno/rat159.html - f170-1r

2. See http://en.wikipedia.org/wiki/Taras_Bulba-Borovets https://www.jewishgen.org/Yizkor/Ratno/rat159.html - f170-2r

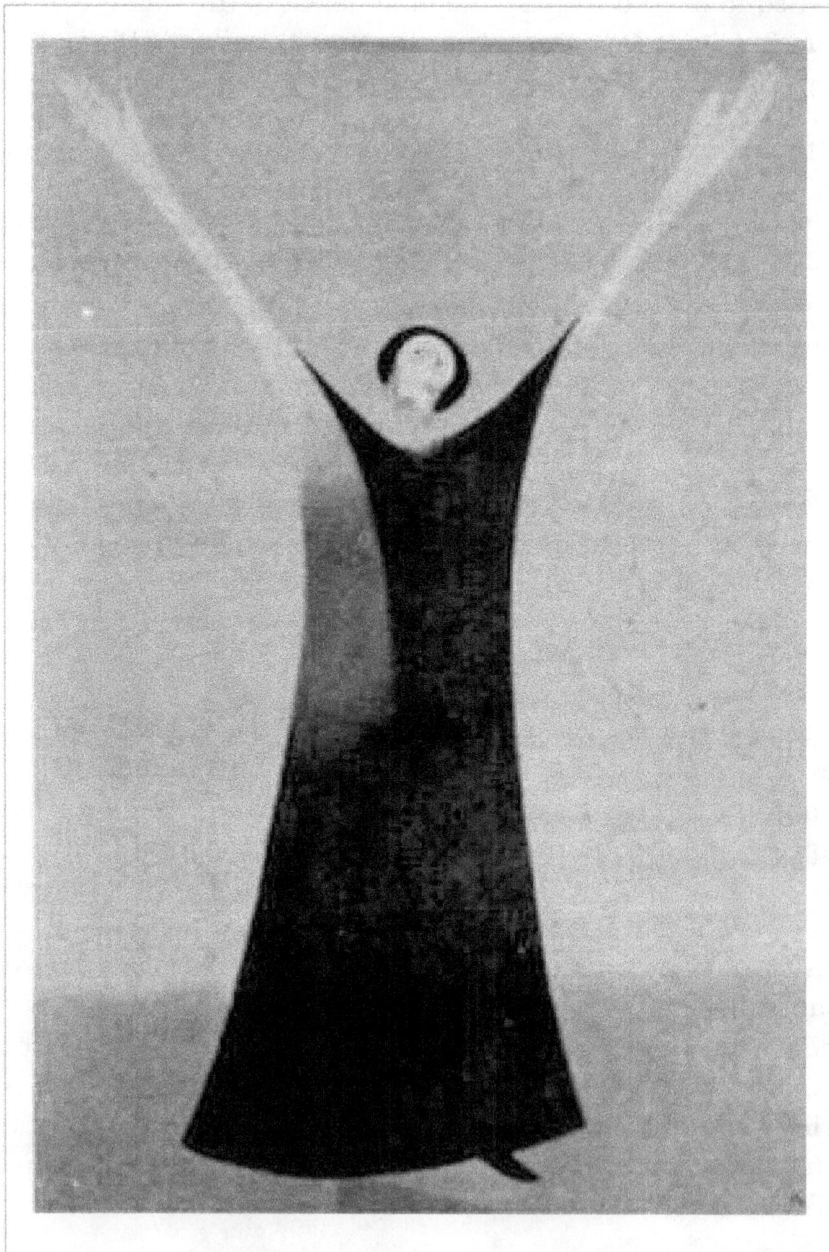

"To the mountains I will lift my eyes, from whence will my help arise" (Psalms). The artist - Ben

Roads and Dreams

by Yisrael Chayat

Translated by Jerrold Landau

I am pacing along a tortuous path toward the destroyed shtetl of Ratno. Along the way, I passed through Jewish cities and towns whose Jews way of life for many generations was now covered with dust, ashes, and thousands of graves. The Holocaust survivors are now wandering over these ruins; brands plucked from fire, gases, and shards remaining from the axe of the executioner, one from a city and not even one from a family, who now look as stalks cut from desolate fields. To anyone who did not witness it, my journey along paths that I had sworn never to return to seems strange. I cannot bypass them. All of the roads here are paved with Jewish blood.

*

It was Ratno at the end of 1945, on a Sunday morning. The sun is warming and shining beams of light today, as always. I was contemplating: For whom? Petrified, I was walking as a wanderer in the darkness, with one thought afflicting me incessantly: Is it indeed possible for the sun to light up and bestow warmth upon the murderers and victims together? I walked along the ruins and grassy hills of Jewish Ratno. Between walls about to fall and mounds of ash, Jewish houses still stand that appear to Jewish eyes as canopies in the cemetery... Living beings peer out from these houses, asking in astonishment: "Is there still a living Jew in Ratno?" I linger next to a garden that is turning green today as it did in those days. Alas! Children are dancing and singing in a circle, but my eyes are directed to another place - to that part of town that has turned into a heap of ruins, to the children buried under the piles of bricks and ashes, and perhaps to the sin that they sinned by planting these gardens?

I meet my former neighbors as they are dressed in their holiday finery, on their way to worship their god who chose them as murderers and us as victims, and I contemplate: My G-d in heaven, were you to grant me now the powers of the mighty Samson in order to shake the sacred objects of the murderers, and "Let my soul die with the Philistines!"

*

The sun is setting, night is approaching, and I am still lying beside the graves in the Prochod Hills. Everything around is desolate and deathly. Only the clouds are moving across the dark sky - clouds whose source is the smoke of the crematorium that carried them here, the smoke of the burned bodies. These clouds make me drowsy and envelop me in dreams.

*

Today as always, my beloved wife greets me, but her dark, glowing eyes are now extinguished; her pink, smiling face is now pale as never before; and her delicate lips that would drop me motherly kisses now whisper: "Do not come here again, don't come..."

My child, my treasure, my diamond comes to greet me, but today he comes to me without his childlike language... With his soft hands that would always hug my neck he shows me today his small head that was shot, and from which warm, childhood blood flows.

I wake up in a cold sweat, with a broken heart and in agony and pain. The clear moonlight shines upon my dream heroes... I lit memorial candles for the elevation of their souls. To the light of the candles, I begin to read bloodstained pages of books that I collected from the ruins of Ratno:

The heavens shed tears, and blood pours from my heart.

I close my eyes so that I can plunge into my agony... If I had read these words that emanated from the hand of a Jewish lyrist, whom long ago I would have understood differently than I do today, but even today - I do not understand why the heavens did not shed tears when the Nazi murderers shot at the hearts of Jews, and why they continued to give light during the days of the murder of the Jews as they did during the days of Jewish life?

How were the Sparks of Revenge Ignited?

by Yaakov Grabov

Translated by Jerrold Landau

At times I have some sort of feeling that a mysterious, invisible hand, perhaps the hand of a baby, is sticking out from a pit, throwing innuendoes and saying to me, 'Tell, tell Yaakov, tell everything, so that they will know until the end of all generations what happened to us."

I left Ratno in 1938 and went to hachshara in the city of Rovno. When the First World War[1] broke out, a directive was received from the central leadership of Hashomer Hatzair to liquidate the hachshara, to return to our homes and our families, and "to guard the coal until the wrath shall pass." (Who knew then for how long this wrath would continue...) We acted in accordance with the command. I returned to Ratno via Luck and Kowel, and I already saw signs of the war in every place through which I passed. When I arrived in Ratno, I already saw caravans of the retreating Polish Army on their way to the railway station in Zabolotya. We slept among the vegetable patches, hiding from the retreating Polish troops. When the Russians arrived in the wake of the Molotov Von Ribbentrop agreement, it was clear to me that the grave had been covered over all of our Zionist ideals, over Hebrew culture, over the activities of the national funds, and over much more. Our only hope was that the Russian occupation would not last long, and with time, we would be able to "Renew our days as of old"[2].

When the war between Russia and Germany broke out in 1941, the Russians began to leave the town, and several Jewish families left along with them. My eldest brother Shmuel and his family were among them. The town was without government for several days, and the farmers from the extended region streamed into town in order to pillage it. Some of them entered the home of Avraham Hochman, the son-in-law of Liber Karsh. At that time, his brother-in-law Binyam Frajman from the village of Krymne was sitting there. When he saw the hooligans, he grabbed an axe and cut off the head of one of them, but he himself fell victim at the hands of the rest of them, who left the house empty handed. There were two days of quiet in town, but German troops quickly arrived. Their first command was that all the Jews of Ratno were to gather on the road and arrange themselves in rows according to families. When the Jews set out for the designated area, the Germans decreed that if there are any Soviet soldiers among the crowd, they must leave the rows. Two Jewish youths who had served in the Soviet army left the rows, even though many people tried to prevent them from doing so. The lads said, "We do not want destruction to be perpetrated on the Jews of Ratno. You acted relatively well toward us, and we will not pay you back with evil instead of good. Perhaps the Germans will satisfy themselves with the two of us, and no evil will befall you."

After this, a bespectacled German with a severe facial expression passed through the rows and identified 30 young people who were to leave the rows. Among those who were taken were my good friend from Hashomer Hatzair Leibel Steingarten, Yisrael Kanfer, Yankel Klodner, and others. When the thirty youths were collected at the side of the road, Eli Janowicz approached the German who had chosen the victims and said to him in German: "My master, I was the mayor of the city during the First World War, and I served the German authorities faithfully. Here are my documents." The German slapped him on the face and said to him, "The Germans of today are not the Germans of that time. to your place!"

As is known, all 30 were taken to be killed, except for Anyuman the water carried who escaped without being noticed, and Yaakov Klodner, who fell on the ground with the first shot and was left for dead, but who later left the pile of corpses.

Night fell upon Ratno. A frightful night that lasted for years.

*

The Germans confiscated the cows in the town and it was necessary to transport them to Kowel. Moshe Zamel, Yisrael David Fajntuch, and I were among those who transported the cows. When we reached the approach to Kowel, one of the cows fell behind the others. Yisrael David approached it, and whipped it with a stick to prod it. When the German who was with us realized that a Jew was raising a stick to the cow, he called him aside, removed his hat, took out a pair of scissors, and cruelly cut and pulled out the hair of his head. Then, the spark of revenge was ignited within me.

The day would come when I would take revenge for the Jew who had been denigrated - I thought in my heart.

*

A flood of decrees poured down upon us. Each day had its decrees. I was an eyewitness to the following event: The Germans ordered a certain quorum of people to present themselves for work at a certain hour. The Judenrat determined who must go. At the set time, not all of the people who were supposed to be present were there. Even the Judenrat secretary, Yitzchak Karsh, was a few minutes late. When he appeared, the German called him and began to whip him with the whip that he held. Blood flowed from Itzel's head, but he did not say a word. When he collapsed completely, another spark of revenge was ignited, or perhaps the first spark became stronger. I thought in my heart: If only I would remain alive, I will take revenge also for the blood of Itzel.

*

The Judenrat was again ordered to provide workers. There was no choice but to gather the rest of the men who remained in town. Among others, the lot fell upon the only son of Shimon the musician (Sdovnik). His mother and blind father screamed frightening screams: "You are taking our only son, who will sustain us?!" Despite the fact that this draft did not fall upon me, I left the line and said, "I will go in his place." Leibel Grabov approached me, hugged me and said, "Yankele, you are a man of valor, a true proletarian."

The immediately took us to Kowel, and we were told to gather all the belongings from the ghetto, whose residents had been murdered the previous day. We worked the entire day until sunset. Suddenly, the German who was supervising our work noticed that two lads put something in their pockets. He motioned to them to come to him, searched their pants, and found two bars of soap. "This is theft!" the German shouted. He took out a long rope, tightened it, and ordered the lads to run without stop around the rope as he whipped them mercilessly with a whip. The rest of the workers stood around and were forced to watch the spectacle. I closed my eyes, for I was unable to look. The fire of revenge burning within me increased more and more.

*

After several days of work in gathering the property and belongings of the murdered Jews, they transferred me to work on cleaning railway lines. Avigdor Fajntuch of Ratno worked together with me. They worked us hard, and demanded a great deal of productivity. One day, my strength weakened, and thoughts of escape entered my mind as I was working. A mysterious voice echoed in my ears commanding me to get up and escape. I stopped working for a moment, and suddenly I felt on my back the rubber whip with a heavy lead ball at the end. A German stood next to me, "You are lazy[3], you are slacking!" The desire to attack him and kill him awakened within me, but I saw his gun and recoiled.

The next day, I did not go to work. Avigdor Fajntuch and I set out in the direction of Ratno. They captured Avigdor next to Butsyn and killed him, whereas I reached the home of my parents in Ratno through a tortuous route. Mother hugged me, but ordered me to escape to the forest and to search for my brother David who had disappeared and was no longer here. I went to the forest and joined the partisans. The sparks of revenge that pulsated inside of me ignited more and more, and in the various actions in which I participated I had a number of opportunities to fulfill the vows that I had sworn to myself, and to take revenge upon the Germans.

Translator's Footnotes

1. I believe there is a typo in the text here, and the intention was the Second World War. https://www.jewishgen.org/Yizkor/Ratno/rat159.html - f173a-1r
2. Lamentations 5:21. https://www.jewishgen.org/Yizkor/Ratno/rat159.html - f173a-2r
3. See http://en.wikipedia.org/wiki/Taras_Bulba-Borovets https://www.jewishgen.org/Yizkor/Ratno/rat159.html - f173a-3r

There Were Also Such as Those

by Yaakov Grabov

Translated by Jerrold Landau

(Memoirs of a Partisan)

I spent most of the winter in attics and barns of local farmers without them knowing. Only one of them was prepared to give me a hiding place in the barn for a few days, after which I was forced to leave the place out of suspicion of being noticed by the neighbors. The farmer apologized to me and gave me a loaf of bread. I left the place at dark, and went to the city in which the house of the Polish forester, who had left the place at the outbreak of the war between Russia and Germany, was located. The farmers of the area had removed the windows, doors, and any other item that could be dismantled. The only things remaining were the walls and the attic that held the fodder and hay for the cows.

I entered the ruin, went up to the attic, and covered myself in fodder and hay, for otherwise I would have frozen from the cold. I fell asleep... I got up in the morning, broke the bread in my sack into pieces, and placed the sack over my shoulder in such a manner that the farmers would not suspect a simple person. Two bats were hanging from a beam next to me. I thought: For them, it is good. Nobody is bothering their rest, and they will revive and be free in the springtime; whereas I am lying here persecuted and thirsting for revenge. And the lice are eating me alive...

I peered through a crack and saw that everything was covered with white snow, and the pine trees were standing with their green foliage covered with snow like white cushions. According to my calculations, it must have already been the end of the winter. Thick snow fell all night. I could not go out, and if I went out, I would leave footprints in the soft snow, which would be liable to give me away.

All night, as I slept, I had visitors in the hut. That night, my eldest sister visited me and caressed my head. The previous night, I was at a Chanukah celebration in the school. One night, my father also came, covered me in his tallis, and took me to the cheder of Reb Motel "Sarpad". Mother came adorned in a Sabbath kerchief. Her white hair poked out onto her pure forehead, and her blue eyes shone. She covered me and said, "You will remain alive, and it is up to you to avenge our blood. Do not forget!" I woke up and looked outside. Perhaps this time I would succeed in seeing somebody from my family, but the sheet of white snow still covered everything, and the shining sun moved along the heavens, casting rays that broke into all colors of the rainbow. I was situated in a white prison...

One night, I heard from afar the crunching of snow under people's feet. I looked through the crack and noticed two young farmers approaching the hut. I saw their red faces and their small eyes. They stood and looked around. One of them said to his friend:

"Perhaps some little Jew[1] is hiding here?"

His friend answered, "Let us go away. Since the hut had been abandoned, only ghosts and spirits live there. The Yids are big scaredy cats. They would prefer to die than to enter here. Bats also find refuge there." He crossed himself as he said this. Two ravens began to call out and to fly around the hut, filling the entire forest with the noise of their crowing. One of them stood on a pine tree and the other on the roof of the hut, as they continued to quarrel. Their crowing filled my heart with joy, as if this was a Divine melody in the world that was being destroyed, whose time had come to end...

At night, I felt a light wind blowing, and I became warmer. Even the lice were rustling more. Toward morning, I noticed that the bats also began to move their antennae. It seemed that spring was approaching, that the snow would melt, and that I would be able to leave the hut that was on the road leading to two Ukrainian villages, populated by murderers who collaborated with the Nazi enemy.

I still had enough bread to last for a few days. I quenched my thirst with the snow that piled on the roof. In the morning, I would peer through the hole and see black stains on the white sheet that covered the ground, as well as a few blades of green grass. I could leave, and my footsteps would not give me away...

In the darkness of night, I covered my feet with straw and rags, and took the bread in my bag. I hid the knife deep in my shirt, bade farewell to the bats, thanked the ravens and left the hut. Only the lice were bound tightly to my body... It was dark around me. The howls of the wolves, crying over the hunger in their bellies, could be heard from afar. A lone star twinkled through the thicket of pine trees, and it seemed that today, it too was persecuted...

I set out for a lone house standing at the edge of the forest, a distance of about an hour of quick walking. If I would succeed in reaching the house without incident, I would go up to the attic over the barn and remain there for a few days. Even if the farmer would notice me, he would not turn me in. At the very most, he would ask me to leave, and might even give me a loaf of bread.

I tied up my tired feet and measured my steps so as not to make any noise. Who knew from where a murderer might be lurking, who would get a kilo of salt and a bottle of liquor from the Germans for turning me in. I carried a grooved stick in one hand, and grasped tightly with my other hand. Soon I would ascend the attic in the barn and I would be able to sleep without fear.

I opened the door to the barn and entered. The warm mist given off by the cows filled the barn. I found the ladder and went up. I sensed the smell of the fodder and hay, and lay down. I was warm, and I fell asleep.

Dawn broke, but it was still dark in the barn. I heard a voice in Yiddish, "Rachel, I think that someone else is here." A woman's voice responded, "No, Meir, it is your imagination." The two names were known to me, Rachel and Meir from the village of Khoteshiv. I girded my strength and responded, "It is me, Yaakov, the son of Pesach and the brother of David Grabov of Ratno." When more daylight penetrated into the barn, I approached them. When they saw me, they were astonished at my thick beard filled with lice like a hive. Meir said to me, "Yaakov, let us go down and I will cut your beard between the cows. Otherwise, there will be a flood[2] here, and we will not be able to sustain ourselves."

We went down the ladder, and stood between the cows. Meir began the task of cutting my beard. Suddenly, we heard the screech of the heavy door turning on its hinge.

One of the sons of Farmer Duda entered. He stood in astonishment as he looked at us and our actions. Meir turned to him as he caressed my head covered with hair white as flax and said to him, "Yoske, don't tell your father that someone else is with us. Right, you promise?" Yoske looked at Meir with his blue eyes and did not say anything. He turned to his chores, gave fodder and water to the cows, left the barn and closed the door.

"Will he tell his father?" "Yes, he will tell! Duda taught his children from their early childhood not to lie and to tell only the truth to their father". When he finished cutting my beard, we returned with stumbling feet to the ladder, as everything seemed to us like an open abyss. The three of us sat silently and waited for what might come.

The hours passed by slowly as we awaited the frightful verdict. We heard the heavy footsteps of Duda approaching the ladder. He went up, and as his head reached the attic, he turned to Rachel and said, "Come here Rachel? Are you not embarrassed to teach my son to lie to his father who bore him?" Tears streamed from the corners of his eyes and flowed onto his black beard that glistened like a sheet of steel. Rachel wished to justify herself, but Duda began to go down before she managed to say a word.

Rachel returned to her place and sat next to us. Once again, a terrifying silence hovered over us. After a little while, we heard the squeak of the gate. Had the end come? Would Duda turn us in? Meir said to me, "We will resist. We are strong. I have a knife, and you do too." They will not receive any salt or liquor from us. Rachel said, "Duda will prefer to die with his family rather than turn us in." We heard the screech of the ladder as Duda was coming up. Before we saw his head, we sensed the warm steam coming from the black pot. Duda went back and brought a smaller pot. There were potatoes in the large pot and warm milk in the small pot. Duda turned to Rachel and said, "Eat, and be satisfied, and may G-d be with you and with me, so that I can withstand this test that I am undergoing." For me, this was the first hot, cooked meal that I had in many months.

Toward evening, Duda came again with black bread and warm milk. He turned to Rachel and said, "Listen Rachel, I am a poor farmer caring for ten children, and I am doing everything so that you will live, as G-d commands. Yesterday, I obtained a bit of wheat. Come into my house tonight, grind it into wheat in my grinder, and bake matzos, for tomorrow is your Passover holiday. You will have matzos for your holiday. I will cover the windows so that no light will shine outside. The young children will sleep, and the older ones know how to keep a secret."

Rachel burst out crying, hugged Duda, kissed him on his forehead and eyes:

"No Duda, there is no need to endanger your life and the lives of your children. If they find me in your house, they will kill me, your family, and all of us, but if they find us in the barn, we will say that you did not know of our existence. G-d will forgive us for not fulfilling the commandment of eating matzos on Passover."

The night after the Seder night in Duda's barn, I left Meir and Rachel. Duda gave me a large loaf of bread for the journey. The aroma of the matzos that I had eaten at my parents' table rose in my nose. The new chain of escapes and persecutions began, until I joined the ranks of the partisans at the end of the summer. I fulfilled the command of my mother, "took revenge, and then some!" Meir fell as a hero in the ranks of the partisans, but not before he also took revenge. Rachel made aliya to the Land and set up her house in Neve Mivtach, and I also succeeded in making aliya to the Land.

Translator's Footnotes

1. Yehudon - a derogatory term for a Jew - could be translated as kike (although kike is an Americanism). https://www.jewishgen.org/Yizkor/Ratno/rat159.html - f176-1r
2. The term used is "flood" but it may mean, "infestation." https://www.jewishgen.org/Yizkor/Ratno/rat159.html - f176-2r

I was Saved by a Polish Woman[1]

by Hershel Mustiscer

Translated by Jerrold Landau

I was drafted into the Polish army in 1938, along with the rest of my age cohorts in Ratno, and I was sent to the city of Zamosc. I was assigned to unit 9 of the infantry soldiers. My friend Simcha Plotzker from Ratno also served with me. We were scheduled to be released on September 15, 1939, but our release was delayed due to the outbreak of the war. I managed to fight against the German Army that invaded Poland near the city of Pulawy, and we retreated to Krasnystaw near Lublin.

The massive, incessant German bombardment sowed confusion amongst the soldiers, who stopped believing in the possibility of a victory. Many began to escape. My friend Simcha Plotzker advised me to escape with him in the direction of Ratno, but I refused to abandon the army ranks as long as our unit was fighting. One night, a fierce battle raged between the Germans and us, and I was wounded. A great deal of blood flowed continually from my foot, and I suffered hellish pains. I was saved thanks to a Polish woman from the nearby village who found me, bandaged my wounds, and calmed me, but left me in the field. German soldiers who found me in the field took care of me despite the fact that I told them that I was a Jew. They transferred me to the hospital in Krasnystaw, where Polish physicians under German supervision tended to me. For a few months, they moved me to various hospitals in Chelm and Lublin. Finally I was transferred to Warsaw, where they removed the cast from the lower part of my body, and I began to walk, something I could not do for many months.

I began to be more optimistic with respect to my future, but the news of the fate of the Jews in the area of Nazi occupation afflicted my spirit. I was treated as a Polish prisoner, so I was able to visit the Warsaw Ghetto a few times, where I was an eyewitness to the suffering of the Jews and the atrocities perpetrated against them.

I was released from the hospital in June 1941, and, in accordance with my request, I was transferred by the Germans to the city of Hrubieszóów, where my friends who served with me in the Polish Army were situated. I hoped for their help so that I would be able to return to Ratno.

When the war between Germany and Russia broke out, I was transferred via Majdanek, which then served as a prisoner of war camp. By chance, I met there Notka Szuster and Yoel Marder of Ratno, who had served in the Russian Army and were taken as prisoners by the Germans. To my dismay, I was not able to offer them any help at all. When I arrived in Hrubieszóów, I no longer found my friends whose assistance I had awaited. I approached the Judenrat to ask for work. After some time I found out that my good friend Reznik of Baranovich, who had served with me in the army, lived in the nearby village of Strzyzżóów. I went to him, and was helped by him to a certain degree. In that village, I met the woman who was later to become my wife - Sara. Her family lived in that village and worked in the cattle trade. I succeeded in finding work in my trade of tailoring. I sewed clothes for the villagers, until I was transferred along with all the Jews of the village to the Hrubieszóów Ghetto in 1942. At that time, the first liquidations of the Jews began, and I had the feeling that the earth was burning under my feet.

We began to search for a more secure refuge. For some time, I worked in an agricultural farm in Rogalin, not far from Hrubieszóów. When the situation grew more serious, I escaped with Sara and her two brothers. We found a hiding place in the barn of Polish friends. We went out from our hiding place at night to search for food. Nine Jews who were with us in Rogalin were captured by the Germans and shot. We survived thanks to a Polish woman, Rybkuba, who is worthy of being considered as one of the Righteous Gentiles, who offered us help to the best of her ability.

After the war, we reached the Displaced Persons Camps in Germany, where our daughter Tova was born. From there, we immigrated to the United States. My brother Meir served in the Red Army and fought against the Nazis. He reached Poland at the end of the war. He too arrived in the United States after a great deal of wandering. Our daughters Miri and Tova made aliya and live in Tel Aviv. The rest of my family (father Chaim, mother Tova, young brothers and sisters) were all murdered.

Translator's Footnotes

1. This entry does not appear in the original Table of Contents. https://www.jewishgen.org/Yizkor/Ratno/rat159.html - f178a-1r

From the Diary of a Brand Plucked from the Fire

by Yehuda Kagan

Translated by Jerrold Landau

June 21, 1941

It was 4:00 a.m. when we heard echoes of the first bombardment from the German airplanes in the town, waking up all the residents of the town from their sleep. Nobody knew what had happened. People began to run to the office of the Communist authorities of the town, where they were told that these were merely training exercises of the Soviet pilots. At 10:00 a.m., people came from Kowel and told us that the Germans had bombed Kowel. Now, it was clear what had happened. At noon, Molotov delivered a speech on the radio and confirmed that war had broken out between Germany and the Soviet Union.

The Russians began to retreat. We pleaded with them to take us along, but there was nobody with whom to talk. They left us to our bitter fate.

June 23, 1941

The town was surrounded by bloodthirsty Ukrainians from the nearby villages, who began to pillage and perpetrate a pogrom. After they took out the first Jews in Ratno to be killed, my father began stating to anyone who was willing to listen that the earth was burning under our feet, and we must escape. We went to a village not far from Ratno, were we remained for about three months. The Ukrainian pillaging continued in the village as well. They murdered and pillaged without end. A Ukrainian police force was set up and headed by a well-known robber. He aroused trembling amongst the Jews by his very appearance. One cloudless morning, a command was issued that all the Jews, from young to old, must gather in the synagogue. There, a tall German and the head of the Ukrainian police, whose appearance instilled fear upon the Jews, were already waiting. Two Ukrainian teachers were sitting on one of the benches, mocking the Jews. A policeman with a gun in his hands and with a Ukrainian beret with an insignia upon his head also sat there. Next to him sat a Ukrainian policeman wearing high boots and holding a whip in his hands. "“Who is the head of the Jews here?”" he shouted. The elderly Reb Meir Olishneker came forth from the row and said that he was the one. In response, the policeman began to whip the old man on the back with his whip. The Ukrainians standing next to him began to count the lashes - to fifty. The old man did not utter anything. His face was covered with blood and tears. At the end of the beating, he was tossed into another room as he was kneeling down.

Next, the turn of my father Nachum came. He was 55 years old, had served in the Russian Army from 1914 to 1922, was in prison four times, had been injured several times, and in his time had also been beaten by the Balachowiczes. My father closed his eyes, kneeled down on his knees, and removed his hat. My younger brother and I were eyewittnesses to the murderous blows with which the Ukrainians whipped him. My father's coat was torn, and his body was red with blood. "“L-rd, G-d, how?”" - this was the call that emanated from the mouth of my beaten father, as he burst out crying. The Ukrainian who was whipping him boiled with anger and issued the verdict: "“You will get 20 more lashes for your crying.”" After my father fainted, the Ukranian tossed him outside. Now my turn came. I bit my lips with my teeth, but I stayed standing. It was not the lashes that hurt so much, but rather the pain and suffering of my father. When the turn of my younger brother came to endure the lashes, I screamed to him, "“Maintain your stand, Yosel-Ber!”" He maintained his stand to the point of sobbing. This was the fate of all the Jews who were present there. Blood flowed from their bodies and their clothes were tattered and torn.

At the end of the whipping, the Ukrainians lined us up and ordered us to march through the muddy streets, singing Jewish songs. In this manner, we reached the Turiya River, with Ukrainians standing on both sides of the road, their mouths filled with laughter. We were given the choice of either drowning in the river, or pulling out 30 meters of entangled wood from the river and arranging it in rows. We worked with the last of our energy until late at night. When we finished the job, we were allowed to go home, where the despairing, weeping mothers were waiting for us. When we entered our house, Mother fell upon our necks with heartrending weeping. Father removed his coat that was flowing with blood, and his skin was literally black as coal.

Days, weeks, and months passed. We worked at hard labor cutting trees for the Ukrainian police, with our feet covered with diapers or rags, and our hands frozen to the point that they could not be warmed up at all. One day in the month of Adar, I returned from work with my brother Yosel-Ber and we sensed the spirit of Tisha B'Av in the house. The reason became immediately clear: my brother and I had been requisitioned to go to a labor camp in Kowel. Mother was already weeping for us, for she knew the meaning of a "“Labor Camp.”" Father was also weeping bitterly and praying. There was no morsel of bread in the house, and the cold was penetrating all the bones. I suggested that I alone remain to wait for those who were to take me to Kowel, while they go out to the forest. One victim was sufficient. I went outside, and a wagon quickly appeared upon which ten Jews were sitting. The Ukrainians wanted to know where my brother who did not show up was. Without waiting for an answer, they began to rain beatings upon me. They broke into the house, tore up the bedding, and destroyed everything that came into their hands. We meandered from village to village as they gathered in the wagon the poor Jews who had lived and worked in those villages for many years. The sobbing and weeping of the families whose sons were gathered into our wagon was indescribable. I recall that at one of the stops, a woman burst forth from the forest, wanting to take leave of her husband for the last time, but one shot from the Ukrainian policeman felled her to the ground, as her blood flowed. At the sight of this wounded women, we thought in our hearts: This is the end that awaits us all. We will not even merit a Jewish grave.

The Ukrainians were supposed to take us to Kowel, but after some time we arrived in Ratno. The city was teaming. Jews were brought there from various places with their sacks in their hands. A certain degree of "“business"” was also conducted there. Youths "“redeemed themselves"” in exchange for gold watches and placed the children of the poor in their stead on the wagons going to Kowel. Suddenly, I saw my father, my mother and my aunt Slava. I gestured to them to disappear. They brought us to the German Commissariat office, which was surrounded by German police. One Ukrainian, a former Balachowicz, was beating the Jews who had gathered left and right, to the pleasure of the Germans. From there, we were taken to Kowel, but when we reached there, the command was given to return home. I arrived home late at night, and everyone was sad and agonized. Rivers of tears poured from Father's and Mother's eyes. Everything that had been in the house had been pillaged and destroyed. When they suddenly saw me, the weeping in the dark house increased.

Kowel 1942

The winter was difficult. There was no firewood, and the house was as cold as outside. We waited for spring, but things did not get any easier. We had become somewhat accustomed to the tribulations. One night during the month of Iyar, there was a knock on the door of our house. This was a representative of the Judenrat in Ratno who came to inform us that Yehuda Kagan must present himself at the German Commissariat in order to go to work along with 50 other Jews. This news dumbfounded all the members of the household. I immediately sent my parents to Ratno, and remained to wait. The next day, a telephone message reached me from Ratno saying that I must come quickly. I parted from my brothers thinking in my heart that this might be our final parting. I arrived in Ratno. Mother and Father were downtrodden and hunched over. They gave me several small packages, which the police tossed onto one of the three wagons that were laden with packages, whereas we had to walk to Kowel, a distance of 50 kilometers, by foot. There were 55 youths, including the leader of Hashomer Hatzair Moshe Pogatch, Wolf-Ber Tenenbaum the son of Motel the shochet, Avraham Kagan, and others. The parting was literally heartbreaking. My father looked at me with confounded looks. My mother was wailing. I already wanted to be far from there, for it was hard to watch the agony of my parents. We began to march, and at the end of the day, we were already bereft of energy. We arrived in the region of a Russian prisoner of war camp and we were ordered to refrain from looking in the direction of that camp. Our eyes noticed the barbed wire fences and the tall towers surrounded by Gestapo men riding on horses. Guards with hunting dogs stood around, as well as soldiers with machine guns. The march drained our energy, but we arrived at the approach to the city of Kowel. They brought us to the Kowel Judenrat, and two Ukrainian policemen gave our names to the head of the Judenrat. From then on, the Jewish policemen who were making the rounds with sticks in their hands to ensure that none of us escaped were responsible for us. The next day, we were taken to the German work office in Kowel. We were divided into groups, and my lot fell into a T.A.S. group. We marched to the area of "“Nowa Kolyuwa”" near the train station. From there, my group was sent to perform excavation work to repair the railway tracks.

My first day of work was backbreaking. I hauled cement in a wheelbarrow that slipped from time to time, and the cement spilled out. We were surrounded by S.S. men who prodded us and whipped us right and left with their whips. Vehicles came at noon to take the S.S. men to their lunch, while we were taken to the Jewish kitchen. The price of a meal was 1.50 marks. Many of us did not have a cent, for our payment for a day of work was 250 grams of bread. Our work day ended at 8:00 p.m., when we lay down on our beds drained of energy. The next day, we presented ourselves again at the work office, where we were again divided into groups for various jobs. Each group was led by Jewish policemen wearing white armbands. This time, I ended up with an easier job on a grain threshing floor. Russian prisoners worked alongside us. We continued working in this manner at various jobs for several weeks, with our food ration being 200 grams of bread per day. The situation grew more serious from day to day.

Ghettoes

Days and nights passed with fear, threats and endless worry. The murderous aktions of the Nazis became more frequent and frightful. We were constantly surrounded by Ukrainian policemen and German S.S. men. After some time, a decree was proclaimed: The Jews were to go to two ghettoes - one to the civic ghetto and the second to a special ghetto for workers. Nobody knew which ghetto they had to go to, but everyone knew that anyone who was not prepared by 12:00 would be shot. Everyone was busy with farewells and packing belongings. Rumor had it that the boundaries of the civic ghetto would be Brisk Street and the market, whereas the workers' ghetto would be located on the sand dunes near the railway station. People trudged along with their bags in the direction of the ghettoes, and the sick people were loaded on wagons. The panic increased from hour to hour. Parents could not find their children, and the children did not follow after their parents. There were literal scenes of horror, all witnessed by the Ukrainians and Germans who were laughing at us and mocking us. Noon arrived, the sounds of the first shots were heard, and the first victims fell. Whoever did not reach the designated area within the bounds of the ghetto on time was shot. I too arrived at the street that was designated as the ghetto. This ghetto could accommodate 600 people, but 6,000 people were crowded into it, with 20-30 people per dwelling. The crowding was terrible, and many people slept outside due to a lack of space. Even worse - there was nothing to eat. People gathered potato peels, and there were long lineups to obtain a bit of water. The ghetto was fenced in with boards covered with barbed wire on top. At noon, a vehicle arrived with 12 S.S. men and high captains who demanded 120 people. I was among the 120 people. Everyone was sure that they were hauling us to our death. They placed us in fine vehicles and brought us to nice houses in Kowel whose owners had abandoned and locked them. We were ordered to break the locked doors. Physicians who had abandoned their property and escaped had lived in many of these houses. Everything that was found in those houses was to be loaded on vehicles, and we were forbidden from taking anything. A German officer checked our pockets to ensure that we did not violate the command. A bar of soap was found in somebody's pocket, and he was shot on the spot. When we returned to the ghetto, they looked at us as if we had risen from the dead....

Yehuda Kagan as a soldier in the Red Army (1945)

An order was issued that only people with work permits were permitted to live in the workers' ghetto, but such permits had only been issued to several hundred of the 6,000 people. Everyone else was obligated to move to the civic ghetto. I was among those did not receive such a permit. It was decreed that anyone who remained in the workers' ghetto without a permit would be taken to be killed. Fear prevented people from running to the civic ghetto. Many people hid in abandoned attics. Four other people and I without permits hid in a small attic in the workers' ghetto. The first shots, accompanied by frightening screams, were heard at 1:00. They were shooting our sons and daughters. Many were forcibly dragged out by the Ukrainians and S.S. and S.D. men to Brisk Square and loaded onto wagons. 100 people were shot on the spot. We looked for hiding places in the water sewers, ovens and any place in which it was possible to hide for a brief time. The Judenrat men were hauled to Gurka, and shot after being tortured. We heard shouts of Shema Yisrael, and the screams of women and children throughout the entire night. The entre city was turned into one huge slaughterhouse. Those who were not murdered were hauled to the synagogue. Many of them wrote their names and their family names in blood, and added a call for revenge over the spilled blood.

We waited for our turn to come as well. Knocks on the door were heard at daybreak. It was the Jewish police, who were informing everyone to not leave the house until the order was received from the commissar who was appointed over the district. At noon, a group of Jews were enlisted to bury the dead scattered throughout the entire city. We came out of our hiding places and were also enlisted in the task of collecting the vast amount of scattered Jewish property. The S.S. men pillaged anything that came into their hands. I turned to my friends and said, "“We must escape from here. We should remove our yellow patches and escape!"” So we did. We tried to get to a certain German driver who was known as a friend of the Jews. We followed him from our workplace and asked him to take us out of the city. When the German heard what we were requesting, he began to shout, "“Accursed Jews, why did not you kill at least 100 Germans and Ukrainians?"” He was afraid to endanger himself, but he showed us the way to go. We appeared as Ukrainians, and also spoke a good Ukrainian. We took our lives in our hands and went toward the railway line. Siddurs, chumashes and tefillin were lying along the way. We stopped a Ukrainian and asked him what was new. He told us that trains of Jews were arriving every half hour, and the Jews were being shot. We again heard the shouts of Shema Yisrael. The voice of the city rabbi was heard, "“Murderers such as you, you are shooting us and burying us, but you will be shot like dogs and will not even have a burial!"” He was hit over the head with a gun, and he fell into the pit while still alive.

We turned leftward in a single line, but kept a distance of several hundred meters from one to the other. We set out toward a small village 15 kilometers away that had no police. We walked over valleys and pits. At one place, we had to cross a brook of water. A farmer promised to bring a boat for this purpose, but suddenly four Ukrainian policemen came who searched our clothes and bags, and took razors and several bars of soap that we had. We were left naked as on the day of our births. We continued to wander through various villages, and after some time, we arrived in the village in which my family members lived. Everyone was surprised to see me. They were sure that I was no longer alive. We did not want to and were not able to remain in the house. We set out to the forest - to the partisans.

Yehuda Kagan in the War of Independence

Yehuda Kagan[1]
Translated by Jerrold Landau

Yehuda Kagan was born in Ratno in 1922, and studied in the yeshiva in the city of Kobrin in Pulisia until 1938. He joined the Beitar Movement in 1937 and was active in that movement until the Russian conquest of that area in September 1939. At the outbreak of the war between the Soviet Union and Germany at the end of June 1941, he was in the city of Birky near Ratno along with his family, and was sent to hard labor in Kowel, as is related I the article on the following pages. He succeeded in escaping from Kowel and arrived in the village of Birky, where his family was living. At the time of the liquidation of the Jews of the region, he escaped to the forest with his family. His father fell at the hand of the Ukrainians and Germans while attempting to defend 50 Jews who were hiding in the forest. After some time, his mother and the rest of his family were murdered. He and his brother, who today lives in the Soviet Union, were the only ones of the family to survive. At the end of 1943, he and his brother joined a partisan unit under the command of General Feodor Chernigovski, and participated in many actions. He later moved to the front and enlisted in the Red Army. He participated in battles on the fronts of Finland, Vyborg, Leningrad, Estonia, Lithuania, Warsaw, and Poznan. At the front in Poznan, he joined the communications division of the

Red Army (S. M. R. Sh.) in the role of translator from German to Russian. In that role, he participated in interrogations of the captains and soldiers who fell into Russian captivity. When 150 Jews who had been in the Gerdenlagen Labor Camp were arrested in the city of Stünzel for possessing German and American documents, Kagan freed them from prison on his own accord. For this, he was imprisoned by the security services. He was held under house imprisonment and interrogated by army interrogators. He escaped from his place of confinement, and after many tribulations and serious danger, reached Frankfurt in the American occupation zone. He was the commander of the guard in the UNRA camp in Zeilsheim, and was also active in the Etzel[2] at that time. He completed an Etzel course in Germany, was involved in Aliya Bet[3], and assisted in the smuggling of immigrants to the Land of Israel. Yehuda Kagan made aliya to Israel in 1948 and participated in the War of Independence in the second division of the Palmach. Later, he served in the Negev Brigade[4]. He was discharged from the Israel Defense Forced in 1949 and set up his home in Givatayim.

In 1963, when he participated in an organized trip to the Soviet Union, he was arrested by the Soviet security personnel, placed in a KGB prison, and accused of deserting the Red Army when he served as a military translator in the S. M. R. Sh. unit, as well as transmitting military secrets to the Americans and acting as an Israeli spy. He was sentenced to ten years in prison. He served the sentence in seven different prisons: Kiev, Gorky, Penza, Kaluga, Rashucha, and Vladimir. He was active among the prisoners, telling them about life in Israel, and even distributing postcards of Israeli scenes. For this crime of "Zionist Propaganda" he was transferred to labor camp 17/358 where political prisoners were imprisoned, and which was known for its most stringent level of guarding. He was imprisoned in Camp 17 in the district of Mordovia along with the Leningrad prisoners[5]: the pilot Dymshits, Chanoch Kaminsky, Korenblit and others, who are today in Israel. He was freed from prison after he served his sentence.

Translator's Footnotes

1. This entry does not appear in the original Table of Contents. https://www.jewishgen.org/Yizkor/Ratno/rat159.html - f180a-1r

2. See http://en.wikipedia.org/wiki/Irgun https://www.jewishgen.org/Yizkor/Ratno/rat159.html - f180a-2r

3. See http://en.wikipedia.org/wiki/Aliyah_Bet https://www.jewishgen.org/Yizkor/Ratno/rat159.html - f180a-3r

4. See http://en.wikipedia.org/wiki/Negev_Brigade https://www.jewishgen.org/Yizkor/Ratno/rat159.html - f180a-4r

5. See http://en.wikipedia.org/wiki/Dymshits%E2%80%93Kuznetsov_hijacking_affair https://www.jewishgen.org/Yizkor/Ratno/rat159.html - f180a-5r

Meir Blit, a partisan from the village of Datyn

My Revenge!

by Eli Zisik

Translated by Jerrold Landau

When the war between Germany and Poland broke out in 1939, I was serving mandatory duty in the Polish Army as a regular soldier. As is known, the Polish Army collapsed quickly, and the Russians occupied Western Ukraine and most of the area of Poland in accordance with The Molotov von Ribbentrop agreement. I was sent back to Ratno, along with many other soldiers who were also sent to their homes. It seemed to me that our town did not suffer especially, in particular not from an economic perspective, during the era of Soviet rule. "Bourgeois" families were indeed sent to Siberia, and those who were suspected of ideological crimes against the new regime were deported. In general, however, the residents got used to the new regime. Zionist activities ceased, and many people began to learn Russian and Ukrainian. At that time, information began to arrive from the cities of Poland that were under German occupation that the situation of the Jews was increasingly declining, and many Jews began to escape in the direction of the Russian border in order to escape from the Nazis.

I worked as a technician and projectionist in the Ratno Theater. In that capacity, I would frequently travel to Kowel to bring films from there. I remember that when the first air raid took place over Kowel, nobody believed that this was the era of German airplanes. Rather, they thought that these were nothing more than training exercises of the Russian Army. That was how great the surprise was. Only after the Russians confirmed over the radio that the Germans had opened an attack, did the situation become clear to everyone that the Second World War had broken out. Immediately after this, the cities near the border were conquered by the Nazi Army. On the day that the ware broke out, I returned from Kowel to Ratno and was an eyewitness to the German attack. There was complete chaos in Ratno. The Soviet authorities proclaimed a draft, but, in practice, the Russians were the first to start to escape in the direction of Kamen Kashirsk. The Jews in town were perplexed, and could not decide whether to escape or remain put. The first group to organize immediately was the band of Ukrainian murderers who began pillaging and plundering. After that, a Gestapo Unit arrived in Ratno and decided to take out 30 Jews to be killed as a punishment for the alleged shooting by the Jews. I was among the 30 Jews who were designated by the Germans to bury the youths who were shot. We dug the graves, and there is no need to describe what was going on in our souls as we were digging. As far as I recall, only one of the 30, who was only injured in his foot, succeeded in escaping at night and was saved. Only after this act of the Germans did the residents of our town began to sense and understand what was awaiting them at the hands of the Nazis. Many began to escape to the villages, but the majority of the Jews remained in the town and were witnesses to the collaboration of the Ukrainians, who turned Jews over to the hands of the Nazis and even earned prizes for every person turned over. As a technician, I was taken to work along with other professionals. Our payment was one loaf of bread a day. I was able to wander freely about the area, and knew about everything with respect to the German decrees. The Judenrat that was set up in Ratno could not stand by all the decrees of the Germans, which became more serious with each day. Some of them served as guarantors. My father Chaim and my sister Chaika and her children were among those murdered. I, my brother Yoske, and several other Jews received permission to bring them for burial. After the Germans liquidated the Kowel Ghetto, aktions began in all the settlements of the region. Screams of Shema Yisrael by those who were being hauled to be murdered were heard throughout the area, and reached my ears as well. I continued to work in Kowel in a garage next to the flour mill along with several other Jews whose professional services the Germans required. After news began to reach us of the defeat of the Germans on the Stalingrad front, we took council and decided to escape at the earliest opportunity. We began to equip ourselves with food, and gathered anything that appeared to us as useful for the escape effort. One night, we escaped from Kowel and set out in the direction of the nearby forest. We walked at night on a path parallel to the road that led to Ratno. Some Jews who worked in an Artel (workplace) in the service of the Germans remained, and we wished to include them as well. There was another reason aside from this one: I had hidden weapons, and wished to retrieve them.

We arrived in the area of Ratno toward morning. Three members of the group remained in the forest, and I continued on to Ratno through the marshes. I knew that the daughters of Gitel Karsh had found a hiding place with a gentile whom I knew, so I went to their house. As soon as I entered, they informed me that the day before, they had gathered up the remaining Jews of the town and took them out to be killed. I immediately severed my contact with this gentile and escaped from there. I knocked on the door of Chaicha Janowicz. She opened up immediately and also told me that the day before, they had taken all the Jews to be killed, and her brother had escaped and was with her. She brought me to the hiding place, and in a brief conversation, we decided to go that night to get the weapons from the hiding place and escape from Ratno to the forest. That is what we did. We took the weapons, cleaned them well, crossed the bridge, and went to the forest via the fields. We could not find the youths who had gone with me and who had remained waiting in the forest. We entered the home of a Ukrainian who used to pillage the wagon drivers who brought merchandise to Ratno. He received us well and told us that he knows of several Jews who were hiding in the area, and that he was prepared to show us their hiding places. At night, the three of us (I, the aforementioned Chaicha's brother, and this gentile) went in accordance with his directions, and found Shlomo Perlmutter and Moshe Chaim Fuchs, who found a hiding place in some barn. We gave them food, took them with us, and went out to resistance activities. The Ukrainian gave us the weapons that we used to pillage the Jewish wagon drivers in the region in return for the Jewish property that we would gather together with him. From him we also received information about what was going on. Among other things, he told us that everyone was talking about a group of Jewish partisans who are fighting against the Germans and also taking revenge on Ukrainian collaborators with the Nazis. They were of course referring to our small group. We continued to go around to the villages during the nights with the intention of searching for partisans and including them in larger scale resistance activities. We succeeded in making contact with a group of partisans called Luginov. At first, they wanted to take our weapons, but they forewent this after the intervention of several Jews, including Meir Blit, and agreed to include us with them.

*

After some time, and after they began to trust us, we were sent to carry out resistance activities on the railway lines. However, they insisted that we not act as one group. Instead, they divided us into different groups, thereby breaking up our group. I transferred to the unit of General Feodorov, who received commands directly from Moscow. In this unit, I met Shlomo Perlmutter once again, who told me that the partisans of that general are the true partisans, and while we are in their ranks, we are able to take actual revenge for everything that the Germans and Ukrainians did to our family, and to the Jews in general. With his own hands, Shlomo had hanged one of those Ukrainians, who had served as a translator for the Germans. That was Ivan Makomachora, who had murdered many Jews in Ratno.

There were many Jews of the area in the units of General Feodorov. Those units acted as military units in all matters. They also received military equipment from airplanes that landed nearby, and imposed fear on the population of the region, who changed their attitudes and cooperated with the partisans. At times, we encountered Banderowches (nationalist Ukrainians), and battles broke out between us and them. With the advance of the Red Army, these groups disbanded, whereas we, the partisans, joined the army and advanced along with it to liberate the soil of Ukraine.

I was with the Red Army also at the gates of Warsaw, where we were forced to remain for about a half a year, and I participated in its liberation. We suffered losses daily, including Yitzchak Szapira, whom I had met by chance. Later, I participated in the conquest of Berlin. This is how things went until the end of the war. I can state without hesitation that I fulfilled the vow that I vowed to myself and the Jews of Ratno. I took revenge for the spilled blood of our brethren.

Yakov Grabov a soldier in the Red Army

The Way of the Partisan

by Yaakov Grabov

Translated by Jerrold Landau

(From a testimony presented to Magistrate Motta Hollander, under the auspices of Yad Vashem)

I was born on October 18, 1921 in Ratno. I was 18 at the outbreak of the Second World War.

In my childhood, I studied in a cheder and later at the "Tarbut" School. I completed grade 10 at age 16 and began to help my father in the lumber business. Two years later I joined the "Hashomer Hatzair" movement and went to Rovno. The Second World War broke out while I was there.

When the wartime actions abated, I returned to my parents' home in Ratno. A few days later, I was sent by the Russians to work in Ludmir, Volhynia. I worked in the erection of army bunks and received a salary. Despite this, after three months, I decided to leave my workplace and return home. The Russians found me in Ratno and put me on trial for the crime of escaping from work. I was sentenced to three months of hard labor, and that same day I was transferred to a camp in Zaporoza, where the punishment of people sentenced to 15 or 20 years of imprisonment was carried out.

After being in Zaporoza for two months, I was transferred to Berdiansk[1] in Ukraine. Berdiansk is located on the Azov Sea (today its name is Osipenko). This was also a hard labor camp. I worked in digging a canal from the factory to the sea. I was sent home after one month. This was in the spring of 1940. In Ratno, I received work in pouring concrete. I worked at this job until the outbreak of the war between Germany and the Soviet Union in June 1941.

The Ukrainians Pillage Jewish Property

Complete chaos pervaded in Ratno at the outbreak of the war. The local Ukrainians as well as those from the nearby region began to pillage Jewish property. They broke into the private houses and Jewish stores, and pillaged everything that came to their hands. Binyamin Freiman killed with a blow from an ax a Ukrainian who broke into his home for robbery. Another Ukrainian who was a witness to the death of his friend shot Freiman dead.

The Germans entered Ratno after two weeks. Already on the day of their arrival, they commanded the Jews to gather together in one place on the main street. The men, women, and children stood there all night. The women and children were sent home toward morning. The men remained in the place, and then the Germans began the murder aktions.

One of the Germans chose six Jews who were taken outside the city, where they were commanded to dig pits. Later, thirty men were selected from the crowd and sent to the place of the pits. Shots were heard after a few minutes. All thirty men were shot and killed. My good friend Leib Steingarten, whose father was one of the six pit diggers, was among the murdered.

Around the time of their entry to Ratno, the Germans sent 60 Jewish men to work in Kowel. I was included in that group. We were sent to the ghetto. In Kowel, we worked on repairing the railway tracks. I escaped from Kowel after two months.

The Escape from the Kowel Ghetto to Ratno

There were two ghettos in Kowel: the large ghetto and the small ghetto. After one of the aktions that took place here, the men of my group were called together to count and organize the belongings that were left by the local Jews who were murdered. During the enumeration, I suddenly felt a blow upon my head from the hands of a German. I immediately heard the scream of one of my friends: "Escape!" I hid in one of the cellars and decided to flee back to Ratno. I begged other Jews of my town to join me, but none of them wanted to move from there. Avigdor Feintuch was the only one who joined me. I escaped from the ghetto with him.

We spent the first night in an abandoned house outside the city. In the morning, I saw a horse hitched to a wagon on the road. A woman was sitting on the wagon driver's stand. I knew the Ukrainian language very well, and my face did not give away my Jewishness. I asked the woman to take us to Ratno. She explained that she was traveling to a village 30 kilometers from Ratno, and she agreed to take us as far as the village. I seated Feintuch on the other side of the wagon due to his Jewish appearance. When we arrived at the bend in the road leading to the woman's village, we suddenly saw a group of Germans approaching us.

Feintuch was nearsighted. I shouted to him, "Let us escape, the Germans are coming!" However, it was already too late. I indeed escaped and hid between the bushes. Feintuch was caught and was asked on the spot, "Where is the other one?" Feintuch answered, "There was no other person!" Shots were heard and Feintuch lay dead on the ground. (His brother and sister are alive today in Israel.)

I lay down in the bushes throughout the day, and at night I set out in the direction of Ratno. After walking for the entire night, I arrived home at dawn. I found my parents and two sisters in the house. This was the autumn of 1942.

The Hiding Place in the Village of Jakosza

Since I was the youngest son in my family, my mother had a special bond with me. When she saw the murderous aktions that were perpetrated by the Germans, she pleaded with me to leave town, for everyone knew me there.

I listened to her and went to the village of Jakosza, a distance of 5 kilometers from Ratno, on the banks of the Prypiat River. Only two Jewish families lived in that village. My friend Mendel Krein, who was partially deaf, lived there with his mother and sister. I would hide along with Mendel in the forests throughout the day, and at night we would return to his house to sleep in the attic on a straw mattress.

One day, I woke up sleeplessly from a nightmare that I had that night. I told Mendel, "I am going home!..." It was not yet dawn when I left the house. I arrived at the riverbank at a place that could be crossed by swimming, for its entire span was one and a half meters. From the other side, one could walk on foot to Ratno. The riverbanks were filled with quicksand. It was easy to sink in it and even to drown. A German foot had never trodden there, and if I were to have arms, I would have been able to fight even against a hundred Germans there. I approached the place where it was said there was a boat available to transport people to the other side of the river. However, no boat was found there. I therefore decided to go on foot, even though I knew that the path was boggy. The 3.5-kilometer path along the shore was longer and more difficult.

Suddenly I saw a boat approaching. Suddenly, I heard clear shouting directed to me from the other side of the river. The shouts emanated from the direction of Ratno. I froze on the spot out of great fear. In the meantime, the boat approached the shore, and a Ukrainian, an acquaintance of mine, said in

Hebrew, "Yaszek, they are murdering everybody, do not return to Ratno!" I returned to the home of Mendel Krein. We both set out for the forest. These were the Pulsia Forests, which spread out endlessly from there. We hid in the forests for two weeks. At night, we stole food from the framers of the area. We finally decided to approach the village of Samorowycze, where rumor had it that there were still Jews there.

The village of Samorowycze was located 20 kilometers from the town. When we arrived, there were still Jews living in their homes, for the Germans had not yet reached there. We met many Jews who had escaped from Ratno and were hiding in the village. We decided to remain there. My friend Mendel Krein decided to return to his village to transfer his belongings to our new place of residence.

He went in the company of a young lad, Gershon. On the return trip, they were attacked by Ukrainian strangers who were not from this region. They murdered Mendel by cutting off his head. They cut off a finger from the hand of 14-year-old Gershon. Then they stole all of the property. Gershon returned to Samorowycze and told us what had happened. I cut off the stump of his finger that was connected by a hairbreadth strand, and bandaged up his hand. I set out to the place where Mendel was murdered with Gershon and a few other friends. We brought his body to Samorowycze and buried him there.

I wandered through cities and towns. At night, I would steal food from the farmers, and during the day I would hide in the depths of the forest. One day, I met an acquaintance from Ratno, Eiden Janowicz, who used to own a restaurant in Ratno. I wandered with him through the forests, searching for some partisan group that we could join. Finally, Janowicz decided to return to Ratno. He attempted to persuade me to do so as well, for the Germans had left 30 Jews in Ratno after the last slaughter. They were working for them, and would certainly be left alive, for the Germans needed them.

"Come with me to Ratno", he attempted to convince me, "And we will join those Jews." I gave him a firm answer, "I will never go to the Germans as long as I am still alive!..."

Janowicz returned to Ratno, and was murdered on the day he returned. A few days later, the last 30 Jews in Ratno were murdered. The only one who had survived and succeeded in escaping was Eli Zask, who today lives in Netanya, Israel. I was again left alone. From the village, in which only one hut was still standing, I returned to the forest to search for my brother. It was late autumn, and the cold afflicted me greatly, for I had no warm clothing. One day, I happened to wander to the village of Bordiatyn. There, I met my brother and his wife in the forest that borders the village. It became clear that they had been hiding there for two weeks, and that they intended to remain in that place. I told my brother, "Let us leave this place, for we can travel within a five kilometer radius and continue our search for family members." My sister-in-law Dvora (nee Papir) said, "We will not go, we will remain here..." I then went myself to the midst of the forest.

One day, I saw a bonfire. I approached and did not believe my eyes. My father was sitting on a tree stump. I saw a man before me, wearing poor clothing and with a beard... It took a few minutes until my father recognized me. When he saw me, he began to complain, "Why did I not go with Mother and the children to the grave? For what purpose am I being tortured here..." My father gave into Mother's urging and escaped to the synagogue through a back door when the Germans broke into our house prior to the aktion. From there he escaped to the forest. He had Ukrainian acquaintances throughout the area, and he hid in their homes for two weeks. Then he wandered in the forest for weeks. He was dirty and afflicted with lice. I took him to my brother. We dressed him in other clothes, and cast away the clothing he was wearing.

No Jews were left in Bordiatyn except for our family: my father, my brother and my sister-in-law, and me. My brother had 50 dollars. We used that money to house our father with a Ukrainian acquaintance. The farmer lived in the village of Gurniki and had his own house. Thick forests surrounded the area. The farmer housed my father in his attic. My father spent two months with that farmer in Gurniki. I visited him every week. I would come to him from the forest in which I was hiding. Once I succeeded in stealing a fur from one of the farmers, and another time, a jar of honey. I brought everything to my father.

One time when I went up, as usual, to the attic from the yard, I did not find anyone there. I went down and entered the house to ask what had happened to my father, and where he was. Then the farmer told me that his neighbors had discovered that my father was hiding in the attic. Father escaped to the village of Melnyk.

Melnyk was a large village, the same size of Gurniki. Many Jews hid there, but that time, the farmers besieged the Jews who were hiding and expelled them all to the village of Chocieszow, where there was a German and Ukrainian police station. They were all murdered there. I returned to my brother in November 1942, and told him that Father is no longer alive.

Continued Wandering and the Successful Escape from the Ukrainians

We wandered together in the forest, sleeping under bales of hay, and stealing food at night. The bales would be gathered in during the winter, when they would freeze. We slept under the bales for the entire month, and when the cold began to afflict us, we had no choice but to go to the farmer with whom my father had previously stayed. The farmer permitted us to sleep at his place. We went up into the attic before nightfall. At 10:00 p.m., the farmer came to us, breathing heavily, and said, "Escape quickly... Ukrainians who are searching for Jews are with me...!"

We escaped. Snow mixed with rain was falling. It was dark, and difficult to see the path. The Ukrainians heard us and began to chase after us. They chased after us in the dark but could not catch us. We reached a small river that was impossible to cross by foot, since its water was deep. At the last moment, my brother-in-law saw a plank spanning both banks of the river. We ascended the plank, and crossed to the other bank of the river. We took the plank with us.

We rested on a small island for the rest of the night and the next day. It was muddy all around, and no traces of people could be found. In the evening, we decided to leave the place. My brother-in-law and his wife decided to approach the nearby village of Rechitsa, and I intended to find refuge somewhere else.

The Murder of 25 Jews and 20 Gypsies in the Village of Miszitz

The village of Miszitz was located on a side route. At that time, there were still 25 Jews and 20 gypsies there. The Jews all worked, and there was complete calm in the town. Rachel Wiener and her brother, whose origins were from a different village, Siderowycze, were there. Despite the apparent calm in the town, it was evident to us that danger was lurking. We decided to go to the village of Bordiatyn, two kilometers away from Miszitz. Wiener turned to me and said, "Wake me in the morning, and we will go together." However, when I woke her up at 4:00 a.m., she said to me, "Go yourself!" I went myself. A few hours later, the son of a Ukrainian acquaintance approached me and screamed, "Flee! They are shooting Jews in Miszitz!"... I escaped very quickly.

Later, I found out that the Ukrainians had murdered all of the Jews and gypsies who were in the village that day. This was late autumn of 1942. Rachel Wiener was the only survivor. Her two brothers were murdered.

The Murder of the Jews in the Village of Likow

Winter was approaching, and I continued to wander about in the forests. I would steal food from the farmers at night and sleep in the barns of the farmers on the warm fodder. The farmers who owned the barns for the most part did not know about this. Thus passed the entire winter of 1942/43. I wore light clothes the entire winter, and the cold afflicted me greatly. Each night, I would sleep in the barn of a different farmer, covered in the fodder, sometimes even standing up. That way I could keep warmer. Almost every night I would dream about my mother who was convincing me that I would not freeze from the cold. I spent a few nights with one of the farmers who knew of my presence. One day, a woman who came from the village of Likow came to that barn. She refused to leave, for she did not have any other hiding place. The village of Likow was approximately 30 kilometers distant from Ratno. The Ukrainian farmers who lived there were known throughout the region as the cruelest murderers of Jews. They murdered the Jews of their villages and the Jews of the entire region. The next day, those Ukrainians murdered 12 Jewish children who were hiding in that village. Two daughters of Leib Grabov, a member of the Ratno Judenrat, were among those murdered children. A woman named Rachel Perlmutter, who hid with her husband in that village, took care of those children. By chance, Rachel Perlmutter was away from the place during the time of the murder of the children. She apparently went to search for bread. Thanks to that, she was saved. Her husband was also saved from that slaughter.

The winter of 1942/43 was particularly harsh, and the cold forest was difficult to bear. I went to one of the farmers whose farm bordered the forest, and asked him to permit me to enter his barn. The farmer refused. I went to the cottage of the forest guard, which was empty at that time. I went up to the attic. Everything was ruined and broken. There were no windows or doors. There was not even any fodder there. I had four gigantic loaves of bread with me, which I hid in the attic. As I was resting in the attic, I heard the footsteps of people approaching me. They spoke Yiddish amongst themselves. They were Reicha Kladnir of Ratno, Yankel Kladnir, and one other Jew whose name I do not know, who came from the village of Zamszeny in Volhynia. Yankel Kladnir was the only one who survived from the 30 Jews who were shot to death in the first aktion of Ratno in 1941, which took place immediately after the Germans entered the city. Immediately after the shooting, Yankel laid himself in the with corpses, Yankel waited until the Germans left the place. Then he left the pit and escaped to the forest. Thus did he pass through the war.

I hid for two days in the cottage of the forester. Groups of Ukrainian workers on their way to work passed by the cottage. One of them wanted to enter, but his friends warned him, "Do not enter, for demons live on top!" Thus did the workers pass by me. I was unable to remain there any longer, for death by freezing was awaiting me.

At night I walked two kilometers and arrived at the yard of a farmer who was an acquaintance. I recognized him and realized that this was a poor, unfortunate family, because four of their children died of typhus within one week. I knocked on the door and they let me in. I gave the farmer a few German marks that I had in my hand, and requested of him, "Allow me to stay in your attic for several days..." The farmer refused. He gave me a half a loaf of bread and a piece of bacon and said, "Come here in two weeks, and then I can take you in." I went away. I did not realize that my brother and his wife were hiding in that attic at that time.

I again wandered around aimlessly and searched for an opportunity to warm myself up with one farmer, but the farmer did not even let me enter and camp out in an empty house at the edge of the pond. I reached the pond that was next to the village where all of the Jews and gypsies had been murdered. I spent eight days in that abandoned house. My food was carrots and beets, and my bed was straw.

Eight days later, I returned to the farmer who was hiding my brother and his wife in Bordiatyn. The attic was empty and the farmer allowed me to enter. It was -35 degrees. The sound of cracking ice could be heard from the ponds and banks. I was happy to find a hiding place. I hid in that attic for two weeks. The farmer brought me a pot of soup with potatoes twice a day. I did not pay him for the food and he did not request payment. Since the cold was unbearable, I once went downstairs to his house to warm up by the oven. When I went from there, I left behind a mass of lice. His wife turned to me and said, "You have too many lice!..." I did not come down to the farmer's house again. I knew how to differentiate between the different types of lice on my body. There were hungry lice that stuck to the body strongly, and satiated lice that quickly fell off from the body when they found a warm place.

I was forced to leave the farmer's house after two weeks. I went to a different village and went to the barn through a hole in the pigpen. During the day I would lie in the fodder, and at night I would sneak into the pigpen, where the sheep and cows live. I slept under the feeding trough in the pen, for that was the warmest spot. One day, an adult Ukrainian woman noticed me in the pen. When she saw me she shouted, "Yankel, are you still alive? It is better for you to go to Ratno, for they are not murdering there anymore" I answered her, "It is better for me to hang myself than to return there... I will leave here and hope that I do not freeze from the cold." Nevertheless, I did not leave there that day or on the coming days. The woman gave me bread and warm milk. She came in the evening and brought me my food along with the food for the cows. I hid there for one month.

Then I went to a different farmer in Mezritsh. I knew that he was a fine person, but nevertheless, he did not allow me to enter. He gave me bread and claimed that the police come by often. I left and went to a different farmer in Moszko. Without asking for permission, I sneaked into the attic, and lay in the fodder for a week. The farmer did not notice me even though he came each day to fetch fodder for the cows. Only after a week did he notice me in a corner of the barn. When he saw me, he began to shout, "Do you want them to kill us all here? You know that various people come to me from Lelikow, where the worst murderers live. Get out of here!" I answered him, "You know that my brother and brother-in-law remain alive. Know that if you turn me over to the murderers, they will burn everything!" The farmer brought me bread and sausage, and calmly requested that I leave. Having no other choice, I returned to the farmer in Bordiatyn who knew my brother well. The farmer took me into the attic. I spent another month there. He did not ask for any payment from me. He provided me with food for free. I do not recall the name of the farmer...

The First Encounter with Russian Partisans

Winter was ending, and the spring of 1943 was approaching. I often heard from the farmers that there were partisans in the forests. When I went out of the barn after a month, I encountered two Jews in the forest from the village of Siderowysze. We went into the depths of the forest together to search for partisans.

After a few days, we met five men in the forest with weapons in their hands. We approached them. They were Russian partisans. They realized that we were Jews who were hiding in the forest. They read to us a booklet that they had received from Moscow in which it was written that the situation of the Russians on the front was good, and they were advancing. We requested that they take us into their group. They refused because we did not have any weapons.

We continued to wander in the forests. A few days later we encountered a group of Jews from Kamien Koszyrski who were hiding in the forest. Kamien Koszyrski is a city in the district of Pulsia, 25 kilometers from Ratno. Approximately 50 people were hiding there. This was a wild place. The forests were thick and impassable. No human foot had trodden there.

We joined this group. The conditions were very severe. The people were dirty and frozen, and they did not have anything to eat. Someone died from typhus every day. Various groups of partisans passed through who would rape the women, but would refuse to take anyone into the ranks of the partisans. Having no choice, we remained with this group for only two weeks.

We Join the Ranks of Russian Partisans

At the end of two weeks, I realized that there were partisans camped in the village of Mawyr. We set out to that village.

The brothers Shalom and Anshel Zricki of Siderowysze joined me. We quickly found the group of Russian partisans, but they refused to take us. We did not have weapons, and they did not need us.

At the last minute, one of the partisans turned to us and asked if any of us knew the way to Brisk on the Bug River, through the passage in the forest that leads to the town of Maloryta. (That town had a railway station, and is located between the city of Brisk on the Bug River and Ratno. Many Jews lived there at the outbreak of the war. Maloryta was nicknamed "The Jewish village.") I answered that I knew the area very well, and was able to guide the group to Brisk. I was immediately accepted into the group of partisans. My two friends, the Zricki brothers, were not accepted. (They survived the war and live in the United States.)

The group of partisans to which I was accepted consisted of 25 Russian men. We set out immediately to go in the direction that I showed them. Along the way, I was given a heavy sack that must have weighed 15-20 kilograms. I did not know what was in the sack. We walked through the forest without resting for two days. We arrived at the place where the railway tracks between Brisk and Maloryta were located. There, I heard the explosion of weapons for the first time, and saw the crushed railway tracks. The sack that I was carrying carried gunpowder that my friend and I placed under the railway tracks.

We continued to advance through the forest. We would turn to farmers' houses at night and take the best food and clothes for ourselves. Along the way to Brisk, we constantly blew up any railway tracks that we came across. We also met other groups of partisans in the forests.

We advanced toward Brisk on the Bug River. We first ran into Germans near the village of Kowriniec. The Germans surrounded the town at the time we were approaching it through the forest.

We began to escape. As we were escaping, I saw a sack under a tree. I picked it up and continued to run. We arrived in the village in which our commander Nikolai Komianov was stationed. When we arrived, our commander lined us up in order to check if any of us was missing. One of the partisans pointed to me and said that I had lost a sack with a mine. Then I showed Komianov two sacks, mine and the one I had found. Komianov approached the partisan, removed his weapons and gave them to me.

It was the spring of 1943. Along with the group, we entered into our camp that was located in Maniewicze near Kowel. We received mines that we were to use to bombard the railway lines. There I was placed before my commander, and there I was officially accepted into the ranks of the partisans.

There were 200 people in the camp at Maniewicze. The forests there were very deep. There was a bathhouse, a well and a kitchen there, and there was a medical service. The partisans also had their own flock of cattle. The commander of these partisans was General Feodorov.

The Killing of a Ukrainian for Collaborating with the Germans

One day, at the table in the Maniewicze Camp, one of those present asked me, "Yaakov, are you also here?" It seemed that he was a Ukrainian, one of my close acquaintances. His name was Johan Onishechuk, and he was a Communist. His mother and brother were killed by German collaborators. In that partisan group, there were many Ukrainians who fought with Germans. Onishechuk came from the village of Jakosza, and his nickname was Sokolov. This Sokolov was a very talented lad, and I went out with him for my first partisan roles.

My first activity was to blow up railway lines and to lay traps for Ukrainians who collaborated with the Germans and Benderovchiks. Once I went with

Sokolov to the village of Jakosza in order to carry out an attack. I ran into a Ukrainian who was the brother-in-law of Danialovich, the police chief of Ratno and German collaborator. Knowing the character of this Ukrainian, Sokolov and I searched him and stood him next to a wall. I shot and killed him with my own hands. This was toward evening, and it was still light outside. This was the first time in my life that I killed a person. Later, I could not sleep for several weeks.

At that time, Russian airplanes landed near Pinsk and brought us weapons. They landed on frozen ponds, for the area was full of bogs.

We were twelve partisans, including Sokolov. From the village of Jakosza we arrived at the courtyard of a farmer whose farm was near the village of Zyczycz. A farmer named Waweram lived in a cottage in the yard. At one time, he had hidden Sumak Papir in exchange for 1,000 dollars, and later cast Sumak into the outside and killed him. When he noticed me, he called several other farmers from the village and all together they chased me for several days.

We surrounded Waweram's cottage. It was toward evening. Later we set the buildings on fire. Since there was a great deal of hay in the area, the fire spread within a few moments. When all of the buildings were engulfed in flames, we began to shoot at the cottage, so that nobody could be saved therein. Waweram's entire family was burnt alive. From there we returned to our camp for rest, which lasted several days. Then I realized that there were also Jews among the partisans.

The Killing of Three Benderovchiks and the Anti-Semitic Reaction of a Russian Partisan

After a few days, we were ordered to go through the forests to Kowel and to plant mines under the railway tracks along the way. One day, we met three Benderovchiks who were hiding in the depths of the forest. We caught them. Our commander issued the command" "Kill all three of them!" Then he asked, "Who wants to shoot?" I offered myself, and I immediately opened fire. When their bodies were already lying on the ground, one of the partisans cast his glare at me and uttered in anger, "Jew boy, a son of a bitch such as you!..."

I did not answer him immediately, but after some time, at an appropriate chance, I reacted appropriately to his anti-Semitic outburst. I then tried to distance myself as far as possible from this anti-Semite.

We returned to our camp at Maniewicze after carrying out al of our assignments, and remained in the camp for an entire week. After a week, a command came from Moscow to choose 25 men from our group who will cross the Bug with other partisan groups and penetrate the forests of Lublin. I was among the 25, as was the anti-Semite of our group. I turned to our commander and told him that I cannot work in this group, and told him the reason. The commander removed the anti-Semitic partisan from the group. I thanked him for this.

We set out in the direction of the Bug River, carrying with us our automatic weapons, grenades, and all other necessary equipment. Our principal task was intelligence operations and blowing up railway lines.

(Here it is worthwhile to mention that after one of the operations, General Feodorov told me, "You will receive the highest Russian decoration of excellence!"...)

Crossing the Bug River. Conquering a Village Near Chelm Lubelski and its Reconquest by the Germans

The spring of 1943 was in full force. We marched day and night in the direction of the Bug River. There were 200 people in our group. Our group was composed of various partisan groups who united, and included many Jews from Poland and Russia. Along the way we ran into other partisan groups, mainly Russian. We crossed the Bug together. We advanced very quickly, without looking backward and without stopping. We also had with us many horses that served us in a most exemplary manner.

We reached the banks of the Bug at evening. The ice had not yet melted, and big chunks floated in the river. We crossed the river at night, transferring the weapons and all of our belongings on the other side. Many horses drowned as we crossed the river, but we had no other means.

That night, we arrived at the forests in the region of Chelm Lubelski. We conquered one of the villages, and did not meet even one German. We spent the entire next day in the village, and toward evening, we saw German airplanes. I slept, and during my sleep I felt the walls moving and shaking, with the mortar crumbling. I woke up and mounted a horse. We immediately heard a command to set out in the direction of Bilgoraj. We succeeded in leaving the village without any losses. We had intended to rest in that village for several days.

The Burning of German Automobiles, The Killing of Several Germans, and Approaching the Forests of Bilgoraj

We again marched forward. We walked on foot or rode on horses all night, through fields and forests, until we came to the main road leading to Lublin. There we stopped. On the road, heavy German trucks passed endlessly. We stormed the convoy of vehicles. We burned approximately 25 vehicles, and killed a similar number of Germans. Someone from our group saw two Germans escaping to the barn. He pursued them and killed them on the spot. After we crossed the road, we again escaped into the forest. The forest was small and meager. I left the horse along the way, for it was weak and could not continue along the route. The Germans figured out where we were and began to shoot at us from airplanes. To our good fortune, only one of us was injured lightly in the foot. We hid in that forest all day, and set out in the direction of Bilgoraj in the evening.

*

-- -- -- We returned to our gathering place in the forest from the banks of the Weiprz River. We received an order to travel to a different gathering place in Zamosc. At that time, Zamosc was a liberated city, and a Russian command operated there. We were a total of 300 people coming from the forest. Some of them volunteered for the regular Russian Army in order to continue the fight against the Germans and the rest of them, about 200 people including myself, received a command to return to the city of Luck, which was also liberated at that time.

We returned to Luck by train. There we found out that we had to travel to Kobrin. Since Ratno is situated on the way to Kobrin, I asked the commander if he would permit me to travel to a closer place and to go to my home. Another Russian partisan, Nikolai Komienov, asked the same thing. He wanted to go to the village of Wydranica, five kilometers from Ratno. We received a permit of passage and set out together in army vehicles and other available vehicles. We were wearing American shirts, and I also had my personal arms: a revolver, grenades, and an automatic gun.

In Ratno I met several Jews who survived the war. I recall that one of them was Avraham Berg who today lives in America, as well as Pearl (nee Vernik today Karsh) who was married to Shapira and spent the war in the forests. I also met several other Jews who came from Ratno, but I do not recall their names.

I remained in Ratno for one day. The city was gray and gloomy. I discovered that our house was completely demolished. Only one tree remained, that was planted by my brother Rafael before he left the city. I found out there that my brother David was killed in the forests by shots from the Germans. From Ratno I went to Brisk, and then, according to the command, to Kobrin.

(In the continuation of the testimony, Yaakov Grabov describes his activities in various partisan units in the forests of Bilgoraj, Janow Lubelski, Zaklikow, Rozwadow, Torodowoka, Zwierzyniec and various other places until the partisan units joined the army units. We are glossing over his activities in these places due to a shortage of space, and concluded with a section that describes his return to Ratno.)

Translator's Footnote

1. It was called Osipenko between 1939-1958. It is now called Berdyansk. https://www.jewishgen.org/Yizkor/Ratno/rat187.html - f1r

One Day in Ratno

by Sh. Perlmutter

Translated by Jerrold Landau

August 27, 1945

7:30

I am in Ratno, my native city!

Three years ago yesterday, on August 26, the despicable slaughter of the Jews took place here. My mother and grandfather were included. I was sitting at the entrance to the "Goriasfulkum" (city hall during the Soviet era) of Ratno. It was early, and the officials had not yet arrived at work. The "Gorozbik" (transport trucks with an open crate) in which I had arrived stopped by the Marsyk House, and I got off. Another traveler who was sitting inside the vehicle also got off. From his dress, he looked like a government or party official. He asked me what I was doing there, and offered to help me. I told him that I was a Ratno native who was now living in Moscow, and I had come here to collect material on the cruel actions of the Nazis. He asked me to accompany him. Now I am sitting in the entrance, waiting for him. He entered one of the rooms and asked me to wait. As I am waiting, I have taken out my diary, and I am writing (in the new notebook):

At 5:45 I was already

at the Kowel "Goriasfulkum", and I set out on my journey at 6:00. I sat for the entire time on the open crate that served as a seat. The cold wind was pounding me in the face. I was watching the familiar landscapes of the journey. The road was full of pits until the village of Buchi, and I was afraid that I might be thrown outside. We were alone on the car, and only one army vehicle passed before us. We stopped for several minutes in the village of Zamshany, and the driver gave a package to a youth who was waiting next to the town hall. We continued through Wydranica, and passed through the sand hills and pine groves. Nothing had changed...

8:40

Am I really here?

I am sitting in the shade of the old pine tree next to the "Yentl" bridge. The road is quiet, and there is no movement. My heart is overcome with the strong memories that are sweeping through me.

The man who had offered to help me was the second secretary of the party. He invited me into his office and offered me tea. He spoke to me about the development of Ratno and even asked if I intended to return there. I thanked him and asked him if he could help me with a return connection to Kowel. What luck! He himself was returning there and was prepared to take me on the condition that I would be there at 16:30. I thanked him again and set out by foot in the direction of the home of Michalko Chawowich.

I passed by the ruins of Droog's house, and the houses of Vernik and Klein, the Onisko Infirmary, the public school that served as the prison for the final Ratno survivors before they were taken out to be murdered, and the ruins of the house of the Steinbergs into which all of the Jews of the city were concentrated when the Germans entered. The first 30 martyrs of Ratno were selected from among them, including Leibel Steingarten and my cousin Yosef Perlmutter -- -- -- The "Yentl" Bridge was there. I used to play on that bridge with my friends and swim beneath it. My mother, my grandfather, and all of my townsfolk crossed it on their final journey to Prochod. I escaped over that bridge when I fled from the Germans. Here was the house of "small" Andreiko Pinkowich, in which I found refuge... Here are the bathhouses of Syuma and Kolya Lenertowich. Here is the house and barn of

Golobowjow, where I hid for many days...

And here are the straw roofs of the houses of Polkowa. Nothing changed there. Everything was standing. Everything, everything -- only the Jews are not there. Soon I would surprise my good Michalko. This time I would come to visit my friend in broad daylight, not like when I would come to find a hiding place and get bread in the middle of the night...

10:00

Michalko and his family did not wait for my visit, even though I hinted to it in one of my letters.[1] We wept from joy. He greeted me like a member of the family. I gave them the presents that Klara had bought for them, including a pipe for Michalko himself. He looked happy. His wife covered the large wooden table with homemade cheeses and cream, and I ate with them. Michalko spoke about those nights when I would come to him with my young brother Motele, and how his heart was broken when he saw us. He always, always opened the door for us. He even reminded me of the scene that his wife put on for us when she accused Michalko of endangering the entire family. (At that time, he had with him two Soviet prisoners aside from us) -- how he slapped her over the face and quieted her...

How brave and generous a man was Michalko?! He did not forget even to mention the good deed that I did for him when he fell into difficulties immediately after the war, and when his neighbors, of his own people, accused him before the government and requested his death. I cleared his name with the help of Elia Ehrenberg.

Now they were all going out to their work in the yard and the field. Michalko himself also begged my pardon for a brief period and entered the shed. I remained alone... and I am recording. Soon I will also go to Amalian Lenertowich.

Michalko knew a great deal about the final days of Ratno Jewry. Many of those who escaped found temporary refuge with him. He told me a great deal about the family of the pharmacist Mogilenski. According to him, he especially liked him. I record the following words from his mouth:

"When the Germans arrived to murder all of the Jews in Ratno in the summer of 1942,

Berka Mogilenski and his wife Gittel escaped to me and hid with me for 17 days. I must note that these were particularly difficult times. The Germans and the Ukrainian police searched in every place and turned over each stone -- while the Mogilenskis were sleeping in my barn. Somehow, this became known to my neighbor Onisko and his wife. Another person came in and said to me that he wants to ask Mogilenski's advice regarding a medication that his wife is receiving. I told him that Mogilenski was indeed with me, but I sent him away. At night I told this to Mogilenski, and he decided to complain, to go to Onisko, claiming that Onisko is his friend and some of his belongings are hidden with him. Indeed, the next day he went to him and remained with him for three days. His wife was with me during that time. When he returned to me, I placed him and his wife on my horse, and took them through the bogs and the forest to the home of one of his friends in the village of Samorowycze. After a few days, Onisko reported on me and my family, and the policeman Jochim from the village of Komarowo conducted a search of our barn and stalls. Mogilenski's son Janos[2] and his daughter-in-law Genia were also in Samorowycze. They had succeeded in escaping Ratno during the day of slaughter. After a few weeks, policemen arrived in the village from the town of Diwyn in order to murder the Jews of the village. His daughter and daughter-in-law escaped, but Berka was shot as he was escaping and fell next to the pond. His wife Gittel ran after him and drowned in the pond. His son Janos and his daughter-in-law were also captured in the winter of 1942 and brought to Ratno. When I found out about this, I bribed the policeman who brought them, and he gave them over to my hands. At that time, several professional Jews worked in the 'Ortel' factory. Janos stayed with me and then moved to Frunyushkin He had no desire to live. They gave themselves over to the Germans and were shot at the 'Cheplik' house."

Text footnote

I met Janos and his wife during the time that I was in Ratno. The following is written in my entries from that period: When I met Janos when he was with Frunyushkin the veterinarian, he was working in his barn. First he was with

Michalko Chawowich. He asked me, “What should I do?” This was not the Janos that I knew, but rather another person, broken and without faith. I told him that he must prepare arms and escape. He smiled at me and said, “We are the living dead.

So why would we need arms?...” The Germans arrested Janos and his wife on January 15, 1943 and imprisoned them in the school building. I found out that before they took Janos out to be killed, he sang Hebrew and Russian songs all night. The next day when they took him to Cheplik, he smiled to the passersby. That day, they shot 15 Jews of Ratno.

I am with Oleksei Pinkowich, the son-in-law of Amalian Lenertowich. Michalko brought me there in his wagon. Oleksei and his wife received me warmly, putting themselves into no small amount of danger, when I escaped from the German work camp in Bitnia in the beginning of September 1942. I remained for a day or two with them. In those days, two days were like two years, if not more. I remained at Michalko's side and we traveled slowly. His gray horse dragged the wagon with difficulty. Michalko hurried it on from time to time. When I pointed out to him that the horse appeared weak and was dragging the wagon with two people with difficulty, he told me that were it not for the feelings he had toward it, he would have “freed himself” from it some time ago. “It passed through the entire war with us, so how can I be ungrateful to it?” We passed by all the houses of the residents of Polkowa. They had not changed at all since I last saw them. Here was the house of Michalko's brother. In contrast to his brother, he behaved cruelly toward my younger brother and me, and sent us away in broad daylight when he found us hiding in his barn without permission. When I asked him, he answered, “Don't remind me of this evil beast, there is no connection between us.”

The house of the Polish forester Jankowski stood at the edge of the road. I had taken ill with typhus there. We went to the main street and passed by the house of Zelik the wagon-driver, who had been beaten to death by the policeman Ivan Lukianuk for being found without the yellow patch on his coat. Someone else was living there, as was obvious from the laundry drying on the clothesline in the yard. Michalko turned the wagon toward the “Malczes” hill, where we used to bathe in the river during the summer, and which was the name of the road. At the house of Olka's son, we turned right to pass the “Roskes” pasture.

I asked Michalko to stop next to Olka's house. I entered the yard and Michalko waited for me. I overcame the dog that had attempted to attack me and presented myself before the old woman, who did not recognize me. "Are you Oleksei?", she said as she crossed herself. "Come, sit down and drink something." She immediately began to tell me that her son Sasha had told her about my nighttime visits to him during the time of the Nazi occupation.

"You know that my daughter was almost killed because of your brother?"

"How?", I asked

She called her daughter from the barn, and told me how my brother Sheikele was shot.

"I was pasturing the cows in Roskes. Suddenly I heard shots, and bullets were flying over my head. I lay on the ground. I noticed a child running toward me. Suddenly, another shot was heard, and the child fell near me. I saw the policemen coming. I fled, for I was afraid." -- -- -- "He fell near me, about as far away as from here to the barn. I heard him calling, "Mother, Mother." Later it was said that this was the son of the Olczyks."

This eyewitness report of the death of my brother Sheikele almost overcame me as she told me the story. I immediately thanked her mother and her, and ran quickly to the wagon that was waiting for me. I left them confused and perplexed. I begged Michalko's pardon and told him that I had just heard a testimony about the death of my brother Sheikele when he was being brought to Cheplik. Michalko was thinking and did not speak. He brought his horse to the Roskes pasture. Across from the areas of the bogs and water, one could see the lone houses of Prochod standing out in the dim image background of the forest. There, on the Roskes, flourished the loves of the youths of Ratno who are no more. Michalko took me to a place near the house of the Pinkowiches and parted from me. He asked to see me again, and we spoke of meeting before I would travel to the house of Brener.

The Pinkowich's house had barely changed. Only the roof was covered with wooden shingles rather than bales of hay, and the shutters were colored gray and black. The garden was destroyed and several bean sprouts were growing over the gate. Old fishing nets were drying or resting on the embankment that surrounded the house. I knocked on the door and a woman who I did not know opened it. I asked about Oleksei and she answered that he had taken his wife to the doctor. She invited me to enter and asked me to wait for him for a bit. The house of the Pinkowiches was considered to be modern, and stood out with its innovations over the rest of the houses of the Ukrainians in Ratno.

From both the exterior and the interior, it resembled more the former houses of the Jews rather than the local Ukrainians. There was a covered, painted porch at the entrance, and there was a wood floor in all the rooms. It was not a large room with an oven, but rather three spacious, nice rooms. There were wooden doors, shutters, and electricity (from the time of the war, there was no electricity, and they used kerosene lamps.) I sat next to the table in the large room. I took out my notebook and began to write my updates. The surrounding village was calm, even though it was close to noon. If the Pinkowiches do not arrive soon, I would go to visit the Cheplik area, where hundreds of my townsfolk were murdered. Then I would go to the old cemetery, where my brother Motele is buried.

13:35

Oleksei and his wife finally arrived. They had not anticipated this surprise of finding me in their home. They hugged and kissed me. “We heard about you that you are a 'shishka' in Moscow”, joked Oleksei, as he invited me to join them for lunch. His wife did not feel well, and went to lie down. The woman who was in their home, apparently their maid, spread a peasant's tablecloth on the table and served cooked fish and potatoes, garnished with cream. Oleksei told me that his wife was pregnant, and apparently there was no doctor in the city. We also spoke about Nazi collaborators who were still living in Ratno and going about freely, whereas his brother-in-law Fedya had been imprisoned. He complained that the Jewish survivors of Ratno were not returning to the city, and thereby they were completing the “wiping out” of the Jews. I retorted that the number of survivors was small, and they did not have the strength to live in the cemetery of their families. He mentioned to me the names of all of the Jews who survived and who had visited Ratno: Moshe Chaim Fuchs, Chaicha and Hirsch Leib Janowicz, Fruma Bergel, Pearl Shapira, Dvora and Avraham Berg, Eliahu and Itzka

Blubsztejn, Magolczia Szpetel, Reicha and Yankel Kladnir, Yankel Grabov, and the Steingarten family. Oleksei offered to take me to the old cemetery at the other edge of the city. He went out to hitch his horse and I waited for him to return. His wife was sleeping for the entire time.

15:30

Once again I am at the entrance to the "Riasfulkum", leaning on the fence. There was still one hour left until the journey, and Michalko had not arrived. Many things were going through my head. -- -- --

Like Oleksei Pinkowich, Michalko had many stories about the last days of Jewish Ratno. It was unfortunate that I could not remain there for more time in order to record his words. He was a witness to the murder of my brother Sheikele, Tzalik Mogilenski and Yehudale Reiskes. He gave over his testimony to me when I had visited Ratno last year. Now he told me about the final journey of the Klein family, who were among the owners of the flour mill. "The entire family hid in a hidden cellar and were found several weeks after all the Jews of Ratno were murdered. When they were brought out to Olianka Street across from Cheplik, I was by chance traveling with my wagon behind them, and Motel shouted to me, "Oleksei, you should know that Unis Zhuk and Petru Mechnik slandered us. We are going to our deaths because of them. Later I found out that the veterinarian Frunyushkin was the one who was truly guilty for their deaths, for he went to search in the home of the Kleins and revealed their hiding place to the police. I followed the Kleins to Cheplik and was a witness to their murder. They ordered them to strip, and one of the daughters rebelled, refused to strip, slapped the police, and wreaked havoc until they shot her." Oleksei traveled through the Roskes and pointed out the nearby Cheplik valley of murder, the trench in which they were shot. Grass grew everywhere. I descended from the wagon for a moment and stood in silence. Oleksei also descended and stood in silence beside me. Then we traveled the length of Olianka Street, and passed the house of Avraham Gleizer the smith. This was the only house that remained in the row of houses on the right side of the bridge. Even behind the bridge there were no houses until the corner of the market. One the wall of the public bank that remained standing, there was a placard in white Hebrew letters, "Woe to the people whose leaders protect the murderers" -- a remnant from the battle of the Jews from the era of the murder of Arlosoroff[3]. The placard remains but the Jews are no more.

We passed through the area that had once been the market square -- it now has white mounds and remnants of trees. From the well, I was able to recognize the place where our house had stood. -- -- -- Oleksei stopped for a moment and pointed out, "Here was your house." Tears choked my throat. The only house that remained intact in the market square was that of Itzel Grabov. The sign of the "Reipotrosioz" (regional cooperative shop) was above his closed shop. Pearl Shapira (Vernik) worked there during the time of our visit last year. I could not understand then how she could continue to remain in the city of ghosts. Her husband Itzika, with whom she had endured all the tribulations of the war, enlisted in the Red Army. I received letters from her for a period of time. Now she has left Ratno and stopped writing. Oleksei drove me to the house of Tyktyner on the highway. From there I went on foot to the old cemetery. Along the way, I passed the Polish cemetery, and stopped for a moment at the graves of Yosel Zikner and Meir Palit, two Jewish prisoners of war who were shot along with 30 Russian prisoners on the day that the Germans entered Ratno. There was no marker on the communal grave -- only grass and thorns. From there I set out to the old Jewish cemetery. I found the grave of my brother Motel. The antitank barrier that I had rolled atop the grave last year had sunk. I spread out over the grave. I hid my head in the grass and sighed. I had the strange desire to open the grave and see Motele, to hug and kiss him... When I stood up I could not move my feet... I walked slowly backward, and forced myself to move -- -- the hour was late. Michalko had not yet arrived. These are the last words that I am writing in Ratno.

Translator's Footnotes

1. The way it is worded does not seem to make sense. Perhaps he intended to say "could hardly wait for my visit, since I hinted to it.." However this does not match the translation. https://www.jewishgen.org/Yizkor/Ratno/rat187.html - f1ar

2. There is a footnote in the text here, describing Janos. See at the end of this paragraph. https://www.jewishgen.org/Yizkor/Ratno/rat187.html - f2ar

3. See http://en.wikipedia.org/wiki/Haim_Arlosoroff https://www.jewishgen.org/Yizkor/Ratno/rat187.html - f3ar

With the Covering of the Grave

by Simcha Lavie (Leker)

Translated by Jerrold Landau

Four letters flashed through my mind today
And I was effortlessly transferred to a different world,
Far far off and very near,
A world that caused all of my 248 limbs to tremble and that evoked aromas and sights
Landscapes and personalities, which I had only seen in a dream of night, and during my childhood
In those days, before the world was ignited with the flames of Satan.

The four letters Reish Tet Nun He (Ratno) stand themselves as living in the eyes of my spirit
They shone and flashed with al the colors of the rainbow.
On their wings I returned to you, Ratno my town,
And I again breathe your scents and your realities:
Dipping in the waters of the Pripyat, walking along Holenki Street,
Feasting my eyes on the flowerbeds of many species
Meadows and marshes, windmills and spiritual occupations
Tottering houses, fruit withering after the autumn,
Haberdashery shops and women chatting on their thresholds,
Waiting for a customer to come, as in the son of Leissin,

The entire world of childhood -
unfolds before my eyes.

Now, I am again standing among
the Karlin Hassidim
In the Stolin Shtibel of my father Reb
Asher
And with my grandfather Reb Shlomo
Aharon, may their light shine and be
bright
Enwrapped in their tallises and
wearing their ceremonial belt as was
their custom,
Their image spreads from the physical
world to the supernal world
Engaging the Heavens with sublime
ecstasy, on the wings
Of the Karlin melody of "Yah
Echsof" [1], which was like a hymn
Of the Hassidim of Karlin from the
time of Reb Aharon the Great

And suddenly, the four letters
Of your name, Ratno my town, took
on different hues,
They changed their colors, and
brought me to other places.
In the afternoon, I was sitting in
Chevrat Shas, bent over a book
of Mishnayos,
Listening to the lesson and shaking in
the manner of all straightforward
Jews,
Swallowing every statement and every
innovation of the scholar, and
answering every question
Like one of these simple folk, who did
not delve into the sea of Talmud,

But who nevertheless has chapters of
Psalms upon their lips, and they
sufficed themselves with such,
And it was good for them with such.
Blessed be you who come, righteous
women, It has been ages since I have
seen you,
And again you are running to bring
ice to a seriously ill person, to bring
salvation
To a woman who is having difficulty in
childbirth, to ensure that an orphan
bride be brought to the wedding
canopy
As your day is laden with mitzvos and
good deeds as in days of yore.

Good morning, Reb Zelig the
teacher, and good morning to all the
teachers
Who did not spare the rod with me,
but who with dedication made sure I
went over the weekly Torah portion,
You taught Pirke Avot. Following after
you were enlightened teachers
With Noach Kotzker at the head, and
all the activists of Tarbut, paying
tribute
To one of your students, who adopted
their doctrine with seriousness, and
with effectiveness.
Behold, a large song ascends from
Krojna Street, the Hassidim of Turisk
And the Hassidim of Stepan, the
people of the Beis Midrash, with silk
cloaks
And woolen belts, among them are the
youths of the youth movements and
members of the parties

Of the various factions, their arms at
their sides, and their eyes fiery bright,
They are dancing together as
on Simchat Torah or as on the day
that the entourage
Of Rabbi Elimelech of Zabolotya
arrives in Ratno. L-rd God! How great
is the entourage,
How tremendous are the scenes, how
sublime is the devotion!
Without division between factions,
there are no differences of opinion,
and all excuses are ended.
Brotherhood has ignited among the
Jewish people, all screens and fences
have been removed, and all
Are one large community, everyone is
a brother to each other, bound and
stuck together.

Again the colors of your letters,
Ratno my town, have changed, and I
see

All of them at the edge of Prochod,
the heap of annihilation. Now I know:
They are being hauled to slaughter!
Trembling overtakes me, yes - to
slaughter, the units of shooters are
standing ready.
I raise my eyes upward and to the
sides, I am searching for mercy, the
good and beneficent G-d,
The wings of the Divine Presence, my
righteous and merciful Father who
will peer down from the clouds,
Who will gather under His wings His
Jews, all who are near and dear to me

as well as to Him,
The flock that He tends, the Hassidim and reciters of
Psalms, parnassim [administrators] and gabbaim [trustees],
All the clergy, the children and the "Holy Flock" -- --
I did not see Him. Specifically at such a moment He is not there.
Where are You, Master of the World - all 248 limbs and 365 sinews [2] are shouting out,
Look, Your Jews, the Jews of Ratno, are hauled like sheep to slaughter,
Look at the prepared pits, look at the units of shooters,
See their faces, examine their conscience and hearts,
Turn Your ear to their prayers and confession, save, have mercy Father of mercy,
Extend Your hand, Oh G-d, please save!

Ratno. The letters exchange colors,
And I remain alone. All of them were swallowed by the pits, and I was saved,
And am standing before You, I Simcha the son of Reb Asher, am
reciting Kaddish in their memory,
Yes, "Magnified and Sanctified may be the Great Name," I call out, I do not protest,
I only ask: In what merit was I saved?
How am I better than they?
Am I better than my father and mother from whose wellspring I drew and from whose tradition I was fed?

I try to resolve the riddle - but it is
beyond my power.
Mighty G-d! Please enlighten Your
servant with the explanation of the
double riddle:
Why did I remain, and where were
You
On the 13 of Elul, 5702 (1942)
When the grave of the Jews of my
town of Ratno was covered over?

Translator's Footnotes

1. See (and listen to) http://www.youtube.com/watch?v=oeNIz96mTfo https://www.jewishgen.org/Yizkor/Ratno/rat187.html - f199-1r
2. A traditional description of all the parts of the body. https://www.jewishgen.org/Yizkor/Ratno/rat187.html - f199-2r

Memories of the Holocaust

by Pearl Karsh

Translated by Jerrold Landau

1939 – The Poles had left the town. For two weeks, it was left without a government, at the mercy of the Ukrainian murderers. They robbed and pillaged anything that came their way, and perpetrated pogroms. It is hard to describe how two weeks could be so long, seemingly endless. The Red Army took control over the Jewish property and nationalized our large businesses in the city, such as the building materials shop, the soda factory, the general store, the wholesale liquor store, and the agricultural machines business. All of these passed to the government, leaving us without any livelihood. Furthermore, the right to work was taken from us. Our identity certificates were replaced with certificates stamped with the letter J. From that time, we no longer had rights of citizenship. The government produced lists of candidates for deportation to forced labor camps in Siberia. Due to my fluency in Russian, I received a work permit and directed a government sick fund with several branches. Thus, I was able to help my family and my husband's family.

The situation was easier for my parents, because my two brothers were able to work and somehow arrange themselves with the new government. Since we were not among the wealthy, the government did not pay that much attention to us, and we were able to obtain work permits. My older brother worked as a carpenter and my younger brother was engaged in commerce.

Life continued in that manner until 1941, and I raised two children: one was mine and the other as my sister Batya's.

On July 6, 1941, after the German-Soviet war broke out, two brigades of Nazis entered our town along with a commander, an S.S. unit, and the Gestapo.

The Ukrainians, who were in the town and were occupied with plunder and pillage, met the Nazis with shots. The reaction of the Nazis was not long in coming, but it was directed against the Jews.

The next day, all of the Jews were called to leave their houses. They arranged us in lines, and then chose thirty young people to be taken to be murdered. A deep pall of mourning fell over the city, and the fear of what was awaiting us under the Nazi boot increased.

The first demand of the Nazi command was to organize a Jewish community so that they would have a reliable address to present all of their demands.

The first demand was that all Jews must wear a yellow patch on their chest and their backs. The affixing of these patches further oppressed and degraded us. We suspected that "the earth was burning under our feet," but who would dare not obey? The community organized itself with several good and trustworthy people to help, who carried out their work with dedication. The head of the community was my father-in-law Reb David-Aharon Shapira. Yitzchak Grabov, his son Leibel Grabov, Yitzchak Karsh and others worked alongside of him.

The Nazis ordered the community to provide them with clothing, furs, gold, and furniture. The Judenrat acted to the best of their ability to respond to the demands of the Nazis, if only the Jews would not be swallowed up.

First of all, the chairman gave over everything that he had, and he received the rest from the Jews in the town, who responded and gave over everything that was imposed upon them. We had hoped that thereby we would exempt ourselves from being sent to forced labor, from which, as we knew at that time, nobody returns. However, the turn for this decree also arrived.

The Germans began to demand people for work. Members of the committee organized the shipment of people in such a way that, at first, children of three-child families were sent, then children from two-child families, and only at the end would children of single-child families be sent. At first, only bachelors were sent, but in the next phase, as the demands increased, the decree also fell upon people with families. This decree caused a commotion in the city. Members of the communal council said that they would go to jail as guarantors, but they would refuse to send married men to forced labor.

My brother, Shlomo, was among the lads sent to forced labor. He was sent along with other men from the town to Zabolottya, where they worked day and night in a large carpentry shop manufacturing furniture that was sent to Germany.

When the turn of my brother, Aharon of blessed memory, came to go to forced labor, my father, of blessed memory, volunteered to go in his place. He was sent to work in Kovel. After two months of backbreaking work, an aktion of 2,000 people began in Kovel. Father succeeded in escaping and wanted to return to Ratno. Along the route to Ratno, some Ukrainians warned him that a return to Ratno would be fraught with mortal danger. However, Father held his own. He had to see the family, and he continued on the journey – as became clear later: on his journey toward death.

Finally, the heads of the community were forced to give themselves over as guarantors, and they were sent to prison. (Yitzchak Grabov, Yiitzchak Mrasiuk, Shaul Gafman, Yosef Kamfer, Meir Toker, and two named Sofer). However the Nazis left the head of the community, Shapira, in the town for the time being, since one of the Ukrainians interceded on his behalf, despite the fact that he himself urged them to take him as well, and even informed them that he would no longer send innocent Jews to their deaths.

The townsfolk, confounded by the terrible decrees that fell upon their heads, pleaded that the imprisoned guarantors be freed. After much pleading and intercession, they succeeded in obtaining freedom from prison for the heads of the community. One of them, Toker, could not withstand the prison, and died.

On the 1st of Tammuz, 5702 (1942), the partisans conducted a revenge operation against the Nazis and killed two captains of the gendarmes. The Jews of the town were worried about the reaction of the Germans, and fled to nearby villages, forests, or to the houses of Ukrainians whom they knew and trusted.

After a few days, when the Jews found out that no revenge operations against the partisan operation were taking place, many returned to their homes. That evening, my father of blessed memory arrived in Ratno, after he had escaped, as has been mentioned, from the action in Kovel. Our joy was indescribable, but it did not last. That night passed quietly. In the morning, my parents took their two grandchildren that were with them, left the house of Yaakov Shmuel Rider where they were staying, and returned to their home. That morning, Germans entered our home and demanded that my husband present his work certificate. When they saw our certificate indicated that we had one child, they asked where the child was. I answered that he was with his grandparents on Pilsudski Street. They said that the child was no longer alive, for he had been killed. When they saw that I fainted, they asked me if we had a place to hide. My husband led them to a room which had a closet, behind which was the opening to the cellar. A German urged us to hide in the cellar, and he himself placed the closet in its place in order to cover the opening, as we were in the cellar!

My husband and I sat in the hiding place and wept. We heard the shouts and weeping of Jews being dragged to their deaths, and we sat and wept, and wept. In the evening we heard my father-in-law and mother-in-law walking through the room, weeping for us, for they were sure that we had been taken along with all those hauled to their deaths. We began to knock on the ceiling of the cellar, which was the floor of the house, and they opened the opening to the cellar. I immediately ran to see what happened to my child and my entire family. When I arrived at my parents' house, I did not find anyone alive. The door was open, and on the stove there was still a pot of soup that my mother had prepared in honor of Father's return.

They went together and met their deaths in the single communal grave: Father, Mother, two grandchildren, and my beautiful 14-year-old youngest sister, Breindele.

I ran to the street as if overtaken by insanity, with the hope of finding them, until I arrived at the place called Rycz Sponczyk. This was a windmill, and all the 120 martyrs lay there in a large heap, for they still had not been buried.

Without knowing what I was doing, I began to search through the martyrs for my dead. I found my father holding one grandchild in his hands, my mother holding the second grandchild, and my sister Breindele between them.

I sat among them, looked at them, and was confounded.

Suddenly, a German who was apparently assigned to guard the place approached me and said, "Get out of here!" I was unable to answer, for my throat was choked. I took his hand and pointed, "Kill me here, this is my place, I am not leaving here!" He stood his own, "Get out of here!" I continued to sit. He gave me several blows, and I, like a stone, did not move from my place, until he lifted me up with force and chased me away. I went, and returned, and he once again chased me away and forcibly prevented me from returning to my beloved martyrs.

I returned home with nervous tension, sick, broken, and enveloped in deep depression. I refused to see anyone, and the following questions constantly went through my mind, "Why did this tragedy afflict me? What was my sin? Why has my entire family perished? How bitter is my lot?"

My brother, Shlomo, who worked at forced labor in Zabolottya, sensed that a disaster had struck in Ratno. The people who worked together with him in the work camp knew what had happened to our family, but hid it from him; however, his heart told him that he must hurry home. He requested from the Gestapo a permit to go to Ratno. He arrived during the days of Shiva [the seven day mourning period]. Many had gathered in the house for prayers for the elevation of the souls of the martyrs. When Shlomo saw those gathered and heard about the tragedy, he fainted. My younger brother Aharon would also faint when he recited Kaddish.

During those difficult moments, I was not only a sister to my brothers, but a mother and father. I encouraged their spirit, spoke to their hearts, and did everything that I could to protect them. It seemed that the tragedies both strengthened and weakened me.

In the meantime, the Gestapo began preparations for the aktion in Ratno. Opinions in the town were divided. There were those that said we should leave the city, go to the forests and hide. On the other hand, others felt that it was appropriate to remain and wait, for "perhaps G-d will have mercy", "until the storm passes." Others looked for hiding places in the town.

My brother-in-law Niska, who owned the soda factory, prepared a hiding place in the cellar, beneath the pile of ice that he used for his business. There, he stockpiled sufficient food provisions for the family, and he was certain that nobody would expose the hiding place. My brother-in-law advised me to come hide with his family, but I strongly refused. I felt that the end of Jewish Ratno was approaching.

My husband and I joined a group of Jews who went to one of the Ukrainians on Zabolottya Street. We entered the barn and hid in a high pile of fodder. There was a lad from Ratno, Ziska Marin, with us. The gentiles found us out and immediately told the Germans that Jews are hiding in the barn. The Germans entered, and first took Ziska Marin down. They asked him if there were other people in the barn. We heard him answer with self assurance, "No, there is nobody there." They believed him, did not continue to search, and left the place. Through his answer, Ziska saved our lives. After a few minutes we heard the sound of a shot: Ziska fell there. The Ukrainian who turned us in did not live long. He stepped on a mine that was hidden in his field, and thereby met his death.

We remained in the barn for some time, and then returned home.

About two days later, many units of German soldiers arrived in the town along with the Gestapo and S.S. soldiers. It was clear to me that our fate was sealed. I decided that I would not remain in Ratno. For what was left for us in the city? My only child would not return to me, and I would never be able to hug and kiss him. I would never see my dear parents again. I turned to my brother Aharon and urged him to leave the city with me. My brother refused. He hid with a Ukrainian neighbor, who promised to protect him. About a week later, the neighbor turned him in to the Germans, and they took him out to be killed.

I requested that my mother-in-law, whom I loved very much, join me, but she explained to me that she could not leave Ratno, for my father-in-law David Aharon, saw himself as responsible for the Jews of the town, and would not leave them as sheep without a shepherd. My husband attempted to convince me to hide with his brother Niska, but I did not agree.

I set out on my journey without knowing to where or to whom. I remembered that our former assistant, Matrona, lived in the village of Shmenky, near Ratno. In the past, I had helped her and her family, and I hoped that I would be able to find a hiding place from the Germans in her home. I did not know where exactly she lived, and it was very dangerous to knock on a strange door in those days, for they would be likely to turn you in immediately to the Germans. However, I had nothing to lose. Death was lurking in every place and every time. I approached the first home, and recognized Oksani, Matrona's father, through the window. A thought flashed through my mind: G-d is with me! He led me to precisely the right place. For all the houses of the villages were similar to each other, and I arrived exactly at the place where I intended!

Matrona brought me into the home and hid me under the roof of the barn, endangering herself and her family, for the Germans decreed that anyone who would hide Jews would be killed along with their entire family.

I sat alone between the piles of hay and wept incessantly. Matrona brought me bread and milk from time to time. They themselves were very poor and suffered from hunger. There were seven children in their home, and Matrona, the oldest, was only 16. On the third day, I suddenly heard the sound of footsteps. I became very upset, but I immediately saw that it was my husband, Itzka. I was happy, and this calmed me greatly. We were together again. Together! He was as always, with his perpetual smile on his handsome face. He said to me, "I had hoped that you would change your mind and return to town, but when I saw that your decision was firm and that you were not returning, I decided to come to you, for what is life without you?"

We both wept from joy, for we were together again. He told me that they had already taken out many Jews from Ratno, brought them to a hill in the village of Prochod, shot them, and buried them on the spot.

Matrona gave us information from the town. She would go to the pharmacist, who was our friend, hear from him everything that was taking place, return, and tell us. Thereby, we found out when my brother Aharon was murdered, how they removed my brothers-in-law and their families from their hiding place, and when they took the Judenrat members to be killed. From her mouth we found out how my father-in-law stood bravely before the Germans and refused to send additional Jews to their deaths, and how he was cruelly beaten until he died.

We continued to remain in the hiding place, and realized that Ratno was already Judenrein. The sky continued to be blue; the sun continued to shine, and the world itself was still in existence.

Our Ukrainian neighbors were now living on our account. They lived in our house, they murdered and also took possession[1]. They collaborated with the Nazi enemy. They earned a prize for every Jew that they turned in and for every Jewish child whom they brought to be murdered. My heart was filled with feelings of revenge, and the desire for revenge inspired in me the will to live. The essence of my thought, that the day of recompense and revenge would come for the pure blood that was spilled, gave me a great deal of energy to continue to live.

About two weeks went by. One day, Matrona informed us that they were being suspected of hiding us. We hurried to leave our hiding place and hid for several days among the bushes. The Germans searched the house of Oksani, and left when they realized that there were no Jews. We returned to the piles of fodder in Oksani's home. He was a merciful and kind Ukrainian, honest and upright. On occasion he would tell us, "It does not matter to me what happens to me myself, but I feel bad about the children. If the Germans find you in my house, they will take us all out to be killed."

At times when we sat in the fodder at Oksani's home, we heard steps. The fear of death took hold of us, but we immediately realized that our friend Michalski the pharmacist, had come. He recommended that we agree to accompany him to a village near Vladimir. He told me that his cousin had died there, and he would provide me with her papers, so I would be able to work as a Ukrainian maid, and nobody would realize that I was a Jewess. I was fluent in the language without any strange accent. I had long locks of hair and a thin figure, and if he were to give me appropriate clothing, nobody would suspect me. But what would happen with my husband?

I pushed off all urgings and logical reasoning with one statement: if we would be saved, we will be together, and if we were to be captured and murdered, then too we would be only together! The pharmacist realized that he would not move me, and he returned from whence he came. We remained together and waited for a miracle from heaven. But there were no miracles.

The Ukrainians once again came to search after the Jews. We were forced to leave our relatively secure place and continue with our wandering. Matrona gave me some of her clothing, atop of which I wore a warm winter coat with a belt, in the fashion of the gentiles. I wore felt shoes (Pustules in Ukrainian) on my feet, which were wrapped in rags.

Thus did we wander in the forests for a few days. Then, we returned once again to Matrona's barn, tired and desperate.

A ray of hope greeted us. The pharmacist informed us through Matrona that in the Samolna Forest, 18 kilometers away from Ratno, they were searching for woodchoppers. They were not particular if they were Jews or gentiles, as long as they were familiar with the trees of the forest. Oksani took us to Samolna, where the elderly forester name Buchhalt met us. He seemed like a good man. We hoped that he would be kind to us. We parted from Oksani as from a dear family member. We hugged each other and wept on each other's neck, with hearts full of gratitude.

We met several people from Ratno with Buchhalt: the Steingarten family – a couple with two children, whose son Aryeh was killed with the 20 who were the first victims of Ratno; Avrech, Sheftal – eleven Ratno natives in total.

The men worked in the forest, while Bat-Sheva and I performed domestic work. We tended to the cows and pigs, and baked bread for al the workers. The work was not easy, but it enabled us to continue to live. We wandered around with relative freedom, and we were registered with the gendarmes of Ratno. We lived!

My husband traveled frequently to Ratno with Buchhalt for shopping and to arrange various matters. In this manner, we found out that several of the most beautiful girls of the town – the daughter of Gittel Karsh, Reizel Gutman and Feigele of Krymne – were in the hands of the gendarmes of Ratno. There were also a few Jews who had remained alive and worked in Ratno, but we all had the feeling that the end was approaching.

At night, Jews who had remained alive and hid in the forests came to us in Samolna.

They came to ask for a piece of bread. Shlomo Perlmutter, W. Kagan and others were among them. They hid among the bushes in the forests throughout the day, with their torn, worn-out clothes, starving for bread.

Indeed, we also did not have sufficient bread, but I always gave them a piece of bread without worrying about the next day. It was clear to me: death would come, if not today then tomorrow, so why should I worry about bread?!

We suffered greatly from lice when we in Samolna. We waged a constant battle against filth and scabies, but our hand was the weaker one. The lice overtook the head, the body and the clothing. We used to say that even a baby emerging from its mother's womb would not be free from scabies, and it would even penetrate its eyes.

After some time we parted from the Steingarten family, who set out to search for partisans, so they could join them. We hoped that among our Ukrainian friends we would find someone who would be willing to hide us until the wrath passed. We wandered about for a week searching in vain for a hiding place. Our Ukrainian acquaintances were concerned for their lives and refused to take us in.

We returned to Buchhalt, and he agreed to hide us. We hid behind the double wall during the day, and at night we went out to help Buchhalt with his night farm work, such as the night milking, feeding the pigs, preparing food for the animals for the day, and baking bread for the next day.

Wanda, Buchhalt's wife, a pious Catholic, would show us that the New Testament states that "The Jews crucified Jesus," and therefore the punishment had come upon us, and we "were obligated to accept the judgment." We had no choice other than to be quiet. She made our lives bitter in various ways. Among other things, she claimed that I did not milk the cows properly. When my husband came to help me, she sent him away, claiming that "a man's hands are always filthy." Buchhalt saw her many attempts to afflict me and asked her to leave me alone, but she did what she wanted. We felt that the earth was burning under our feet. The hatred of Wanda, the frequent visits of the Ukrainians who were searching for Jews, the constant, repetitive claims of Wanda that she did not want to endanger herself on account of us, her threats that she would move to Lutsk and leave Buchhalt with us – all of these made it clear to us that we must leave.

Buchhalt, the good, upright man, dreamed that the war would end soon, and that he would come to dance with us on the streets of Ratno as a man who succeeded in saving a Jewish couple. He decided to join the partisans along with us and fight the Nazis.

On a cold winter day, Buchhalt went out to the partisans to inform them that we would be joining. However, Polish collaborators with the Nazis attacked him. They beat him fiercely and left him lying on the frozen ground.

He arrived home with his last strength. My husband and I tended to him, plastered and bandaged his wounds, and helped him with his illness.

One day we heard knocks on the door. My husband and I hurried to our hiding place, and Buchhalt strengthened himself and opened the door. In the past, we were accustomed to Buchhalt calling us after a few minutes, for the visitors were usually friends. This time, nobody called to us to come out from our hiding place. We worried greatly about Buchhalt. We left the hiding place and did not find Buchhalt in the house. The house looked as if it had been hit by a pogrom. The hunting gun that had been hanging on the wall was also gone.

We decided that we could not remain there with the homeowner not present, for it was dangerous for us. We left the place. We found Buchhalt lying dead between the trees, a few meters from his home. We could not bury him because the ground was frozen. We covered his body with tree branches and bushes. We wept over the death of this good man who had been kind to us, and we swore that that we would return again to bury him. It was clear to us that he had been killed because he refused to turn us in to the Ukrainians. He preferred to die.

Our tribulations began again. We were forced again to find a place of refuge. We decided to go to Samarovich, the village in which our acquaintance Ivan Shtoch lived. He was a trustworthy Ukrainian, and we hoped that he would agree to hide us.

Most of the residents of Samarovich were Ukrainian. We required the grace of heaven to enter such a village without being detected and turned over to the Germans, but our desperate situation gave us no choice.

We entered the village at night and immediately turned toward the home of Ivan Shtoch. He immediately took us to the attic of the barn and hid us among the piles of fodder. His wife and children did not know about us. They would have objected were they to have known.

Ivan took responsibility for the care of the horses and cows upon himself, so that nobody would wander around near us. He brought us food once a day: potatoes, milk, a piece of pork and sometimes even a piece of bread. The place was not ventilated, it was impossible to stand, and there was not even enough room to lie down. We had to go down to the barn at night to relieve ourselves.

The Dream and its Interpretation

Ivan would bring me wool so that I could knit scarves for his children. I knitted in the darkness on the roof, and he brought the scarves to his family as if he had bought them as gifts. Once, he asked me to knit gloves. I did not know how to knit five-fingered gloves. My husband Itzka and I struggled for two days until we overcame the problem. I also knitted gloves for Ivan's family.

We hid with him for six weeks.

One night, my father-in-law Reb David-Aharon appeared to me in a dream and warned me that the place was dangerous. He urged me to move on.

I got up and woke Itzka up. I told him about the dream, and urged him to get up and leave immediately. Itzka opposed the idea and claimed that we must not leave as long as Ivan agreed to keep us with him. However, I did not give up, and my husband finally agreed to my suggestion, but he insisted that we part with our host before we left.

Ivan did not urge us to stay, but asked to know where we were going. We told him that we would try our luck with Nikon Krybsky in the village of Kortelesy, 14 kilometers away from Samarovich.

We set out on our way when it got dark. Walking was very difficult for me. My legs had become stiff after six weeks of sitting in one place.

Itzka carried me on his shoulders and dragged me for 10 kilometers. He was stronger than I, and was able to overcome many obstacles.

I was concerned that even were I to remain alive after the hell, I would be lame and blind, for the long sojourn in darkness also affected my eyes. However, hidden powers were apparently awakened within me, which helped me to prevail. We succeeded in reaching Nikon Krybsky.

He was a well-to-do, perhaps even wealthy Ukrainian. He was a good acquaintance of ours, but he refused to hide us with him even for one day! We begged him to permit us to wait with him until the partisans arrive in the village, and we would then be able to join them. He finally agreed to let us hide in his field, so that he would not be held guilty in the even that we were to be caught.

We hid in the piles of fodder in a corner of the field. We were without food or water, and without cigarettes – which was very hard for Itzka. However, at least it was warm. We were not concerned with the cold in the winter that was all around.

Ivan Shtoch came to us on our second night. He told us that on the same night that we left, a group of Banderites[2] came to him and searched the house thoroughly. They went through the entire farm, and took down all the fodder as they were searching for Jews. Of course, they found nothing, and left him alone. He came to us to ask why we left suddenly. What was the interpretation of the miracle that took place to him and us, for it was clear that had we remained, neither we nor his family would have survived!

I told him about the dream that moved me to leave. Ivan was deeply affected by these words. He kissed the ground, crossed himself, and could not calm himself for a long time. We kissed and hugged as if we were beloved family members.

He left us a piece of bread and some tobacco for Itzka, and then returned to his village.

We sat in the fodder, and Krybsky sought ways to connect us with the partisans. He finally succeeded in forging a connection, and arranged a meeting for us.

In the Partisan Camp

The partisans in Ukraine were primarily Soviet citizens who had not been able to escape from the Germans. They did not have great faith in Jews, especially because we did not have weapons, which they needed.

One group of partisans agreed to take us in. We went with them for some distance, and then they suddenly ordered us to lie on the ground. We lay down, and they began to beat us cruelly. I asked them to kill us, for I could no longer breathe from the beatings. They shouted "You are spies!" They claimed that we must have certainly helped the Germans, for if not, they could not understand how we managed to survive to that point. They finally took my wedding ring, searched our bodies, and said that they would not take me because they had no use for women. However, they agreed to take Itzka. They brought me to the home of a Ukrainian whose name I do not recall, and told him to protect me so that no harm would come to me. They took my husband, Itzka, with them.

I found myself once again in a Ukrainian house, this time with a family that did not know me, in a remote village near Kortelesy.

With the partisans, Itzka did his best to prove that Jews are not fainthearted, as the partisans thought.

He took upon himself every difficult and dangerous task, and bravely carried out in full everything asked of him. After he proved his trustworthiness and dedication to the partisans, they responded to his requests and permitted him to bring me to their camp. We were together again!

I was sent for two weeks to study first aid: tending to wounds, giving injections, making bandages, and other such tasks. I also went through training in the use of weapons. When I returned to the camp, I received a band with a red cross for my arm and a satchel for my shoulders. I went out with the soldiers to fight against the Nazis.

My primary role was to rescue the wounded, move them off the battlefield, and tend to them. When I now think about everything that I did among the partisans, I am astonished that a woman of 31-32 could have gone through everything that I did.

I had a sort of field hospital in the village of Burobni, in the area of Samary-Kortelesy. Aside from the wounded, there were also many people ill with typhus. This terrible illness spread among the partisans due to the poor hygienic conditions, as well as the large lice infestations. We knew that, if the lice settled upon you, your chances of contracting typhus was certain...

A special hospital in the home of a Ukrainian was opened in order to isolate those ill with typhus. I was responsible for tending to these sick people. The entire burden fell upon me, and I was not able to rest for a moment, day or night. I gave them medical aid and especially moral support. I told them stories to encourage them. I talked about the awaited end to the war, about the defeats of the Nazis on the battlefield, about the fortunate times that would come to humanity after the Nazis were defeated.

We did not have medicinal compounds or pills, of course. I utilized ordinary cups instead of cupping glasses[3], and vodka instead of alcohol, which was lacking. I do not recall even one case of death in my unit.

It is worthwhile to relate one episode, from which one can learn about the anti-Semitism that pervaded among the partisans.

One day, while we were in the camp, all 40 of us were summoned for a roll call, and were brought to the place where there had been a fire. The names of two Jews who were with us were called out, and they were accused of setting the fire. They were accused of spying due to the fact that poison was found during the search of their possessions. They rejected the explanation offered by the Jews that they carried the poison with them when they fled from the Germans. The partisans unanimously held that the Jews set the fire, and that they were spies and traitors. They shot them to death on the spot as we stood there.

On the way back to the camp, I poured out my dose of poison that I constantly carried with me, without anyone noticing. There were two reasons for this: a) the danger in carrying poison, and b) the knowledge that the end of the war was approaching, and I should not be thinking of suicide, which is a sin against both the laws of G-d and man.

The news from the front was very encouraging. The defeat of the enemy was approaching. We were approaching the awaited day of salvation. At that time, they enlisted Itzka to the Red Army. I accompanied him to the place of his draft. I recall that we walked together for about an hour until we arrived at the place where all the draftees were gathering.

Itzka urged me to return to my workplace in the hospital. We said that we would meet in Ratno. I parted from him with a feeling of deep oppression. My heart prophesied that I would not see him again. I went along my way, weeping and in despair. I was pregnant at the time.

I did not remain at the partisan hospital for long. The news reached me that Ratno had been liberated by the Red Army. I received a letter of recommendation from the partisans for my good and dedicated work, and set out to my town of Ratno.

The sight revealed before my eyes in Ratno was horrifying. Everything was destroyed and in ruins. There was no trace of the houses and streets. Everything was mounds of ruins. I recognized every stone, tree, and corner, but people did not recognize me. They were new faces – the faces of strangers. I had nowhere to go. Only one house remained standing, the house of Avraham and Dvora Berg. I heard that they had survived. They told me that my brother Shlomo survived, and was in Zabolottya. I did not know if this was true. I entered the house of the Berg family. The house had been taken over the by Red Army authorities, but one room remained empty and they allowed me to live there.

I began to work immediately after my arrival. I directed a large cooperative with many branches. My job was to receive the provisions and send them to various branches. I was given a free hand to act in accordance with my judgment, as long as I protected the government property.

I received a coupon to obtain food from the cheap restaurant, where they served a form of liquid that was called soup. I also received a dress, which I have kept as a souvenir to this day. It was as if I was divided into two. Half of me worked and lived, and the other half wandered as a shadow in my Ratno, Ratno without Jews! I was searching for a sign or remnant of the near past, but in vain.

From time to time, some survivor of the city came to search for relatives or acquaintances who survived.

Those who came included Yechezkel Kotler who had been wounded and injured in his hand in the Red Army, Yaakov Klodner, his wife Reiza, Golda Sheftal, and Shlomo Perlmutter.

With every survivor who came to town, the pain and mourning increased, for nobody remained alive, there was no remnant from the home of Father and Mother – everything had gone up in flames. Therefore, they returned from whence they had come, in despair and mourning, with each person going along his path of suffering and loneliness.

Shlomo Perlmutter urged me to leave Ratno, which was full of gentiles, but I remained put, for I had promised my husband, Itzka, that I would wait for him there.

One day, as I was walking on the street, I saw the Ukrainian murderer, Yurek Yandovich, wandering free opposite me. I knew no peace in my soul. I immediately turned to the K.G.B. commandant Nikishechenko, and told him about the murder that Yandovich perpetrated against innocent people on Mount Prochod. I had heard about the entire incident from Prozina of Prochod. The commandant was interested to know whether there were "only" Jews among the victims, and I responded that there were also Soviet citizens. He summoned Prozina and received testimony from her, confirming everything that I had said. I did not meet Yandovich again in Ratno...

My due date was approaching, and there was no appropriate medical supervision in Ratno. Avraham and Dvora came to me from Kovel and asked me to come with them for the duration of the birth and recovery, but I decided to not leave Ratno, and placed my trust in G-d.

I prayed that I would give birth to a girl, for the issue of circumcision was complicated, and the thought that I would raise an uncircumcised child caused me great suffering.

The labor was very complicated, and the elderly Ukrainian woman who had been called to assist did not know what to do. When she realized that she did not know how to proceed, she ran outside and began to call for help. Finally my daughter Rivka was born. She now lives with her family in Israel.

Avraham Berg came to visit after the birth. We both drank Lechayim and he gave my daughter her name, Rivka. He left a book of Psalms with me. I placed it at her head when ever I left her alone, and it protected her from all evil.

After some time, I received a letter from Itzka, who wrote that for him the war had not yet ended, but he hoped to return soon. He requested again that I wait for him in Ratno.

One day I was called to the command, and given the terrible news that my husband had fallen. I went into shock and took to bed. It was only the urgency of caring for my daughter that gave me the strength to overcome the terrible shock. At that point, the period of wandering, suffering and great tribulations began, until I arrived in the Land of Israel.

Translator's Footnotes

1. A reference to Kings I, 21:19, where the Prophet Elijah asked Ahab "Did you murder and also take possession. https://www.jewishgen.org/Yizkor/Ratno/rat202.html - f1r

2. See http://www.encyclopediaofukraine.com/pages/B/A/Banderites.htm https://www.jewishgen.org/Yizkor/Ratno/rat202.html - f2r

3. See http://medical-dictionary.thefreedictionary.com/cupping+glass https://www.jewishgen.org/Yizkor/Ratno/rat202.html - f3r

From right to left: M. Tiktiner, Yisrael Chayat and Shalom

Tiktiner

Yitzchak Shapira, who fell in a battle near Warsaw as a soldier in the Red Army; Meir Grabov

From right to left: Pearl Karsh-Vernik with her daughter in line to receive a meal at a detention camp in Cyprus

The First Days of the Nazi Regime

by Shlomo Perlmutter

Translated by Jerrold Landau

(From the diary of a 14-year-old child)

July 7, 1941

It took place at noon. I stood with other children next to the school, when a young, tall man wearing white clothes and black pants, with a revolver in his hand, suddenly sprouted up as if before our eyes. "Lie down, don't look! I am shooting," he ordered us in Ukrainian. The sound of shooting was quickly heard. The doves standing on the roof of Liber Karsh's house were startled. They spread their wings and disappeared... At that time, a new reality began in the town. It was as if things suddenly became dark at midday. Images of armed Ukrainians fluttered through the streets -- -- -- I did not heed the command "Lazshis!" (Lie down). I fled. Two bullets sliced through the air, as if pursuing me. I reached the entrance of my house frightened and confounded.

"Daddy, Mommy, a pogrom! Flee!"

The windows were open wide. At that moment, they were sitting and drinking tea.

The atmosphere in the house changed immediately. The escape began... Everyone tried to hide to save his life. I ran in the direction of the river and hid in the bulrushes. I lay there with my entire body immersed in the water, and only the tip of my head sticking out.

After a few minutes, I began to sense the extreme cold, and my teeth chattered. The shots and screams did not cease. I saw how Binyamin Friedman was taken out of the house of our neighbor, the wagon driver Yitzchak-Hirsch. Two strong hooligans tied his hands. A shot was heard, and Binyamin fell dead. He was 32 years old, healthy and strong. When the Ukrainians broke into his house, he split the head of one of them with an axe. After that, they caught him and killed him.

The intensity of the pogrom increased from moment to moment. At first, they tried to defend themselves a bit, but they quickly gave up. Everyone knew that the German government stood behind the Ukrainian hooligans. Jewish property became open for all. The Ukrainians began to empty out the houses of the Jews who had left to find hiding places. The heads of the rioters were (here, there is a list of the full names of 12 rioters)[1] .

-- -- -- When the shooting abated, I left the river and went to a Jewish home. The elderly Tzvia (Efraim Kotler's mother) was standing at the entrance of her house, with her grandchild beside her, weeping bitterly. Her lips were whispering: “Master of the World! In sanctification of the Divine Name.” With her own eyes, she witnessed the slaughter, how tens of Ukrainians broke into Jewish homes, and how everyone ran to hide. However, she was already elderly, and she had no energy to run. Therefore, she sat and waited for death. I broke into her house as a madman, with my clothes dripping water. I was prepared even to slink into the oven in her house and hide there, but I quickly left her house, and ran with all my might to the house of Yankel Prossman. As I was running, I recognized three Ukrainians with “Nagans”[2] in their hands, walking the length of Zabulotia Street. I knocked on Prossman's door:

“Open the door, have mercy, it is me, Shlomke!”

The door opened, and Reb Yankel, with his long, splendid beard stood before me. He was trembling. He clapped his hands together when he saw me and said, “A bitter and difficult time has come.” His wife sat there confounded, muttering something silently.

I also could not find a place for myself in the Prossman home. I went up to the roof many times and surveyed the area, wanting to know what was going on. My ears heard incessant shots. At that moment, we heard loud knocks on the door, with shouts, “Open up the door, accursed Jews!” The Ukrainian hooligans began to break the door. Without giving too much thought, I jumped out the window into the garden next to the house, crawled to the vegetable patches, and lay down among them.

It was only then that I understood for the first time the full meaning of the word pogrom. My heartbeat became more rapid, and I was literally afraid to think about Mother, Father, and my brothers. Who knows where they were located at that time? Where did they find a hiding place? Were they able to escape? For how long will the pogrom continue? The situation intensified at night. Ukrainians arrived from all the neighboring villages in groups of hundreds, armed with guns and revolvers.

I got up quietly from where I had been lying down. I carefully crossed the street, climbed over and crawled through gardens and barbed wire fences, and reached the home of Shefa Lander. I spent the night in the garden of Anatolio that was next to Shefa's yard. It was cold, my clothes were wet, and groans and the thunder of shots were heard from time to time. Avraham Gutman and his daughter Reizel, Berish the son of the scribe, and other Jews hid there.

July 8, 1941

It was a cold, dewy night. We were startled by the explosion of grenades already before dawn. The earth literally shook, and large flames flashed up. The Germans had entered the town.

Suddenly, I heard a voice ordering: "Halt! Las!" Somebody in green fatigues grabbed me by my sleeve. He ordered me in German to raise my hands, and began to lead me somewhere. Along the way, he ordered other Jews to raise their hands and join the row of those being led. Nobody knew where they were taking us. Everyone who seemed to be age 13 and above joined the row, which continued to grow. This was a Tuesday. As if to mock us, it was a lovely summer day. Not even one small cloud appeared in the sky. Birds chirped, and a light wind was whispering. The universe seemed happy. Announcements that had recently been posted on the walls informed of the showing of a new movie. Lines from the well-known poem of Bialik came to mind, "For G-d called spring together, the sun shone, the doctrine grew, and the slaughterer slaughtered." We, hundreds of Jews, were now marching with raised hands as the armed Germans accompanied us the entire way. They were chasing Jews from their houses, and the same question afflicted everyone: Why and to where? In this manner, we were led to Steinberg's home on the Kovel-Brisk road. We were all arranged in a row on the left side of the road. During better days, we used to meet the bus arriving from Kovel in that place. Aside from Jews, several Poles and 15 Ukrainians were arranged there at the side of the church. I was also among those standing there. A German who noticed me began to mock, "Children, go home!" Without thinking, I began to run in the direction of our house, but some demon in green fatigues with a revolver in his hand stopped me and ordered me to return. I passed by our house. The windows were shattered, feathers were scattered, and pillows and washing utensils rolled in the street.

When I arrived at the hundreds of Jews who had been captured, I heard a voice, "Oh, woe to me, Shlomole, you are also here?" This was the voice of my father. I turned my head. His face had darkened. Who knew where he had been during the last few days. When I reached him, he hugged me strongly and kissed me. I felt how good it was to have Father... It had only been two days since I had seen him, but in my eyes it seemed like two full years. “What is your opinion, Father, to escape?” “Do as you wish,” he answered me. In circumstances such as these, even Father could not help. Various thoughts went through my head: To escape? Not to escape? Perhaps I would be killed as I escape? And perhaps all of this will end with simply a fright? I weighed the options of what to do. The faces of all those standing there were in mourning. One could not see the faces, just the sadness. Hundreds of Jewish women whose husbands were standing here in a row were now wailing in their houses. Yossel and Meir, two Russian soldiers who found temporary refuge in Ratno, were also standing there. When I turned my gaze toward them, I saw that they were suddenly removed from the line. They were taken by eight German soldiers. I followed after them. Rumors spread through the row that a Polish Jew who had a bad reputation in the town had turned them in. Others said that Ukrainians, who knew all the Jews of Ratno very well, informed the Germans that those two were there. The Germans selected two Jewish youths as undertakers (Moshe Leker and Yossel Mostishter). The former Soviet soldiers went quietly to their deaths. The undertakers later said that along the way, Yossel tossed his watch into a sewer, and before he was murdered, he asked that the town of Kozima in the region of Odessa be informed as to what happened to him and his friend. After they were shot, their bodies were tossed into a pit in which there were also the bodies of the three hooligans from Yakush had who had been shot earlier by the Germans due to the fact that weapons were found with them. A large unit of Germans surrounded us. Machine guns were set up at different vantage points on the road. Groans and murmurs of “Master of the World,” and “Shema Yisrael” were heard. People clasped their hands. At that time, the Nazis freed the few Ukrainians and Poles. Their wives greeted the Germans with gifts: sour cream, butter, eggs, and milk. The Ukrainians gave testimony that the “Communist” Jews were those who shot the German soldiers on the night of July 5. This testimony was sufficient for the Germans. So that they would not be surprised that the Jews were such “wanton” people, they added that the Russian prisoners who found refuge in the town perpetrated the attack. The German captain ordered all the Jews to arrange themselves into fours, decreed loudly “Achtung!” (Attention!) , and began to read the verdict:

“When we entered this town, the Jews and Russian prisoners began to fire at us. Therefore, I order that one out of every 15 Jews be taken to be killed, as well as 35 Russian prisoners.” As the verdict was being read, his face became inflamed and he began to curse the Jews as follows, “You Jews have always been provocateurs of war. Because of you, our blood was spilled on the battlefields. We will annihilate you!”

After he concluded his words, the military prosecutor, wearing white gloves on his hands, began to select the Jews who were to be killed. One, two three. When he reached number fifteen, he commanded him to turn to the right. Then he repeated this. Thirty-eight Jews stood at the right, and they all knew what their verdict was. Aharon Reisman begged to be allowed to bid farewell to his wife, whom he had married only a week ago. Leibel Steingarten wept and Yisrael Steingarten chain smoked. I witnessed with my own eyes how all of these people who were chosen for death were hauled along with the Russian prisoners to the designated place. I heard with my own ears the shots that put an end to their lives. After some time, the Germans freed all the Jews who were gathered in the square, and accompanied them with the following warning, "Go home, but know that in the event that one more shot is heard in Ratno – it will be a clear sign that weapons remain among the Jews. We will then kill you all."

July 9, 1941

German captains are wandering around the town. They are apparently conducting the local enumeration. For the purposes of this enumeration, the homes of Yehuda Leib Vernik and Motel Tiktiner were expropriated. Many Ukrainians arrived in the morning to celebrate along with the new rulers. They marched through the streets of the town, waving their yellow and blue flags as well as German flags. A German captain, a Ukrainian translator, the Ukrainian commandant Danilevich, and the mayor Chatzovich greeted the marchers. The German captain issued his words of greeting from atop a stage that was set up next to the firefighters' building: "The Bolsheviks have been defeated. Only small bands of them are still fighting, but they have no power. In order to achieve the final peace, it is necessary that you Ukrainians assist our fighters through your work and with your wheat. May the new regime live throughout the world! For the Jews we will prepare a 'Sabbath', for the Poles – a Sunday, and for you and us – a wedding" (Translated from Ukrainian).

The speech was translated into Ukrainian, and the crowd received it with applause. The Ukrainians did not like the innuendo regarding the wheat that was to be placed at the disposal of the Germans. They awaited taking rather than giving. However, the final words hinting that everything would be given to the Ukrainians once again raised the morale. Not one Jew was seen on the streets throughout the celebration. Only children ran about the area. I sat in the home of Avraham Barg near the place of the celebration, and heard everything.

July 10, 1941

Tidings of Job arrived from Kovel. The Germans surrounded Warsaw Street, took out 300 male Jews from their houses, hauled them to the area of the barracks, and commanded them to dance. After the dance, they brought all the Jews into the barracks. The Jewish community of Kovel made efforts to save the Jews. The Ukrainian residents of Ratno also knew about this. A few of them even said, "Tomorrow, you too will dance for us."...

July 12, 1941

I am presently sitting next to the window in the front room of our house and writing. It is quiet around, but this is the calm before the storm. There is a deathly silence in the market. All of the stores are closed. A child is coming out from the lane of Shaya Bakler, and he disappears immediately. Nobody knows what the day will bring. There is no newspaper or radio. We are living as in the days of our ancestors, as grandfather had told us. We are afraid of every rustling leaf. The Beis Midrash is the source of news. All of the frightening news comes from there. The atmosphere around is like that of a cemetery.

July 14, 1941

Two decrees were issued. Decree number 1 states, "The police chief of Ratno decrees in the name of the German civilian government that the entire Jewish population, from age ten and up, must wear a white patch with a blue Star of David on their right arm. Anyone not fulfilling this command will be liable to justice. The City Commander: Mironiok. Decree number 2, signed by Danilevich and Mironiok states that "From tomorrow, Jews are forbidden from talking to and greeting Ukrainians. From 5:30 p.m. until 6:00 a.m., Jews are forbidden to leave their houses."

It was very sad in the house. Father sat all the time with his book of Psalms (he had become very pious), and mother was busy preparing bean soup from the beans that grew in our garden. Shaykele was reading "Children of Sailor Garnet." Motele was not in the house, and I was sitting and writing. In the evening, I read what I wrote to my grandfather. He was the only one who had the patience to listen to me...

-- -- -- In the afternoon, I and several of my friends fell into the hands of Wonka Komorover. He ordered us to burn the garbage and to come the next day to chop wood and light the stove in the kitchen. We suffered beatings from him. I heard my mother tell her aunt Chasia-Breina, "This is some evil affliction, who runs through the streets all day."

July 17, 1941

A Judenrat was set up by command of the German civilian authorities. The chairman was David-Aharon Shapira, and the members included Leibel Grabov, Fishel Shuster, Yossel Shniter, Asher Leker, Nachum Reiskis, Izel Grabov, Yisrael-David Feintuch, Mendel Blatt, Yitzchak Chayat (Leibel's son), David Steingarten, and Yankel Liberman. The policemen were Yona Stern, Ozer Klapech, Lerber, and Yossi Leivont. Iserke Stern was the messenger of the Judenrat. The Judenrat was located in the house of Yankel Liberman, and a Ukrainian sign fluttered above. Toward evening, I brought David-Aharon a letter which stated that he must send, "a blue Boston suit, three blue silk shirts, two blue ties, and towels." Signed by S. Danilevich.

Pages from a Diary

by Yisrael Chayat

Translated by Jerrold Landau

Ratno, June 25, 1942

Around, it is still verdant and sprouting. It is only on the Jewish street that autumn winds are blowing. The pall of the Day of Atonement is hovering over us. Here and there, one can still see a woman scurrying about. The yellow patch on her clothing makes her recognizable from afar. During these perplexing times as the ambushes of the Ukrainian police increased, she is the only one who can still concern herself to some degree with the needs of her family. Children are playing in the streets and yards around the houses. They are screaming, making noise, acting wild, and attempting to mimic the deeds of the adults with their childhood enthusiasm. Now, they arrange themselves into two camps, and everyone is "girded for battle" against his fellow. For a moment it seems that nothing will distract them from their game. However, the "Green fatigues" approach, and again, they are no longer innocent children. In the bat of an eye, they turn into wise "tourists." The news is given to the adults. The houses empty. Life goes underground. Only the few Judenrat policemen still walk around "securely" through the streets of the city. They greet the Ukrainian policemen with an honorary bow. The white band is on their sleeves, its purpose to create an air of importance. In truth, it adds to the disgrace of its owner in the eyes of the Jews who see it.

The Judenrat members, headed by David-Aharon, enter into a council meeting in the morning. The frightful news of the slaughter of the Jews in Kovel does not let up for one moment. Has our end not arrived, and can it not be stopped due to the severity of the decree? It seems that such is the case. The feeling of death overtakes everyone. Jewish cities are burning. Cities are being wiped out, and entire communities are marching to oblivion.

June 26, 1942

After midnight, our ears heard the rattle of dozens of cars that arrived for the Ukrainian command, with their headlights extinguished. That year we became accustomed to the noise of cars, and every time they arrived, we became more afraid. The heart prophesied atrocities.

The eyes of Jewesses peered through the cracks of the closed shutters and covered windows, searching in the dark, trying to figure out the meaning of the incessant rattling and the bustling around the police station. The darkness aroused fear just like the darkness of the shadow of death in the cemetery. Nevertheless, the Jews prayed that the night would continue on forever. They were more afraid of dawn than the previous nights. Our hearts suspected that this would be our final night in the town.

At 5:00 a.m., the echoes of gunshots heralded the beginning of the end. Half naked men, women and children, with unkempt hair, were running in confusion through the streets and alleyways of the city, frantically searching for an exit. They wanted to escape to somewhere beyond the bounds of the town. Others made efforts to get to their hiding places that they had prepared while there was still time. Those who were more settled went to the Judenrat house to find out anything. Some of them went out to sweep the streets, a job that was given to them the day before.

The shots did not stop. At 6:00 a.m., Gestapo men accompanied by Ukrainian policemen appeared on the streets. They arrested Jews and brought them to the open area next to the house of Eliahu Ivanovich. Berl Held, the first Jew who did not obey the command and attempted to continue on his way, was shot on the spot. Ratno was surrounded by 400 Germans – Gestapo men and death squads – like bloodthirsty leopards running through the streets. They passed through the Jewish houses, searched the cellars and attics, removed their victims, and dragged them to the square of slaughter. From there, they were transported to the sand dunes of Prochod – to the pits into which 1,300 people were buried in one day.

It was 4:00 p.m. The shots stopped. The murderers and our Ukrainian neighbors celebrated on the ruins of the town, pillaging and stealing Jewish property.

The eternal night had just started.

Yisrael Chayat

My way in the Land

by Pearl Vernik-Karsh

Translated by Jerrold Landau

I met Ben-Zion Karsh in Lublin. He was one of the activists in Peta"ch (Pioneering Partisan Soldiers) who was connected with the "smuggling" of the Israeli brigade. Together with him, I left Poland and arrived in Italy. I was together with my young daughter Raya in the U.N.R.A. camp in Carmona. My wedding to Ben-Zion as well as the wedding of my brother Shlomo with his wife took place one night in Milan. Our son, Yehuda, was born in February, 1947, and we began to prepare for aliya to Israel. Leaving Italy was fraught with many dangers. In the darkness of the night, we waited at the seashore in Genoa until the small boat arrived, which took us from the port to the midst of the sea, where we were transferred to a larger, shaky ship. The men busied themselves with fixing the boat throughout the entire journey, for water was coming in from all sides. We did not believe that we would arrive to our destination in this ship, but we arrived. As soon as we saw the coast of our homeland, we began to sing Hatikva. Our joy was boundless, but did not last long. The British policemen and soldiers who used to fight with the illegal immigrants exposed us and transferred us to a warship that brought us to Cyprus, before we could set foot on the soil of the Land.

At that point, a new, sad chapter began – the chapter of Cyprus. We were housed in a camp of bunks on the coast. The camp was surrounded by a wire fence. We were given food in minimal quantities, and if our behavior was unacceptable to the British, they would not give us food. There was a shortage of fresh water. The suffering of the families with babies, mine included, was especially great. My husband Ben-Zion of blessed memory would set out to a second camp and remain in line for an entire night to obtain water for our baby. Illness spread among the children due to the inhuman conditions in which we were placed. At first there was no doctor there. Dr. Falk arrived only after some time, bringing with him two volunteer nurses and vital medicine. An epidemic broke out among the babies and many died. They separated the mothers from their children for health reasons, and I was not able to hear the crying of my child. Despite the ban, I entered the room of the babies and sat beneath the cradle of my child so that they would not detect my presence. I recall that one morning, Dr. Falk came to visit the infants. When he saw me sitting beneath the cradle, he ordered me to leave the room, but I strongly refused. He took his camera in order to "perpetuate" this strange scene, where a mother was sitting beneath her child's cradle. Only then did I accede to his request, and left.

Who knows how far our suffering would have reached were it not for the fact that a certain group of certificates arrived for the Cyprus deportees on the occasion of the birthday of the Queen of England. My family and I made aliya with the first group, and arrived in the country one day after the declaration of the state. We were greeted with great joy in the aliya camp in Raanana. The first letter that I received was from our fellow native Shmuel Goldman, who was then the secretary of the labor council of Rishon Letzion. He offered us his assistance in our first steps, and he gave his assistance willingly.

Pearl Vernik-Karsh

Translator's Footnotes

1. In the actual book, the list of names did not appear. https://www.jewishgen.org/Yizkor/Ratno/rat202.html - f1ar

2. A brand of Russian revolver. https://www.jewishgen.org/Yizkor/Ratno/rat202.html - f2ar

In Honor of the Ratno Survivors

by Tova Gandelsman (Bokser)

Translated by Jerrold Landau

I frequently see our town in a dream at night, or as I lie sleepless at night. There was a vibrant Jewish life in Ratno, and the existence of a different, gentile environment right next to us did not bother us at all. Aside from rare instances, a sort of peaceful coexistence existed between the gentiles and us. In our street at the edge of town, life carried on as if literally in a village. There were plots of land around the houses, and all the residents had cows. Our land reached the Pripyat River, and the gardens around the houses instilled a veritable village spirit. Our family lived together with another family in a shaky house with a straw roof. My father earned his livelihood by transporting mail to Ratno from the Zabolottya railway station. The other resident of the house, my mother's brother Zalman Kolpac, earned his livelihood by teaching. I recall that as children we spent most of our time in the home of my father's cousin Sheindel Prigal. This was not only because of the family closeness, but also because there was something in the atmosphere of that home that attracted our hearts. It is difficult for me to recall exactly what this was.

In January 1941, during the time of Soviet rule in Ratno, I was sent to Lwow in order to complete studies in the area of Soviet cooperatives. I did not think that I had a special aptitude toward that topic, but this was apparently the only chance, and I took advantage of it. I wanted to return to Ratno when the war began, but this was no simple matter in those days when the chaos was great, and the trains were bombarded incessantly. The train that I traveled upon from Lwow to Ratno was also bombarded during the first night. I somehow reached Tarnopol and enlisted in the army assistance unit. I was sent to work in the military pharmacy, and after some time, I accompanied those wounded in battle to the trains. In accordance with an ordinance of Stalin, former Polish citizens, I among them, were fired from such roles. I returned my uniform and began to search for some refuge. I wandered endlessly. In the winter at the end of 1941, I arrived in the district of Starovo[1] along with a group of other refugees. There had been an autonomous German republic in that area, and they deported all the Germans from there to Siberia at the beginning of the war. I remained there until the end of the war. I suffered from loneliness, cold and hunger, but not from anti-Semitism or any form of degradation. I worked as a secretary, bookkeeper, cashier, warehouse official, etc. There were times when I worked at three jobs, and even then it was difficult to earn a reasonable livelihood. Simple people helped me during the times of tribulation, and many of them related to me as if to a family member. I recall this very well to this day.

During the time that I was in that area, I learned that Russian people known how to adjust to suffering and tribulations.

When we received the first news of the German retreat and the liberation of Ratno, I began preparations for the trip "“home,”" even though I knew that I no longer had a home there. I sent letters to all sorts of institutions in order to receive any sort of information as to whether any of my family members survived. I received a response from the town council of Ratno that nobody survived from the Bokser or Kolpac families, but from the Prigal family, Reicha (Raaya) Kolander-Prigal survived. I began to write to her even though she was not a relative. When I arrived in Ratno, she was no longer there, for she had traveled to Kowel and then moved to Luck. When I arrived in Ratno, I first went to see the house in which we had lived. I found plowed up land in the entire area of our and my uncle's garden. I walked the entire length of our road, and reached the home of my uncle Baruch-Hirsch - and there was no trace of an acquaintance or a relative. The sounds of gramophone music emanated from the home of my uncle Yaakov-Pinchas. These sounds oppressed me to the core. I returned to the plowed up area of our house, lay down on the ground, and had no desire to get up. After some time, Yisrael Chayat arrived there. He brought me to the home of the aforementioned Raaya, where the "“Lame matron”", the new owner of the house, greeted me. I slept over in our former house - now her house[2]. Yisrael Chayat came the next day and convinced me to travel to Kowel with him. He brought me to the home of Avraham and Rachel Wiener. I remained there for some time until Raaya came and took me with her to Luck. Their home served as a form of refuge for anyone who survived. There, I met the man, Yosef, who later became my husband, the Ratno native Motel Tyktyner and his girlfriend Fruma Bergel, as well as others whose names I have now forgotten.

We were not Zionists, and my husband and I wanted to remain in Luck, but there were no opportunities to set up our life there. We moved to Poland, but when the wave of anti-Semitism increased there in 1956, we decided to make aliya to Israel. We arrived at the Yavne transit point in March 1957, and were helped greatly by the Ratno natives Pearl Vernik, Aryeh Wolk, Chaya Grabov, and others, who worked to the best of their ability to ensure that we would be properly acclimated in Israel. After some time, we decided to move to Kibbutz

Ein Shemer, where we built our home. I wish to point out that only the aforementioned Ratno natives, as well as Mordechai and Zelda Gefen, gave us the feeling of being at home when we arrived in Israel, and we will always be grateful to them.

Tova Gandelsman (Bokser)

Translator's Footnotes

1. An area in the Kirov Oblast on the Volga. https://www.jewishgen.org/Yizkor/Ratno/rat202.html - f215a-1r
2. According to the story, this may not actually be the house of Tova's family, and the term "“our former house"” may have been used somewhat vaguely. https://www.jewishgen.org/Yizkor/Ratno/rat202.html - f215a-2r

The Tribulations of Freedom

by Yisrael Chayat

Translated by Jerrold Landau

The thunder of the cannons echoed incessantly and increased from hour to hour. The walls of the stable in which I had found a hiding place were almost falling down. I began to feel that I was liable to meet my death under the ruins exactly at the threshold of the liberation. The retreat of the Nazi occupiers brought a great tumult, with the terrifying screams of the confused residents, the movement of the vehicles, etc. However, now silence pervaded around. Hidden, wonderful feelings were awakened within me and swept away the gloom, dampness, cold, and fear that had been my lot throughout the long months that I lay covered under the dung heap upon which stood the cow of Cecilia the butcher woman. The tense wait for liberation and freedom overtook the precautions that I observed to this point, thanks to which I succeeded in evading my German and Ukrainian persecutors. I no longer had the patience to wait for the signal that was agreed upon between Cecilia and me, and I freed myself from the pit.

A deathly silence enveloped the suburb of Znatica, the lanes of which I walked that morning. It seemed as if a wave of thick water silenced the pulsation of life in that suburb. This is how the Jewish alleyways looked at the beginning of the Nazi occupation, now with the addition of ruin and destruction. A completely different environment existed there only a few weeks earlier, including acts of pillage, attacks, and murder through the joint efforts of the Nazi demon and the Ukrainians. Only the yelping of the dogs testified that a living being was present. I recalled the motto "If the dogs are yelping - it is a clear sign that the Angel of Death is in the area." Who was he stalking this time? Perhaps me, myself? This deathly silence around and the cannon shots that were getting stronger awakened in me the faith that the hour of vengeance and recompense was approaching. The murderers will be brought to an accounting over the murder of millions of innocent people. These feelings in my heart accompanied me as I left gentile Ratno on my journey eastward.

I continued along my journey through fields, forests, and frozen rivers. Wagons of Ukrainians from the villages of the areas, laden with women, children, and belongings, were hurrying along in front of me and behind me. The increasing thunder of the cannons frightened them from their comfort, shook up their certainty of a Nazi victory, and instilled fear and trepidation in them. They hastened to escape before the feet of the Red Army would trample there, and before judgments would be passed on them too.

I thought about the irony of fate. A lone Jew such as I was able to walk without fear along these roads, which until this point were dangerous for any Jew, while the thunder of the cannons that he could hear was like the shofar of the Messiah. Whereas the "brave ones" of yesterday who instilled fear on all Jews were now running frantically like mice in a trap. Perhaps it was worthwhile to suffer so much in order to see - and not just within one moment - that which I was seeing at that time, the world of tomorrow, the world of peace and brotherly love that also includes the Jewish nation. I longed for and waited for that day when the liberated world would begin to repay the angels of destruction that which they deserved.

I sat on a sawed off tree stump in the forest of Luchichi in order to rest a bit. The shooting stopped. I glanced around and noticed that the surrounding landscape and vegetation had also changed. The forest was imparting a benefit to a wandering, hungry, barefoot Jew who was going on a journey to nowhere, with no destination. Various strange thoughts ran through my mind. Pictures from the terrible recent past blended in my mind with visions of the future. These were random thoughts that I could not organize. The shout of "Stay!" (Stand!) that pieced the air put an end to these mad thoughts. Five fighters of the Red Army stood next to me. They began to interrogate me vigorously while

I was standing next to them with my hands raised, answering all their questions. Only after they were convinced that they had some business with one of the Jews who had survived, and that no danger was coming from that Jew did they order me to put down my hands. They even treated me to a slice of bread and a piece of sugar. The commander ordered them to transfer me to their bed.

The bed was located in the house of farmers in the village of Luchichi. When we entered the house, the person accompanying me disappeared for a moment. The old farmer woman came out of the kitchen, noticed a living Jew, and looked at me as an other-worldly creature. She muttered something, perhaps a prayer or perhaps a curse, crossed herself and left. The door of the next room opened, and I was ordered by the person accompanying me to enter. There was a table in the corner upon which there were statues of Jesus, Mary, and other Christian saints. A Red Army captain sat at the table, looking at military maps. He did not turn his head to me or even respond to my greeting as I entered the room. He only turned to me, smiled, and responded to my greeting after he finished what he was doing and folded up the maps. The person accompanying me left the room, and I was invited to sit next to him.

"So, what do you have to say, my friend?" he asked me, with a soft, loving tone of voice. This pleasantness moved me to open my closed heart and tell him about all the tribulations and suffering that I endured, about my wandering through forests and fields, about the persecutions, and about the great destruction that I had witnessed with my own eyes.

The captain sat motionless. It was possible to see from his facial movements that he was moved and emotional, but he tried to the extent possible to withhold any sign of emotion. After a brief silence, he said, "Yes, my dear one, we already knew about and had heard a bit about these things. We will certainly hear much more. We will pay them all back with the full force of the law!"

I was unable to control myself. I sighed. The words of the captain regarding justice for the murderers echoed in my ears as if they came from Divine providence. After I calmed down, I asked him to draft me into the Red Army.

The captain politely explained to me that he understood my spirit very well, and furthermore that he understood my reasoning, but that the matter of enlisting in the army could only be decided upon by the higher authorities who were now far from the front. Therefore, he recommended that I enlist in the ranks of the partisans who were fighting in the area, for he was certain that I would be able to bring great benefit to them, for I knew the area well, and I would be able to identify all those who collaborated with the Nazis in those areas, so that they could be brought to justice.

I began to explain to him that the partisans in this area did not willingly accept Jews into their ranks. However, he retorted and said, "This is not the case, but if it is the case, they will accept you with our recommendation." As if to end the discussion, he instructed me to go to the partisan command in the village of Vydryche. He extended his hand and wished me success.

I dragged my feet with difficulty through tortuous paths parallel with the main road from Ratno to Kamin-Kashirsk. It was difficult for my tired legs to bear my emaciated body. The few words that I heard from the captain regarding judgments against the Nazis stayed with me and encouraged me throughout the journey. I hoped that this time, as opposed to previous times, I would be accepted into the partisan camp and they would not present me with their usual conditions: weapons, gold, etc.

At the entrance to the village of Vydryche, I ran into a partisan guard post. Three typical villagers with murderous expressions on their faces stopped me. "What are you doing wandering around here, little Jew[1]?" I responded quietly, "I have come to you in order to enlist." A smile came across their faces, and one said to his friend, "Here you have a new fighter. Take him out to the depths of the forest and show him how we fight..."

A cold sweat covered my body, and my legs weakened. I attempted to not lose consciousness, and said, "I have come to you in accordance with the recommendation of the captain responsible for the district of Luchichi. He also informed your captain of my arrival, and I am supposed to give over important information to him."

When the guards heard my serious words, they changed their tone, and consulted with each other. Instead of hauling me to the thickness of the forest, they accompanied me to their command post. There was a great deal of movement surrounding the command post. Fighters both in uniform and out of uniform, armed and not armed, were running around. Among them was someone I recognized - a Jewish partisan from the village of Datyn, named Blit (today in Canada). I stopped him and asked, "Are you not from the Blit family of the village of Datyn?" He responded in the affirmative. I continued asking, "Do you not recognize me?" He responded, "Yes, I recognize you. You were an official in the people's bank of Ratno."

"Perhaps you know of any other Jews of Ratno who survived?"

"Yes, yes, Yaakov Grabov, Hershel Leib and Reicha Janowicz."

To each of my questions about what happened to him, and his past, he responded with mechanical responses. It was impossible for me not to realize that this "fortunate" Jewish partisan was suspicious of the evil eye of gentiles around us who were following after the conversation of two Jews.

I separated from Blit, and in the eyes of my spirit, I saw myself as a partisan like him, with a belt and weapons, wearing the vest of a Nazi soldier who had been shot.

Three of the partisan commanders were sitting in the room designated as the weapons warehouse in the command building and were discussing technical problems of dismantled weapons. One of them, short, hairy, and with an athletic build gave me an evil glance from the side when I entered the room. The conversation among the commanders continued, as I was immersed in thoughts about what was awaiting me and about the good fortune that fell into my lot to be a fighting partisan. I thought to myself, "Who knows, perhaps tomorrow I will reach destroyed Ratno not as someone seeking refuge among its ruins, but rather as someone taking revenge for the blood of my family, my townsfolk, and my nation..." I recalled from my childhood school days the statement that gentiles only recognize the power of the G-d of Israel after he conducts a fierce battle against them. The question suddenly directed to me interrupted my thoughts. The following is a transcript of our conversation.

"What is your name?" asked one of the commanders.

"Yisrael," I responded.

"A Jew?"

"Yes."

"Your occupation?"

"An official."

"Where did you hide during the period of the Nazi occupation?"

"In various places. At first in the fields, forests, huts, and pits, and later with a butcher woman from a village."

"Is she still a butcher woman currently, even after she received some of your gold?"

"She did not receive any gold from me, for I did not have any gold. She is still a butcher woman."

"Why did she give you refuge if she did not receive any reward from you?"

"Because she knew my parents, who used to give her presents in a generous fashion. She also believed that it was a good deed to save a human being."

"Is she religious?"

"Yes."

"How old is your butcher woman?"

"Over 70."

"Who of your family is still alive?"

"I do not know. It is possible that someone survived, and it is possible that nobody did."

"When did you separate from them?"

"I parted from my wife and children on October 26, 1942."

"Where were they on that day?"

"As in all the previous aktions, my wife and children entered the pharmacy that day, and she began working as a pharmacist. This seemed to us to be the best course of action, for it was forbidden by the Nazi directives for a Jew to enter a pharmacy."

"If that is the case, how could she, as a Jewess, have worked in that pharmacy?"

"Since the supervisor of that pharmacy, the Pole Koblaski, gave her support, and her external appearance and fluent Polish accent would not give her away."

"And if your family members are no longer alive, do you want to continue to live alone?"

"Under no circumstances do I wish to be murdered by a Nazi."

"Why not?"

"Perhaps due to the hope that someone of my family is still alive. I do hope for this."

"Are you prepared to be killed by one of our bullets?"

"If it comes to this - yes!"

"Why do you wish to be a partisan?"

"I searched for such an opportunity throughout the time of the war, but I did not succeed. The partisans wanted me to provide them weapons, and I was not able to."

"And now do you have weapons?"

"No."

"Enough!" One of the captains sitting in the room cut off the interrogation. "At this point, we will continue the war without him."

To me these words seemed to be a death sentence, without any chance of appeal. I wanted to remind them that I was sent to them through the agency of the regional commander of the partisans, but an armed partisan was already standing in front of me, and I was ordered to follow after him.

We reached one of the houses of the farmers in the village in which the partisans of the region and from other areas of Russia were gathered. Some of them were smoking and drinking, and others were playing music, and dancing and singing songs of the awaited victory. I noticed Motel Tyktyner on a bench in the corner of the kitchen. He looked terrible. It was clear that he was emaciated from hunger. Parts of his body appeared blue through his torn clothes. He rested on his two hands and tears were flowing from his eyes. Two female Jewish partisans were baking and cooking next to the farmer's oven. A partisan with a freckled face tried to tend to them, but left the house after a few moments. The partisan Blit, whom I had met earlier, came in from outside, and crossed the room without even glancing at us and apparently without noticing that he was in the presence of two Jewish youths who were in danger. Then, the two Jewish partisan women left the house. A villager who was breathing heavily entered and announced that the pit that he had been ordered to dig was already prepared. My brother in danger, Motel Tyktyner, reacted to this declaration with the groan of a dying person in his death throes: "Yisrael, they are going to shoot us!" In the murderous eyes of the person who dug the pit, staring constantly at my pants with the intention of getting them after he killed me, I found reason to believe what Tyktyner said. At that moment, I was standing at the threshold of the house, immersed in nightmares and frightening thoughts. I concluded the thoughts with the realization that I was standing on the threshold of death.

"Master of the World," I shouted as if to myself, "is this indeed how the life of freedom looks?" In those moments, I began to feel that the bleeding wound in my soul would never heal. The fear of despair and lack of hope would accompany me as long as I lived. What was worse than anything: I would not have anyone to participate in my grief and agony, for I would never find my relatives. It was getting dark outside. A small flame, like a Yom Kippur candle, was flickering on the farmer's oven. A tall, blond "shegetz"[2] entered, took down a gun from the wall, put a magazine with bullets into it, locked the lock, smiled and gestured to his friends and said, "My friends, come to the event!"

I walked first, after Motel. When I opened the exit door, and saw the darkness of the night outside, I began to shout to myself and Motel who was following after me, "Escape! Escape!"

As I was running, I heard the sounds of the shots and saw the red flares. I ran for my life. Only after I found refuge behind the stable of a farmer, did I begin to feel the pain in my left foot. I took off my shoe that had been pierced by bullets, and bandaged the wound with my last shirt that I took off my body.

(Translated from Yiddish by Simcha Lavie)

A group of women Holocaust survivors from Ratno in Munich

Translator's Footnotes

1. The Hebrew word here is an insulting diminutive for a Jew. https://www.jewishgen.org/Yizkor/Ratno/rat202.html - f215-1r
2. A derogatory term for a gentile. https://www.jewishgen.org/Yizkor/Ratno/rat202.html - f215-2r

The Fateful Escape

by Shlomo Vernik

Translated by Jerrold Landau

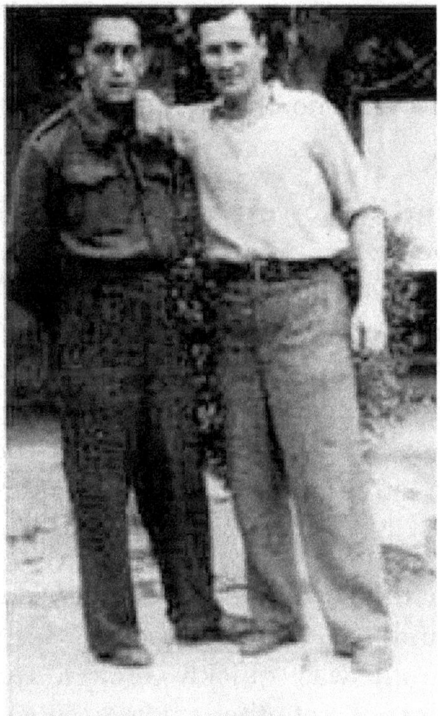

Shlomo Vernik and Yisrael Steingarten in Carmona (Italy)

Many years after the Holocaust, we continue to ponder one question: Why did Jews go to their mass deaths as sheep to the slaughter? Why were there not many resistance actions in every place? Why was there no mass escape? Where were the leaders?

I do not pretend to be able to answer all these questions, but it seems to me that every deliberation of this nature must take into account the circumstances and conditions of that time. First of all, we cannot ignore that the heads of the community, especially in the small towns such as Ratno, were religious men who tended to see all tribulations and harsh situations as decrees from Heaven, regarding which there can be no guile or means of escape. The younger leaders, members of the youth movements, left the stage during the era of Soviet rule, and the "conductors" of the adult community were primarily the religious men who were suspicious that any escape or opposition would cost us dearly. Therefore, there was no choice but to make peace with the situation and go along the path of "sanctifying the Divine name."

This concept was not acceptable to us, the youth, but in the absence of appropriate protection, we had no choice but to accept the judgment - and so we did.

I myself was drafted into a two-year compulsory period of service in the Red Army in 1941, while we were still under Soviet rule. We, a group of eight youths from Ratno, set out together in the direction of Kolomyja, where we were required to present ourselves: M. Sheinis, Sh. Chayat, Z. Bender, Sh. Prigal, M. Hornstein, Tovia ("Mokeches"), D. Eilbaum, and me. We were together in a labor camp next to an army camp, under very difficult conditions. We worked at backbreaking work and the food was insufficient, but we supported each other in the Soviet "Garden of Eden" in order to sustain ourselves.

After four months in this camp, the war between the Soviet Union and Germany broke out, and we found ourselves as Soviet soldiers on the Ukrainian front. The front was quickly broken up, and we were taken prisoners along with thousands of other soldiers. Since the prisoner camp was not guarded stringently and the conditions inside were unbearably terrible, the Ratno natives took council and decided to escape at the first opportunity. This is what we did, with the intention of returning to Ratno. Our friend D. Eilbaum of Ratno decided to not join us, and I do not know what his fate was. After escaping from the camp, our first stop was the town of Tlumacz in Galicia. There, the Ukrainians caught us and put us in jail. They housed us on the third floor in order to make another escape difficult.

When the Jews of the town found out that there were Jewish prisoners in the local jail, they quickly made contact with us, brought us food and clothing, and worked to the best of their ability to free us. Indeed, we quickly succeeded in being freed. They provided us with food and we left the town with the good Jews, for this was the condition of freeing us. The Ukrainians pillaged, perpetrated pogroms, and rejoiced at any opportunity given to them to attack the Jews. We, the group of Ratno natives, went together to Lwow. When we arrived at the gates of that big city, we were told that it would be best to avoid the city, for the Ukrainians were pillaging therein. We were tired, fatigued, and hungry, and we did not follow the advice that we were given. There, the group disbanded, with each person going in his own direction. We talked about meeting a few days later in the Great Synagogue of Lwow. The parting was difficult for each of us, but we had no choice, for it was very dangerous to continue going as a group.

I continued walking sad and depressed, when I met a Ukrainian woman along the way who told me incidentally during a conversation that her only child was serving in the Red Army. It turned out that her son had been a good friend of mine in the army. She invited me home, and treated me to a good meal and a place to sleep without knowing that I was a Jew. In brief - all the comforts. After three days in her home, I decided to go to the synagogue as we had arranged to meet the rest of the group from Ratno. There, I found out about the large pogrom that had been perpetrated by the Ukrainians against the Jews of Lwow, which ended with 8,000 murdered Jews. I never met my friends from Ratno again, and I do not know what their fate was.

I remained alone and did not know what to do. After much deliberation, I decided to advance in the direction of Ratno to see my family. When I consider today the conditions and circumstances of that time, it is hard for me to understand why I endangered myself to such an extent. However, in fact I arrived in Ratno on the evening of August 4, 1941. I was the only one of the group of Ratno natives who went out to Soviet Army service to return.

I told my family members and anyone else willing to listen about the tribulations that I had endured and about everything that I had seen on the journey - about the pogroms perpetrated by the Ukrainians, the atrocities of the Germans, etc. However, I saw that it was hard for them to believe that the situation was such. They said openly: Perhaps the Ukrainians are liable to perpetrate the atrocities about which you have mentioned, but regarding the Germans, it is impossible to believe what you have said, for we know them from the time of the First World War... In short - the people of Ratno believed that this would not happen to them -- -- --

The Germans began to draft people for work, and I found myself in a group of 30 people who were drafted for work at the sawmill in Zabolottya. I worked in the sawmill together with 15 other people. The labor camp consisted of several dismal bunks containing two levels of crowded beds. We worked under very difficult conditions, and I was always thinking about how to escape. I even encouraged other people in this matter, but few were interested in this.

The Germans began to conduct selektions in the work camp in stages. People were taken out to be murdered or were transferred to an unknown location. Finally, only A. Berg, his wife Dvora, and I remained in the sawmill. Three other Jews remained under guard in the city for service work.

According to the news that reached me, the German director of the sawmill, K. Kraus, promised Avraham Berg that no harm will come to him and his wife, and that they did not have anything to worry about, for he intended to take them to Germany.

One night in the autumn of 1942, I saw my father of blessed memory in a dream, who had come to warn me that I must not remain in the camp, but that I must rather escape to the forest. This dream gave me no rest. I got up in the morning, opened the sawmill, and began to work. In the meantime, additional workers came, and the work whistle was sounded at 5:45. I left the sawmill, quietly entered our bunk where A. Berg and his wife were still sleeping, took a small pack of food, and told Berg and his wife, "I am leaving you and going to the forest." I slammed the door and set out with sure steps.

After traveling along the way a bit, I heard the voice of A. Berg from behind me, "Wait, we are following you!" I waited and continued along with him and his wife. We were already in the forest after walking for about half an hour. Two days after the escape, I was accepted into the ranks of the partisans, and I fought against the accursed Nazis for two years. After that, I served once again in the Red Army until the end of the war.

After the war, I passed through the cities of Ukraine, visited Luck, Kowel and Ratno, and saw the great destruction with my own eyes. From our large family of about 200 people, only two of us remained: my sister Pearl and I. We both succeeded in actualizing the desire of our souls, as we arrived in the Land of Israel through the illegal immigration. My fellow escapee, A. Berg, settled in the United States.

A Passover Seder in the "Achdut Yisrael" group in Santa-Cesaria, Italy (1945). Yaakov Steingarten is at the head of the table

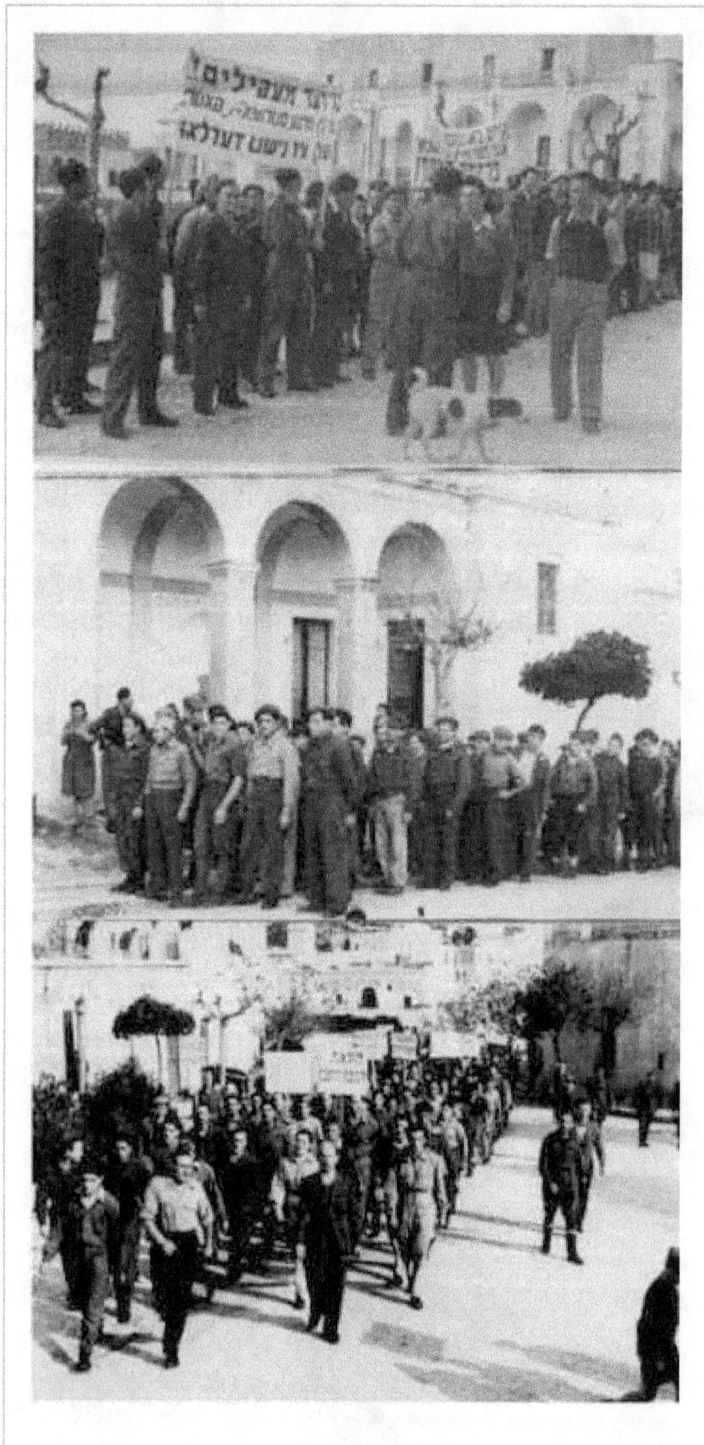

Elchanan and Yisrael Steingarten at the head of a demonstration against the White Paper in southern Italy

From the Stories of the Fighters
Two Brothers with the Partisans

by Elchanan Steingarten

Translated by Jerrold Landau

To a large degree, I was saved from the Holocaust thanks to one man named Buchwald who lived in Ratno. This Buchwald served as a forester in the government guard, even though he was not an expert in forestry. When the Five Year Plan ("Piatletka") was declared, and it also included the forestry business, Buchwald began to feel that he would be unable to stand up to the demands placed before him in accordance with this plan, and that he would therefore be liable to a punishment of imprisonment or deportation to Siberia, as was the custom of the Soviets. Therefore, he approached my father, who was a professional forester, and asked that he take the job instead of him. My father agreed, freed Buchwald from all responsibility, and carried out the work in the best possible manner. Buchwald owed a debt of gratitude to my father, who saved him from a great deal of unpleasantness. Two years later, when the Germans entered Ratno, and their first activity was to murder 30 young, local Jews as revenge for the supposed attack by gunfire upon a German unit. My brother Aryeh of blessed memory was among those murdered. When Buchwald[1] found out about this, he approached my father and recommended that he come with him to the Smolna forest, where he would protect him. He would be able to do this, for he was considered by the Ukrainians to be a Ukrainian, by the Russians to be a Russian, and by the Poles to be a Pole; and when the Germans entered, he declared himself as a Volksdeutche who was close to the Germans.

We took advantage of the generosity and protection of this Buchwald. Whenever there was a fear of danger, my parents, my brother Yisrael, and I escaped to the city and found protection with this Buchwald. This situation continued until August 1942.

On Thursday, 13 Elul 5702 (August 26, 1942), the Germans began to liquidate the Jews of Ratno. On the first two days (Wednesday and Thursday), we hid in a hidden cellar in our house, and on Friday night, we escaped to the Smolna Forest. After some time, Buchwald obtained a permit from the Germans to employ us in forestry work. Pearl Vernik and Itzka Shapira were with us. We worked in the forest for a few months, until the Ukrainian police appeared on December 5, 1942 (26 Kislev 5703) and brought us under guard to Ratno. Along the way to Ratno, the Germans also captured the family of Elkana Szeftel and joined them to us. When we arrived in Ratno, Buchwald began to negotiate with the Germans until they freed us. The Germans informed him that they would take us to the place where they took Jews to be killed on the route to Cheplik, and would free us there. When we arrived at the bridge over the river, one of the Germans asked my father, “Where is your family?” When my father pointed to us, for we were nearby, the German instructed us to stop. We were returned to the prison in Ratno, and toward evening, we were brought to the Artel[2] that existed in Ratno. We remained there until Tuesday, and then we were returned to the forest where we remained until February 7, 1943, the day of the liquidation of the remaining Jews of Ratno, including Gittel Karsh and the girls. We found out about the final liquidation of the Jews the next morning. From that time, our only hope was to go to the partisans. Throughout the entire time that we were in Smolna, we knew that Buchwald maintained contact with the partisans, and even gave them information about the various actions that the Germans were preparing. We pressured him to bring us to one of the partisan camps that operated in the area. On Friday night, we agreed with Musyuk, one of Buchwald's assistants, that we would go to one of the places in the area that was known to my father, where the partisans would accept us into their service. That is what took place. On February 12, 1943, two Ukrainian partisans accepted us into their unit. (It is appropriate to note that to the best of our knowledge, Buchwald's grandfather was a Jew who converted to Christianity. Jewish blood flowed through the veins of our benefactor, but this did not stop himself from presenting himself as a Ukrainian, a Russian, a Pole, etc.)

*

I wish to tell about one of the partisan activities in which we participated. This was in December 1943. Our unit camped around Pinsk and received a directive to go out to an action in the area that was known as a German supply route to the front. A group of 30 people, including my brother Yisrael of blessed memory and me, went out to this action that was to be conducted in the area of Ratno. After we arrived in the designated spot by vehicle and by foot, we hid a distance of a few kilometers from the Brisk-Kowel railway line. The number of people who went out to each action varied from between four and five, all volunteers. The active groups would alternate, and the same group would not go out to an action day after day. After two weeks, my brother returned from an action of bombing a train on the Brisk-Kowel line. The same evening that he returned, I went out with a different group to attack a train. Of course, we would conduct scouting observations before going out, for the Germans would patrol the railway line incessantly. Most of the time, we would wait with our explosive material until literally the last minute as the train approached. That was the way it was this time as well. We would place down our explosives when the train was a distance of about 100 meters from us. We would hear the sound of the explosion right after we placed down the material. It became clear that another unit had placed explosive material a minute before we did. We were forced to dismantle our load, but instead of returning to the base, we camped for the night in one of the houses of the area. In the interim, the Germans managed to repair the railway line, and we returned to the same place in order to place down our load. We did not have enough time to conduct a scouting observation before the action itself, for the train was already very close to where we were. We placed down the load and remained in hiding. When we saw the lights and the steam, we began to retreat from the area. The explosion would take place when we were close-by rather than in the forest, as we usually were. The train and the railway line were damaged. We returned to our base in the morning hours. I knew that my brother Yisrael said he would be at the base, for he had returned from an action the day before I went out, but I did not find him. I was tired, and I went to take a brief nap. I saw Yisrael when I woke up. I asked him where he was, and he answered, "I knew that you went out to an action, and instead of sleeping here and thinking about what might happen to you, I preferred to go out again to an action in a different place." After a few days, we received a notice from our mother camp in Pinsk that the Russian Army was advancing through Ukraine in a significant fashion, and we must unite with the army that was fighting at the front. We moved from the area of Ratno to the area of Pinsk, and, in January 1944, we met up with a patrol of the Russian Army that was advancing toward our base.

My Journey to the Land, and my Activities in Italy

After the liberation, we began to search for the shortest route to get to the Land of Israel. We arrived in Lublin as repatriated individuals, but we did not want to remain on Polish soil. Rumor had it, that there were unutilized certificates in Romania, and we therefore wished to reach Romania as quickly as possible. We indeed arrived there through a roundabout route that took us through Czechoslovakia and Hungary, but we were too late. There were no certificates. We therefore traveled to Italy in order to be as close as possible to the Land of Israel. In order to ensure the possibility of aliya, I began to work in the Revisionist Movement, to which I was connected while still in Poland. There was a Lechi[3] representative working in Italy at that time, and my friends and I decided to collaborate with Lechi until an Etzel[4] representative would arrive. It was not long before such a representative indeed came, and he was actually a Volhyner (a native of Luck), with whom we had a common language. He chose several dozen members from amongst the activists and brought them to a special course in Torrecuso. Officially, this was a course for Beitar leaders, but in actuality, it was a course for resistance attacks, use of weapons, etc. At the end of this course, my brother was sent to an Etzel activity in northern Italy, whereas I was given a task in the area of Rome. I began to work at obtaining weapons and in leadership. After the Mandate Government suppressed all aliya from Italy, and the Etzel command decided to carry out a serious resistance attack upon the British embassy in Rome, other members and I were given the task of providing the necessary explosives. The action was set for the night of October 31, 1946 at 2:45. Five hours before that time, I arrived in Rome by tram from Grottaferrata with two suitcases of explosives. The action was carried out successfully, and Etzel confirmed its responsibility for this action by proclamations and notices in newspapers. The Italian investigators began to follow the perpetrators of the action. Since at about that time, I had given to one of the Etzel commanders (a native of Kamin-Kashirsk) my documents for the purposes of a specific action, and the documents were captured, the investigators began to suspect me and to search for me. In accordance with a command of the Etzel commander, I was to leave Italy immediately. Since the first ship that I was able to board was travelling to Cyprus, I travelled to Cyprus. While there, I read in a newspaper of December 26, 1946 that the police were searching for Steingarten. I suspected very much that my brother Yisrael, who remained in Italy, would fall into the trap (the police investigators did not know that there were two Steingartens). I wrote to my family that was still in Italy that I was very worried about my brother Yisrael. Their response was, “We know who has to worry about whom.” In any case, I changed my name, and after some time, Shlomo Reiner (my new name) arrived in Israel from Cyprus. I began my new existence as an Israeli. A trial against the perpetrators of the bombing of the British embassy in Rome took place on October 31, 1951. Among the accused in absentia was Chona the son of Yaakov Steingarten, as the person who hid the explosive material.

Translator's Footnotes

1. In the analogous story on page 207, the name is written as Buchhalt. https://www.jewishgen.org/Yizkor/Ratno/rat202.html - f221a-1r

2. See http://en.wikipedia.org/wiki/Artel https://www.jewishgen.org/Yizkor/Ratno/rat202.html - f221a-2r

3. See http://en.wikipedia.org/wiki/Lehi_%28group%29 https://www.jewishgen.org/Yizkor/Ratno/rat202.html - f221a-3r

4. See http://en.wikipedia.org/wiki/Irgun https://www.jewishgen.org/Yizkor/Ratno/rat202.html - f221a-4r

With a Song on Their Lips

by Shlomo Perlmutter

Translated by Jerrold Landau

We were three:'Sheikele, Motele, and I.

Sheikele was a pale child with curly hair. A thin film of blue showed in his sad eyes, and the dimples on his cheeks added charm to him.'He was diligent in his studies, and his graduation certificate showed excellent marks, and imparted honor to father's table with the various prizes and silver certificates.'He was only 12 years old.

He never asked me, his older brother, for protection.'He always expressed his opposition to my opinions and attempted to compete with me in every area.'He was stubborn, and at times he permitted himself to even mock grandfather.'Among everything else, he claimed, “Is it any wonder that father shows preference to Sh. over me?'For he bears the name of his father - Shlomo Aharon?!”' In general, there was a battle between him and me over one topic:'who will have more influence over the youngest brother, Motele.'We attempted by all means to win over his heart, especially with sweets, and Motele would always tend toward the one who seemed to show a weakness.'At times, he befriended me and preferred me over Sheika, and at times he turned his back to me.'As long as he was at my side, we together covered Sheika with the small decorative cushions that we threw at him.'If he was at Sheika's side, they both would toss the cushions at my head...

Our pranks ended when the war broke out.'I was taken away to a far-off labor camp with Father, and mother remained with my two younger brothers.'Later, Mother was forced to hand'them both over to one of the farmers that we knew in the area in order to save their lives. They worked as shepherds for the farmer.'At that time, at the end of the summer of 1942, many Jewish children were working as shepherds for the flocks of farmers in the pastures and forests of Pulsia and Volhynia.'Among them were "well pedigreed" children such as the son of the pharmacist Mogilenski of Ratno (Betzalik), and the son of the elder firefighter of the town, Yehudale.'Betzalik was a thin, blond child.'He was a student in grade six, and baby eyes peered from'the shadow of his thin, yellowish eyelashes.'Yehudale had black hair, and his eyes were recessed in their sockets, adorned with thick, black eyebrows.'The testimony that I collected is dedicated to the three of them.

Motele related:

I visited the community of Ratno a day before the slaughter.'Mother gave us much love as usual, and a great deal of food for the journey.'She accompanied us to the house at the corner of the large street and the Post Office Road - Brener's house.'I urged her, "Mother, do us a favor and come with us to the village, for my heart foresees evil".'Large tears fell upon her cheeks as she heard our request. She responded, "I cannot leave Grandfather alone."'She kissed us.'We left her standing and looking at us, as she was drying her tears.'We felt bad for her.'I did not cry, and neither did Sheika.'It was not appropriate for me to cry in front of Betzalik and Yehudale.'Thus did we take leave of Mother.'I never saw her again after that.

The next day, as I lay down in the pastures near the town, I heard the thunder of shots. I was very afraid, but I did not imagine that they were murdering the Jews of the town, including Mother and my grandfather.'When it got dark, I returned to the village with the cows, with a great heaviness in my heart, that prophesied evil tidings.'Suddenly I heard the sound of the footsteps of Alexander "the American."'He was my gentile, whose flocks I tended.'"Motel," he said to me with a hidden tone of satisfaction, "they slaughtered the Jews of Ratno, all of them"...

I felt the need to visit Sheika, who tended to the horses of Emilian at the edge of the forest.'I went to him in the darkness.'Betzalik and Yehudale were sitting next to him.'They were whispering among themselves.'They were ten and twelve years old - big boys, not merely shepherds, but rather workers of horses.'They were also very worried, and told me that they would consult with the Jewish shepherds in the village the next day.

I returned to "my" farmer.'Sheikele and Betzalik led me through the fields.

I snuck into the barn like a bewildered rabbit.'I did not close my eyes that night.'I thought only about our house, about Mother, about Grandfather.'Who knew what happened to them.

The first light of day found me awake.'I went out once again to the flock in the meadows next to the town.'Shots echoed endlessly.'I had never heard so many shots.'It seemed to me that the cows were also disconcerted, and were mooing fiercely at the sound of the shots.'They jumped from one grassy area to the next, and barely ate.'They returned from the meadows hungry, and there was no milk in their udders.

Avraham Cohen (perished) and Shlomo Perlmutter – Ratno natives

Alexander greeted me next to the barn.'He told me that he was in Ratno, and he saw with his own eyes how they captured and murdered the Jews.'He also saw Mother as she was walking arm in arm with Grandfather, who was wearing his tallis and tefillin.'Uncle Asher, Shevale and Beila were next to them.

That night, "my" gentile did not invite me to the table as usual, but rather brought my supper to the barn.'

After everything became silent in the barn and the yard, I realized in the darkness that Alexander, his wife, and children were busy unloading the loot that they had hauled from town.'It was impossible to fail to notice their joy in undertaking that work. I could not remain there.'I placed my two shirts in the shepherd's sack and fled to my brother Sheika.'I knew that I would find him in Emilian's grove, and that was indeed how it was.'He was waiting for me. That night, we fled in the direction of the forests of Zabrody.'Yoshke Ginzburg, Yisraelke Zisik, Zeligl Bukler, Betzalik, Yakovle Hochman, Yechielik Weiner and others were with us.

We remained in the forests of Zabrody for no more than three weeks.'We sustained ourselves with the potatoes that we stole from the fields of the farmers and from the bread that we would get as a gift from the gentiles at night.'I ate anything that was available.'Later, we wandered to the forests of Adamivka which were denser.'The farmers in the region were evil, and even threatened us with knives.'We remained there for a few days, and then continued to pass through the known marshes of Wielimcze.'The farmers quickly detected our presence, and warned us, waving axes, that they would take care of us appropriately if we did not disappear from their area.'Our situation deteriorated.'Sheikele, as well as the oldest among us Yehudale and Betzalik, decided to go to the town, for there was a rumor that any Jew who returned to Ratno of his own free will would not be killed.'In Ratno, there were approximately 30 Jews who had returned of their own will.'They organized themselves into a collective of workers. Sheika even promised me that after he would arrive in peace, he would do everything to bring me to him.'He went.'I ran after him. I wept.'He left me alone, as Betzalik and Yehudale returned to Ratno with him.'The next day, I heard of their deaths.

This ended Motele's story.

I heard and wrote the following from the mouths of Reizele Gutman, Feigele Fyuler and Golda Karsh:

The Ukrainian policeman Borysiuk from the village of Postupel was walking home minding his own business one Sunday.'When he reached the shallow brook at the edge of the village of Luchichi, he noticed three pale, emaciated boys sitting at the brook.'He asked them where they were going, and when they told them that they wanted to go "home", he "offered" to accompany them.'He turned them in to the police and received the specified reward:'50 marks per head, and products that were more valuable than gold, such as tobacco, salt, and cigarettes.'All the efforts of the few remaining Jews of Ratno to free the children failed. They were held in a dark cell that served as the final stop for the many refugees from Ratno who were found in the forests, villages, and various hiding places.'In the evening, a Gestapo man ordered the children to come out of the cell.'The children ran about like trapped rabbits, as if they were seeking refuge in the bosom of their friends.'They were marched through the roads of the town. They passed through the marketplace near their houses, went up the bridge and continued to walk in the direction of Cheplik.'Ukrainians saw the procession of the children on their way to their deaths, but their hair did not stand on end.'For them, this was a regular, daily scene.

When the "procession" reached the home of Avraham the smith, many shots were heard from all directions.'Sheikele escaped from them despite the barrage of bullets.'He was seen jumping over the fences and running toward the fields that were behind the row of houses on Olianka Street.'The policemen were certain that he had escaped from their barrage of firing.'Suddenly, he slumped down and fell.'A stray bullet hit him.'The policemen approached their victim, and heard the tune of Hatikva coming from the mouth of Sheikele.'Heavy clods of earth covered him and put an end to him and his song. -- --

The Gestapo man ordered Betzalik and Yehudale to strip.'They joined arms, and before they were shot, they also began singing the hymn of the Jews that they knew so well.

One more testimony - from the mouth of the farmer Oleksei Pinkovich of 24 Zabolottya Street, who lived approximately 150 meters from the communal grave in the plots of Cheplik.'I recorded his testimony on September 22, 1944:

Sheikele was shot next to my house.'I accompanied him to Cheplik.'Throughout the entire journey, he was singing the song that all the Jews sang while standing in silence. (I attempted to sing various tunes to the farmer to verify the song that Sheikele was singing before he died, and only when I began to hum Hatikva did the farmer say that that was it.)'The blond policeman Borysiuk ordered me to hitch up the horse, to tie the body behind it, and to bring it to the pits.'I was forced to carry out the command.'They murdered the majority of "your people" next to my house.'I was a witness to the deaths of many of the Jews of the town.'At first it was difficult, but later I became accustomed to all this, just as my brother-in-law Fedya had become accustomed to the abattoir situated near his house.'Nevertheless, this scene was different from all the other scenes that I had witnessed to this point.'My horse was dragging a live child, bleeding and singing.'Believe me:'I could not look at his face. I could not.'When I brought him there, the policemen shouted at me as they would to their dog who had fetched game.'They kicked him into the pit, and from the pit - to G-d -- -- --'The policemen stood next to me and ordered me to bury the children while they were still alive.'They wanted to see how I would do this.'I recall that the spade slipped out of my hands, and a wave of tears flowed from my face.'I fainted.'Vanka Halstim restored my consciousness with a blow from the butt of his rifle.'He warned me, saying, "Stop lamenting. From now on, you will only bury live Jews, and you will weep every day."

"A Survivor's Story"

by Eliahu Liberman

Translated by Jerrold Landau

I left Ratno in 1937 and went to Brisk to study in the ORT trade school. When the Russians entered our area, I continued my studies in the Technikom of Brisk, which replaced the ORT school and the Polish technical school. At the beginning of June 1941, a group of students, I among them, was sent to Vitebsk in Byelorussia to complete our studies. When the war broke out on June 22, I asked to return to Ratno, but I was told that there were no trains going west. I remained in the factory in which I was training, but it was not long before our factory began the evacuation. All the equipment and machinery was loaded upon the trains traveling eastward. After about a month of travel in "echelon," we reached Yalach, and began to set up the enterprise. With the German advance, we had no choice but to retreat again. After a journey of six weeks, we reached Chkalov in the Urals along with all the equipment of the enterprise. There, thousands of miles from the front, the enterprise was reestablished, and I worked in this enterprise until I was drafted into the Red Army in the summer of 1944. Life in Chkalov was more or less punishing. We worked for 12-14 hours each day, however we were not lacking anything from a physical perspective relative to the situation of that time. The news of the murder of tens of thousands of Jews by the Germans even reached the far off Urals, but we did not want to believe this. In the spring of 1944, after Ratno was liberated, I wrote to the secretary of the division (or the head of the council) in Ratno, asking for information about what happened to the Jews and to my relatives. The daughter of the head the council responded to me and described the great disaster in detail. She gave my letter to Avraham Berg, and I also received a detailed letter from him. My Jewish friends and I who studied together with me in Brisk decided to enlist in the Red Army and to find a way to get to the land of Israel. After two months of training in the region of Chkalov, I was sent together with nine other soldiers to the command of the communication division in the district of Bucharest. We crossed the Russian border in Galatz[1], a town in Transylvania. In this town, I met a Jew who had survived along with his family. From him, I learned that many Jews survived in Romania. Among other things, he told me that the main leadership of Hashomer Hatzair was functioning on 2 Olimpului Street in Bucharest. I did all that I could to get to Bucharest. I went to the address that he had given me, and found several youths there. At first, they were very hesitant to tell me anything, but after I convinced them in Hebrew that I was not a provocateur, and no danger awaited them from me, they told me that activities of the Zionist movement had restarted in Romania, and that they were organizing aliya to the Land. They hinted to me that if I were to defect from the Red Army, they would begin to concern themselves with my aliya. However, I decided to continue with my army service, and to make aliya only later. I joined a unit that worked in expanding and strengthening the telephone lines and electric stations. News of the conclusion of the war reached me when I was in Bratislava, Czechoslovakia. They began to sort the units, and all professionals from my unit were transferred to Moscow, where we worked in the central workplaces of the communications division.

With the beginning of the repatriation in March 1946, I presented my request to return to Poland, and expressed my willingness to forego my Russian citizenship. After some time, I was told that I must return my army equipment. I was placed on a train, and after several days of travel, I arrived in Brisk, the city where I had studied for several years, along with several dozen other Jews and Poles. In this city that had once bustled with Jewish life, I did not find even one Jew. I was not given the opportunity to travel to Ratno. After wandering, I reached Walbrzych, where there was a group of the Dror Kibbutz that I joined. I was appointed the head of the group, and after several months, we began to advance in the direction of the land of Israel. This included stealing across borders at night, and following various circuitous and complicated routes along with the “smugglers.” We spent some time in the camps in the district of Frankfurt in Germany, where I got married. Later, I moved to Munich to work in the Dror center. In March 1948, I arrived in the Land of Israel along with my wife as part of the Fourth Aliya.

Translator's Footnote

1. Possibly Galaţi, Romania, but that is not in Transylvania. https://www.jewishgen.org/Yizkor/Ratno/rat202.html - f226a-1r

"A Survivor's Story"

by Dvora Dorner (Teitelbaum)

Translated by Jerrold Landau

I know that many of the Holocaust survivors tell that they wore the yellow patch with pride. I confess that I was embarrassed of it, and I attempted to hide it to the extent possible. I recall that I once passed by the house of Mogilenski, where the Ukrainian policemen were housed. I held in my hand the coat upon which the yellow patch was sewn. One of the policemen noticed this and asked me why I was not wearing the yellow patch. Without waiting for my response, he began to beat me with murderous blows. When I arrived wounded and injured at the home of my Aunt Mindel, my aunt broke out in hysterical weeping.

After the liquidation of the ghetto in Dubove, I escaped with my sister in the direction of Hirnyky. We searched for survivors of the Jews of Ratno, so that we could join them. We met Yidel Janowicz in the forest, who recommended that we join him and go to Brody, for Jews remained there. There, we met Nechama Melnik along with her mother and brother, who were working in construction. This was on a cold winter night. We asked them if we could stay over in their small house, but they did not agree. They claimed that if we would be found with them, we would all be taken to be killed. We found refuge in some barn at the edge of the village. Yidel went to the house of farmers who were acquaintances, and waited for their help. At night, we heard screams and shots. The Germans, with the assistance of the Ukrainian farmers, took out the remaining Jews of the area, including Yidel Janowicz, to be killed.

We escaped to the forest, and arrived in Samary, trembling with fear and cold. We went to the house of a Ukrainian widow with four children, that was isolated and far away from the other houses of the city. We hid in the barn until morning. When the woman entered to milk the cows, she began to cross herself. She recognized us and was certain that we had already been dead for some time. We begged her to give us refuge for several days, but remained with her for over a year.

At night, we helped her with all types of housework. We sewed, knitted, ground wheat in her home mill, and did all tasks that she asked. She told us that our mother had been thrown into some building that was used for preserving ice during the summer. Our tension during the time that we were with her is indescribable. We sat in the attic and listened to the laughter and songs of the Ukrainian children. At that time, I thought that I would never be able to listen to sound and laughter again. I covered my ears at the sound of their laughter. With the help of the partisans, we later reached Rafalovka and Manevychi. When I later reached Ratno, I did not recognize the place. It was a heap of ruins. From Ratno, I returned to Kowel with my sister, and from there to Luck and Breslau. Later, we reached Germany via Czechoslovakia and Austria. I succeeded in arriving in Israel with my husband in 1948, before the declaration of the state. My husband was immediately drafted into the communications brigade of the Israel Defense Forces at the rank of sergeant. He was the only one of his family to survive.

Revenge and Recompense

by Shlomo Perlmutter

Translated by Jerrold Landau

One January day in 1944, as I was riding on my horse in the snowy forest path during the course of carrying out my tasks in the Kotovski Unit, I suddenly noticed a man whose appearance alone caused my heart to beat so strongly that I literally almost lost consciousness. Was this indeed him? I refused to believe the image before my eyes, but the personage was clear – the image of Vanka, the infamous murderer of the Jews of Ratno, the murderer of my brother Shaykale and his friends Yehudale and Betzlik. Here he was in the partisan camp, armed with automatic weapons, wearing the partisan cap with the red ribbon on his head. Was it possible? Was he also among the partisans? This murderer? Was it possible that he was wandering around securely in the area under the command of the unit commander Feodorov? I felt myself covered in a cold sweat. It was as if thousands of hammers were banging at my temples. I could not even turn my head backward to check if I was not mistaken – if my eyes were not misleading me. I placed my feet in the stirrups of my horse, urged on the horse, and galloped directly to the communications unit. I continued to think about this Vanka throughout the entire way, this wild murderer of myriads of Jews, this frightful monster, who was now serving in the same unit as I was...

I quickly gave over the transmissions and mail that I had with me, and decided that, before I returned, I would discuss this Vanka with the command. My feet carried me to the office of General Feodorov himself, whom I had met a few days earlier when he visited our unit. I was so emotional that I did not even make efforts to ask permission of the general's office guard, who was completely astonished at my brazenness. I entered the office of the general as if I was one of his confidantes. I walked properly, but my legs trembled, and the words choked in my throat. I was unable to control the level of my voice, and I literally shouted"

"Aleksei Feodorovich, Comrade General, a wild animal is walking outside here!"

The general rose from his chair, approached me, sensed that something had happened to me, and attempted to calm me. Perhaps he sensed that some sort of evil spirit had overtaken me, and I had gone mad.

"Sania, what happened to you? Tell me, what happened?"

His loving voice and calm manner of speaking gave me back my sense of self- assurance, and I calmed down somewhat. I explained to the general that the murderer of my family and many Jews of my town was now a partisan in our unit, and I had just run into him on the path.

"Are you sure you are not mistaken?", said the general in the same calm voice, "What is his name?"

"Ivan Lokianioch, Vanka, from the village of Komarovo near Ratno. I am not mistaken. He is the man, and he is the one who murdered my family members.

Members of the partisan headquarters with General Feodorov (in the center) Standing at the right edge – Sh. Perlmutter

Shlomo Perlmutter and Yaakov Kaldner in Moscow

The partisan unit of General Feodorov
Third from right in the top row – Sh. Perlmutter

Shlomole on a journey with the partisan unit

I saw it with my own eyes, Comrade General."

Feodorov sat down in his chair, and requested that the person in charge of special services as well as the commissar be brought to his office. When they arrived, they asked me many questions, and I attempted to respond to the matter as calmly as I could, despite the fact that inside I was all stormy and emotional. The next day I heard that Vanka was imprisoned...

*

The investigation of the murderer lasted several days. During the first stages of the investigation, he insisted that he did not know me, and he denied everything. He only admitted that he had served with the Banderites for a brief period, but deserted them after he became convinced that their way was not correct. He never attacked Jews, and never killed any of them. On the contrary, he offered help to the Jews at every opportunity, and even saved a Jewish girl whose name was Caroma[1].

However, the investigators were not satisfied with his admission. They continued pressing him, and he broke down and admitted to his investigators that he had been sent by the Germans and Banderites to spy in the partisan camps. Among the tasks imposed on him, there was one additional one: to kill General Feodorov. He also confirmed that he knew me, and even began to call me by my name Shlomo rather that Semion or Sania, as I was called by the partisans.

During one of the meetings of the investigation, I told about all of Vanka's atrocities in Ratno, and recalled how he murdered a Jew by beating him with a stick only because he had gone out without the yellow patch on his back. The murder took place next to Berger's house on the road, as tens of local Ukrainians were standing and watching the deed, and even encouraging this "hero." The investigator Zolotoronko asked me if I wished to repay him for this. I responded affirmatively. I took a stick from the linden tree that stood in the corner and beat him until I ran out of energy. The Ukrainian "hero," the murderer of my brother, screamed like a wounded animal, and rolled like a ball off the bench upon which he was sitting all the way to the corner of the room, overturning the heating oven with its coal in the process. "The two-gun murderer," as he was nicknamed by the Jews of Ratno, now sat as a captured, bleeding rat. I was only sorry that only a few people were able to see this varmint lying and wailing at my feet. I only told one person from Ratno, Eli Zesak, who also served in Feodorov's group, about the imprisonment and investigation of Vanka. He encouraged me, strengthened my spirit, and told me to not let up until justice is served. Zesak said that this was the purpose of our lives now – this is why we had remained alive.

*

In the meantime, days and weeks passed. I went out with my units to action in the expanse of Sarny. I was concerned that Vanka's investigators might have mercy on him and free him. At the end of our action, I immediately galloped to the command to find out what the situation was. Zolotoronko calmed me and informed me that they were dealing with Vanka "Pa Partisanski" (In the manner of the partisans), and I had nothing to worry about. He would receive his punishment.

A few days later, I met Michael Glider, our cameraman and photographer. He told me that Feodorov decided to hang Vanka. I did not hide my joy, and asked that they not forget my role in this matter when the time comes.

On the evening of February 11, I was informed that I must immediately come to the command of the general. When I arrived, I was officially informed that the general decided to execute Vanka, and I was one of those designated to accompany him to the gallows. At that meeting, I was also told that the procession to the gallows was to be filmed by Michael Glider, to be included in a movie that he was preparing about the partisans, their lives and activities. Feelings of joy, depression, and powerlessness all converged together upon my heart. I had to take control of myself, and I did so by bringing to my memory my brethren of my nation, my brothers Motele and Shaykale, and my parents; and by imagining their joy about my being able to take the revenge for which they had so yearned.

*

When they took Vanka out of his jail cell, he recognized me and smiled at me as if he had seen an old friend. I did not return his greetings... He was wearing a short farmer's cloak. A beard had sprouted on his face, and his hands were tied with strong parachute rope. He was commanded to march forward, and I marched behind him. We brought him to the partisan gathering area, which had been prepared from the outset in a cut-down area of the forest at the edge of the camp. Vanka turned his head backward several times and asked me where they were taking him. I responded that he was been taken to a partisan court. He appeared calm, but when we left the area of the camp and crossed the dirt path, he was suddenly overcome by a spirit of madness, and his entire body trembled.

"What does this mean?", he asked.

"The time of revenge has arrived," I answered. "Did you think, Vanka, that you would escape? Did you think that you would not be brought to justice for all your deeds? Did you think that you killed them all, and nobody remained who would settle the accounts? You were wrong, Vanka. You will surely be repaid, you will pay with your life! All the Jews of Ratno whom you murdered are accompanying you now on your journey to the gallows." I do not know if he heard all of my words, but he realized full well that his time had come. At times he stopped and refused to move, but we prodded him on with the butts of our rifles.

When Vanka stood next to the partisan gathering area, and Zolotoronko read out the verdict that had been signed by the general, the commissar, and the head of the unit, I felt as if had I soared off the snowy ground upon which I was standing, and was floating upward to far-off, holy places, among my parents and my brothers. I felt as if the last wish of thousands of martyrs had been fulfilled, and that the Revenge and Recompense had finally come.

One by one, Zolotoronko enumerated all the atrocities of this poisonous snake who had fallen before us. When he finished, we brought Vanka to the rope that had been tied upon one of the tall oak trees. Two partisans of the unit tied the noose to his neck. I took the noose knot in my hands, and my hands began to tremble. The ancient blessing of my fathers and ancestors came to my head. I recited it silently, with only my lips moving: "Blessed art Thou, oh G-d, our L-rd, the King of the Universe, Who has kept us alive, preserved us, and enabled us to reach this time." I was obligated to recite this blessing for myself as well as for the thousands of martyrs for whom I was acting as their emissary at this moment! They, all the martyrs, held the knot of the noose along with me, and they, together with me, tightened it around the neck of the disgraced murderer. A strong fire was kindled in my eyes. I could not maintain my strength, and I fell.

I recall that when I arose, I saw Michael Glider, the photographer and filmer, standing by me and giving directions, as if we were in a photography or movie studio. I turned my eyes to the direction of the gallows. I saw Vanka swinging. A wave of tears broke out in my eyes.

These were tears of joy.

Translator's Footnote

1. There is a footnote in the text here: This refers to Fruma Bergel of blessed memory, who fell into the hands of a nationalist Ukrainian Banderite unit.https://www.jewishgen.org/Yizkor/Ratno/rat231.html - f233_1r

Shlomole decorated with medals

Shlomole at the time of the giving of the verdict on Vanka

The Traitor

by Michael Glider

Translated by Jerrold Landau

(A chapter from the book "With a Camera on the Neck of the Enemy" by Michael Glider, published in Moscow, 1947.)

In January, a tall, strong youth joined our partisan unit. A young, 15-year-old partisan, Semion, who fought in the Kotovski Unit, recognized him. Semion immediately ran to the head of the unit and told him that this youth, Ivan, had been a policeman in the German ranks in his hometown of Ratno, that he had been cruel to the Jews, and had murdered his family members, among others. The youth Semion had served in the unit for approximately 2 ½ years. He was pleasant and talented, and had witnessed more than enough atrocities during his brief life as a Jew and a partisan. He immediately recognized the murderer of his family, and swore that he was not mistaken. He trembled and wept when he related this. An investigation was opened, but I will not describe the details here, so as not to go on for too long. I will only include the essence of the words of testimony of the subject of the inquiry himself after he broke down during the first stage of the inquiry. His name was Lokianioch, I. L., born in 1923, served in the tractor brigade of the M. T. S. in Bucyn, in the region of Ratno. He was drafted into the Red Army, and deserted with a bicycle and revolver. When he arrived in Ratno with the entrance of the Germans, he took part in the organization of the Ukrainian police, imprisoned Russian soldiers and captains, pillaged the local population, Jews in particular, and beat Soviet citizens on the streets if they did not wear the recognizable symbol (the yellow patch) on their backs. When the Germans began to enlist people for work, this Lokianioch behaved with great cruelty, separated the men from their wives, and removed babies from their mothers' breasts. As a payment for his actions and his faithfulness to the German fascists, the Germans sent him to the school for field gendarmes in Kovel. After he completed three months there, he received the designation as gendarme guide. He later went to Ratno, Turisk, and Kupichev along with the Gestapo men. Then he returned to Kovel. His job was to expose Jews and other citizens who collaborated with the Russians during the era of Soviet rule in the district. The prisoners were shot, and Lokianoch took an active part in taking them to be killed. According to his words, 18,000 men, women and children were killed in the district. Their property was pillaged by the Nazi troops. He also took part in the looting.

In May, 1943, following German directives, he met with the commander of a partisan unit who had known him previously. This commander, who did not know about his past and his deeds, recommended that he join the unit. Lokianoch did not yet agree to the recommendation, for he said that he did not yet know who would be victorious. In 1944, the Germans sent him to a partisan unit that was active in the district, and instructed him to tell them that he was now already convinced of their victory, and that he wanted to switch to their side. He was given the order to go through several units, and then to penetrate the camp of General Feodorov. His tasks were 1) to verify if the partisans had a connection with Moscow; 2) to verify the type of assistance that they received from Moscow; 3) to discover the names, origins, and history of the commanders; 4) to determine the morale of the partisans, the number of fighters, and the types of arms that they possessed; 5) to discover their signals for the landing of airplanes. Aside from all this, he was promised a reward of 50,000 marks if he succeeded in killing General Feodorov himself. In the verdict against him, it was stated among other things that he had demonstrated that he was an enemy who was not fitting to support the homeland. The verdict was unanimous - hanging. The verdict was signed by the commander of the unit, the commissar, and the head of the division.

The command was read before a gathering, and the partisans greeted the verdict against the traitor with shouts of hurray. He was brought to a tree from which hung a rope with a noose. The partisans were silent during the hanging of the traitor. Only Semion, who revealed him, wept, of course not because he had mercy for the hanged traitor, but rather because he remembered all of his victims. That day, there was not one partisan in the unit who did not express words of congratulation and support to Semion.

*

I often had the chance to talk to Semion, who felt closeness and trust toward me. Several days after the verdict, he approached me and said, "David Mishka, take me with you."

I said to him, "How can I take you? I cannot teach you, for this would require specific conditions. I already have an assistant. Perhaps I can take you as a rider, responsible for the horses." Young Semion answered me, "Whatever you want, just take me."

I told him that he was a fighter in the ranks, and the commander would not free him, for it is not right to turn a fighter into a rider. He was stubborn and said, “If you ask – they will free me, and I will also go with you to the battles.”

Eventually this worked out. I obtained a new rider – Semion. Feelings of friendship quickly developed between Semion and Pomzanka, but at times this friendship caused unpleasantness for the youth. He caught a cold, and Pomzanka decided to cure him in his customary manner with “Samogon” (a type of homemade liquor). I did not know anything about this, and I got very angry when I found Semion drunk. In my anger, I raised my hand to him. As he received his beating, Semion said to me, “Now I know that I also have a father.” I could only smile when I heard this response.

In its time, the story of the execution of the enemy of the Jews Ivan (Vanka) earned great acclaim and special interest from famous Soviet writers such as Ehrenburg, Markish, the Hidden (Der Nister)[1], and many others. Shlomo Perlmutter was often asked to explain how he discovered the traitor in the partisan camp of General Feodorov, and how he tied the noose to his neck. In 1965, the Ministry of Security of the Soviet Union published the story of General A. P. Feodorov, who twice earned the title of “Hero of the Soviet Union.” On pages 224-236 of this book (“The Last Winter”) the general discussed that period of time at length, going into minute detail. He even mentions the name of Semion Olitzky (as Shlomole was known among the partisans) as the person who exposed the traitor and took revenge upon him for his people and family members, who were among his victims.

Translator's Footnote

1. Three Yiddish writers. See http://en.wikipedia.org/wiki/Ilya_Ehrenburg, http://en.wikipedia.org/wiki/Peretz_Markish, and http://en.wikipedia.org/wiki/Der_Nisterhttps://www.jewishgen.org/Yizkor/Ratno/rat231.html - f235_1r

Next to an Open Album

by Yisrael Honik

Translated by Jerrold Landau

Yisrael Honik and his wife from Argentina at a meeting with Ratno natives in Israel

We have just returned from the memorial evening for the martyrs of Ratno. Pictures and images from there floated before our eyes: the house, the friends, the youthful dreams, the happy, bright days and nights. Shnitzel, a native of our town, described everything that took place there – the Holocaust with all its details: "You are obligated to know everything; you are obligated to sense and remember everything just as I do. The images from the valley of murder must accompany you throughout your life. The fact that all of us sitting at this memorial survived is only a coincidence. You must see yourselves standing next to the large graves, watching how they tossed children into the open pits, hearing the shots. I come from the pits into which my children, brothers and sisters were thrown. I am standing and talking to you, and with my eyes I see this frightful march, the march of death, when the entire town, young and old, women and children, were marching through the market street to meet their deaths... I went to these graves after the awaited liberation and relived the frightful scene. I lay down next to these graves for hours, and then began to run like a desperate animal – I ran to you. To this day, my soul cannot find rest. Thus, I continue to run endlessly across seas and lands -- -- -- The pits with all of the victims are located in the large garden of the town, the garden in which you used to stroll with your girlfriends during the evenings. There we debated, wove our dreams, and dreamed of a better and more just world. -- -- -- There, all of our dear ones are now bound in the bonds of death – they along with all their dreams."

*

The Ratno native who was saved from the hell told us this and similar things. We all listened to his words with trembling. We felt ashamed, and feelings of guilt also rose up within us, for we have now experienced 21 years of satiety and peace since the years of the great, tragic destruction.

After this memorial, we went to Velvel's room. He took out from some drawer his album with hundreds of photos of Ratno. We began to leaf through this album with tears in our eyes. The world of yesteryear was revealed before our eyes. We saw our boys and girls at various ages, our houses, our parents – everything that was once there and no longer is. Here is my entire family at my sister's wedding. My elderly grandmother is sitting in the center surrounded by her grandchildren. Here are her in-laws, here are our dear parents. Joy radiated from all faces – and the date was 1938. Here is the whole gang sailing in two boats on the Pripyat. Zelig was playing his mandolin and Aharon-Yankel his violin. The girls are singing songs of love and songs of freedom and revolution. -- -- -- We filled all of the gardens of the town with youthful mirth, tricks, competitions and races. – Ah, how I remember those days and nights, the long strolls on white, winter nights, the ideological debates regarding both important and unimportant matters.

Here is another photograph: Jews going to Taslich on Rosh Hashanah. The entire street is filled with Jews going to observe the commandment. This was a religious parade. These Jews are standing at the bank of the river, their mouths murmuring the prayer, and their eyes staring at the river foliage. Here are the photographs of organizations and movements; musicians and wagon drivers; the Tarbut School with its teachers and students, the pride of the town; fighters returning from prison with their faith in the revolution, prepared to fight and actualize it.

Thus did we sit for a long time, glued to the pages of this album. Velvel's small room was filled as if with hundreds of people who knew each other and loved each other so much. A world that once was and ended rose to life. The distant past turned into the present reality. The album remained open. We could not close it, but we felt the need to disconnect for a moment from the reality that its pages were telling us. We escaped to some small coffeehouse, and tried to summarize the former times in friendly conversation. “You remember Velvel,” I said before my friends, “how our parents and grandparents sat at twilight between Mincha and Maariv in the Beis Midrashes and told wonderful stories about landowners, noblemen; and, to differentiate, about great Tzadikim and wonder workers? They always concluded their conversation with the same sentence, 'What a wonderful world it was in those days, and perhaps we will yet merit a wonderful world in the future.' The soul of the nation was woven in a wonderful, better world. Now look at what type of a world they actually receive, what type of bitter end they suffered. They went to meet their end without power and without hope. Will we merit a different world?”

A memorial of the martyrs of Ratno in Buenos Aires

The committee of the Organization of Ratno Natives in Argentina (1946)
Sitting right to left: H. Cohen, A. Feigelis, Y. Tucker, Ch. Steinberg, M. Honik, M. Telison
Standing: Y. Honik, Y. Wilkomirski, Y. Fuchs, Y. Werag, A. Y. Rief, B Tanis

The End of the Story

by Shlomo Perlmutter

Translated by Jerrold Landau

(From the diary of a 14-year-old child} For five hours straight, Shlomo Perlmutter told his daughter, at her request, about his town of Ratno, about the way of life of the Jews, about the school, about the realities, etc. At the end of the story, he told her the following (recorded on tape):

This is, more or less, the story of this town. I wanted that you should know about it and also that your children should know about it. I have lived in the Land for 36 years, and this story accompanies me with every step. I cannot forget what was there. I live with it, and I cannot disconnect. Not a day goes by when I do not think about my parents. Sometimes this "comes to me," as you say, in the middle of a class that I am giving at the school, during a meal, or at many other occasions. In my story, there are "vitamins" that you will probably not find in the story of other Holocaust survivors. This is because I endured the Holocaust in a somewhat different, unusual manner. Few were able to tie the noose with their own hands on the neck of the murderer of the Jews, as I merited. Do not forget that the fear of the persecutors pursued me for a long time, and do not forget that I was a child at that time. Perhaps it was to my good fortune that everything took place when I was still a child. Many of those who went through the Holocaust at an older age remained afflicted in spirit throughout their lives. It is difficult for me to describe the feeling that constantly accompanies me, that they are pursuing me, that I must escape, escape... There was a time when I wished to commit suicide, but I did not have the strength to climb up a ladder and throw myself off. Despite this – and this will certainly seem strange to you – I had then the will to live, to survive, and to tell others about everything that I experienced. Have you seen my diaries? Even today, I cannot explain to myself what moved me to maintain a diary at all times, to tell what I was seeing, sensing, and hearing. Today I am a history teacher, but then, during my oppressed childhood, I still did not have a sense of history. Time did its work. Many things descended into the depths of forgetfulness, and perhaps I myself pushed them to those depths, for otherwise I could not continue on. Now, even the dreams of the persecutors no longer afflict me every night. Here I am speaking to you now, telling you about various events, but it is as if I myself am passing by these events, as if I was not there, as if these things did not take place to and with me. It seemed as if I was constantly walking by a pit, but I never descended into it, but rather held myself with great strength at the edge of the pit. I know that I am unable to impart to you a full picture of what was there. I now see before my eyes the motto that was written on the wall of one of the houses in Ratno after I returned there one day, and found it empty of Jews – "Judenrein" as the Germans said. The motto is "Woe to the nation whose leaders protect the murderers."

This motto had survived from the days of the elections to the Zionist Congress of 1934, and was referring to the murder of Arlosoroff[1]. I am incapable of describing to you, and you are incapable of feeling the sensation that I felt in my soul at seeing this motto in a town where all the Jews had been murdered. My father loved the poems of Bialik very much, and apparently, he also instilled this love to me. I walked through the alleyways of

Ratno and saw myself walking in the "City of Murder" of Bialik. Many verses and lines of that poem sounded within me:

"With your eyes you will witness, and with your hands you will feel the fences
And upon the trees and the stones, and atop the plaster of the walls
The clotted blood and the hardened brains of the victims."

Indeed, I did not see clotted blood here on the fences and the plaster of the walls. However I certainly saw the "hardened brains"... In this manner, and through this manner, the masses of Jews struggled with the threshold of the abyss on the eve of the great slaughter. I was embarrassed and horrified at the sight of these mottos, and I hoped that there would be nobody there who could translate them for the Ukrainians that remained...

Translator's Footnote

1. See http://en.wikipedia.org/wiki/Haim_Arlosoroffhttps://www.jewishgen.org/Yizkor/Ratno/rat231.html - f1r

On Martyrdom and The Violin
(Not fiction, but rather a true story.)

by Shlomo Perlmutter

Translated by Jerrold Landau

Unpaved roads covered with mire and swampy mud in the fall and layers of dust on the scorching summer months go forth from Ratno toward the fields. Among the small houses that stood on those roads are some plastered, wooden houses covered with tile roofs or white metal sheets. The latter testified that their owners were among those "burnt out," who rebuilt their houses after the fire. In one of those houses, very close to the streets of the gentiles, lived the family of Dovidl.

His father, Avraham, was a blacksmith with a black, curly beard. His face was always covered with soot, and he had good, fiery, eyes. One had only to take one glance at Avraham to realize that he was a pure, honest man. He was one of the Hassidim of the Rebbe of Stepan. On Fridays in the mikva [ritual bath], he did not suffice himself with the seven immersions that the Hassidim of Stepan felt obligatory. Rather, he poured several additional jugs of hot water on himself, and went up to the highest level of the sweat rungs in order to be flogged and to purify himself from any taint of secularity, so that he could greet the Sabbath Queen that was about to arrive. He was from the simple folk. His words would only rarely be heard in the synagogue, and he regarded himself as one of those who cleave to the dust of the feet of the scholars and serve them. To that point, but no further. Avraham raised three sons in his workshop, one of them being Dovidl. He was a tall, handsome lad, with especially shiny teeth. His thick, black eyebrows decorated his fiery eyes like those of this father. Dovidl learned all the trades of the hammer and anvil from his father; but after he learned these thoroughly, he went to Shmaya the tailor and requested that he accept him as an apprentice. "I do not want any more soot," he said to Shmaya. However, after he had studied and learned how to make fine men's suits, he rejected tailoring too, and went to the elderly baker in the shtetl and requested that he teach him the trade of baking. This too did not last long. Something mysterious nestled in the heart of the lad. He sought and searched. Nobody knew what he was looking for, and perhaps he himself did not know.

I myself barely knew him. At times I would see him at the banks of the river that passed through our shtetl, swimming wonderfully, arousing admiration from the entire group. I was lucky, and we became close with each other. We became friends.

The following is the story that took place. When I turned nine, my mother, may peace be upon her, decided that the time has come for me to study violin and to prove my musical talents, which doubtfully existed at that time, and certainly do not today... In the marketplace, she met a villager from Konysche who exhibited a fine, handmade violin. My mother jumped on the bargain and purchased the violin for me. The next day, she invited Aharon Reizman, who was known as an expert violinist, to our home and asked him to teach me to play the violin. She said that she would pay him very well. He agreed. Several months passed, and one summer evening, a few years before the Holocaust overtook our shtetl, Dovidl's face suddenly peered through the window of my room as I was practicing my music. I stopped playing and snatched a hurried glance at the lad. He was also a bit frightened. His face blushed, and he uttered a few garbled expressions, the meaning of which only became clear to me after a little while: he asked me in all manners of request that I permit him to listen to my playing. I was apparently very moved by the fact that there was a "connoisseur" for my music. I invited Dovidl to enter my room, and I played an étude for him that I knew thoroughly. When I finished, Dovidl asked me to teach him how to hold the violin. When I acceded to his request, he opened his heart to me and told me that he wished to play the violin. He wanted to take lessons from Aharon Reizman who was teaching me, but his father opposed this.

His words touched my heart and I told him that I was prepared to teach him gratis the little that I had succeeded in learning. Dovidl could not control his emotions, and tears streamed from his eyes.

A year passed. It became clear that of all his endeavors, Dovidl displayed perseverance only in violin playing, and this reached the level of professionalism. He played day and night, got a violin, and quickly became known in town, especially amongst the klezmers [popular musicians], as a lad with an absolute pitch. They took him under their protection, and included him in their appearances at weddings and celebrations. Sometimes, he would even play a duet with Aharon the Great himself. At times when Aharon did not appear with the band, and the hosts were concerned that their joyous occasion would be marred, Dovidl succeeded in enchanting all hearts and ears. Even the musicians themselves, who were not free of the taint of jealousy, praised him effusively and said that one day he would reach the highest levels of musical playing, and the town of Ratno would be too small for him.

They prophesied and knew about what they were prophesying. It was not long before Dovidl left Ratno and all its weddings and joyous events. He left his parents' home without asking for permission, went to Lwow, and was accepted in the conservatory, where he quickly became known as one of the best students of that institution. He would send me letters from time to time, all with the same theme: It was in my merit, in the merit of that summer evening when I taught him how to hold a violin, that he attained all that he attained. In one letter he told me that he had already appeared in a special concert, and had earned the recognition of his teachers who foretold a great future for him. He wrote, "Music purifies my soul, and I am happy that I have become acquainted with the wonderful world of music. One day, I will return to Ratno, we will gather together all of our friends, and I will play tunes for them that you have never heard before."

The war broke out. Many people's plans became spoiled in our world, Dovidl's among them. Emptiness, void, and waste. Dovidl, who was a stranger in the big city, decided to return to his shtetl Ratno. He set out by foot through the roads that bustled with human and vehicular caravans. Masses of people fled eastward out of fear of the Nazi beast, but Dovidl was among the few who went north. He would hide in the groves throughout the day, and would wander at night, hungry and perplexed. At times, he would feel the desire to go along with the stream that was flowing eastward, but he pined for his home, his parents, and his small shtetl - so he continued northward. He continued on - until he fell into the hands of the Germans at the entrance point to the city of Zbaraz.

He was administered many beatings, placed in a car of prisoners and taken to Zloczów. There he was placed in a large courtyard along with thousands of Jews who were rolling on the ground, crawling on their bellies, licking pavement stones. Armed officers stood next to them, beating them until blood flowed and not leaving them be until they completed licking the entire courtyard. In the evening, they were taken outside the city along with many Jews, where volleys of bullets put an end to the lives of masses of Jews. However, Dovidl miraculously survived, and, under the cover of darkness, dug his way out of the pile of bodies that covered him. He covered his nakedness with whatever clothing he could pick, and continued to run through the side roads, hungry and tired, until he came close to the city of Dubno. There too he was captured and brought to the police. After he claimed that he was a pure Pole, they put him in a car that was traveling to the interior of Poland. Thus did he arrive in Toruń, the birthplace of Copernicus, thousands of miles from his shtetl of Ratno. They dressed him in work overalls, brought him to the large foundry, and put him under the care of a young Pole who was commanded to include him in the work circle.

Dovidl looked at the young Pole and became pale. This was Alek, the son of the police chief of Ratno from the days that Ratno had been under Polish rule. He had studied in the Ratno elementary school along with this Alek. Dovidl thought about hiding his identify from this Alek, who did not recognize him, for he remembered well that Alek did not maintain especially friendly relations with the Jewish students. However, he finally decided to identify himself to him with his name and family name. It was surprising: Alek expressed love and related to him in a special way. Furthermore, he also invited him to his home, the home of the Nawara family of Torun, where they welcomed him politely and granted him the feelings of a warm family home for a little while. The Nawara family took care of all his needs during those days. After the war moved to the depths of Russia, they furnished him with identity papers and put him on a train that was going directly to Brisk, near to his Ratno.

One day during the time of the Nazi occupation, news reached me that Dovidl had returned to his parents' home. Avraham the blacksmith and all the family members were very happy at the return of Dovidl. However, during those days, no joy lasted very long in a Jewish home... Dovidl had not yet been able to shake off the dust of the road when his younger brother was ordered to be sent to a hard labor camp in the Kowel ghetto. Dovidl saw himself as more experienced than his younger brother, so he packed his bag and presented himself at the Judenrat in the place of his brother. One summer evening, he was loaded on the wagon before the eyes of his bitterly weeping family and sent to the far off Kowel ghetto along with approximately 80 young Jews.

From that time, we had no news of him. The 50 kilometers that separated Ratno and Kowel was literally an exaggerated distance at that time. An opaque curtain separated those who were sent there from those who remained in Ratno. One day, I was called to the home of Avraham the blacksmith. I imagined that I would hear the tidings of Job that my dear friend Dovidl was no longer alive, for we had been informed that many of the youths of Ratno had been murdered in Kowel. As I opened the door to their house, there was Dovidl extending his arms to embrace me. I did not believe what I saw. He was the only one to escape from the field of death, as a bird who escaped from the birdcage prior to slaughter. My tongue failed me - as did his. Only after some time did he tell me about the seven departments of hell that he endured until he reached his parents' home.

On the 13th of Elul 5702 (1942), the S.S. troops surrounded the shtetl, took all the Jews out to the Prochod sand dunes and shot them. Only very few succeeded in escaping the besieged shtetl that was going up in flames and reached the forest. That time as well, Dovidl was among them, for he hid in the hidden cellar of his father's smithy.

He wandered for a year through the Smolna forests, passed through villages at night and collected bread. He fell into the hands of the Germans more than once, and succeeded in escaping. When the cold winter days arrived and the snow covered the entrance to the forest, hunger forced Dovidl to seek refuge with a farmer in the village of Konysche. This was the same farmer from whom my mother, at that time, had purchased my violin, which also served as Dovidl's first violin. The farmer's neighbors noticed the entry of the young Jew to the village, and followed him from a distance. When he entered the house of the violin-maker villager, they also entered, bound him in ropes and tied him to a harnessed wagon that was setting out for Ratno. Dovidl was turned in to the police. Their reward for turning him in was tobacco, salt, cigarettes, and other such luxuries of those days.

When Dovidl was brought before the police, he was asked about his profession. When he responded that he was a violin player, they hurried to bring him a violin and commanded him to play. Dovidl refused to take the violin in his hands. This instrument, which had become part of his body, an inseparable part of his essence, through which he expressed his longings and desires, enjoyment and tribulation, was now strange to him, and he would not play for these Germans and Ukrainians who were pursuing and murdering his nation. He would not violate the holiness of the violin. Over and over, the Germans ordered him to play. They brought him new clothes as would befit a professional musician. They also attempted to entice him that on account of his playing, he might be able to save his life. However, Dovidl stood firm in his refusal. He did not accede to them even when he was badly beaten.

On January 15, 1943, Dovidl walked along Holianka Street, along with many other Jews who were surrounded by German and Ukrainian guards, toward the pits on the property of Cheplik in Prochod. This time, he did not escape death. He fell in sanctification of the Divine Name and in sanctification of his violin.

How the Jews of Ratno were Murdered

by Shlomo Perlmutter

Translated by Jerrold Landau

The Murder of Nachum Reiskis and his Family

Their house was in the market square, next to the house of the Yonovitches. Nachum was about 50 years old, and a painter by trade. He was also a contractor for matzo baking between Purim and Passover. Aside from his business occupations, he served as an intercessor before the Polish authorities to obtain business permits and passports. When the Germans entered the town, he was appointed as a member of the Judenrat. He served on the Judenrat until he was taken by the Germans as a hostage along with seven other Jews of Ratno, when the Jews of Ratno were falsely accused of sabotaging the telephone lines. During the slaughter that was perpetrated after the partisan attack on Ratno and the killing of two German gendarmes on 1 Tammuz, 5702 (1942), his wife and children were murdered by Ukrainian policemen in the district of Reiskis. This is what Shlomo Licht, who was murdered at a later time, told me.

The eight hostages, Nachum included, were freed thanks to the bribes paid out by the Judenrat. From that time, he stopped working in the Judenrat and went out to work in his trade as a painter in the villages. On the final day of slaughter (August 26, 1942) Nachum and his son Yehudale tarried in the village of Zabrody. His oldest son Leizer–Ber was hauled to Prochod, and exited the common grave alive. After some wandering around, he found his father and younger brother. They hid in the forests for about a month, but when the news that the Germans set up a professional cooperative (Artel) in Ratno reached him, he returned to Ratno, leaving his son in a village next to Luchichi. When he arrived in Ratno, his "friend" Tomas Chochovich, who served as the Ukrainian mayor of the town, recognized him. He was imprisoned and taken out to be murdered by the Ukrainian policemen of the Cheplik division. When the Germans entered, his oldest son, about 16 years old, was sent by the Judenrat to work in a German equipment warehouse. He succeeded in stealing a gun from there, and hid it under the foundations of Yonovitch' house, which was turned into the local "Masloforom" (center for dairy products). Boris, the son of the Ukrainian secretary Fedya Lanterovich, later found the gun.

On the day of the liquidation of Jewish Ratno (13 Elul, 5702 / 1942), he hid in the attic of their house, but the Ukrainian policemen found him and brought him to the gathering area (Ramiza) in the fire station. They ordered him, and everyone else, to get undressed. Then they brought him by covered automobile to Prochod. Leibel Grabov of the Judenrat was also brought with him. According to Leizer–Ber, he was the only one whose spirit did not fall. He encouraged all the Jews sitting in the automobile, telling them, "The Jews who survive will avenge our blood!" Leizer–Ber succeeded in tearing the sheets that covered the automobile in which they were being transported, and sneaked out, but the car that was driving behind them

stopped, and a Ukrainian policeman named Kuzmitz came out, captured him, and brought him into his car. He was hauled to the dunes of Prochod, where there were already pits dug to gather the victims. He was ordered to run to the edge of these pits. Leizer–Ber told me, "I heard explosions, shots, shouts, and groans. Suddenly I became hot and felt a wetness. I opened my eyes and saw hands, feet, heads and a great deal of blood. I opened my eyes and recognized the blasted head of Leibel Grabov. I escaped in the direction of the grove and hid until it got dark. Then I went to Zabrody, where I found my father and brother."

Leizer–Ber wandered through villages and forests for several months. One night, he arrived at the home of one of the farmers, a friend of his father, in the village of Luchichi, to ask for several belongings of the family that were given to him to guard temporarily. The farmer promised to prepare the belongings and asked him to return on Sunday. When he returned along with Moti Mogilenski at the set time, he ran into Ukrainian policemen who were invited by the farmer. The two lads tried to escape, but the policemen opened fire on them. Leizer–Ber was injured and fell, but Moti Mogilenski, as I later discovered, returned several days later and avenged the blood of his friend by setting the house, stable and barn of the farmer on fire. The fate of his younger brother Yehudale is described in another article in this book.

The Kotzker family

I recall my first teacher, the good Noach Kotzker, from my early childhood. I would frequently visit their house. Chayale, the daughter of the teacher, was my friend. I was in the same class as she was. I recall very well their house, with three clean rooms and a kitchen, which also stood out in its cleanliness. In the eyes of my spirit, I see my teacher's wife, Tzvia, sitting in a large room and knitting, with my friend Chayale playing or looking into a book. She had calligraphic handwriting, which I can still recognize today from amongst thousands of manuscripts. Her grandmother Necha was busy with cooking and baking in the kitchen.

My teacher Noach was short in stature, goodhearted, and very diligent. Almost all of the youths of Ratno were students of this man, and all of them felt appreciation to him.

On August 27, 1942, the day after the beginning of the large slaughter, when their neighbor Hela Peikovich and Korsevich's wife went to search out the Kotzker's house, they found the owners of the house hiding in the cellar of their house. All their pleas were to no avail, and they were turned over to the Ukrainian police. Feigele Foiler, a native of the village of Krymne near Ratno, who worked for the Germans until the final liquidation of the Jews from Ratno, told me about the final moments of the Kotzker family. “Chayale was very hungry, and begged me to give her something to eat before she died. I tried to save her life, and pleaded before the Gestapo chief, but he did not give in. Chayale told me how she was exposed by the neighbors.”

She, her parents, and their eldest son were hauled to Prochod the next day. Theyounger brother Yosele was together with me in the Byten work camp next to Holoby. He was murdered on September 3 in the town of Mielnica along with all the forced laborers of Ratno.

The Honik Family

The head of the family, Zecharia, and his wife Yocha (Yocheved) died before the war. Their sons Yisrael and Moshe immigrated to Argentina. The rest of the family, Berl, Feichia, her husband and their children Feiga, Michael and Zalman were murdered.

Berl was an active member of Hechalutz Hatzair. He was a refined, and goodhearted lad. After the death of the father, he undertook the yoke of livelihood. He was murdered along with his brother-in-law Shimshon Weisbord of Turisk on 1 Tammuz next to Rycz-Sponczyk.

Feichia, the wife of the aforementioned Shimshon, was murdered in Prochod along with her children, three-year-old Sheikale and year-and-a-half old Yisraelik. Their sister Feiga was murdered along with them.

Zalman, a 16 -year-old lad, was together with me in the Byten camp. He escaped from there to the forests of Skulyn under a volley of bullets. From Zelig Langer, who also succeeded in escaping from the labor camp, I found out that Zalman was murdered in the city of Neschiz.

Michael, 19 years old, escaped to the forests of Smolna on the day of the slaughter, where I met him when I arrived there after I escaped from the aforementioned camp in the autumn of 1942. He was a very faithful friend, and instilled in us hope for the future. I wandered together with him for many nights in order to search for partisans, but it was for naught. When we were accompanying Mindel Ides, the wife of his brother Moshe who was with us, in the district of Melnyky-Richytski, the Ukrainian policeman Piven opened fire at us from a distance of 30 meters. We began to run and we scattered in every direction, and we met again later that day in the forests of Komarove. We slept in the barn of Pavel the lame of Nisniscki. From there, we set out for the forests of Smolna, which were familiar to us. We intended to set up caves there so we could hide when the heavy snows began. However, the winter came early that year, and the snow covered the entrances we had prepared. We crouched down next to a bonfire, for we were afraid of moving lest our tracks be found. We remained without food. A heavy snowstorm occurred one night, and we were covered with snow to a great height. Michael did not lose his composure. He shook himself out of the snow, gathered branches, and lit a bonfire once again. Having no choice, we decided to exit the cave and to connect with the families of Yankel Steingarten and Itza Shapira, who worked in Smolna at that time with the forester Buchhalt with a German permit. The forester promised to obtain a permit for us to join the Artel in Ratno. Sheva Steingarten and Pearl Shapira (Vernik) fed us warm soup, and provided us with a bit of food. We then returned to our hiding place in the forest. Two days later, we received notice that the forester had obtained the required permit for us, and we had to decide whether or not to go to the town. Michael and I opposed this, claiming it was better to freeze in the forest than to turn ourselves into the hands of the Germans. However the majority (Wolbish Kagan, Yosel Karsh, Chaim Trajanow, and Motel Leibman) determined that we would go to Ratno. We reached the home of the forester with broken hearts and slept for one night on the straw mattresses that the Steingartens had prepared. The next day, six German policemen arrived and took us to Ratno, where we were imprisoned in the police office. It seemed that the entire "endeavor" was a German trick. Three of them had good luck and were freed: Yosel Karsh thanks to the connections of his brother–in–law Sheika Telzon, who was one of the chief pillars of the Artel since he was an expert tailor; Chaim Trajanow since he was a good locksmith; and I, on account of my friend Feigele Foiler who worked for the Gestapo chief and introduced me as her brother.

From the window in the room of the last Jews, to whom I was brought, I saw how Michael, Motele and Wolbish walked along their final journey with raised hands. They were murdered in the small, private church next to the "Ramiza" and buried in the pits next to Cheplik.

The Family of David–Aharon Shapira

Despite his age, for he was about 70, David–Aharon was strong and full of energy. He owned a tavern during the interwar period and was considered to be one of the wealthy people of the city, even though his way of life and mannerisms were not exceptional. He and his wife Chava had four sons: Motel, Nota, Niska, and Itza, and one daughter Riva. David–Aharon was appointed as the chairman of the Judenrat when the Germans entered Ratno. He responded to the demands of the Germans and Ukrainians with the assumption that every passing day shortens the suffering and brings the end nearer. When the German gendarmes accused the Jews of the town of sabotaging the telephone wires, and demanded hostages until the identity of the saboteurs was established, David–Aharon told them that he would under no circumstances provide hostages. The Germans beat him, but David–Aharon was not broken. He continued to protect and represent the Jews of the town until the day of slaughter, August 26, 1942.

Feivel Langer told me about his final moments when I met him in the forests of Smolna.

“On August 26, 1942, David–Aharon left his secret cellar and went to the Judenrat office as was his usual custom. A Ukrainian nationalist youth from the village of Richytsya, Omtako Silchuk, recognized him, stopped him, pushed him into one of the alleyways and told him that he would permit him to escape the city if he told him the location of the hiding place where he hid his gold and silver. David–Aharon claimed that he had already given over everything he had to the Germans. Omtako did not believe him, beat him with the butt of his gun, pushed him to the ground, and trampled him with his feet. The Germans later brought him to the gathering area in Ramiza. The Ukrainian policemen also demanded that he turn over his treasures, but David–Aharon told them that his silver and gold would go down to the grave with him... Before he ascended into the death car, the Ukrainian police chief Danilevich approached him and whispered something in his ear. David–Aharon gathered his last strength, extended his third finger, stuck it in Danilevich's mouth, and shouted, ‘Only this you will get from me.’ He was among the first to be murdered on Prochod Hill.”

Hirsch–Leib Janowicz, who was together with me in the partisan camp, told me about the final moments of Niska Shapira (David–Aharon's son) and his son Nachman:

“They hid in the forests between Luchichi and Zabrody. One day, a farmer from the nearby “Kotor” arrived and warned us that the Germans and policemen had arrived in the village of Luchichi, with the aim of murdering Jews. He advised us to go to a different town, for they knew of our presence in the area. He began to prepare to leave, but Niska broke out in hysterical weeping and shouted, 'We have nowhere to go!” He took his young son Nachman and disappeared along with him into a thick grove. They both swallowed poison, and then left the grove and sat down next to us. Niska began to talk, saying that his life would end shortly. He wished us well and asked that if any of us survived, we should perform the kindness of providing them a Jewish burial. They faded before us like Sabbath candles. The child shouted, 'My throat is burning, bring me water!' Then he fell asleep on his father's lap. The poison took effect, and both of them expired.”

The rest of the family of D.A. Shapira also met their deaths in various manners.

The Droog Family

This family was one of the families to whom all the Jews of Ratno felt appreciation, especially due to their sons and daughters who were beloved by all. The father Avraham owned a grocery store and beer hall. His wife Reizel was a proper housewife. Their house was close to the Kowel–Brisk Road[1]. Their son Moshe completed his studies in the gymnasium in Kowel, and was the head of the Hashomer Hatzair chapter. He made aliya to the Land of Israel. The second son completed elementary school and was 15 years old when the war broke out. Their daughter Pnina was a member of Hechalutz Hatzair. She made aliya to the Land of Israel and lives on a kibbutz. The second daughter Amalia graduated from the Teachers Seminary in Vilna and was a teacher at the Tarbut School in Ratno. The third daughter, Golda, was the head of the Hashomer Hatzair chapter. The fourth daughter, Devora, graduated from the Teachers Seminary. The entire family perished. Henech, 15 years old, hid together with his father in an apple field next to the brick kiln. One of the Ukrainians, Kutik, exposed them and turned them in to the Germans. Amalia, Devora, and the mother Reizel perished in Prochod. Golda and her husband Shlomo Karlin succeeded in escaping, but the mayor of the village of Konysche, in whose house they stayed for a few weeks and for whom they knitted sweaters and socks, turned them in and hauled them to Ratno in chains. 75 other Jews who were captured in the villages and forests were taken out together with them to be murdered in Rycz–Sponczyk.

The Szpetel Family

All the members of the Szpetel family in Ratno and Prochod, numbering 20 souls, succeeded in escaping to the forest on the day of the great slaughter. The manner in which this large family managed to sustain itself in the forest is beyond belief. My friend David Gleizer, whom I met in the forests of Smolna, brought me to them through paths that had never previously been trodden by a human foot. These paths went through groves in the forest and patches of quicksand. We crawled most of the way to avoid being spotted. We found the family behind a thicket of willows. The entire family, including elders, women, and children, sat next to the extinguished bonfire. Nachum took out unpeeled, cooked potatoes from a large tin pot and distributed them to the family, and Elkana (Kuna) distributed thin slices of bread to everyone. The children also received a bit of milk. They invited us to dine with them as well.

After it got dark, all the men went out to perform various tasks. Nachum's sons Eliezer and Alter went to their native town of Prochod to fetch bread. The teacher Karlin and David went to the village of Hirnyky to fetch potatoes. Kuna, Magolczia, Chava and Bracha went to gather wood in the forest of Kniazna next to the bog. Nachum's wife and elderly mother remained with the children. Everyone returned before dawn having successfully performed their tasks. They lit a fire, and the smoke blended with the pre–dawn clouds that covered the large marshy area around. The men recited the Shacharit prayer, and then the entire family ate around the bonfire. Throughout the day, they ate some of the red–sour seeds (zurchlins) that grew abundantly in the area. The men dozed or recited verses of Psalms responsively, and the women tended to their children and knitted socks or sweaters, which they used to exchange for food in the villages. The family had a second meal toward evening, and then the men went out to perform their tasks once again.

That is how the Szpetels lived for many weeks in the bog. When the autumn came and the entire area turned into one big pond, they left the bog and moved to the pine forests of Kniazna. Their situation worsened, especially after the farmers locked the doors of their houses in their faces and did not want to provide them with food. Rumors spread at that time that the Germans were permitting the Jews to return to the villages. This was of course a false rumor spread by the Germans so that they could hunt the Jews who had managed to escape. The Szpetel family then divided into two. One part continued to hide, and the other part exposed itself. Nachum, Elkana, and Alter returned to Prochod to operate their weaving machines, whereas the majority of the family continued to hide in the barns of farmers who were considered to be friends. The teacher Karlin and Golda moved to the village of Konysche where they knitted sweaters and socks for the family of the mayor, Tokarsky. On December 15, Ukrainian and German police spread through the villages of the area. The members of the Szpetel family escaped, but some of them were captured by farmers and turned in to the Germans. Nachum's younger daughter Bracha, Magolczia's husband Chuna and their young child, and Nachum's elderly mother were murdered. Kuna Szpetel and his family escaped to the village of Hirnyky, and found a temporary hiding place with their former maid Yevka, but she later turned them in. I was a witness when they were taken out to be murdered. I was living then in the house of Oleksei Pinkovich near Cheplik, and I saw a group of Ukrainian policemen headed by Vanka Lokianioch and a German known as Czechi (perhaps due to his place of origin) bringing the family to the pits. Davidl was the first to be shot by Vanka. He fell next to the pit. Then they shot his father and Heniale. Finally they shot the mother Ethel and her young child Binyamin. Ethel wailed, shouted and cursed before she was shot. Henia kissed her mother before her death. The police pushed the bodies into the pits and left without covering them. They left them lying one atop the other. Magolczia and her daughter were the only survivors of the Szpetel family. They immigrated to Canada at the end of the war.

"Friend of the Family" - Murdered

Before the war, Avraham Hochman owned an iron shop and was considered to be a well–to–do man. When the Soviets entered Ratno in 1939, his shop was confiscated and turned into a government store. His wife, Esther–Leah the daughter of Liber Karsh, was a good, quiet, housewife. Their children Chaya and Yaakov studied in the Tarbut School. At the end of August 1942, when the Germans began to liquidate the Jews of Ratno, all the members of the Hochman family were located in a secret hiding place that they had prepared beneath the floor of their house. They were exposed by Ukrainian policemen and hauled to the valley of murder in Prochod along with Maraida Liberman, the good friend of their daughter Chaya who was also in the hiding place. Avraham's son Yaakov (Yankele) was ten years old at the time, and his father "set him up" to work as a shepherd with his friend the farmer Alexander "the American" (George) in the village of Luchichi. When Yankele found out about the slaughter of the Jews of Ratno including his family, he began to consult with his friends who were also working as shepherds (Betzalik Mogilenski, Yehuda Reiskis, Sheikele and Motele Perlmutter, Yoshka Ginzburg, and Yisraelik Zesak). They understood that they could no longer continue working as shepherds, so they escaped to the surrounding forests. They wandered from place to place for several months, but decided to return to Ratno out of fear of the approaching winter. A few Jews remained in Ratno in the service of the Germans. Gitel Karsh and her daughters Chana and Golda adopted young Yankele and took him into their home. In February 1943, when the Jews of Ratno, including Gitel Karsh and her daughters were murdered, Yankele succeeded in escaping. He found a hiding place in the barns in the district of Koznitz. There, he met Moshe Chaim Fuchs, who was also hiding in some barn.

I met both of them by chance in the winter of 1942, in the barn of Michalko Chawowich. Our meeting was short and terse. Yankele was forced to separate from Moshe Chaim Fuchs. He hid for a brief time with Ulka Seshko, across from the "Kliatkes." I found out that Yankel returned again to the home of Alexander "the American" in the village of Luchichi. One night, this "friend" whom Yanekele's father trusted greatly and even gave over some of his property, murdered Yankele while he was sleeping in his barn.

Translator's Footnote

1. Also known as Kovel–Brest Road.https://www.jewishgen.org/Yizkor/Ratno/rat242.html - f242-1r

How the Jews of Ratno were Murdered

by Shlomo Perlmutter

Translated by Jerrold Landau

The following words are selections from articles that I wrote under very difficult conditions during the years 1943–1944, when I served with the partisans of General Feodorov of Cernigov[1]. I finished some of them a year later when I was in Moscow. In these articles, I attempt to describe the murder of the Jews of Ratno as I saw and heard, without any cover–up. In accordance with the recommendation of the chairman of the Jewish anti–fascist committee, Shlomo Michaels, these articles were scheduled to be published in a special booklet published by Emes, with the title, 'The Destruction of Ratno, a Jewish City in Volhyn – The Testimony of a Young Partisan." However, they were edited and modified beyond recognition by the editors of Emes. For example, they erased the word "Ukrainians" from any place that described the murder of Jews by Ukrainians, replacing it with "Germans" or "Nazis." On the other hand, in places where I described the help offered by several Ukrainians, the matter was exaggerated beyond all proportion, to the point that it gave the impression that we survived only due to the generosity and goodwill of the Ukrainians... The word "Jewish" was also removed from the title, which then became "The Destruction of Ratno – A City in Volhyn." I expressed my opposition to these "emendations" to the editor L. Strongin[2]. He attempted to placate me, but my colleague, the well–known Jewish writer, "Der Nister"[3], advised me to retract my submission. He expressed his opinion that it would be better for these things to not be published at all, given these changes and omissions. In the meantime, I left Moscow with the pages of the first draft in my hands. I was later informed that the booklet had not been published. A portion of the original articles about the murder of the Jews of Ratno reached me in a wondrous manner, as well as pages from a diary that I had written at that time (those pages were published in booklets 33 and 34 of Yalkut Morsehet under the title "Chapters of Moscow").

Translator's Footnote

1. See http://encyclopedia2.thefreedictionary.com/Fedorov,+Aleksei+Fedorovichhttps://www.jewishgen.org/Yizkor/Ratno/rat242.html - f242a-1r

2. Leib Strongin was a Jewish publisher in the Soviet Union. See http://www.jta.org/1968/03/07/archive/leib–strongin–veteran–soviet–jewish–publisher–dead–in–moscowhttps://www.jewishgen.org/Yizkor/Ratno/rat242.html - f242a-2r

3. Literally, "The Hidden One". See https://en.wikipedia.org/wiki/Der_Nisterhttps://www.jewishgen.org/Yizkor/Ratno/rat242.html - f242a-3r

Ratno

by Zeev Grabov

Translated by Jerrold Landau

Ratno, my hometown,
I see you
On sleepless nights
Filled with nightmares:
Two or three streets,
The market, two bridges,
And a river surrounding you as a belt,
Two cemeteries,
A sea of tears and agony,
Seven synagogues,
Thousands of supplications and prayers,
And youth pining for Zion.

I wander among your ruins,
All the days of my life,
Wandering about on the way to Cheplik,
Rycz–Sponczyk, and the Prochod hill.
I gather the dust of your feet,
From your final journey,
And carry it on my shoulders
As a monument.
I gather every drop of your holy blood,
That rages within me and does not let up,
I gather up your final screams
That were cut off as a curse,
And I do not know upon whom to place them,
On man or on G–d.

Two out of 130

by Shlomo Perlmutter

Translated by Jerrold Landau

At the beginning of 1942, the Judenrat was commanded to provide Jews to the German building company "Johannes Jezrich–Shreltonburg–Berlin." Among other things, this company was involved in the expansion and repair of the Brisk–Kowel Road in the area of the village of Smolna. The company office was located in the house of Liber Karsh. It was fenced with barbed wire, and surrounded by guard towers manned by Ukrainian policemen.

In accordance with this edict, tens of youths presented themselves to the offices of this company every morning. They were taken to the Smolna area on platforms attached to large tractors. The only compensation given to the workers was work permits issued by the arbeits–amt (Work Office) in Kowel, stating that they were workers in the service of the German Army, and they are not to be employed in any other work. The work overseers and foremen were veteran Germans who wore red bands with black swastikas on their sleeves.

When the repair work undertaken by the company in the region of Ratno concluded in the spring of that year, it moved its operations to the section of road between Kowel and Luck, but some of its offices still remained in Ratno. A fenced in camp with wooden bunkers was set up near the road in the Holoby area next to the town of Byten. 130 Jews of Ratno were housed there. These Jews were promised that they could visit their families in Ratno frequently, but the promise was not kept. Several young people, including me, were permitted to travel to Ratno to fetch provisions only once.

Our work and living conditions in the camp were too hard to bear. Over and above everything, our connection with home was severed. We felt like prisoners and slaves. Tens of Ukrainian policemen supervised our work. Our food consisted of coarse bread and water. We were able to escape despite the supervision of the Ukrainians. The only thing preventing us from doing so was our concern that our families might be harmed in the wake of an escape. The Germans warned us several times what would happen if we attempted to escape from the camp.

News of mass murder of the Jews of Kowel and its region began to reach us in August of that year. The tension in the camp increased, and we even felt that the Germans were behaving in a stricter manner toward us, beating us for any small transgression. We were afraid of any whisper and rustling leaf. We were especially afraid when the Germans found out one day that five workers had escaped from the work camp.

The “Schachmeister” Pinka threated that if the missing people did not present themselves within 24 hours, we would all be taken out to be killed. We did not know what to do, and waited for the worst to happen. That night, the escapees returned to the camp. They were convinced that they had no choice other to return, due to concerns for the lives of the many Jews in Ratno and in the camp.

The next morning when the customary siren sounded, we once again all paced to work in rows, but we could not help but notice that the number of Ukrainian policemen accompanying us had grown considerably. A roll call was taken next to a grove at the side of the road, and the “Schachmeister” Pinka ordered those who had escaped the day before to march a few steps forward. We had the feeling that they would shoot them first, and then shoot all the rest of the camp workers. One of those who had escaped the day before, Yisrael Wyslowa, escaped to the grove and fled once again. The rest were ordered to lie on the ground, and the Ukrainian policemen administered 30 lashes to each one. My friend Alik Blostein-Kotler was among those who were whipped. I did not believe that he would be able to stand up again on his feet after the blows that he suffered, but to the surprise of everyone, he recovered, stood on his feet, and continued to work on the road like the rest of us.

That night, the night of September 2, several youths escaped through a breach in the fence in order to fetch a bit of food from the surrounding villages, as they used to do all the time. Zalman Honik, the aforementioned Alik, and the writer of these lines were among the escapees. One our way back to the camp with the several loaves of bread that we succeeded in obtaining, Alik recommended that we escape to one of the forests of the area and not return to the camp. Zalman and I opposed this. The three of us returned to the camp. The usual work siren was not heard the next day. The German supervisors arrived at the camp, accompanied by tens of policemen. It was clear that something was about to happen. Someone called out in our bunk that we should use our work implements to break through the police chain, for our fate was sealed and we had nothing to lose. However, others quickly claimed that we should not do so, but rather wait for the work to start up again. As we were still deliberating about what to do, we heard a volley of shots. My friend Alik jumped out the window, and ran behind the camp gate where there were many Ukrainian policemen stationed, who were astonished by the brazenness of this youth and began to aim their weapons at him. We as well, the camp inmates, stood open mouthed and watched with fright as this youth forged a path between the policemen, ran and fell on occasion, without the bullets hitting him. At that moment I also made the decision to escape, come what may. I told this to my father who was standing next to me. He hugged me and said, "Shlomole, let us stick together, and die embracing each other." Some strong force pulled me away from him. I jumped out the open window and decided as well to run through the open gate while the guns were firing from all sides. I escaped through the gate and ran to the road. I knew that everything was lost, and it made no difference in what manner I would be killed. In a wondrous manner, I managed to reach the grove. That day, September 3, 1942, all the Jews who worked in the camp, including my father, were brought to the town of Mielnica by the Ukrainians and taken out to be murdered along with the Jews of that town.

After some time, I met Zelik Langer in the forests. He had succeeded in escaping from Mielnica. I heard from him that Zalman Honik and Isser Rozenbaum had also escaped from the camp, following us, and succeeded in reaching the forest. However, for some reason, they decided to go to the town of Neschiz, where they met their deaths. Zelig also told me about the final moments of the Jews of Ratno, who were murdered in Mielnica (he himself perished some time later). The two survivors of the Byten camp are Alik Blostein–Kotler, who today lives in Canada, and the author of this article.

After Forty Years – A Public Dialogue Among Holocaust Survivors

by Shlomo Perlmutter

Translated by Jerrold Landau

Editor: I did not want at this meeting to repeat matters and topics that have already been included in the book published in Yiddish in Argentina, nor topics that you have written for the book that is to be published in Hebrew. Nevertheless, I find it appropriate that we take advantage of this meeting to give clear answers to the questions that your children and grandchildren who read the book might pose. They will want to receive the most exacting response possible regarding anything that they read here and there. I assume that the many years that have passed since that time have caused many issues and details to be forgotten. It is also possible that you want to bring many details down to the grave. Therefore, I will not use this occasion to collect a comprehensive or exacting testimony about side matters. But I do request that you express your opinion on three topics, which I will present one by one.

a) The question that is asked incessantly, that particularly interests those who were not there, and that appears endlessly in all the books of martyrology: Why was there no attempt at resistance, of self–defense, and on standing up for one's life in Ratno? This begins from the murder of the thirty and continues until the final phase of the murder of the remnants of the Jews in the town. Nobody stood up to take revenge. Why did something such as what took place in Lachwa (Pulsia) or other places take place in Ratno? There were Zionist pioneering youth movements in Ratno, such as Hechalutz and Beitar. Where were the leaders of these movements? Did they all go down like sheep to the slaughter? You will certainly forgive me for raising this matter. Perhaps I do not even have permission to raise it, for I myself was not there. However, I imagine that your children and grandchildren will pose this question. They will also want to know what role the Judenrat played in the town. There are various theories regarding this topic in the material that has reached me. In contrast to the majority who believe that the Judenrat worked to the best of its ability, and particularly praise the Judenrat head David–Aharon Shapira; there are those who state that after the murder of the thirty, or perhaps after all of the bachelors were commanded to go to forced labor, they pelted his house with stones. I think that despite the fact that we now are sitting in the home of the daughter–in–law of D. A. Shapira, the living spirit of the Judenrat, it should not bother us to discuss these matters in her presence. One more thing: I came across several manuscripts that state that all of the communal leaders during the Holocaust era were religious men, who regarded what was happening as the "Finger of G–d," and therefore unanimously upheld the concept of: Not attempting, G–d forbid, to take revenge; fulfilling the will of the Germans and acceding to all their demands. Was this indeed the case?

Shlomo Perlmutter: After 40 years, and with the lack of many details upon which to base judgment, it is indeed difficult to reach a proper and objective conclusion regarding the role that the members of the Judenrat played. However, it seems to me that there is no basis for a negative assessment of the role that Jews such as D. A. Shapira, David Steingarten, Asherl Leker, Nachum Reiskis, Mendel Blatt (the representative of the tradesmen) and others played in that era. Within their limited confines of action, they attempted to avert the numerous harsh decrees that fell upon the Jews of Ratno each day. Let us consider: what could they do? What would we have done had we been in their place? True, most of them were religious men, and their philosophy was "we must survive this". Some of them recalled the behavior of the Germans toward the Jews during the First World War, and could not image that members of that nation would be able to murder and annihilate Jews. We must not forget that the Jews of Ratno were cut off from the world. The means of communication that exist today did not exist then. The Jews did not know what was taking place even in nearby Brisk and Kowel. The Jewish communal activists, to the best of my memory and judgment, were primarily concerned about the general rather than the individual, even though it is possible that there were some exceptions. Throughout all the time of my wandering, the personage of D. A. Shapira stands out as an image of a national leader in the form of Don Isaac Abravanel[1], who marched in front of the camp and spoke in the name of the entire community. He did not display any fear, and never attempted to save his own life. He appeared before the murderers and asked for their requests, knowing that he had no choice other than to fulfil their requests to the extent possible, otherwise things would be even worse.

It is true that the Judenrat did not call for a revolt. In their way of thinking, every additional day of life brought the end and the redemption nearer. They sanctified life. Even when they produced a list of people to send to the labor camp in Kowel, they were certain that this was the lesser evil. They did not think that these people were sentenced to death. I am certain that had they thought such, they would not have provided the list. They did not call for revolt, for they knew that there was no possibility of such a revolt under the conditions of Ratno, and any failed attempt would result in a great many victims.

If I had to classify or define the Judenrat of Ratno, I would state that they were among the best, and they cannot be blamed for what took place.

Shlomo Vernik: I agree with the words of Shlomo (Pearl Vernik: this is also my opinion and the opinion of others who recall these matters well). We related with trust to those people who fulfilled their tasks on the Judenrat, which was in reality a continuation of the Jewish communal council. I did not know that they stoned his house. I was in the Zabolottya Labor Camp. The trains transporting people to extermination passed before our eyes. We knew that they were being transported to extermination. I recall that on one Sunday morning, I was in Ratno, and I saw from the porch of my house Reb David–

Aharon Shapira standing with Zecharia Honik, Fishel Levant, and others. I went to them and asked: For what and for how long are you waiting? The Germans are slaughtering and murdering Jews throughout the area (this was at the beginning of 1942). Reb David–Aharon answered me: "Shegetz[2] what do you want, to hasten our deaths? And if we escape – where will we take the young children, the women, and the elderly?" That was the mindset of those days. We cannot ignore the fact that the chief activists were pious Jews who believed in Divine providence. My father never hid from the Germans. I once asked him, "Father, why do you not seek out some hiding place?" He answered me simply and tersely, "That which is supposed to happen, that which is decreed from Above – will happen."

Yaakov Grabov: If the Shapira's house was ever stoned, it would have been done by individuals, the parents of those sent out to labor. I was one of them, and I also know that the Judenrat had no other option other than to send the men. Itzel Karsh, a young man, was the Judenrat member responsible for the shipment of men to work. In addition, we must recall that the Germans poisoned us and put us to sleep in stages. Many have already written about the Nazi strategy of silencing the Jews. One could not stand up against this in the big cities, and certainly not in a city such as Ratno.

The editor asks: Where were the leaders of the youth movements and Hechalutz? Most of them made aliya to the Land. Those that remained had endured the era of Soviet rule that for all intents and purposes liquidated all Zionist activities. It seems that nobody remained in Ratno who would have been capable of calling for or leading a revolt. Do not forget that we had been under the shadow of Soviet occupation for two full years. Their apparatus had a great effect on us.

Yehuda Kagan: There is no basis for the assumption that the Jews went like sheep to slaughter. I and many others escaped to the forest with weapons. I know from my experience that in the Jewish villages surrounding Ratno there was leadership that urged the Jews to escape to the forests and fight. The village Jews placed their trust not only on G–d, but rather primarily on weapons. Even Zalman Kamfer from Ratno, who was responsible for the Jewish National Fund, was with us in the village. Masses of Jews escaped to the forests. Things crumbled in the town, but we must recall that the Ukrainians came to Ratno by the thousands, and they hated the Jews with their guts. I point out once again: In the villages, the Jews stood up for their lives, fought and defended themselves.

Chanan Steingarten: I want to deal with what Shlomo Vernik said about his conversation with Shapira. This was not the whole story. The truth is that many thought, and were even certain, that "this will not happen to us." Even when news reached us about the slaughter in Kowel and other places, people surmised that there were unique reasons (partisan activity, the murder of some German, etc.) I was very young at that time, but I remember well that we also spoke a great deal about defense, going out to the forests, etc. However, we were too tied to our families, and we were particularly afraid about what the Germans were liable to do when steps were taken toward defense.

Nobody wanted to take responsibility for what might happen in such a case. It may be that were we to have had experienced and brave leaders at that time, they would have said: In either case we will die – let us escape come what may. However, the fact remains: there were no such leaders, and therefore there was no mass escape to the partisan ranks. Everyone saw themselves as responsible for the public. Only after the large aktion did everyone regard themselves as free to act as they felt appropriate. I remember that we were once sitting with Shlomole on some roof. We had a gun and we practiced with it, but we were afraid of endangering ourselves by using weapons, for the Germans were liable to murder hundreds of Jews if they found out about this. Incidentally, the Ukrainians did not act in this manner when the Germans liquidated the Ukrainian village of Kortelisy on account of partisan activity. The young Ukrainians did not think about their parents and family members. Rather, they took weapons and escaped to the forests, abandoning the elderly and children.

Those who claim now that we went "like sheep to slaughter" fail to take into account all the circumstances of those days. Several years ago, they captured the Jewish athletes in Munich – did they attempt to resist then?[3] They murdered them all one by one. The conclusion is that there are cases where resistance is impossible. It is easy to discuss resistance when you do not stand in front of a gun. (Perlmutter: and what took place in the bus on the coastal road when the Jewish drivers and travelers stood before Fatah members? Was there resistance?[4]) I always think about the incident that took place in Munich. Our best athletes, proud, brave, Israelis, did not attempt any resistance under the conditions that they found themselves at that time. And under what conditions did the Jews of Ratno find themselves? It cannot even be compared. I know very well the feeling of being led to slaughter. They led me to slaughter, and they sent me back along the way (Pearl Vernik: such things happened to me more than once).

Shlomo Perlmutter: I want to support Chanan's words regarding the issue of Jewish leadership. It is true, in Ratno there were no youths of the type that there were in the Warsaw Ghetto, who called for revolt and perpetrated a revolt. It is also true that the Soviet government that preceded the Nazi government removed the potential leadership who would have been able to rise to the occasion during the times of tribulation. However, it seems to me that first and foremost, we must stress the sense of responsibility that the individual felt toward the public. I know of several cases where young Jews held back from carrying out some activity that was liable to bring destruction upon the Jewish public. We felt that we must not do any act that was liable to lead to German sanctions against the entire town. Perhaps this was not the correct decision in the face of a long–lasting slaughter, but this was the feeling that accompanied us during those times.

The following fact shows how far this feeling of responsibility went. A similar thing took place even in the Holoby forced labor camp, where about 130 Ratno natives were imprisoned. I, Zalman Honik, Eliahu Blostein, and others went out from the camp on the final night before the slaughter to gather bread from the surrounding villages. We were able to not return to the camp, and some of the people proposed that. However, we imagined what would await the Jews of Ratno in such an event, and our sense of responsibility (we were young lads at the time) led us to refrain from doing so. I recall well how we lay down on sheathes in the field and one person from the group (I am not sure whether it was Zalman Honik or Eli Blostein) proposed that we do not return. However, after a brief discussion, the proposal was rejected by everyone. Even the person who proposed the idea understood that this was a faulty idea, for it could result in a disaster. Only the following day, when they came to liquidate the work camp, and they transported the Jews to nearby Mielnica, and Eli Blostein and I escaped under a volley of bullets, did I begin to feel that I was free of the feeling of responsibility for the Jewish people in general.

The day after the escape, when I returned to the camp and discovered that they had murdered all the Jews of Ratno in Mielnica, I realized that I was free to go (more correctly – to run) anywhere, and I was not subject to mutual responsibility.

Chanan Steingarten: I will add one thing: As is known, my brother Leibel (Aryeh) was among the first 30 to be murdered by the Germans. I know from Yankel Kladnir that he was among those who was transported to the valley of murder, and he was saved, because on the way to a certain death, someone proposed that they attempt to escape, and whomever luck would favor might survive. My brother Leibel rejected the proposal. His reasoning was that this step was liable to lead the Nazis to murder all the Jews of Ratno, Heaven forbid. They marched toward their last breath with this sense of responsibility.

Nachman: Perhaps it is justified that they did not escape during the first days of Nazi occupation, but it is surprising that they also remained in the town and did not escape later, when news of the mass murder of Jews in Kamin–Kashirsk, Kowel, and all neighboring settlements began to arrive.

Shlomo P.: This question points to a lack of understanding of the conditions that pervaded at that time. All the rumors that arrived were unverified, and, as has been stated earlier, we did not believe them. We were cut off completely, and had no communication with the nearby settlements. When we worked on the Kowel–Luck road, and the Ukrainian farmers who passed by told us that they were slaughtering Jews throughout the area – we did not believe their words. The Nazis had succeeded to this extent in putting us to sleep from a psychological perspective. As has already been stated: In all places the Jews thought that this would not happen to them.

They preserved their hope and opened themselves to various delusions even on the threshold of death. The Nazi psychologists developed special theories and techniques, and succeeded.

Nachman: Perhaps we will now try to examine the issue of relations between the Jews of Ratno and their Ukrainian neighbors. When I read the material that I have collected on this topic, I asked myself: The Jews of Ratno had lived for so many years in very close proximity to the Ukrainians. They nurtured business relationships and the like. How could it be that all of this did not lessen the great hatred between the Jews and Ukrainians? The description of the behavior of the Ukrainians toward the Jews was frightening. Their level of guilt was no less, perhaps, than that of the Germans. How can we understand this phenomenon? Why were there so few who agreed to give refuge to the Jews? Perhaps the Ukrainians bore a grudge against the Jews. If so, what was the source of this grudge? I was greatly moved by several songs that were written by young lads from Ratno that gave expression to a protest against the business practices of the Jews with respect to the gentiles. Perhaps the behavior of the Germans toward the Jews during the war was some sort of recompense or revenge for them not behaving properly toward them?

Chanan: This is a topic worthy of research. Based on my own experience I can state: if there were still Ukrainians in western Ukraine who still gave refuge or assistance of any sort to the Jews, there was almost no instance of such help to the Jews in the eastern portion of Ukraine which had been under Soviet rule from the time of the 1917 revolution.

Yaakov Grabov: The good Ukrainians who were exceptional only confirm the general rule.

Pearl Karsh: With this it is worthwhile to note that there were numerous exceptions, and I am able to tell about one of them. There was a farmer named Ivan Shtoch in the village of Smorivitchi[5] who brought us food throughout the period of four consecutive months. This farmer's son was a keeper of cows, and his father was concerned that his son might expose us and turn us in to the Germans, or pass judgment on us himself. Therefore, he attempted to keep him far from our hiding place. One night I dreamt that my father–in–law David–Aharon Shapira commanded me to immediately leave the place where we had been under the protection of this Ivan. When I told my husband Itzka about this dream – he mocked my dream and said that if we leave the place, we will never find a Ukrainian who will give us refuge, for no such people exist. I stood my own and acceded to his request to remain there for only one additional day. A day later, we left and went in the direction of Kortelisy where we had an acquaintance named Niko. When he saw us, he crossed himself and said that the Banderovcis(Ukrainian nationalists) were swarming through the village, and that he could not even exchange one word with us. That is how all the Ukrainians acted, even those who were considered friends.

Yaakov Grabov: There was only one primary reason for the enmity of the Ukrainians. They wanted to benefit from our destruction. They had seen Jews who were successful and amassed property. Their desire for the money and property of the Jews overcame them.

Aryeh Wilk: The interesting thing is that it was specifically the Ukrainian intelligentsia, the upper class of the society, that were the worst behaved, and the most murderous toward the Jews.

Chanan Steingarten: Many Jews made the error of hiding their property with Ukrainians whom they regarded as friends. When these “friends” discovered the type of treasurers amassed by the Jews, it is no wonder that they coveted that property for themselves, and literally awaited the death of the owners of the property.

Aryeh Wilk: It is hard to believe that the intelligent and educated son of the local priest acted in an evil manner. He murdered Jews without any sense of conscience, whereas one of the locally known prostitutes granted Jews refuge in her house.

Pearl: Kodrinski's son worked with me in the courthouse. However, when the Germans arrived in Ratno, he ignored my existence and turned his head as if he did not recognize me at all. He would not even say hello to me.

Shlomo P.: The question presented here by the editor is one of the questions that has been or will be presented to us by our children or grandchildren. They will not be able to understand how we did not succeed in finding an opening with the Ukrainians, our neighbors for hundreds of years. These relations should have obligated them to come to our assistance during our time of tribulation. This is also the question that is posed in one form or another by the researchers of that era. In various circles of the Ukrainian people, there was a push to prove that many Ukrainians came to our aid, and that their level of collaboration with the Nazis was not that strong. However, the testimony of many survivors, including the survivors of Ratno, points to a different conclusion. There is no doubt that there were Ukrainians who came to our aid, and I myself was witness to such during the time of my wandering, however these were a negligible percentage. Their hatred to the Jews was literally pathological. The Banderovcis, who were at times worse that the Nazis, were very great examples of such. The incident with Kamintzky and Fruma when they found themselves in a unit of Banderovcis and were saved was a rare, isolated incident, and we cannot derive any general principle from it. Pearl also mentioned someone who was good to her in the village of Smorivitchi, and I will also remember positively Michalko Chawowich, whom I did not know before and was known previously as a person who did not like Jews, but nevertheless later displayed very generous traits in extending assistance to my brother and me. Nevertheless, we must stress again and again: these are only individuals. I also surmise that the Ukrainians who were good to us were from among the lowest classes of society, but I suspect we cannot be hasty in reaching such a conclusion. An incident such as that with Maria, the wife of Arjon the water drawer of Ratno, who held four Jews in her house, was unique. Her husband contracted typhus from the Jews that were hidden in the house, and died. Eli Blostein, his brother Itzka, Magolczia Szpetel, Fruma Bergel, Moshe Chaim Fuchs, and I hid in his house. We said to him that when peace came, we would buy him a gold chain, affix a large gold cross to it, the same type that hangs from the neck of a priest, and hang it on his neck. He answered, “I do not need any crosses. I have a wagon but I do not have a horse. When peace comes I will go to Prochod and borrow a horse from my friend there, hitch the horse to the wagon, and place all the Jews of Ratno that I have saved upon it. A meeting will take place in Ratno, and I will stand on the podium and say, 'Here are five Jews whose lives I saved – and what did you Meishchines do?'"

I do not believe that the business relationships between the Jews and Ukrainians determined their behavior. They were enticed by the promises made to them by the Germans, by the promise of the establishment of an independent Ukrainian state, by the rewards offered for turning in Jews, etc. In any case, the situation demands further serious research.

Shlomo Vernik: I also want to add that the German threats of fines and severe punishments for anyone caught hiding Jews in their house also caused them to recoil. The Germans gave products to the collaborators that "could not be purchased with gold," such as tobacco, salt, and vodka, free of all taxes and fees. There was one Jew, named Yosel, in the village of Zabolottya, who gave over all his property to a Ukrainian farmer who hid him in his house. Later, that farmer murdered him and brought his body to the Germans. It was hard for them to resist the strong enticements.

Pearl: A similar incident took place with my brother Aharon, who found a temporary hiding place with our former neighbor, Ivan Chachby. That Ivan later turned him in to the Germans. On the other hand, there were Ukrainians who had no connections with Jews, but when they were able to help, they did so.

Nachman: I suspect that the question that has been presented is still waiting for a fundamental answer. You repeated and stressed that the kind acts of the Ukrainians toward Jews were isolated and rare, but no convincing explanation has been given as to why the situation was such and not otherwise. Was it only the desire for reward that influenced so many of them (and perhaps also their religion)? I am certain that this question does not interfere with the daily regimen and research of the historians, but we have no choice but to state here that we do not know the answer.

{Photo page 256: At the editorial board of "Einikeit" in Moscow (June 1944), with one of the Jews of Moscow.}

We will now move to the third question, which in my humble opinion is not sufficiently clear in the manuscripts of the Holocaust survivors, or at least in those that have reached me. The question is: How were the Jews who escaped to the various partisan camps and units around Ratno received? I read hair-raising stories about the brutal treatment they received in partisan camps. On the other hand, I read about heartfelt relationships. Are both versions true? Was there no definitive political line, based on directives from on high, that bound the partisan units together?

Yehuda Kagan: From my experience, I know about several partisan units that treated the Jews who came to them with actual cruelty. However, I do not think that this behavior was a result of a political stance that was defined or legislated from on high.

Chanan: Many Jews were murdered by partisans. This is an irrefutable fact.

Yaakov Grabov: This was only at the beginning, when the confusion was great in the camps themselves. My oldest brother David fell in battle with the partisans. As time went on, there was a noticeable change in their relationships with Jews. This is a fact.

Yehuda Kagan: Your brother fell with weapons in his hand. I recall that when I arrived at the partisan ranks, I found Yaakov and David Grabov there. Later, I was informed that they escaped from the unit. Why? Because two Jews from the village of Zalukhiv who had spent some time with the Banderovcis, arrived at their unit. The partisans claimed that this was a sure sign that they were spies, and took them out to be executed. They also interrogated me for a long time with the "Suvorovches",[6] and this was not one of the most pleasant things at all. Every Jews was a suspect to them at first. In nearby Kamin–Kashirsk, there were young Jews who set up a Jewish partisan unit, for they were afraid of joining the Russian and Ukrainian partisans. I was also advised to join that group. The farmers in the area spread rumors that the Jewish partisans were plundering them. The Suvorovches then came, removed the weapons from the Jewish fighters, took off their boots and clothes, and murdered them.

Y. Grabov: They tied the Jews of Kamin–Kashirsk to trees and killed them.

Sh. Vernik: It is appropriate to note that tens of Jewish fighters from Kamin–Kashirsk succeeded in escaping with weapons.

Y. Kagan: Those Suvorovches had no supervision at all from Moscow, and they acted however they pleased.

Chuma (Sh. Vernik's wife): I myself met Jews from Kamin–Kashirsk who escaped from the "Suvorovche" camp.

Sh. Perlmutter: Everything that was said here regarding the relations of the local partisans toward the Jewish fighters is completely true. This also includes the general relationship between the Ukrainian population and the Jews. The relationships with the Jews were completely different in the large units that received direct commands from the partisan headquarters in Moscow. I am referring to the units of generals Kovpak[7] and Fedorov (the Chernigovy and Rovany), but these only arrived in the area in 1943. The Jews of Ratno did not have arms, and therefore were unable to escape with arms. Those who escaped – the number estimated at several hundred – were unarmed. The Jews who escaped from Ratno with weapons were Eliahu Zesak, Hirsch–Leib Janowicz, and later on, Moshe–Chaim Fuchs and I. All joined the partisans.

Y. Grabov: The Jews were always commanded to be careful even in the large, famous partisan units mentioned by Shlomo. Their situation was not the same as that of the rest of the fighters.

Chanan: The Jews of Ratno never had weapons in their homes. This was in contrast to the Ukrainians who always had weapons in their homes. The local partisan units did accept armed Jews into their ranks[8]. Shlomo told me that were the Jews of Ratno to have had weapons, many would have been saved. I agree with this. The proof can be seen in the liquidation of the Jewish fighters of Kamin–Kashirsk. My family and I reached the partisans thanks to our connections with the forester Buchhalt, who served as a link with the partisans.

Sh. Perlmutter: As I recall, there were attempts to liquidate Kruk[9], the commander of the local unit in the district of Manievich, most of whose fighters were Jews, before he reached the district of Fedorov the Chernigovy.

Chanan: In our partisans units, which were composed mainly of prisoners of war and locals, there were partisans who murdered Jews. The captain in charge of us, Adilat, murdered Jews with his own hands, and even removed the gold rings from their hands. Even Jews who arrived from Ratno armed with cannons and guns were not accepted.

Y. Grabov: They would first take all of their weapons.

Pearl: When I arrived at the partisans together with my husband, they called us traitors and cowards. They made us lie on the ground and beat us. Finally, they agreed to accept my husband but not me. This is how things were in the unit that was called "Boyavoy."

Sh. Perlmutter: I wish to note that at around the time an independent Jewish unit was set up in Kamin–Kashirsk, we, a group of four youths from Ratno, were active. We went around to the forests and villages, offering assistance to escaping Jews. The weapons in our hands were very simple: one gun and and an "otriz" sawed off rifle without a magazine. In one of the areas near Rechitsa, there lived a farmer who was known as a highway robber. It is interesting that it was specifically this robber who gave us a gun in exchange for stolen Jewish property that we promised to give over to him. On one occasion, he even joined with us in an attack we made on the village of Prochod, where most of the Jews of Ratno had been killed. Magolczia Szpetel, who lives today in Canada, asked us to return to her some of the property that her father had given over to a farmer who had been considered to be a friend of the family, and was appointed by the Germans as mayor of the village. Magolczia had found a hiding place with Maria, the daughter of Arjon[10] the water drawer, and required this property in order to sustain herself. We succeeded in enticing the village guards, in whose eyes we were partisans. After they showed us the house of the mayor, we entered and took control over all the residents. They gave us a portion of the property of the Szpetel family. We also furnished ourselves with some food, and left without shooting even one bullet. Later, this incident became known throughout the area, and many people who were holding Jewish property began to worry about revenge from our side. The news about Jews armed with weapons roaming about the area spread throughout the area.

We were fortunate, and we found our way to a partisan unit that did not check our origins, and accepted us as we were.

I can tell about my personal experience regarding the relations to Jews in the large partisan units, such as those of the Fedorovs and of "Diadia Petia"[11] on the border between Volhyn and Pulsia. Throughout a certain period, I served in the position of communicator in the Kotovski Otriad [Unit] of Fedorov the Chernigovy. Our unit was composed of Soviet prisoners of war who had escaped, local youths who were supporters of the Soviet Union, as well as a few paratroopers who had parachuted in to us. We were four Jews in this unit: the cook and her daughter, a brave, limping youth who joined us for two weeks as he was fleeing Poland and spoke at all times to the Russians in

Polish, and I. We were four Jews among 400 non–Jews. More than once when I was lying on my mattress, I caught snippets of conversation that expressed strong anti–Semitic views. When I warned them about this, they attempted to silence me. On the other hand, Fedorov himself and his staff related to the Jews properly, and even with affection.

10–11 Tammuz 5701 (July 8–9, 1941): Ukrainian attacks against the Jewish population.
13 Tammuz 5701 (July 11, 1941)[12]: German invasion, murder of the thirty.
1 Tammuz 5702 (June 16, 1942): Murder of 110 Jews next to Rycz–Sponczyk.
13 Elul 5702 (August 26, 1942): Mass murder of Jews in Prochod.
20 Elul 5702 (September 3, 1942): Murder of 130 Jews of Ratno in Mielnica.
7 Tevet 5702 (December 15, 1942): The first liquidation of the "Artel", 32 murdered.
2 Adar 5702 (February 7, 1943): The second liquidation of the "Artel" on the way to Zhyrychi. Drawing page 260: Star of David, Sabbath candles, Holy Ark)

Translator's Footnote

1. See https://en.wikipedia.org/wiki/Isaac_Abravanelhttps://www.jewishgen.org/Yizkor/Ratno/rat242.html - f249-1r
2. A derogatory term (often, but not here, used for a disagreeable gentile). Literally "Disgusting one."https://www.jewishgen.org/Yizkor/Ratno/rat242.html - f249-2r
3. This took place in 1972. See https://en.wikipedia.org/wiki/Munich_massacrehttps://www.jewishgen.org/Yizkor/Ratno/rat242.html - f249-3r
4. This took place in 1978. See https://en.wikipedia.org/wiki/Coastal_Road_massacrehttps://www.jewishgen.org/Yizkor/Ratno/rat242.html - f249-4r
5. Likely Samary–Orikhovihttps://www.jewishgen.org/Yizkor/Ratno/rat242.html - f249-5r
6. A follower of Suvorov. See https://en.wikipedia.org/wiki/Alexander_Suvorov . Even though Suvorov lived many years before, his legacy lived on as:

https://en.wikipedia.org/wiki/Order_of_Suvorovhttps://www.jewishgen.org/Yizkor/Ratno/rat242.html - f249-6r

7. See https://en.wikipedia.org/wiki/Sydir_Kovpakhttps://www.jewishgen.org/Yizkor/Ratno/rat242.html - f249-7r

8. The original Hebrew says "did not accept," but I believe the "not" may be in error, as it is not used in proper grammatical context in the original sentence, and does not make sense in the context of the paragraph. I omitted it in the translation.https://www.jewishgen.org/Yizkor/Ratno/rat242.html - f249-8r

9. See http://www.infocenters.co.il/gfh/notebook_ext.asp?book=21670&lang=eng&site=gfhhttps://www.jewishgen.org/Yizkor/Ratno/rat242.html - f249-9r

10. On page 256, Maria is noted as the daughter of Arjon.https://www.jewishgen.org/Yizkor/Ratno/rat242.html - f249-10r

11. See the reference to this in "A Child Without a Childhood" in http://www.jewishgen.org/yizkor/melnitsa/mele047.htmlhttps://www.jewishgen.org/Yizkor/Ratno/rat242.html - f249-11r

12. The English date had 1942, which is an error. I changed to 1941.https://www.jewishgen.org/Yizkor/Ratno/rat242.html - f249-12r

After Forty Years
– A Public Dialogue Among Holocaust Survivors

by Shlomo Perlmutter

Translated by Jerrold Landau

Approximately 40 years after the Holocaust, during the holiday of Chanukah 5743 (1983), Holocaust survivors of Ratno, who now live in Israel, gathered in the home of Pearl Vernik in Rishon LeZion to engage in self–reflection, to bring forth memories, to discuss from their hearts, and to try to find an answer to several questions that they ask themselves and are also asked by others. The initiator of this gathering was Shlomo Perlmutter, who was in charge of collecting material for the Holocaust section of the Book of Ratno. Aside from the survivors of Ratno, Nachman Tamir, the editor of the Book of Ratno, was also invited. He was asked to pose the questions that came to him as a result of studying the material that was presented by the Holocaust survivors. Almost all of the invitees attended the meeting, the exception being several of them who could not attend for various reasons. This was an open discussion that was conducted without any air of formality. All of the participants stressed that they too felt an internal need to get together and engage in an open and honest discussion to free themselves from the pain and oppression that has accompanied them for many years. There is no need to introduce the participants, for they were all natives of Ratno, and each of them was very familiar with the stories of the paths of tribulations that each of the participants had endured. However, the chairman, Shlomo Perlmutter, felt the need to introduce the participants of the dialogue with a few words in the presence of the "man from the outside," the editor of the book, who is not a Ratno native.

The following are the participants of the meeting:

Elchanan (Chanan) Steingarten, who was saved along with his family, with the exception of his oldest brother who was murdered by the German soldiers as they entered Ratno. He later joined the partisans under the command of Fedorov (the Rovany).

Pearl Karsh endured all the tribulations of the war and the Holocaust. Her story is included in detail in the Book of Ratno.

Yaakov Grabov fought in the partisan ranks, and gave over comprehensive testimony to Yad Vashem about what had transpired. He too describes various experiences in the Book of Ratno.

Yehuda Kagan fought in the partisan ranks. He describes all that he endured in the book that he wrote, which will be published in the near future.

Eliahu Liberman studied in a professional school in Brisk before the war broke out. He was later sent to the interior of Russia, and thereby he was saved. He made Aliya to the Land at the end of the war.

Aryeh Wilk was one of the few who succeeded in escaping from Ratno on the first day of "Operation Barbarossa" (the German attack on the Soviet Union). He spent the wartime period in Russia, and made aliya to the Land of Israel at his first opportunity.

Daniel Merril was a soldier in the Polish army at the outbreak of the war.

After the Polish retreat, he enlisted in the Soviet Army and joined the unit of General Andros, which reached the Middle East in 1943.

Shlomo Vernik was one of those sent from Ratno to forced labor in the village of Zabolottya. He escaped from there. He describes all that he endured in the Book of Ratno.

Eli Zesak was a partisan in the Ninth Battalion of General Fedorov of Chernigov.

Shlomo Perlmutter, whose story and activities are known to the natives of Ratno and were also published in various publications.

Yisrael Chayat could not come to the meeting due to health reasons, but he saw the need to respond through Sh. Perlmutter to the questions presented by the editor of the book. He was saved by a Ukrainian woman, which was a very rare occurrence. In the Book of Ratno, which was printed in Yiddish, several of his articles appear. These articles are included in Hebrew translation in our book.

Ben-Zion Kamintzky also did not participate in the meeting. He sent his story to the editor of the book, where he tells the rare story about how he and his parents were saved because they were in a camp of Banderovches.

Aside from the aforementioned, the following people from Ratno also survived: Avraham and Dvora Berg who went to New York, Eliahu Blostein

(Kotler) who escaped form the labor camp and currently lives in Canada, Magolczia Szpetel who is also in Canada, Chaicha and Hirsch–Leib Janowicz who currently live in New York, Eli Berg who lives in Miami, Moshe Chaim Fuchs who died in Argentina, Fruma Bergel of blessed memory, Yankel Kladnir and his sister Reicha of blessed memory.

Michalko Chawowich was one of the few Ukrainians in the city who provided assistance to Jews from Ratno, including Sh. Perlmutter, the pharmacist Mogilenski, and others. In the bundle of letters in the archives of Yisrael Chayat, we found a letter written by Michalko at the end of 1961. Here is the letter, translated from Russian:

"Dear Yisrael Chayat, I am sending you heartfelt greetings from Ratno, and wish you all the best. I am approaching you at the suggestion of Avraham Berg, for I have been told that you do not live far from Olitzki (Shlomo Perlmutter). I ask that you give him a warm greeting from me, and I would be very grateful if you would send me his address. At the time, I was very disturbed when the news reached me that he had fallen in the War of Independence of Israel. Now, after I found out that this rumor was false, and that he is alive, I am happy and very moved that my efforts to save him were not in vain. I, with the help of G–d, offered help to various people, and therefore I have merited recognition from G–d and people. I ask again, if it is not too hard for you, that you fulfil my request. I wish you happiness and everything good. If Magolczia (Szpetel) lives not far from you, please also give her my regards."

The Responses of Yisrael Chayat

As has been stated, Yisrael Chayat, one of the Holocaust survivors, was unable to participate in this public discussion, but he saw the need to give to us his responses to the questions presented. He did this through Sh. Perlmutter.

To the first question: Only someone who was not there could use the expression "like sheep led to slaughter." Only those who were there are permitted to judge us. In my opinion, the prime factor that prevented us from organizing escapes, revolts, and uprisings was the oppression.

Regarding the matter of the Judenrat, I was there day and night. Its office was with us in the house (with Sh. P.). I saw from up close how it operated, and I have a positive attitude toward it. When the Germans demanded workers to send to labor camps in Kowel, the Judenrat members first sent their own family members. They simply wanted to buy time. In their innocence, they believed that every passing day brings the redemption closer.

To the second question: I have no doubt that the cases where Ukrainians offered help to the Jews were exceptions to the rule, and one cannot deduce the general rule from the exceptions. Katia Ochalik, who hid me in her house for nine months, did this not because she was a Ukrainian, but rather because she was an exceptional human being.

To the third question: When the front approached Ratno, I escaped from the town to the forest, where the partisans attempted to kill me. I described these events in the book. I was saved from their hands by a miracle. This happened on the route from Ratno to Kamin–Kashirsk. There was a Jewish lad, Meir from the village of Datyn, among these partisans. However, it seems that he was unable to give me any assistance.

We Shall Remember

Translated by Jerrold Landau

We shall Remember all the Jews of Ratno who were murdered during the years 1941-1942 in the hills of Prochod, Cheplik, Rycz-Sponczyk and other places, at the hands of the Nazis and Ukrainians, and who did not merit to have a Jewish burial and monument. We will erect a memorial to them in this book, according to their places of residence and the names of their families. Their memory will always be guarded with us.

The list of martyrs on the following pages was prepared by Eliezer Ginzburg (United States). We must assume that it is not complete, and that many families are missing from it.

Translator's note: When transliterating a list of names, spelling variants are always an issue. One can choose the original Polish spelling, or defer to a more Anglicized spelling which would likely be more accurate with the names of any current family members. For first names, I utilized the Anglicized / Hebraized version rather than the Yiddish or Polish version. For surnames, I often used the Polish version. However, in cases where the translation coordinator, Lynne Siegel, indicated personal preferences from surviving family, I deferred to her suggested spelling. In other cases, I used the Anglicized version for simplicity. Thus, the spelling convention used in this list is not consistent. Furthermore, there may be cases where it does not match other occurrences of the name within the book.

The Market Street

Avrech Bracha
Olicki Asher
Olicki Shmuel-Simcha
Eilbaum Moshe
Icikzon Chaim
Aplbaum Moshe
Apel Lea
Akselrod Yaakov
Akselrod Sheftel
Bender Leibel
Bender Binyamin
Bender Sara
Bergel Berl
Bulker Izak
Bekerman Yehoshua
Greenstein David
Greenstein Yoel
Greenstein Yitzchak
Goldberg Alter
Gleizer Wolf
Gleizer Nisan
Gleizer Eliezer
Grabov Leibel
Ginzburg Necha
Ginzburg Moshe
Grabov Yitzchak
Gindgold Lea
Gesko Breindel
Druk Asher
Honik Zecharia
Hoffman Shaul
Hindich Shlomo
Hindich Reiza
Held Fishel
Held Berl
Hochman Avraham

Wolk Chaim-David
Zelcer Zelda
Zelcer Hinda
Zesak Yosef
Chayat Yaakov
Chemler Sara
Telizon Chaya-Sara
Tofolowski Chaim
Titelbaum Alta
Yonovitch Eliahu
Yonovitch Yona
Jakobzon Shimon
Janower Bracha
Kac Aharon
Liberman Chana
Libman Yona
Leker Asher
Leker Moshe
Leker Yaakov
Leibman Yona
Marin Yona
Marin Zusia
Mogilenski Berka
Marin Pesach
Plocker Mendel
Fuchs Avraham
Fuchs Sara
Fuchs Yitzchak-Hirsch
Fuchs Rasia
Furer Batya
Fjuler Hershel
Prusman Dvora
Perlmutter Yosef
Pogacz Gitel
Pogacz Rafael
Pogacz Binyamin
Pogacz Shlomo
Pogacz Sara
Prach Shimon-Ber
Prach Chaim

Prach Sara
Perlmutter Asher
Celin Baruch-Leib
Kirsz Berl
Kneper Yaakov
Kneper Yisrael
Koltszenik Izak
Kirsz Berl
Koniszter Eltza-Feiga
Koniszter Shmuel-Ber
Koniszter Yaakov

Kahn Yitzchak
Kahn Wolbish
Kotler Yitzchak-Hirsch
Kozak Keila
Rajski Nachum
Roizkes Nota
Rozenbaum Aharon
Steingarten David
Steingarten Leibel
Shapira Freidel
Shapira Nisan
Shapira David-Aharon
Shapira Nota
Shapira Yitzchak

The Street of the Butchers

Berg Yitzchak-Hirsch
Berg Kreina
Bender Yisrael
Wilinski Wolf
Zelcer Sara-Ita
Zelcer Moshe
Chayat Berl
Chayat Shalom
Ternblit Berl
Ternblit Yisrael
Langer Bat-Sheva

Langer Shefa
Melnik Wolf
Milstein Asher
Sofer Shefe
Kirszner Tzvia
Kesler Mendel
Reif Dova
Szwabeche

The Street of the Road (Rechov Hakevish)

Brener Wolf
Bjon Asher
Guterman Avraham
Goldman Shamai
Gamernik Meir
Glekl Berl
Droog Avraham
Druker Shimon
Hochstein Zelig
Vernik Yehuda-Leib
Trenenblit Avraham
Tyktyner Mordechai
Marder Natan
Marder Sara
Melnik Miriam
Meir (the shoemaker)
Marsyk Elchanan
Marsyk Yitzchak
Marsyk Chana
Serczuk Yosef
Pogacz Moshe
Klein Mordechai
Klein Mendel
Klein Nachum
Klein Avraham
Karlin Shlomo
Rothschild Yisrael
Rothschild Mordechai-Leib

Slescza Street

Arde Yitzchak
Aplbaum Yaakov
Bender David-Leib
Bender Rita
Bender Feivel
Bender Yisrael
Bender Levi-Yitzchak
Berg Avraham
Grabov Pesach
Grabov Shmuel
Grabov Chaya
Herlich Yisrael-David
Herlich Lea
Zesak Chaim
Chayat Yitzchak
Chayat Leibel
Taub Chaim
Taub Pesach
Taub Yosef
Trajanow Yaakov
Liberman Leibel

Liwent Hershel
Maranc Yosef
Markuza Yaakov-Chaim
Mogilenski Yaakov
Sendjuk Yehuda-Leib
Fuchs Abba
Fuchs Yaakov
Feintuch Henia
Feintuch Aharon
Feintuch Yisrael-David
Feintuch Avigdor
Eplbaum Yaakov
Konifas Sara
Kamincki Meir
Kacan Rachel

Roizkes Baruch
Stern Isser
Stern Malka
Shuster Motel
Szapir Asher

Mitzraim (Egypt) Street

Osowski Kalman
Baumel Yaakov
Wiener Eliahu
Chaim-Yosef (the water drawer)
Hoffer (Anciluk --[translator's note -- "the aimless"])
Wolf (the water drawer)
Wiener Moshe-Meir
Toler Meir
Toker Avraham
Slop Aharon
Slop Yaakov-Leib
Slop Avraham
Kirszner David
Kirszner Shimon
Kirszner Yitzchak
Nachum the shoemaker
Wasertreger Wolf [Translator's note -- Wasertreger means 'water carrier', so this may
be a duplication of the name 11 above.]
Reicher Motel
Reichel Moshe
Reuvenche
Kotler Shlomo-Chaim
Perlmutter Tzvia
Kirszner Moshe

Street of the Mill

Eilbaum Miriam
Eides Hershel

Eides Natan
Brajnhendler Zeev
Brajnhendler Yosef
Blobstein Itzel
Birbrajar Binyamin
Blubstein Hirsch-Ber
Bajan Yaakov
Bajan Yisrael-Yitzchak
Ginzburg Aharon-Yaakov
Hochstein Zerach
Zalichs Chana
Chayat Moshe-Yaakov
Ternblit Yitzchak
Ternblit Wolf-Leib
Ternblit Avraham-Leib
Yosef-Ber
Kohen Nisan
Marin Yehuda
Prusman Yaakov
Prusman Henich
Prusman Dvora
Kuperberg Leibel
Kuperberg Breindel
Kotler Tzvia
Kotler Yitzchak
Kahn Nisan
Kleiner Chaia-Feigl
Kleiner Avraham
Kleiner Moshe
Shuster Fishel
Szpetel Nachum
Shderovitzki Aharon

Rechov Holonka

Bernstein Yaakov
Bokser Yudel
Bokser Zelig
Bronstein Eliahu

Bokser Baruch-Hirsch
Geler Avraham
Gryngarten Chaim (Zwloti)
Henich Bina
Held Yitzchak-Hirsch
Haker Shmuel
Weisblat Chaim
Zamel Zelig
Zamel Monish
Chayat Yisrael-Yaakov
Chmeler Udel
Lewint Wolia
Langer Feivel
Marin Zuska
Frigel David
Frigel Mordechai
Frigel Chaim
Klapcz Yitzchak
Klapcz Zalman
Kaminer Avraham-Ber
Kaminer Chaim
Klein Mordechai
Klein Wolf
Kowel Avraham
Karpels Malka
Kahn Motel (the shochet)
Reizman Aharon
Raf Malka
Rokoter Hershel
Hertzls Rachel
Rokoter Zelig
Steinberg Izik
Steinberg Pesach
Sheins Chaim
Shapira Mendel
Shapira Nota
Steinberg Eliahu

Krywa Street

Avrech Yaakov
Avrech Malka
Olicki Simcha
Bazeder Avraham
Babnik Moti
Bronstein Batya
Goldman Shamai
Grabov Pinia
Ginzburg Berl
Ginzburg Aharon-Yaakov
Wlinic Hershel
Weintraub Mendel
Weintraub Feiga
Weiner Yoel
Chayat Yeshayahu
Chayat Malka
Chayat Menashe
Chayat Meir
Chayat Yaakov
Chayat Carna
Tuker Meir
Toler Moshe
Janowic Shlomo
Kagan Nachum
Marin Zusia
Mostiszer Chaim
Magidcha Chaya
Slawa, the daughter of Itzi-Zalman
Fuchs Abba
Feldman Chaim
Feldman Moshe
Kocker Noach
Kolcznik Izak
Kemper Wolf
Kemper Yosef
Kemper Zalman
Kemper Yehuda
Kemper Tzipora

Kirsz Gittel
Kemper Binaymin
Rozenbaum Moshe-Pinchas
Rothschild Susia
Rider Moshka
Rider Yaakov-Shmuel
Rider Mendel
Rider Izik
Richter Malka-Yehudit
Szapir Tzipa
Szpetel Elkana

The Street of the Smiths

Tyktyner Mordechai
Tyktyner Leibel
Tyktyner Chona
Chayat Falik
Marder Binyamin
Miller Hreshel
Marder Lea
Fier Nechama
Rothschild Yisrael
Rothschild Batya
Roitenberg Moshe

The Street of the Synagogue

Yitzchak Ben-Aharon
Beder Herschel
Bender Gedalia
Blatt Mendel
Bruszniker Eliezer (the teacher)
Geller Zusia
Gewirc Mendel
Gewirc Yisrael
Dobczyner Baruch
Hochstein Nechemia (the teacher)

Herlich Frida-Rachel
Wolkomirski
Kac Eliahu
Liberman Yaakov
Melik Yaakov
Sofer Avigdor
Prusman David
Fuchs Yaakov
Freiman Binyamin
Friedlander Shlomo-Tovya (rabbi)
Kirsz Liber
Kirsz Yitzchak
Koniszter Moshe
Koniszter Aharon-Yehoshua
Koniszter Yisrael-Yaakov
Kosznik Henia
Kosznik Eliezer
Rog Yitzchak-Hirsch
Szinpracht Pinchas
Szapir Pinchas
Szlitan Ezriel
Shuster Yaakov

The Street of the Old City (Alt-Shtadt)

Gabrialcha
Hochman Leibka
Hochman Yaakov
Hochman Moshe
Toler Shmuel-Chaim
Serczok Berl
Koczyk Shmuel
Koczyk Alter
Kladner Asher
Kamelmacher Berl
Shneider Leibel
Shneider Shlomo

Lorber Yitzchak
Fuchs Eliezer

Bina and her son
Reizman and his children
Szwarc Leibcha

Ratno Descendants in Israel and Abroad

The Stories of the Early Olim [Immigrants to the Land of Israel]

The Story of Mordechai Gefen

Translated by Jerrold Landau

The Ratno natives in Israel regard me as the first of the olim from Ratno. I will not contradict this, for it is a great honor for me, and I have a great privilege in being Nachshon the son of Aminadav[1] with respect to aliya to the Land. Nevertheless, from a true historical perspective, I am unsure if this privilege is valid for me. We must not forget that four years before I made aliya, a Jew from Ratno named Yaakov Srochok made aliya to the Land of Israel. He was a tailor. He spent a brief time in Tel Aviv and then returned to the Diaspora. Yaakov Tuker, who fell along with Trumpeldor and his comrades in the defense of Tel Hai, was a Ratno native who certainly earned the rights of being the Nachshon. We cannot forget my friend Moshe Stern who made aliya to the Land of Israel at that time.

On the other hand, I am also prepared to accept the title that the natives of Ratno bestow upon me, for I did not first make aliya to Israel in 1929, the year that I made aliya in reality, but actually much before that. When I was a five-year-old child, I already thought of the Land of Israel as my future home. I absorbed my longing and desire for the homeland from my teachers in the cheders and certainly later from my teachers in the Tarbut School. I recall how my father was moved with emotion at the news of the Balfour Declaration, which he saw as the beginning of the redemption. The words that he said when he read in the newspaper that the Jew Herbert Samuel was appointed as the High Commissioner of the Land of Israel, as a King in Judah, still echo in my ears: "If I was now a twenty-year-old, I would not hesitate for one moment to make aliya to the Land of Israel!" There is no doubt that he was the first to impart Zionism to me, despite the fact that he himself was not an official Zionist, but rather one of the worshippers of the Trisk Shtibel, who believed in G-d and trusted his Rebbe.

The second factor that influenced me and hastened my aliya was the Jewish reality in our town. I would say with the words of Bialik, "My father is the bitter exile, and my mother is dark poverty." I saw with my own eyes how the Jews became disparaged and downtrodden. I saw the hooligans of Petliura[2] and still recall the pogroms of Bulak Balachowicz and his gang of murderers. Although only a few Jews were murdered in Ratno itself, we knew that about 100 Jews were murdered in nearby Kamin Kashirsk. Even after the rise of the new Polish republic, I saw how the fine declarations of national equality were carried out in actuality. I saw what Grabowski and other ministers of the reborn Poland did to the Jews. They literally squeezed them to the bone. I had closer contact with the realities and lot of Polish Jewry after the death of my father in 1925, when I assisted my mother in the store and became familiar with business in a Jewish town, the competition for every Ukrainian customer, the weak foundations of Jewish economy, etc. I recall that, shortly before my father died, a fire broke out in the home of Avraham Ides in Ratno. The house went up in flames after all of the family members were murdered by the Polish commandant who did not want his act of pillage to become widely known. They spoke a great deal about this at home, and when I dared to ask father, "Why are we quiet?", he responded tersely, "We are in exile, my son. Perhaps you will understand the reason for our quiet and restraint when you grow up..."

I was 16 years old when I joined the ranks of Hechalutz. I would declare and announce at every opportunity that I see no reason and no permanence in Diaspora life, and I firmly decided to make aliya to the Land of Israel. Many difficulties came my way after the death of my father. My mother was widowed, and three orphans remained at home: my two sisters, and I, who was the eldest. I had to take the place of my father and assist in the livelihood of our family by maintaining a metal material and locksmith supplies store. However, as I have said, I was unable to come to terms with the reality and the detachment of the Jewish town. At the first opportunity, and this was at the beginning of 1929, I arose and went out to hachshara in Klesowa, which was at that time a beacon to the entire chalutz movement.

M. Gefen and M. Stern, members of Givat Hashlosha, in the Yam Hamelach Group of Hakibbutz Hameuchad (1931)

I had only been on hachshara for six months when I received a permit for aliya. Many were forced to wait for a year, two years, or more to receive the awaited permit. Apparently, I had passed through the proletariatization process in Klesowa in a satisfactory manner; I had become accustomed to work with detonators, rock exploding, and the like. Aside from all this, I had apparently found favor in the eyes of Maharshak, who, as is known, was the living spirit and moving force in Klesowa. The fact was that I was authorized for aliya after only six months of hachshara. When I returned home for my final preparations for aliya, I endured such pressure that I was only able to withstand it through a miracle. Nobody believed that I would indeed make aliya, especially in that tidings of Job came from the Land one after another. I recall that when I was in Brisk after hachshara, I met two people who knew my family - Gutman and Naftali Gloz - and I told them that I was about to travel to the land of Israel. Gloz raised his finger over his head in a gesture that the lad - that is me - has taken leave of his senses... It was specifically my grandfather who placed the greatest pressure upon me. Grandfather constantly complained in my ears, "Upon whom will your mother and sisters rely?" "You are the oldest, where is your responsibility?" When he realized that his words bore no fruit, he tried another method, "You want to go, go. Within two months I can get you an immigration permit to Canada or Denver, Colorado where we already have relatives. You will go, and the entire family will follow." When he realized that my motivation for aliya was much stronger than his practical reasons, he began to use an entirely different method against me, by trying to prevent my aliya by reporting to the authorities that I was avoiding Polish Army service... That is the extent to which things went.

Without any feelings of misery, I can dare to say, that if I look back now with a retrospective glance, with all the obstacles, difficulties and pressure that I withstood, I am full of respect for that 18-year-old lad Mottel Weinstock, as I was called then, who succeeded in overcoming all the difficulties and actualizing his aspiration.

On sleepless nights when doubts and worries overcame me, when the admonitions of my grandfather regarding my rebellion and stubbornness with respect to aliya echoed in my ears, when I saw the tears of my mother and the faces of my sisters - I found support and comfort in the memory of my late father. He was the one who fortified me for the difficult struggle. I comforted myself that my father would certainly have wanted for me to make aliya to the Land of Israel. He understood the spirit of the new generation. He, the Hassid of Trisk, was a progressive man. He always claimed to those who opposed his efforts to set up a Hebrew School, "The world is advancing, and we must advance along with it." He was a Zionist in his heart and soul, and I, his only son, was actualizing the theory of his Zionism.

I will not even attempt to describe what went on at home when I received the certificate, and the day of parting came. There was an atmosphere of Tisha Be'Av, and I can still hear the weeping of Mother even now, as I write these lines. Who could have realized then that on account of my stubbornness, through my aliya to the Land of Israel, I would succeed in saving Mother and my sisters from the bitter fate that was awaiting them?

Zelda and M. Gefen and their children next to their barn in Kfar Sirkin (1956)

In October 1929, when I arrived in the Land on deck of the ship that transported many chalutzim such as I, the "Yishuv," as the Jewish population of the Land of Israel was known then, was suffering from the after effects of the disturbances of the summer of 5689 (1929). The restrictions of aliya were in full force, and, above all, the kibbutzim required additional manpower. I set out directly for Kibbutz Givat Hashelosha, as I had already decided when I was in Klesowa. I did not have many difficulties in absorption. My hachshara in Klesowa was not in vain, and it contributed greatly to my rapid acclimatization. I thought that that they would give me work in building (something which apparently enchanted me from the time that I was a volunteer firefighter in Ratno, when I excelled at climbing over roofs and unstable objects). However, instead, I was assigned by the work office to work at hoeing and porting in the orchards. This was not easy work, and, after a short time I was the only one of my four friends in the kibbutz who remained in this job. I was not a tradesmen and this led them to “peg” me as a hired worker in the orchard.

I did not find satisfaction in this work. My heart carried me to greater things than these. I derived no satisfaction from continuing on a path forged by others. I wanted to be among the path forgers. After a brief period as a hired worker outside the bounds of the kibbutz, I found the opportunity to actualize this ideal of mine, when I was among the forces behind the founding of Kfar Sirkin. This was not an easy task. I dedicated myself to the establishment of this village and my kibbutz with my entire being. It can be said that I attained what I attained with my ten fingers, and of course with the assistance of my wife and family members. We did not receive grants or subsidies, but the village that sprouted up splendidly is a living testimony to the great pioneering efforts that the first settlers imbued in it.

I have been living in this town for approximately 50 years, and even now, close to 80, I still work the land despite the various restrictions imposed by old age. I had thought that my children would continue in my path, but they did not want to do so, and fate did not have it such. Other paths and other lands enchanted them more, but I have remained a lover of this land. When I survey my path and my achievements here - I have nothing to be ashamed of, Heaven forbid. I do not look backward in anger.

Translator's Footnotes

1. By tradition, the first person of the Jewish people who jumped into the Red Sea before it turned to dry land. https://www.jewishgen.org/Yizkor/Ratno/rat269.html - f271-1r
2. See http://en.wikipedia.org/wiki/Symon_Petliura https://www.jewishgen.org/Yizkor/Ratno/rat269.html - f271-2r

Shmuel Marder and Mordechai Gefen with building workers in Petach Tikva

Veterans and new immigrants from Ratno

Top: Maya and Miriam Weinstock-Gefen. Sara Ginzburg, Ethel Gutman

Bottom: Pnina and Moshe Droog, Mordechai Gefen

The Story of Moshe Droog

Translated by Jerrold Landau

Approximately 50 years have passed since I left Ratno, but at times I attempt to recall the days of my childhood and youth, and I see in the eyes of my spirit the events and happenings of those far-off days.

I see myself as a four-year-old child, hiding with my sister in a wagon hitched to a horse standing outside the town as it was going up in flames. A Cossack riding a horse was demanding ransom from Father in return for letting the family live.

I see the Germans, who entered the town during the First World War, chasing the Russian Czarist soldiers. Their captain was housed in a portion of our house.

I see barefooted Bolshevik soldiers, wearing torn and worn-out clothes, breaking into the town. Most of their captains were Jewish lads. They were storming in the direction of Warsaw; however, the regime changed before long and the Hallerczyks of the Polish army attacked the Bolsheviks, who were forced to retreat in the direction of Kiev. On the way, they "incidentally" attacked the Jews of the town, cut beards, administered 25 lashes with their whips for all sorts of imagined transgressions, and plundered and pillaged everything that came to their hands.

I see myself hiding next to some monument in the old cemetery during the days of the infamous Bulak Balachowicz, as his soldiers were running wild in Ratno, plundering and murdering without anyone to stop them.

Behold, the events are changing and the pictures are turning. There is a pastoral silence around, and I am walking on a snowy night from the cheder of Reb Leizer the teacher, with a "lantern", which is nothing more than a candle in a bottle; or I was escaping along with other children from the cheder of Reb Nechemia, who was running after us to bring us back to the cheder.

Again the years pass, and I see myself as a student in the Tarbut School, founded by Noach Kotzker, as I was becoming accustomed to the Hebrew Language with Ashkenazic pronunciation.

Now, our spacious, wooden house stands before me, surrounded by a fruit and vegetable garden, with a granary, stable and barn. The neighbors close to my house were Ukrainian farmers. The house was always bustling with movement. My friends, and the friends of my sisters Amalia and Pnina, were discussing and conversing with childhood enthusiasm about important matters, questions of whether Hebrew or Yiddish was the "eternal" language; the Land of Israel versus Birobidzhan[1], etc. Despite the sharp differences of opinion, friendship remained strong between them all, and the "politics" did not disturb the friendship.

Here I am in the large city of Kowel, dressed in the uniform of the Hebrew gymnasium, with the Hebrew Language in Sephardic pronunciation rolling off my tongue in a most natural manner. This was indeed a great event in my life, and perhaps not only in my life. Many Jews in Ratno regarded the travel of my sister Amalia to study in Kowel as a brazen act with respect to my parents. She was the pioneer, and one year later, I also joined her as a student in the Tarbut Gymnasium. We both joined the Hashomer Hatzair chapter during our studies in Kowel. This movement that blended scouting, pioneering, labor and Zionism, and later also Socialism, enchanted us greatly. It was natural that when we came to Ratno during our vacations we attempted to give over our experiences to the local youth. We founded a chapter of Hashomer Hatzair in Ratno. At that time we felt, and there was definitely a basis for that feeling, that we were thereby enriching the lives of the youths who had no meaning or purpose. We were taking them out of the miry pit of gradual degeneration, and we were imparting to them something that was sorely missing in those days - a purpose for their lives. After some time, about a half year before I concluded the gymnasium, I dedicated almost all of my time to that aim. As I was forced to interrupt my studies due to an illness, I dedicated myself to the activities of the movement with all my means.

As I write these lines, I recall how we performed Lamdan's "Masada" on stage. This performance was a topic of conversation for a long time for everybody. We did not regard Lamdan's "Masada" as merely a literary creation, but rather as a flag, as a call against the degeneration of the Jewish youth in the Diaspora, and the presentation of new challenges and goals that would impart meaning to these youths. I directed the play, even though I had no stage experience at all. Accomplishing this task was a challenge for me.

These and similar occurrences leap before me as a kaleidoscope of my childhood and youth. Many of my generation certainly see the same images and pictures as they recall the days of their youth in Polish Wolhyn.

***

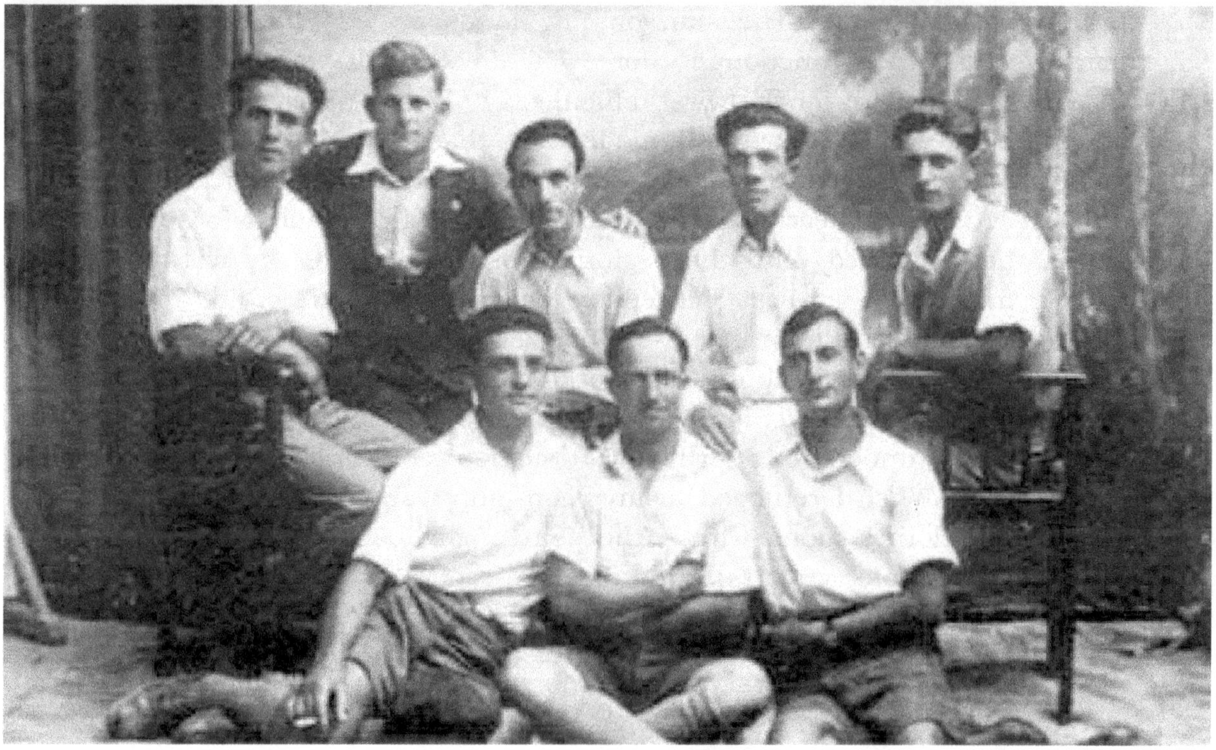

A group of the first Olim from Ratno

On the bottom: M. Gutman of blessed memory, M. Gefen, Sh. Marder

On top: A Kosnik, M. Stern, M. Droog, Sh. Lavie, A. Feintuch

I made aliya to the land in May 1934 on the Polonia ship. For health reasons, I did not go through hachshara on a kibbutz in the Diaspora, and I made aliya as a student with the intention of graduating from the Hebrew University of Jerusalem. I did not remain in Haifa after I arrived, and I immediately attempted to visit my fellow townsmen Mordechai Gefen, Moshe Gutman and Moshe Stern, who left the kibbutz Givat Hashlosha at that time and were later among the founders of Kfar Sirkin. After several days of rest and touring, they arranged work for me with a building contractor in Petach Tikva.

These days of work are etched in my mind. I had never before held a spade or a hoe in my hands, but on my first day, the contractor gave me the task of preparing concrete from a mixture of gravel, coarse sand, sand and cement in a large basin for the purpose of pouring on roofs. I held my own through the workday with difficulty. The skin on my hands peeled off and my hands themselves lost their functionality for a few days. What vexed me especially was that the payment for that first difficult day of work never reached me, for the contractor went bankrupt. I made note that "Working Land of Israel" remains in debt to me for one day of work... I moved to Haifa after I decided to study structural engineering in the Technion, and I attempted to spend the months that remained until the beginning of the semester by working and saving money for my studies. The section for general workers of the Council of Workers of Haifa set me up in digging pits for placing hydro poles in the Tira region. I also remember well my first workday in Tira. This was a fine summer day, and since I was not yet familiar with the strength of the Israeli sun, I took off my shirt and undershirt after two or three hours of work to ease the heat of the sun a bit. When I returned to my room and wanted to take a shower, I removed my clothes along with - the skin of my back, which had turned completely into water vesicles. Thus did my second day of work in the Land end.

I did not despair, for I was prepared for the pangs of acclimatation. After some time, I began to work in one of the many building groups that existed in Haifa at that time, and apprenticed in iron construction and scaffolding. My original plan of studying at the Technion slowly faded to the background. This was largely due to the scale of values that was accepted in the Land of Israel at that time, where the value of labor was supreme.

The lack of work was felt strongly in Haifa during the time of the Italian-Abyssinian War. I and five other youths set up a civic commune. We rented a three room dwelling in the city and divided our meager belongings equally. As time went on, this house of ours became a transit dwelling for many new immigrants who found some assistance there, with the workers kitchen providing the remainder...

After some time, when the employment situation improved, I arranged an independent building group. Our first job was building the Ziv neighborhood in Neve Shaanan atop the Carmel. At that time, I built my own house, but was forced to sell it for I was unable to make the payments during wartime. These were the times of "disturbances" and their effect was felt throughout the entire country, especially in Haifa. In order to reach the Ziv neighborhood, we had to go through the Arabi area of Chalisa and an area of the Jordanian Legion that was stationed atop the mountain. The situation was fraught with danger, and at times we were "honored" with a volley of shots as we returned home. As a member of the Haganah, I was sent to a course for squad leaders organized in the forest of the Carmel after the murder of eight guards on the mountain. At the end of the course, I was given the responsibility of security in the Ziv neighborhood. From that time, my nights were dedicated to guard duty and my days to work. I was not the only one involved in difficult work and uncomfortable conditions. Many others like me lived and worked in similar conditions. Everyone performed to the best of their abilities and even beyond.

Moshe Droog as an iron worker on the roof of a building in Haifa

M. Droog with residents of Netanya digging defense positions in the region of Kfar Yona (1948)

My work group disbanded due to issues of the times. I worked at Solel Boneh for a period of time, and later at a security gate in the north, in "Pillboxim ," and in setting up security walls for the oil tanks in Haifa. At about that time, I was offered the job of supervisor of the consumer's organization in Netanya. I took on the job knowing the importance of these organizations for the workers who were living on meager salaries and having difficulty meeting their budgets. I regarded this as a specific challenge, and moved to Netanya in 1943...

After a few years , the organization that I ran turned into a very important part of the supply chain in the city, first and foremost for the local community of workers. This was in the midst of the era of austerity of Dov Yosef[2]. All the citizens of the state were ordered to "tighten their belts," but even with the belt tightening, there was a need for food. The organization also served as a supply source for units of the Israel Defense Forces that camped and were active in the eastern Sharon during the War of Independence.

In addition to my role as director of the consumer's organization, I was simultaneously active in the Consumer's Cooperative League. In 1956, I was asked to represent it on the leadership of the "Central Provision Depot" (Hamashbir Hamerkazi) as the director of the food department, which was then one of the central departments. I had to do on a national basis what I used to do on a local basis. The supply network of "Hamashbir" was not restricted to consumers' unions but also served kibbutzim of all types, the Moshav movement, government and communal institutions, and other such things. Among other activities, I set up an independent trucking network for the institution. In addition to local branches, I opened up branches of Hamashbir Hamerkazi in Eilat and Kiryat Shmona. Part of my responsibility was the building of a new center on Giborei Yisrael Street in Tel Aviv, the tank in Kiryat Gat, the branch in Beer Sheva, the central warehouse for foodstuffs, and others.

The period of my service also included the years 1956, 1967, and 1973, which, as is known, were years of war. The burden of responsibility for food supply to all of the settlements united by Mashbir, first and foremost for those living near the borders, was double and more. These years placed many difficult challenges before me with respect to supply, trucking, manpower, etc.

After 21 years of activity in Hamashbir Hamerkazi, I left its leadership in 1977 and became involved in the development of a company for cooperative importing of foodstuffs for Hamashbir Hamerkazi and the consumers' organizations, as well as setting up a central warehouse for those institutions. I retired in 1981 and transferred my task to someone younger than I.

Translator's Footnotes

1. See http://en.wikipedia.org/wiki/Birobidzhan https://www.jewishgen.org/Yizkor/Ratno/rat276.html - f276-1r

2. See http://en.wikipedia.org/wiki/Dov_Yosef https://www.jewishgen.org/Yizkor/Ratno/rat276.html - f276-2r

Moshe Droog on a squad leaders course in the forests of the Carmel

Armored vehicles of the Haganah ascending to the forests of the Carmel

Yehudit Sandiok, M. Droog, Dvora Grabov and Feiga Marin at Kibbutz Mesilot

The Story of Shmuel Goldman

Translated by Jerrold Landau

I spent my early childhood years in the Ukrainian village of Dubechno, 17 kilometers from Ratno. Very few families lived in that village. Some of them owned stores, and the rest, who lived near the Kowel-Brisk railway station, worked in the lumber trade. My father was among them, and he expanded his business and even acted as a building contractor for the extensive forestry authorities in the district.

Good neighborliness pervaded among the Jewish families and the Ukrainian population. Many of the Ukrainians worked with the Jewish merchants at sawing lumber in the forests, transporting the lumber, and loading it on the transport trains.

As a child, I played with the children of our Ukrainian neighbors. I would go to their homes, and I even went out to the fields with them during harvest time to watch them bring in their produce. I loved village life, the surrounding forests, and the gathering of various types of berries and mushrooms. I recall the "Brioza" trees next to our house that would drip their natural, tasty sap into the cans that we had hung on them. We had a vegetable garden, a cow, a goat, fresh milk for drinking, and homemade dairy products.

Our large house was next door to the house of my paternal grandfather, Pinchas, a scholar who never stopped learning. He always sat and studied Torah, for the work was primarily the task of Grandmother. She ran the guesthouse and tended to the guests - the various foresters, bankers and lumber merchants. This was the accepted custom in those days: She concerned herself with this world, and he concerned himself with the World to Come.

With anything related to the vanities of this world, Grandfather satisfied himself with very little. He was modest, upright, and forgiving. When Grandmother was railing against someone who owned something and was not paying his debt, Grandfather responded, "If he did not pay yet, it is a sign that he does not have anything now, and when he can afford it, he will pay."

My father Shamai studied during his youth in the Yeshiva of Brest-Litovsk under Rabbi Chaim Soloveitchik, who was an important person in those days, and not everyone was able to be among his students. Later, my father realized that "the way of the world precedes Torah" and that a livelihood takes precedence over scholarship. Therefore, he ended his studies and began to work as a lumber merchant - a common profession amongst the Jews in our district in that era. My maternal grandfather David and his family lived in Ratno, where he had a workshop for tanning hides.

On the High Holidays, all the Jews would leave our village to go to their relatives, so that they could attend the public prayer services in the synagogues with the rest of the People of Israel. Of course, our family did so as well. My mother Breindel was an intelligent woman who knew Hebrew and Bible. She was an exemplary housewife and mother. Through the influence of Grandfather David, my father became a Karliner Hassid. He drew close to Hassidism, and whenever Rev Melechke (Elimelech) came to Ratno, my father turned away from his business endeavors and went to be with the Tzadik. At times, he would even travel to the Rebbe for advice and a blessing.

I am in gratitude to Rabi Elimelech for permitting me to make aliya to the Land. Once, when I was returning from hachshara to prepare for my aliya, there was sadness in the house and my parents were going around depressed. My father traveled to the Rebbe to request his advice. The rabbi listened, pondered, and decided, "He wants to go - let him go in peace!"

When he returned home and repeated what the Rebbe had said, there was calm in the house. My mother even added, "I wish we would merit to also go." My heart is pained because that wish was never realized. May the name of the Rebbe be blessed.

In Ratno, I studied with Leizer Broszniker, Nechemia, and Reb Hershel. Then I moved to Brisk. I was in the Yeshiva of Rabbi Sokolovski for a brief period. I belonged to the "Hitorerut" group that stemmed from extremist Torah education. I began to swim through the "Sea of Talmud." However, at that time, I was also influenced by the spirit of Zionism that had penetrated the Jewish youth circles of Brisk, including the members of the household in which I lived, who belonged to the Gordonia chapter. The Hebrew songs that I heard in that home blended with my Gemara melodies. I was then a lad of 14 or 15. I began to think about the ways of the world and my own path. It seems that, in the Gemara, I did not find a solution to the questions that bothered me, and the Hitorerut group in the Yeshiva was not sufficient to satisfy the way of life of a lad who had witnessed pogroms with his own eyes. I transferred to the Tachkemoni School, and from there to the Tarbut High School. A new spirit began to pulsate within me, that found expression through youth activities in the pioneering movement.

Shmuel Goldman at a formation of watchmen

Along with a few other friends, including Avraham Grabov of blessed memory, Yisrael Honig, Simcha Leiker, Charna Greenstein, and Maya Weinstock, and with the assistance of Mordechai Yanover of blessed memory, we founded a chapter of Hechalutz Hatzair in Ratno. From that time, I devoted all my energies to that movement. I participated in the first summer Moshava of Hechalutz Hatzair in the town of Bereszchka in Wolhyn. The counselors included Chuma Chayes of blessed memory and Moshe Breslewsky of blessed memory from the Land of Israel. This Moshava fortified me ideologically, freed me from doubts and uncertainties that had found expression in poems that I had written at that time, and in my pouring out my heart in my personal diary. I regarded Hechalutz Hatzair as the forger of Jewish reality in the town, and I cleaved to it with my entire essence and soul.

I went out to hachshara in Klesowa. From there I went to the world seminar of Hechalutz in Warsaw, under the direction of Yitzchak Tabenkin. The participants of that seminar later formed the active group of the pioneering movement. According to our plan, we spread out into different districts. At first I worked in the headquarters of Hechalutz Hatzair in the organizational committee. Later I was sent to the Tel Chai division in Niemen, where I worked at organizing the chapters of Hechalutz Hatzair. It seems that there was not one town between Lida and Vilna which I did not visit on business of the organization. I was even arrested by the police in one of the towns, for I was suspected by them of Communist activities.

Later, I was elected as secretary of the Tel Chai division, which saw itself as destined to settle in the Upper Galilee. Indeed, when I made aliya in October 1933 with my wife Sara, who was also an activist of the movement, we went directly to Ayelet Hashachar, where the members of the Tel Chai division of Poland gathered.

First Steps in the Land

Shmuel Goldman with his oldest son at Ayelet Hashachar

Our dream was realized. The stormy period of movement activities in the Diaspora found its expression with our coming to Ayelet Hashachar in the Upper Galilee. We were burdened with the yoke of the kibbutz, of the building efforts, of clearing the fields and preparing them for cultivation and planting, of drilling for water, of guarding the fields, and of defense. I was among the drafted guards.

As every new immigrant in those days, we were afflicted with fever, dysentery and skin diseases. I was chosen for various tasks: secretary of the kibbutz, treasurer, editor of the internal newspaper, etc. I was able to meet all of these challenges. To my great dismay, we became entangled in a certain crisis that led to our leaving the kibbutz. This was a painful and dismaying departure both for us and for the kibbutz. Looking back, it is unfortunate that we did not have the strength to overcome the various difficulties, and were forced to leave. However, we remain connected to the kibbutz with all the strands of our soul to this day. We have deep feelings of gratitude for members who said to us during the farewell gathering, "Whenever you wish to return - the kibbutz is open to you." These words encouraged me when I went out frustrated and perplexed toward a new path of life.

My wife obtained work in a school for abandoned children in Kfar Avoda near Nehalal, under the auspices of the prominent educator Dr. Lubinsky. The school received it support from the institutions of the national committee. We received an apartment in this institution, and we moved there with our son, and my mother-in-law Henya. I wanted to join the Beit Shearim Moshav, but I was lacking the 50 Israeli Lira that was needed for this. I was unable to obtain a loan for this purpose under any circumstances, and the idea of the Moshav was shelved.

Later, the principal of the institution offered me a job as a substitute teacher in the village school, on the condition that I obtain a permit from Professor Shalit, the head of the supervisory committee of the school. After a discussion with Professor Shalit, I received a letter of recommendation for the principal of the institution, authorizing me to be given work.

As a teacher of literature, Bible and history, I developed educational activities within the youth groups for children of various ages that were affiliated with the institution. I entered them into the ranks of the Working Youth, I forged a connection with their families, and with the assistance of some friends from the neighboring kibbutzim, I forged a connection between the oldest group of the youth of the institution and people of the same age from the surrounding settlements. I drew them close to a new way of life, to work and creativity, rather than the life that they knew on the streets to this point.

This work gave me satisfaction and calm. Apparently, I was destined for educational activities. I received significant assistance and encouragement for this work from David Cohen of blessed memory, of the Working Youth.

I am happy to note that a group of the youth whom I educated even joined the kibbutzim, and are members to this day.

At the outbreak of the Second World War, and the organization of the British Army, the buildings of the institution, which bordered an airfield, were captured by the British Army, and we were forced to vacate the place. We moved to Hadera, and from there, after a period of transition, to our permanent residence next to Moshav Herut. On account of the situation, the character of the institution and composition of the children changed, and we decided to leave this work. We moved to Rishon Lezion, where I worked at first as the director of the consumer's organization. After some time, I was chosen as secretary of the Workers Council of Rishon Lezion. My wife worked at first in Sarafand, and later in the kindergarten of the Organization of Working Mothers.

During my tenure at the consumers' union, I searched for ways to draw the community of workers close to the consumers' institution. During that era of work shortages, we found a solution to the pressure by supplying the agricultural workers who received their provisions through special grants. During that period of time, I was also chosen as a member of the advisory council of the consumers' cooperative, and I served on the city council of Rishon Lezion.

My years of work as secretary of the workers' council were dedicated to two areas: the social consolidation of the community of workers by setting up cultural institutions and educational activities. The secretary for cultural matters, the writer Mordechai Taviv of blessed memory, should be remembered positively. He worked a great deal in this area. I dedicated myself to the setting up of communal institutions. We even began to set up a workers neighborhood in the area of the Histadrut institutions as well as an agricultural center. We concerned ourselves with obtaining loans for the workers who did not have the needed sums for a first payment.

During that period, our home in Rishon Lezion was open to new immigrants who arrived from Ratno, thanks to a significant extent to my mother-in-law Henya of blessed memory, who saw it as her duty to assist the absorption of Ratno natives in the land.

The years 1946-1947 were years of economic pressure and work shortages. The danger existed that additional functioning enterprises might close. Among others, the Gavish cooperative, which employed many workers, was liable to close. Upon realizing the danger awaiting the local community of workers, I advised the owners of Gavish to set up an equal partnership between the local workers and the owners. The workers were promised loans to finance the investment that each person was required to invest in this cooperative. This initiative was based on the following assumptions.

a. With the establishment of the cooperative, relations between the workers and employers would improve.

b. Work productivity would increase.

c. The workers would be equal partners with management, which would ease the pressure on the owner of bearing the yoke during that era.

The owners of Gavish, who did not at all want their precious institution to close, agreed to my recommendation. I had to enlist the help of the wives of the workers and explain to them that if the enterprise was not rehabilitated, their husbands might face a long period of unemployment.

The efforts bore fruit, and the plan came to fruition. We raised the first sums that were needed for the shares, and the partnership commenced. To everyone's joy, a positive change began and the period of growth began.

This successful experience of Gavish, and the will to continue along this path of a 50:50 partnership between private capital and the workers' cooperatives obligated the cooperative headquarters to bring this matter to the central committee of the Histadrut for a fundamental decision.

When I spoke before the central committee, I defended this path as a broad opportunity for ensuring employment for workers in failing enterprises during this period of economic straits, and perhaps also as a means of widening the network of creative cooperatives in general.

The executive committee gave its blessings to this path, and the cooperative center began to operate in that direction. I was invited to the cooperative headquarters in December 1947 as a member of the secretariat. One of the first tasks given to me was looking after the enterprises that had formed partnerships between private capital and the workers' cooperatives, in the scope of my role as director of the metals branch.

During this period, Hamalachim, Pliz, Karpuman, Maalit, Keren-Or and others were established. From this, the partnership between Ampa and Haargaz was born, forming the Amcor Concern.

I worked at the cooperative center for ten years, and I concluded my work in December 1957. From then until this day, I am the director of the Amron factory in Herzliya that belongs to the Amcor Concern. This enterprise employs 200 workers, and is especially involved in the export of receivers and ionization devices throughout the world. In the most recent year of 1982, the export revenues reached six million dollars. It also manufactures television receivers under the auspices of the Nordmende Company.

Ratno natives at the drilling of wells in the area of Herzliya

Members of the pioneering movements taking leave of the head of their organization, Moshe Droog, before his aliya to the Land of Israel

The Story of Simcha Lavie (Leker)

Translated by Jerrold Landau

Uncaptioned. Simcha Lavie

I was 20 years old when I left Ratno on my journey to the Land of Israel. From time to time, various visions of the town come to my mind. Some of them, especially of the landscape, I will attempt to bring here in these lines. Perhaps because I left Ratno in the month of December, I frequently see it as covered in the snows of that month. When I left the town, I had a feeling of liberation from the straits, as if I went through a tunnel with a beacon of light on the other side signaling to me the path that I was to follow. I would be telling the truth if I state that it was not just light that I saw in Ratno. Symptoms of haughtiness, heavy–handedness, lording, and the like were very prominent in communal Jewish life. When I was in Hechalutz and the youth movements, I rebelled against all types of symptoms that were not apparent to me at that time. The fact that my aliya to the Land of Israel was not through the official, acceptable channels at that time demonstrates my ability to stand up for myself, to not depend on institutions, and to forge my path through my own powers. It is a fact that I did not follow the well–trodden path at that time, and apparently this trait has remained with me during my time in the Land of Israel.

I arrived in the Land of Israel in the month of Adar 5693 (1933) with the address of one of the first residents of Herzliya in my suitcase, whose relatives in the Diaspora asked me to send him a greeting.

On my third day in the Land, I decided to travel to Herzliya to deliver the greeting. I thought to myself: on this journey, I will pay attention to the landscapes of the Land and perhaps find some ideas for work through conversations with people that I meet.

The journey from Tel Aviv to Herzliya took about two hours. It first went through the narrow road leaving to Petach Tikva, and then through a dirt road with the orchards of the Sharon and the towns of Ramatayim, Magdiel, Kfar–Saba, and Raanana on both sides. Herzliya appeared before me unlike I imagined it. The houses were very low and far from each other. The roads were unpaved. Everything was still under construction. One cannot forget that Herzliya was only ten years old at that time.

When I got off the bus of the Hasharon cooperative, I found myself opposite a house upon which a sign was fluttering: The Workers Loan and Savings Fund. A short man came out of the building at that moment. When I asked about where the person I was supposed to greet lives, he told me that he would bring me to his door. This was Ben–Zion Michaeli, the director of the loan fund and a member of the local workers' council, who took interest in the "Chalutz" (as the green immigrants were called at that time...) He recommended that I remain in Herzliya and he even rented me a room in one of the orchards of Herzliya that was built on a hill. There was a small room appropriate as a dwelling place for one person on its slope beneath the supports of the house. I purchased a sofa from one of the neighbors for 50 grush (1/2 an Israeli Lira). Thus, I became a resident of Herzliya without any plans and without any institution concerning itself with my absorption.

I entered the local Workers Council building that evening. I was received there with great warmth, as if I was one of the locals. I later found out that my "patron" of my first day, Michaeli, had already told his friends in the council about the new immigrant who had come to the settlement, who spoke fluent Hebrew, was expert in what was taking place in the workers movement and the Histadrut, and who would attempt to settle in Herzliya.

At that moment, on the spot, I registered in the Histadrut and Kupat Cholim [Sick Fund], and was told that I should arrive the next morning at 6:00 a.m. and wait for two members with whom and under whose direction I would work in the orchard.

Armed with a borrowed hoe, I stood at the designated spot and met my guides. These were Pesach Krasnogorsky (Yifher) who later became mayor of Herzliya, and Pinchas Zucker (Eylon) who currently serves as the mayor of Holon. Both were active in the community of workers during those days in a fully voluntary fashion as was the norm then. They too worked in the orchard to earn their livelihood. Thus I began my first job in the Land – hoeing and fixed the "plates" around the tree roots to provide irrigation.

Within a brief time, I obtained work in digging wells. I seized this opportunity, for it would be slightly easier on my back, which was suffering due to the hoeing. It would also be better for my wallet, for the salary was almost double. I would travel by van along with the staff of day workers to the place of the boring. I would spend the entire workday hermetically closed below the well under construction. At the end of the work, I would climb up the steps of a ladder, and exit into the air of the world. I would again breathe clear air, and absorb the intoxicating aromas of the blossoming citrus fruits again, and "be guilty with my soul" as it says in Pirke Avot[1], for I said to myself "How beautiful is this tree, how beautiful is this field."...

When the disturbances of 5696 (1936) broke out, I moved to District 3 that was atop the hills, along with my wife and my newborn son Yigal, who was six weeks old at the time. My neighbors and friends at that time were the Mabovitch family – the father of Golda Myerson[2] of blessed memory, and the Lipschitz family. These two families arrived from the United States during the 1930s, and it goes without saying that the Land was good to them in those days. I worked as a regular employee in the orchard of the Lipschitz family for some time.

The backbreaking work during the day and guard duty at night in order to prevent attacks from the Arabs in the neighboring villages did not deter me. I set myself up in the Third District because I felt the duty to participate in the burdens, efforts, and struggles of the local residents. Mendel Lipschitz, a childhood friend of my father of blessed memory, was a bosom buddy of mine. I worked as a regular employee in his orchard.

One summer's day in the year 5697 (1937), the village of Shmaryahu was set up near our settlement. The news that the road that connected the two settlements was to be paved shortly gave us faith and great encouragement. The community of local workers, who earned their livelihoods primarily from work in the orchards, awaited other sources of livelihood, for there was a serious recession at that time in the plantations. Most of the orchards were young and had not yet produced fruit. A great deal of patience and a pioneering spirit was required in order to establish oneself in this settlement despite the difficult economic conditions. The district in which I lived was a separate municipal entity from the settlement of Herzliya. When the bulldozers came to mark out the path of the road that was to be paved, the workers of the area insisted on their rights to fulltime work. The council of workers of Herzliya ignored this demand and wanted to insist on its own supervision of this work despite the fact that this settlement was outside its jurisdictional area. Discord was created between the workers of the two districts. I was divided in this dispute. On the one hand, I was among the spokesmen for the workers of the district, and on the other hand, I had a certain nostalgia for the settlement of Herzliya – my first stop in the Land. I expressed my opinion that a compromise might be found between the two fighting sides, and my opinion gained significant support. However, my “agricultural” era ended with the beginning of the paving of the road to the village of Shmaryahu. My employers, the aforementioned Lipschitz family, were unable to continue with the expenditures needed to develop their orchard, so they returned to the United States, from where they had come. Within a brief time, the uprooting of trees from the orchard began.

From that time, I made a “professional circuit” with some frequency. I worked in paving, moving the paving machines, building, quarrying in “Even VaSid”, marketing, and manufacturing. I always aspired to be independent. Now, after a period of 50 years in the Land, I can sum up and say that I have realized this aspiration. There is one thing that I must point out: I was never satisfied with work for the sake of a livelihood. I was active in the Haganah, in the Israel Defense Forces, and in various other areas of service. I am proud of my work, my modest contribution to the building up of the Land, my family that I have established, and all of my deeds for the sake of my fellowman.

Translator's Footnotes

1. Pirke Avot 3:9. https://www.jewishgen.org/Yizkor/Ratno/rat287.html - f287-1r
2. Golda Meir. https://www.jewishgen.org/Yizkor/Ratno/rat287.html - f287-2r

Childhood Landscapes

by Simcha Lavie

Translated by Jerrold Landau

Shallow water,
marshes and reeds
Gatherings of winged
birds
The Pripyat is
caressing
With its jubilees of
years
My native town
With its greenish
water.
On its mildewy ground
Dark and cleft
In the shade of the
bog, it groans,
equalizes,
Among the briars,
thistles, and thorns,
It is almost always
mired in mud
This is how I recall you
From the days of my
childhood and youth.
White pages as well as
turbid.

Spring

Splendid white
shows
Strong rays of the sun
As sheets yellowed
from age and moths:
Cracking icicles,

Collide and drip
Noisily shattering on
the bridge.

Melting snow,
diluted and flowing
With ice
The gutters are
obscured
By the harnessed
horses.
With the Pripyat River
And its entire backlog
of the month of Nissan
Drifting with the
mysterious secrets of
winter.

The blanket of mud
in the streets,
Like expanding, sticky
dough, malignant,
The sun and the winds
do not succeed
In drying it – it
remains.
It is a landmark of our
town
During the season of
spring – this is its
crown.

Summer

The horizon outside
through the length of
the settlement
Its waters are deep,
flowing, and clear.
Its banks are
frequented

By the washerwomen
and those that beat
the laundry.

Not far from the
long
And narrow little
bridge –
An isolated mound as
if it rises up from the
river.
It is called "meltzes", a
place of bathing
Shallow, half–deep
water.

And across the
"Roskes" meadow
With its chewed up
grass
Where the farm cattle
are raised,
And lone trees,
sending out their
branches
To enjoy, to indulge in
love.

Between "Holianka"
and "Yentel"
There was a path for
swimming and sailing
And in the summer
evenings
Along the banks,
waiting for customers
Were charming,
healthy young girls
Braiding their hair like
flax.

Autumn

At the end of the
summer, in the month
of Elul
The bog turns yellow
as an autumn leaf.
Preparing with the
clear, fresh air,
For the purifying Days
of Awe.

Between "Drolinka"
and "Yentel"
The second bridges,
The route upon which
For half a year
They too dangle
In the streams of
water –
The movement
weakens
Due to the force of the
season.
In the town itself
The sun hides
Between the cloud
cover
The autumn rains, the
change of foliage
In the clear light, as in
the Cheshvan moon.

Winter

Ratno, the town
upon its place:
Is lacking its routes,
and oxygen for

breathing.
Snow, ice, and all the
winds
Do not prevent the
farmers from coming
From all directions.

The galloping of the
horses,
Form a procession
To the fair, to the
market, for business.
And we, the lads,
Skate on the frozen
river –
This is the
entertainment, and
this is the challenge.

The old people
warm up
Next to the ovens,
And we, the youth
Warm ourselves up
with songs,
That burst forth in the
evenings
From the chapters and
the "dens"
Where we guarded,
and molded our
youthfulness.

The Story of Eliahu Feintuch

Translated by Jerrold Landau

I lost my father when I was still a child, and the Hechalutz chapter in Ratno served as a second home to me. I went to hachshara in Baranovich, in a unit of Kibbutz Shacharia. Later, I was in Kobrin, from where I made aliya to the Land. My first stop was Kibbutz Ramat Hakovesh. I remained on that kibbutz for seven or eight months. After I left it, I worked for some time in various agricultural roles in Kfar Saba, and then I moved to Herzliya. I began to work in digging wells. I continued in that work from that time until my retirement several years ago. I dug wells in all areas of the country, from Dan to Beer Sheva, and I am able to tell of the history of the wells throughout the entire country.

Digging wells in those days is not at all similar to the digging of wells in our times. At that time, all the work was done literally by hand, without machines. I would descend to a depth of 50 meters below ground. To this day, scars of various wounds can be found on my body. However, it seems to me that at that time I had a greater feeling of satisfaction than I do now, even though, just like now, I was not lacking anything material. At times, we were attacked by Arabs as we were trudging to the places of the drilling. At times, I would return home from work with serious wounds. None of these, however, dampened my spirit, and I was always content with my lot. It is possible to state that the words of "Work is our life," a song that was song in the Land at that time, was for me more than just words, but rather the content of my life.

I was a member of the Haganah from 1938, and I was one of the first to be drafted to the brigade. I went through training in the Land. Then we continued our training in Italy. At the end of our training, I was sent to the front. I was wounded, and spent two weeks in an Italian hospital. I served in the brigade for six full years, and then returned to my wells of water...

I was drafted into the Israel Defense Forces at the beginning of the War of Independence. I served in the artillery brigade for a year and a half, and fought in various places in the Land. I perhaps could have chosen an army career, but I preferred to work in my field. The drilling devices were a part of my essence and reality. The feeling that we were providing fresh water for new, desolate villages increased my love for our Land. Even now, when my hearing has weakened, I hear the sound of gurgling water when I am awake and when I am dreaming. There is no more pleasant thought than that!

I spent almost all of my years in the Land in the settlement of Herzliya. (For me, Herzliya will always remain a settlement - even when its legal status changed to a city...) I regard it as a merit that my first daughter was born in Herzliya, and her name is also Herzliya. It is like my wife. I am betrothed to Herzliya, I am betrothed to it forever.

Eliahu Feintuch (first from the left on the bottom) with soldiers of the brigade in Italy

E. Feintuch as a soldier in the British Army

The Story of Charna Givoni (Geenstein)

Translated by Jerrold Landau

My lot during the time of my youth in Ratno was not good to me. I started work at a young age. The livelihood was meager. My mother ran our store and I ran the household, which consisted of five children. This was not one of the easy things. I could not attend school like the other children of my age. However, I was fortunate in that the teacher Kotzker gave me private lessons at home – this was a great privilege. I will not speak greatly of his praise, for certainly many others have certainly done so. However, may I say that Kotzker had many talents even as a private teacher. To him, teaching was not simply to earn a living. He saw himself as responsible for the knowledge and education of his students, and his dedication knew no bounds.

At night, I was free from the burdens of the household, and I found diversion in the Hechalutz Hatzair [Young Pioneer] chapter. I was one of its founders. Apparently, there was something special about our chapter, and it was no coincidence that any representative from the Land of Israel who came to Ratno wanted to return to visit our chapter. Avraham Grabov of blessed memory, Avrech, and others left their special stamp on this chapter, which continued to have an effect even after they made aliya. I had good fortune, and after five months of hachshara on the Tel Chai Kibbutz in Bialystok in 1932, I received a permit for aliya. I did not have to wait years for the certificate, for I already had made aliya in April 1933.

I recall the day of my departure from Ratno very well. All of my friends, male and female, who came to bid me farewell, and certainly my family members, wept. To this day I do not know if this was a weeping of bitterness, or perhaps tears of joy for the fact that I succeeded in making aliya. There was no opposition to my aliya even though it left a noticeable hole in the house. Even my father, who was a faithful Karliner Hassid, did not express any opposition to my step in that direction.

I arrived at the port of Haifa on May 1, 1933. That day we were sent to Kibbutz Naan, which had only been settled recently and required reinforcement from the Diaspora. There I met the people educated in the Land of Israel youth labor movement, who formed the first kernel of this Kibbutz, and I appreciated the unique traits of this group. I remained in Naan for about two years. I was forced to leave, for the news of the dire straits of my family in

Ratno gave me no rest. I had to help them. I worked for some time in the workers' kitchen. Then, I moved to Holon where I worked in the Lodzia factory[1]. I sent two Sterling Pounds per month to my family in Ratno. This was a respectable sum in those days, which in any case brought great relief to my family in the Diaspora. As well, I felt contentment in that I was able to help my family.

Uncaptioned. Charna Givoni

.

I worked in Lodzia for nine years, and then I continued in a smaller weaving factory.

There were about sixty people in all branches of my family – and I am the sole survivor.

Translator's Footnote

1. This was a textile factory. https://www.jewishgen.org/Yizkor/Ratno/rat287.html - f292-1r

The Organization of Ratno Natives in Israel

by Simcha Lavie

Translated by Jerrold Landau

The Organization of Ratno Natives in Israel was registered as an autonomous organization in 1960. However, the activities of the natives of Ratno in Israel actually began many years earlier. It can be said that this activity began already with the aliya of the first three youths from Ratno. Mordechai Gefen, Moshe Stern, and Shmuel Marder formed the first kernel, and the first address for Ratno natives who arrived in the Land of Israel after them. They were the first sources of information on the Land for those who made aliya from Ratno. They greeted the new arrivals from their town and offered assistance and good advice to anyone in need of such. Indeed, no small number were in need. The brotherhood and friendship that typified the Jews of Ratno also typified our people in the Land. Every person from Ratno who made Aliya agrees that they had someone with whom to consult, and that the perpetuity of Jewish Ratno would not let them down...

When the Second World War broke out, and we heard the first news of what was taking place in the areas under Nazi occupation, the natives of Ratno in the Land felt great stress. We did not have the resources and we could not offer assistance, but we waited for any sign of life from there, and any information on survivors. Eliezer Heller, Simcha Lavie, Sara Schwartz–Ginzburg, Chaya Yanosovich (of Tel Aviv), Sara and Shmuel Goldman (Rishon Letzion), Mordechai Gefen, Moshe Stern and Moshe Gutman (Kfar Sirkin),

Moshe Droog (Netanya) and others remained in touch to get information and make plans for action between themselves and also among the other natives of the town who had made aliya or lived in the Diaspora: America, Canada, and Argentina. The activities were fruitful. Aid committees were set up wherever Ratno natives were found to raise money from the natives of our town. The collected money was transferred to the Land by Mordechai Gefen, Shmuel Goldman and Simcha Lavie.

In 1944–1945, reliable information came to us about the fate of the natives of our city, especially after our fellow townspeople Yaakov Bender, Aryeh Wolk, and Daniel Marin arrived in the Land under the auspices of the brigade of the Independent Polish Army that was set up on Russian soil, and transferred to the Near East by the Allies. Their stories confirmed the extent of the terrible disaster, and the tribulations of the survivors. At the end of the war, contact was made with several survivors, including Shlomo Perlmutter and the Steingarten family. The picture was very clear.

The first survivors began to arrive from the vale of tears at the beginning of 1946. These included partisans and fighters who had to forge their way to the Land after great difficulties, via France, Italy, and other countries. From there, they made Aliya on the Haapala[1] ships. Every person brought their individual story, some of which are included in this book. We sat around nervous, depressed, and sorrowful.

All we could do was weep over our dear ones and attempt to help all of those who came for any help.

It seems to me that it would be no exaggeration to state that we withstood the test by providing all urgent provisions. The Holocaust survivors felt that they had an address, and found appropriate solutions to the problems of absorption as Ratno natives, appropriate to their professions and inclinations. Every one of us attempted to do our best, some a great deal and some little, to find these solutions.

The next phase in the activities of this organization was the memorialization of the martyrs of Ratno who fell. The first memorial ceremony took place with the initiative of the Ministry of Religion. The name of our town is etched on a marble tablet for eternal memory in the Holocaust Cellar on Mount Zion in Jerusalem. Then, we joined the memorialization activities of the Jewish National Fund, and planted a grove of 1,000 trees in memory of the martyrs of Ratno. For several years, this grove served as a gathering point for the natives of Ratno in Israel on Holocaust Remembrance Day.

Three additional members joined this circle of activity: Shlomo Perlmutter and Yisrael Chayat who were both Holocaust survivors, as well as Zeev Grabov who had made aliya from Argentina. It is especially worthwhile to make note of our role in the establishment of "Heichal Volhyn." Mordechai Gefen, Zeev Grabov, and Simcha Lavie represented our organization in the committee of the Heichal. We rented a room in this Heichal together with the Organization of Natives of Kamin–Kashirsk. This symbolized the strong connection that existed in the Diaspora between these two neighboring towns, and the many family connections that existed between the Jews of Ratno and Kamin–Kashirsk. This room served as a place for meetings and memorials for the natives of these two towns, and a place to unite ourselves with the memory of family members who perished.

In Elul 5711 (1951) the organization published the "Yetomot" booklet – pages of memory for the community of Ratno. When a Yiddish language memorial book was published in Argentina, we joined together with the editors and powers behind that book, and worked to the best of our ability to ensure that this book would reach all the natives of Ratno in Israel.

The board of the organization was diligent in organizing annual memorial ceremonies. The 13th of Elul was the day established for these memorials. We found an additional means of memorial in 1980 when we erected a monument in memory of the martyrs of Ratno in the cemetery on the border between Bat Yam and Holon.

We did not neglect or abandon the mitzvah of mutual assistance – in the literal meaning of the term. We established a loan fund affiliated with the organization, which offered assistance in the form of loans to natives of Ratno who were suffering from economic distress, for the needs of living expenses, household expenses, and the like. The activities of this fund were conducted with great dedication by Mordechai Gefen, who was the prime mover. His followers were the members Moshe Gutman of blessed memory and, may he live long, Zeev Grabov. For a period of thirty years, this fund responded to all requests by granting loans of reasonable sums without any need for security, without the standard interest rate, and collecting only a minimal payment from its members in order to cover the bank service charges. Requests for loans dwindled during the later period (a fact that testifies to the fact that the members had become well–grounded from an economic perspective), and almost all the members reached the conclusion that the time had come to utilize the principle sum of the fund to publish a book of testimony and memory for our town in Hebrew, so that our children and grandchildren, who are not fluent in Yiddish and therefore cannot read the book published in Argentina, will know what Jewish Ratno was. In the words of the poet, they would be able to draw from the wellspring from which our murdered brethren drew. The initiative to publish this book was accepted with appreciation and esteem, and the committee worked to the best of its ability to include anybody who had something to contribute to the book. We regard this as the crowning achievement of our activities, and hope that we have acted to the best of our ability to perpetuate and survey the heritage and past of the Jewish community of Ratno.

The current members of the committee of the organization include: Moshe Droog (chairman), Mordechai Gefen (treasurer), Chaya Grabov, Shmuel Goldman, Zeev Grabov, Simcha Lavie, and Shlomo Perlmutter.

{Photo page 295: One of the walls in Heichal Volhyn. The caption in the photo itself reads: In memory of the martyrs of the community of Ratno.}

Translator's Footnote

1. The pre–State illegal immigration. https://www.jewishgen.org/Yizkor/Ratno/rat287.html - f293-1r

I Thank You, Father and Mother!

By Aviva

Translated by Jerrold Landau

To my parents Mordechai and Zelda Gefen

(Written on the occasion of the 50th anniversary of my father's aliya.)

Fifty years have already passed since you made aliya to the Land, and whenever I see you – the Ratners[1] – gathering together, I never fail to ask myself: What binds you together so much for so many years?

You were only 20 years old when you left behind your remote shtetl, Ratno – and you have already spent 50 years of your life here in Israel. What is the power that brings you so close to each other after so many years – more than the number of years that you lived there together? Is this a nostalgia for the lovely years of your youth? Why is such great and sincere joy awakened when a native of Ratno arrives for a visit as a tourist from America after decades, or when a new immigrant arrives from behind the Iron Curtain after a period where nobody had heard of him or knew of his existence? I too lived in Kfar Sirkin until my adulthood. I had friends and acquaintances there during the years of my childhood and youth, but from the time that I left home, with each of us establishing our families wherever we did, we only see each other at infrequent times and in an incidental fashion, or at organized gatherings once a decade – and even these are not through our initiative.

I wonder to myself: why with respect to my father and mother, as well as with another small group of 50–60 Ratners, is it different? Why do they get together and meet at every opportunity, whether they live in Jerusalem, Afula, Haifa, or even Metulla? On every holiday or joyous occasion, or, to differentiate, at every time of sorrow or disaster, they get together with such great heartiness. Every one catches up with what has taken place with each other throughout the year, about their children and grandchildren, about concerns regarding livelihood, illnesses, and other problems. This is not just about passive news, but also support in the time of need — whether it is financial or moral support, whether it is physical assistance or encouragement in a time of difficulty. When I repeatedly ask myself, I get the impression that there are two answers:

The first one – Apparently, this was a different quality of life. There were values that we – the second and third generation – today refer to as "Diaspora ideas," such as mutual assistance, an open house, a closeness based on language and culture, of common experience of education in the cheders, schools, and youth movement; and memories of common events, a different landscape, and a different climate. In order to guard all of these things, one must return and meet again and again, to spend time together with friends, to reminisce, to tell stories and jokes — so that they will be repeated and relived, and so that they will not be forgotten.

The second reason that brings you together, in my opinion, is the loss. In accordance with the stories from the mouths of Father and Mother with which I was raised, and prior to that from the mouth of Grandmother Yente of blessed memory, I know clearly that from a physical perspective there is not much to be nostalgic about. They did not leave behind great splendor or glory.

[Page 295–alt]

The poverty was very often quite severe, but this too was lost in the Holocaust. The pain over the loss of these things, even though they might have been meager, cannot be cured. In essence, the fact that the shtetl was wiped off the face of the earth, along with the relatives and dear ones who went to their deaths – all this unites and brings together the Ratners in Israel, as if to protect the final ember so that it will not extinguish.

In the midst of all the upheaval that we are living through in the present, this closeness of you – the Ratners – is like a brand saved from the fire[2], which will continue on and shine light as long as you stand on your feet and continue to breathe and live. Therefore I wish to thank you, my father and mother, as well as all the Ratners.

Translator's Footnotes

1. A term for Ratno natives. https://www.jewishgen.org/Yizkor/Ratno/rat287.html - f293a-1r
2. See Zechariah 3:2. https://www.jewishgen.org/Yizkor/Ratno/rat287.html - f293a-2r

A meeting of the Ratno natives in Kfar Sirkin

By Shmuel Goldman

Translated by Jerrold Landau

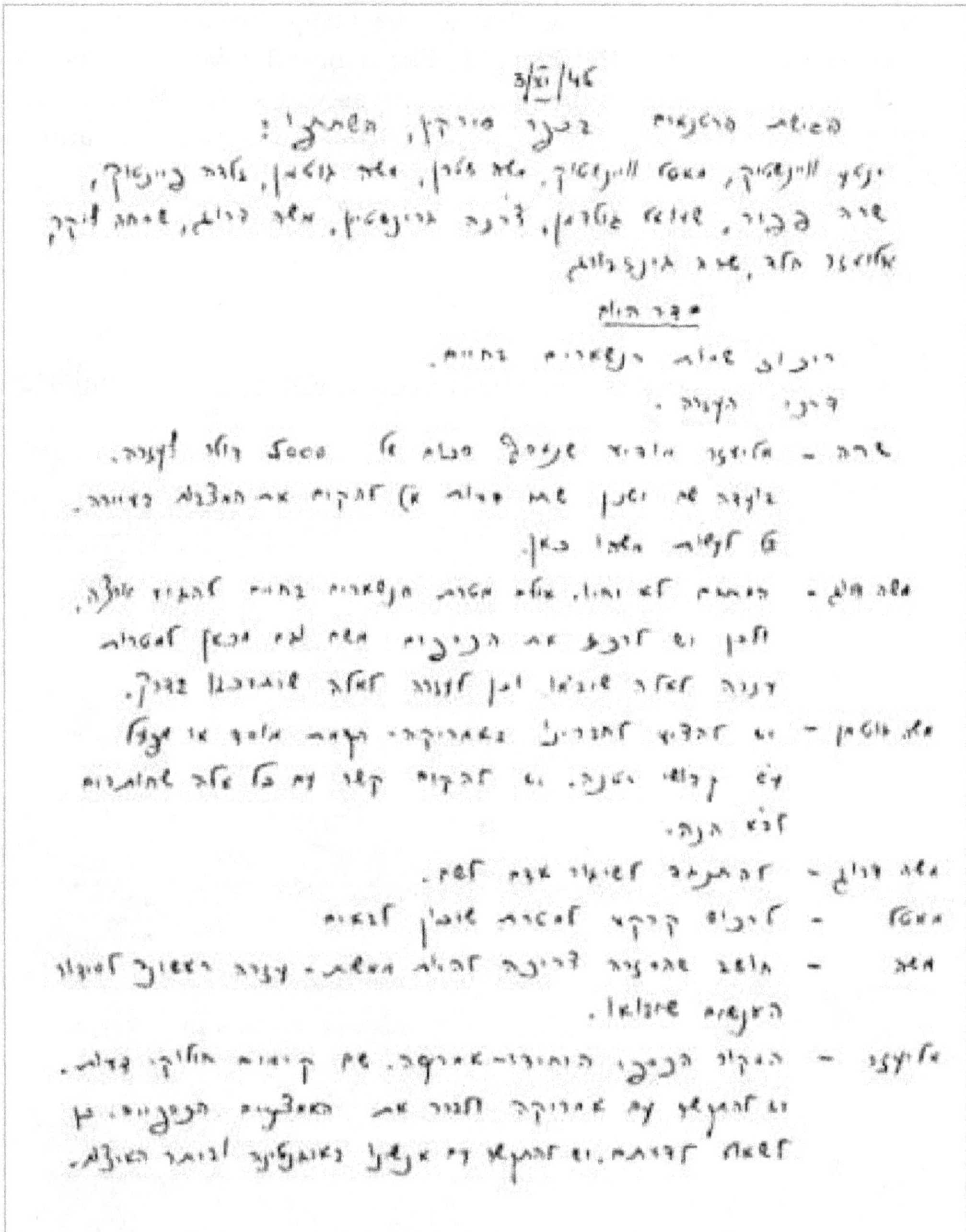

A page of the minutes of a meeting of the committee in 1945 dealing with assistance to the survivors of Ratno. Note: full translation follows

November 3, 1945

A meeting of the Ratno natives in Kfar Sirkin. The following people participated:

Yente Weinstock, Mottle Weinstock, Moshe Stern, Moshe Gutman, Zelda Feintuch, Sara Papir, Shmuel Goldman, Charna Greenstein, Moshe Droog, Simcha Leker, Eliezer Held, Sara Ginzburg.

Agenda

A collection of names of survivors.

Means of assistance.

Sara – Eliezer informs us that a sum of 5,000 dollars for assistance has been collected. Two opinions were expressed at the meeting: a) to build the headstones in the shtetl; b) to do something here.

Moshe Droog – The dead will not come back to life. However, the goal of the survivors is to make it to the Land. Therefore, we must collect money there as well as here for the purpose of helping those who will come, as well as to assist those who may be delayed on their journey.

Moshe Gutman – We must propose to our friends in America the establishment of a foundation or an enterprise dedicated to the martyrs of Ratno. We must establish contact with all those who are thinking of coming here.

Moshe Droog – Opposes sending someone there.

Mottle – We should obtain land for housing of those who will be arriving

Moshe – Feels that the assistance must be concrete – first level aid to help the arrivals set themselves up.

Eliezer – The sole source of financing is America. Differences of opinion exist there. We must get in contact with America and clarify the financial means available. We must also hear their opinion. We must get in touch with our people in Argentina and other countries.

Ratno natives at a memorial in the Ratno Grove in the Forest of the Martyrs in the mountains of Jerusalem

A meeting of the first olim from Ratno in Petach Tikva: Sara and Shmuel Goldman, Moshe Gutman, Simcha Lavie, Mordechai Gefen, Shmuel Marder, Moshe Stern

A group of Holocaust survivors at a memorial to the martyrs in Germany (1946). Among the participants are: Kamintzky and Liberman who made aliya to the Land of Israel, Avraham Berg (died in the United States), Yosef Steinberg, and Malka Yunevitz (Canada)

A meeting of Ratno natives in Israel with Dova and Shlomo Cohen from abroad

The monument in memory of the martyrs of Ratno in the Holon Cemetery

Ratno natives at Heichal Volhyn, where a room is dedicated to Ratno — Kamin Kashirsk

Ratners Will Always Be Ratners

by Zeev Grabov

Translated by Jerrold Landau

Our sages have said, "In the future, the Land of Israel will spread throughout all the lands". From here it would seem that even such a small town as Ratno can spread out and expand... Whoever has any doubt about this will be convinced from the following episodes -- all of which are true.

Once Moshe Droog, a Ratno native, was driving in his large car to an important meeting in an institution of which he was a director. When he approached Rishon Letzion, a policeman of the traffic division stopped him and said curtly and seriously, "Sir, you are driving at more than 100 kilometers per hour, give me your drivers license and all of your documentation. I am writing you a ticket." Moshe Droog stuck his head out the window and began to explain something to the traffic policeman. However, when the traffic policeman looked at the driver, a smile came over his face and he said, "Is it possible? Moshe Droog, the son of Reb Avraham Droog of Ratno, would hold his life so cheaply? Would you have driven in Ratno with such a speed on a wagon hitched to a scrawny horse?"

Moshe Droog was astonished, and the policeman saw the need to add an explanation, "Do you not recognize me? It is not surprising, for when you made aliya, I was a child of about eight years old. A Ratno native finds it difficult to write a traffic ticket for a native of his own town, so here is your warning: Drive slowly and carefully!"

*

Here is a story about Shmulik Goldman who served as the secretary of the workers' council of Rishon Letzion. Shmulik was sitting in his office, pensive and sad. The work shortage in the moshava (at that time, Rishon Letzion was a moshava) was worsening, and today there was to be a workers' demonstration in front of the offices of the workers' council. The workers did not come to work and advised him as well not to be absent during the demonstration, but he was not prepared to accept such advice. He was prepared to negotiate with the workers. He had what to say to them, for he was not sparing any efforts in trying to minimize the work shortage.

As he was still immersed in his thoughts, he already heard the shouts of "bread and work" from the demonstrators who approached the building of the workers' council. Shmulik looked outside the window and saw the throngs of demonstrators, headed by a strong young man who was shouting directions and orders. Shmulik left his office and stood at the outside door, preparing to greet the demonstrators and tell them what he had to tell them. However, the leader of the demonstration started to talk first, and he specifically spoke in Yiddish. He asked the demonstrators to stop their shouts of "broit un arbeit" (bread and work), and gave a fiery speech about the tribulations of the new olim and the urgent necessity for action from the institutions to create sources of work. He spoke a sweet Volhynian Yiddish which was extremely recognizable to the secretary of the Rishon Letzion Workers' Council. Shmulik attempted to say his piece and advise that the demonstrators choose their delegation to discuss the measures that could be taken, however their spirits were afire, and the demonstrators did not want to hear his words. At that moment, an idea flashed through Shmulik's mind. He turned to the leader of the demonstrators, and said to him, "Listen to me comrade, your Yiddish reminds me very much of my hometown."

"What town?" asked the leader of the demonstration.

"A small town in Volhynia, called Ratno," answered Shmulik.

"You are from Ratno? Unbelievable."

Shmulik responded calmly, "Yes I am from Ratno, the son of Shamai Goldman. Does that name mean anything to you."

At the sound of those words, the head of the demonstrators approached Shmulik, hugged him, and then turned to the demonstrators, calling out, "Comrades, stop shouting! We have someone here with whom we can talk! Let us choose a delegation and sit together with the secretary of the council to discuss how we can solve the work shortage."

While Shmulik was still standing in surprise over the sudden turn of events, the youth added, "I am from the village of Datyn, not far from Ratno. When I was still a child, I would often come to Ratno to visit the home of my uncle Woli Levant. During the war, I was a partisan and I fought against the Nazis. I want you to know that from now, you have reliable support from this community, and one can depend on people from Ratno!"

*

That morning, it was very crowded in the Kupat Cholim infirmary on Rothschild Street In Petach Tikva. An official was standing at the main entrance and greeting anyone who arrived with a smile and a good morning wish, in accordance with the new protocols instituted by the order keeper, a former Ratno native. Inside, next to the counter, Moshe Gutman, also a Ratno native, is sitting, supervising the distribution of notes to the doctors. Shouts from inside reached the ears of the order keeper or the supervisor. He went inside and saw that a muddied woman was standing next to Moshe Gutman's desk, and shouting, "I came especially from Moshav Nechalim. I must visit a woman's doctor. I have not yet milked the cows in the village, and there is a bus from Nechalim to Petach Tikva only twice a day. Give me a number for a woman's doctor."

Gutman, who was dedicated to Kupat Cholim with heart and soul, told her that he had run out of numbers of the woman's doctors, and the doctor was refusing to accept patients beyond the established quota. However, his words did not convince the woman. When the argument reached a high pitch, the order keeper approached the woman and asked her to give him her membership booklet. When he looked at her booklet he said to her, "Wait a minute, we will try to see what can be done for you."

He approached Gutman and said to him quietly. "Moshe, see, this woman is from Ratno. Give her a number reserved for the most urgent situations." Moshe smiled upon hearing these words, and gave the woman a number for the women's doctor. He said to her, "Why did you not tell me that you are from Ratno? Who are you from Ratno?"

"What Ratno is in your head?" retorted the woman. "My name is Ratner, and that is all."

"This time you put one over me," said Moshe the Ratner to the order keeper, a native of Ratno. The woman with the number also smiled. She never imagined that there would be so much charm in her name.

*

Here is another episode, that I would not have believed had I not heard with my own ears, for the incident was indeed as follows.

Yaakov Wolonta, who had moved from Ratno to Denver, Colorado, USA, was turning over in his bed at night with a dream that recurred each night. He saw himself at sunrise in the vegetable garden of Melnik the tanner, picking ears of corn and hiding them in a bag. Suddenly he felt as if tongs were clasping his neck, and that strong blows were being administered to his back to the point "that he could see his grandmother", as we used to say in Ratno. He turned his head and saw Shalom Melnik, who was two years older than him, ready to deliver one more blow, however he let up when he saw Yaakov's face turn yellow, and he said, "Do you desire our corn?" Yaakov escaped like an arrow from a bow, but when he was already a distance away from Melnik, he declared, "Wait, wait, one day I will settle my accounts with you. You will not come out clean from my hands, and I will never forget your blows!"

After this "vision" repeated itself for several nights, Yaakov decided, "This is nothing other than the finger of G-d." He must complete his accounting with Melnik, who, as far as he knew, lived now in New York. He told his wife about his decision to travel to New York, and his American wife mocked him, "Have you gone crazy, to undertake a trip of this nature to 'conclude a matter' of more than sixty years ago. The spirit of foolishness has overtaken you!"

That night, he once again dreamed that dream, and he decided, "Let my wife's opinion be as it may." He felt it necessary to travel. He booked a place on an airplane, and the next day, when the streets of New York were covered with snow up to the neck, he arrived at Shalom Melnik's door. Before he rang the doorbell he deliberated about whether he should extend his hand to

Shalom as usual, or perhaps he should deliver a strong blow, the same type that he suffered from him 60 years ago in the vegetable garden in Ratno..."

He rang the doorbell, and a white-haired woman with a pleasant appearance opened the door. She was surprised by this morning visit on such a snowy day, and asked him what he wanted. Yankel answered, "I have come especially from Denver, Colorado to see your husband Shalom. I have an urgent matter to discuss with him." His wife explained that her husband was not well, and was still sleeping. "Nevertheless," said Yankel, "wake him up, for the issue cannot be put off. Tell him that a Jew from Ratno has come to see him." After a few minutes, a bent-over Jew came out of his room, wearing winter slippers and a scarf on his neck. Yankel recognized him immediately. This was Shalom, who had beaten him in Ratno. He walked to greet him. They recognized each other, hugged and kissed each other. Then Yaakov tapped Shalom lightly on the back and said to him, "Here, I have paid you back. I told you then in Ratno that I will never forget the beating that you administered to me regarding the corn in your vegetable garden. Now the repeated dream will no longer afflict me."

"I am happy to see you here in my house," answered Shalom, and told his wife to serve the important guest from Denver, Colorado in an ample fashion. The surprised wife did what her husband wanted. With a good heart, and over cups of whiskey, Shalom explained to his wife the meaning of the "urgent matter" that brought the guest from Colorado to their home...

Dvora and Avraham Berg at the monument in memory of the martyrs in Germany

Translator's note: partial translation of the monument (not all of it is clear in the photograph):

Remember what the Nazis did with our people. They killed six million.
(next four lines are unclear)
May G-d Remember
And may their holy souls be bound in the bonds of eternal life
And may their blood be avenged
And let us say Amen.
May their souls be bound in the bonds of eternal life.

Ratno, 13 Elul 5702
August 25, 1942}

On the Communal Activities of Ratno Natives in Argentina

by Zeev Grabov

Translated by Jerrold Landau

The ordinary Jews of Argentina are likely to think that our Ratno is a large city whose Jewish population certainly reached into the tens of thousands. I have experienced this myself. I once met a Jew from Chaco, about 1,200 kilometers from the capital of Argentina. During our conversation, when I told him that I came from Ratno, he said to me, "What type of city is this Ratno, for this is almost no Jewish communal institution in Argentina in which Jews from Ratno are not involved!" This is the way things are in our times, but this is not the way it was decades ago. I myself arrived in Argentina in January 1937. Difficulties, doubts and many struggles accompanied my first steps. My struggles began even before I set foot on Argentinian soil: how would I get used to life without the Jews of Ratno, without the Hashomer Hatzair chapter, without the realities of our town that was an inseparable part of my essence? My brother who preceded me in immigrating to this country greeted me at the port. With the first hug, I knew that Ratno also existed here, that this was the embrace of Mother and Father, the embrace of a man who understands your soul and is prepared to help.

Isser Kamintzky was the first Ratner who I met. I did not know him previously, but when I heard that he was the son of Yitzchak and Dincha Kamintzky, I felt immediately that a "slice" of Ratno was before me. At that time, Isser was already a powerhouse who supported the Jewish National Fund, the League for the Working Land of Israel, and other areas of communal endeavor. His base was in Lanus, in the province of Buenos Aires. From there, his rays shined upon the capital city... Everyone knew that for Isser, communal matters were more important than issues of livelihood, that were apparently side affairs. As time went on, I met Yisrael Honik, Eliahu Cohen, Bertha Cohen, Shlomo Cohen, L. Buckler, David Goldin, Berla Fuchs, Yaakov Fuchs, Eliezer Feigelis, A. Y. Reif, Yehuda Konishter – all natives of Ratno who gathered in the city of Lanus, whose population was about half a million.

Moshe Honik arrived in Argentina in 1938, apparently directly from the Hachshara farm of Czestochowa, after he did not succeed in obtaining a certificate for the Land of Israel. He immediately immersed himself in the mighty waters of communal affairs. While we were searching for sources of livelihood for the body, we were also searching for sources of livelihood for the soul. Since we all knew that we left behind in Ratno family members who were waiting for our assistance, we dedicated time and energy to affairs not related to livelihood[1]. In Ratno we had worked with dedication for the Jewish National Fund – and we continued that in Lanus, with Isser Kamintzky as chairman, Eliahu Cohen the treasurer, and Zeev Grabov the secretary. Several other Ratners were active: M. Honik, D. Goldin, L. Buckler, A. Feigelis, and Tzvi and Yosef Buber. We left some place for natives of other towns... It was the same situation with the League for the Working Land of Israel. Natives of Ratno were the yeast in the dough, the living spirit, and the moving force. At their side were other new immigrants who had arrived from other cities in Volhyn and Pulisia.

Another important arena was education. There were two small Jewish schools in Lanus, each with several tens of students. We Ratners, former students of Kotzker, attempted to continue his path in a settlement that was 500x500x500 parasangs[2] from Ratno. Our first task was to make one large, serious school from the three small schools. We established a fine school named for Chaim Nachman Bialik, as well as a kindergarten named for Chana Senesh. For the sake of historical accuracy, and so as not to neglect the natives of other cities and towns, we will point out that it was not only Ratno natives who were active in this important arena. One of them was Konobka, the son-in-law of Yosef Buber. He was a native of Kobrin (which is known to be somewhat larger than Ratno). However, when people would ask him from where he came, he would always respond, “Ratno.” He wanted to attach himself to the large tree, to demonstrate how famous Ratno was in Argentina. A hall for all the Jewish youth was built in Lanus in 1938. Where was this set up, if not in the home of Duba Cohen of Ratno, the wife of the shochet Reb Avraham of Ratno who was murdered on the eve of Rosh Hashanah 1921 by the men of Bulak Balachowicz. The Ratners Isser Kamintzky, Noach Cohen, Leibel Buckler, Eliahu and Shlomo Cohen, Moshe and Yisrael Honik, Zeev Grabov, Eliezer Feigelis, David Goldin, Hershel Buber and five or six other people who were not Ratno natives gathered in her home. Thus was the Y. Ch. Brenner Hall (the name was proposed by Yisrael Honik) established in a fashion that served as an example also for other Jewish settlements in Argentina. The Ratners also helped set up the WIZO women's Zionist organization, as well as the mutual assistance committee, headed by our Duba Cohen.

In 1942, two Ratners (Moshe Honik and Zeev Grabov) founded the Hashomer Hatzair chapter in Lanus based on the principles and example of the chapter of Ratno. Moshe Honik later moved over to the Poale Zion party for a short time. He became one of the pillars of that party after some time, and we should note the publication of the Kiyum books toward which he invested great energy and saw great success.

A crisis afflicted the Jewish community in Lanus (Union Izraelita) in 1945. It served as the protector of the first immigrants, and did not look upon the greeners (the new immigrants) positively. The Ratners again came to help, and pushed through a change of guard. Who was chosen as president? None other than Moshe Honik of Ratno. From that time, the Union Izraelita became the representative of all the Jews, supported Zionist activities, and removed all conflict between the long–timers and the greeners. When candidates for the cantor of the synagogue had to be examined, we (Moshe Honik and the writer of these lines) also performed that task, even though we had no previous experience from Ratno in that area...

The activities of the Ratners in the Kovler Bank of Buenos Aires form a chapter unto itself.

The bank was named after the city of Kowel, even though its central activists were natives of Ratno, who gave a great deal to firmly establish the institution and ensure its cooperative nature. This bank went from strength to strength, and earned great acclaim among Argentinian Jewry. We should especially note the dedication of Yaakov Tucker, Motel Telson, Yosef Buber, and A. Y. Reif. The latter headed the bank for a long time, and protected it as the apple of his eye.

There were three centers of communal activities of the Ratners in Argentina: Buenos Aires, Lanus, and Resistencia (Chacho district). The golden chain of Ratno was continued in those three places. From among those active in the areas of education and culture, we should note Yaakov Rag (from among the first of Hatzofim of Ratno), Yoel Steinberg, the brothers Yaakov and Meir Tucker, Chaim Grabov, and Velvel Rajsky (in the leftist circles). The brothers Yosel and Asher Eides excelled in communal affairs in Resistencia. They established a school and library in the city that seemed to be a remote city to us. Later Manes and Tove Eilbaum, whose home was open to any new immigrant, came to their assistance, as did Meir and Beila Grabov, Zelig Bender, Wolf Blostein, and others. It is fitting to stress that many of the children of the Ratners continue in the tradition of their fathers, including Shmuel Eides the son of Yoel Eides (in the Aml"t Organization); the engineer and poet Eliahu Tucker, the son of Yaakov Tucker; the engineer Chaim–Leib

Fuchs, the son of Berl Fuchs. There are certainly many others whose names I do not recall.

Moshe Honik delivers introductory greetings from the community to Y. Zerubavel during his visit to Argentina

In summary, it can be said that Ratno natives were prominent in all central representative organization of Argentinian Jewry. In this manner it can be proved that the chain has not been severed, and that which the parents sowed in Ratno was reaped by the children in Argentina.

A reception for Moshe Honik in Israel

Y. Konishter, his wife, and M. Honik with a guest from Israel — Charna Givoni

Translator's Footnotes

1. This means that they took time away from their personal efforts to earn a livelihood to arrange assistance to their family members in Ratno.https://www.jewishgen.org/Yizkor/Ratno/rat300.html - f305-1r
2. A parasang is an ancient unit of distance that appears in the Talmud. 500 parasangs is an expression for a considerable distance.https://www.jewishgen.org/Yizkor/Ratno/rat300.html - f305-2r

Ratno Natives in Argentina

by Isser Kamintzky

Translated by Jerrold Landau

I arrived in Argentina in 1924, but the immigration from Ratno to Argentina began two years previously. When I arrived, there was already a community of Ratno Jews in that country. The desperate situation in Ratno and lack of means to find a direction in life forced them to immigrate to overseas countries. My family moved to Kowel in 1917, and it was natural that I would search for Kowel natives in my new country. I do not know why, but for some reason I was specifically attracted to Ratno natives: my cousin Noach Cohen and my friends Yaakov Rag, Yoel Richter, Chaim–Yosef Gutman, Yosef Rajsky, Sheptel Melnik, Yaakov Tucker, Mordechai Telson, Yoel Eides and others. Most of the Ratners lived in the capital city of Buenos Aires, but some made it as far as Resistencia. Almost all were lacking a trade. Having no option, they took hold of the only "trade" that was apparently open to everybody, and did not require any training — the trade of peddling, or, as it was called in the local language "Cvantnikes." This trade required a great deal of energy, for those occupied therein had to go from door to door selling merchandise at prices appropriate for villagers and small settlements.

I found my fellow natives in a depressed spirit. They had not yet "made America." They lived in meager dwellings, with three or four people in a single room. However, these conditions did not keep them from fulfilling the commandment of mutual assistance. Any new immigrant that arrived was taken into their rooms and provided with all his needs until he was able to stand on his own and save up about 100 Pesos, which in those days amounted to a significant sum (a dollar was worth about 3–4 Pesos). The Ratners in Argentina observed this commandment with respect to their fellow natives in a manner that was traditional and ingrained in their blood, just as it had been ingrained in the blood of their parents. I recall that my father of blessed memory would not leave the synagogue on Sabbath eves until the last of the visitors who had arrived in town had found a host - that is a householder who invited the guest for the Sabbath meal and to stay over. The Ratno tradition was well recognized in another area in Argentina - in the relations between man and G–d. Even those of our townsfolk who had cut off all contact with the Master of the World while they were still supported at their parents' table in Ratno renewed connections with Divine Providence after arriving in Argentina. They would meticulously arise in the morning for the Shacharit prayer and to don tefillin before going to work. I recall one episode: when my cousin took me into his room in which four Ratners already lived, I found Chaim Yosef Gutman reciting the Shemone Esrei prayer. When I extended my hand in greeting, he only responded after he concluded his prayer and reached "Oseh Shalom Bimromav." We set up places as synagogues for all the Jewish holidays. It seems to me that the decisive reason was: we wanted to feel the feelings of our home in Ratno from which we had been severed, and the feelings of Jewish tradition that were ingrained in us from our childhood.

A large network of Jewish activity and organization already existed in Argentina in the 1920s. Among these were noticeable activities conducted by circles that considered themselves as "progressive, " which in truth were Yevsektsias[1] marked by the hatred of Zion, activities in support of Birobidzhan, and the like. It should be noted that the tendency toward the Yevsektsia was foreign to the vast majority of Ratno natives, even though there were some that were singed by their coals. We cannot forget that were it not for the limitation in the issuance of certificates for aliya to the Land of Israel, most of us would never have arrived in Argentina. However, once we did arrive, we wanted to nurture the values with which we were educated in our town of Ratno even in that country, including faithfulness to Zion with all the practical activities that such entails. It was not easy to plant these values in a foreign land under radically different conditions and realities, but it seems to me that I do not boast if I note that we did to the best of our ability preserve the values with which we were educated. My friends and I invested all our energy into activities on behalf of the various Zionist funds. We were represented in all the conventions and gatherings. We raised the flaming coal of Ratno to the expansive breadths of the Argentinian "Pampa." Our process of becoming rooted in Argentina was not easy at all. We concerned ourselves with the spirit more than the body. At that time, there were several writers and people of the spirit in Argentina, and we made efforts to not miss even one important lecture or interesting article published in the Jewish newspapers from the fruits of pens of serious publicists such as Ragelsky, Botoshinsky, and others. The landsmanschafts were in full bloom, and we, natives of Ratno, took hold of the "east" in the organization of Kowel natives, and we worked toward the development of the loan and savings funds, which with the passage of time turned into an important banking institution. A serious struggle unfolded between the Zionists and the non–Zionists over control of that institution. The writer of these lines served as the first secretary of the fund. Noach Cohen was the vice president and Yaakov Rag was the treasurer.

After the concerns over livelihood eased, and we became somewhat settled, we began to concern ourselves with our families abroad, by providing financial assistance and permits for immigration to Argentina. This is an endeavor which is worthy of its own article, but I will not do so here and now.

Lanus, near the capital city, was an important center for the Ratno natives. This was primarily because Eliahu Messer, who himself was a native of Trisk near Kowel, immigrated there. His business was the supply of various products through peddlers, and he employed numerous Ratno natives. Thus did the direct trans–Atlantic Ratno–Lanus line begin. The home of our comrade Noach Cohen became the headquarters for Ratno natives. There, we planned various activities and made early efforts for communal activities, some of which are outlined in Zeev Grabov's article in this book. As time passed, Lanus became too constricted for us, and the first people to break through this constricted situation and transfer their activities to Buenos Aires were Moshe and Yisrael Honik, Zeev Grabov, and the writer of these lines. The serious and broad–ranging efforts of our comrade Moshe Honik, who served in various capacities such as secretary of the cultural activities of the Hebrew community in the capital, founder and director of the Kiyum publishing house under the auspices of the Labor Zionist Movement, which was the central point for the publication of the community yearbook, and other roles should be especially noted.

After the great victory of the Labor Movement in elections for the 20th Zionist Congress with the active participation of the emissary from the Land of Israel Nachman Tamir, two comrades from Ratno were added to the list of delegates to the congress: I as the representative of Lanus and Meir Grabov as the representative of Resistencia. Moshe Honik served as a delegate from Argentina in a different congress.

At the end of our outline we must state: Ratno did not let us down even in Argentina, and all the good that we received in Ratno remained with us throughout the time we lived in Argentina.

Translator's Footnotes

1. Jewish sections of the Soviet Communist party. See https://en.wikipedia.org/wiki/Yevsektsiyahttps://www.jewishgen.org/Yizkor/Ratno/rat300.html - f305a-1r

Ratno Descendants in the United States

Translated by Jerrold Landau

In the memorial book that was published in Argentina, B. Kahn (Berl Chanech's) tells the following about the first steps of the Organization of Ratno Natives in the United States.

"On a Sabbath late afternoon in 1906, Ratno natives who lived in the Brownsville neighborhood of New York gathered in the home of Yisrael Kahn. In those days, Yisrael's house served as the center for Ratno natives, just as the house at the corner of Clinton and Rivington in Manhattan served as the center for Ratno natives in Manhattan. The prime motive of this meeting was to relieve slightly the loneliness of the Ratno natives in the big city. Some of those present read letters that they received from their relatives in Ratno and that warmed the heart a bit.

In the memorial book that was published in Argentina, B. Kahn (Berl Chanech's) tells the following about the first steps of the Organization of Ratno Natives in the United States.

A group of Ratno natives in New York

Eliezer Ginzburg (Breindl's)

"On a Sabbath late afternoon in 1906, Ratno natives who lived in the Brownsville neighborhood of New York gathered in the home of Yisrael Kahn. In those days, Yisrael's house served as the center for Ratno natives, just as the house at the corner of Clinton and Rivington in Manhattan served as the center for Ratno natives in Manhattan. The prime motive of this meeting was to relieve slightly the loneliness of the Ratno natives in the big city. Some of those present read letters that they received from their relatives in Ratno and that warmed the heart a bit.

At that meeting, the idea of uniting the Ratno natives into a brotherhood and mutual assistance organization was first hatched. As I remember, those present at the meeting included Velvel Kirsch, Eliahu Klein, Hirsch-Leib Klein, Chaim Leib Peshinski from the village of Wydranica, Shemaya Schneider, Yoel and Yehuda Schneider, my father Yisrael, myself, and several other Ratners whose names I do not remember. Velvel Kirsch was elected as the chairman and I as the secretary. Each of those present paid one dollar and decided on a biweekly membership fee of 10 cents. When the Ratners of Manhattan (New York) joined our organization, it was necessary to rent a hall for our meetings. After some time, we used the money collected in the account of the organization to purchase land for a cemetery with regular payments, and also a house of worship on the fourth floor of a house on Firside[1] Street. From that time, we held our meetings in that location. Ratno natives from all parts of New York and also from outside of New York would come to our synagogue for the Hakafoton Simchat Torah, and the house would be too small to accommodate everyone. It is appropriate to note that Shalom Friedman, the son of Yudel the scribe from Kowel, was especially dedicated to our organization. To the best of his ability, he made sure that those in need would receive assistance. He also transferred money to Ratno to renovate the synagogue, cemetery and other institutions. Special subsidies were given by the organization to "Maot Chittin" (Passover charity) for those in need, to the local rabbi, and to the poor of the town. In its peak years, the membership reached 120, however this included some people who were not from Ratno. Hershel Shachna's (who had been a teacher in Ratno) served as the secretary of our organization until his death. Afterward, the chairman was David Sobol, and his son Max Sobol served as chairman.

The following regulations were included in the charter of the organization that was called "The sons of Rabbi Yosef, Natives of Ratno and Volhynia":

-- The official languages of the organization for everything related to correspondence, accounting, etc. would be Yiddish.

-- The main purpose of the organization is philanthropic -- to provide assistance to the needy, and to assist the widow in the event of the passing of a member.

-- The chairman (president) and vice president are obligated to visit the sick at least once a week.

-- Brotherhood and unity must pervade amongst all the members of the organization.

-- Only upright and dedicated men will be accepted as members. A person who has not married within the Jewish faith is not permitted to be a member."

The aforementioned book by Leon Ginzburg, the son of Yosel and Breindel, writes the following about a later period and about the assistance committee of the Ratno neighbors:

"In January 1945, natives of Ratno in New York gathered in the home of Yaakov Kotler in order to organize the assistance for the Holocaust survivors of Ratno and its region. We did not have yet any definitive information about the fate of our dear ones in Ratno, but we were aware of the magnitude of the disaster. At the end of the war we learned that not a trace of Ratno Jewry remains. The following people participated in the first meeting: the brothers Zelig and Avigdor Marin, Pinchas Berg, Shalom Melnik, Yaakov Kotler, Hodel Goldstein, Harry Kirsch, and Leon Ginzburg.

Our first task was to forge a connection with the hundreds of Ratno natives who were scattered around greater New York and other cities in the United States, whose addresses we did not have. We decided to publish notices in the Jewish newspapers and the radio informing of the establishment of our assistance committee, and asking that all Ratno natives join with us. We chose a provisional committee that consisted of Pinchas Berg as chairman, Leon Ginzburg as secretary, Yaakov Kotler as treasurer, and Zelig and Avigdor Marin as auditors. Four months after we began our activities, we received a letter from Avraham Berg, one of the survivors, who was the brother of Pinchas Berg. The letter described details of the bitter fate of Ratno Jewry. This letter included the names of 29 survivors of Ratno Jewry.

The Ratno natives in Canada offered us faithful assistance.

Avraham Berg later arrived in the United States, and became very active among the Ratno natives. He left 5,000 dollars in his will for the activities of the organization of Ratno natives. The Marantz brothers, Yitzchak Leib Kotler, Yosef Fisher, and the Anglo-Jewish poet A. M. Klein helped in particular[2]. Feisi Kreskar and the Kagan and Kirsch brothers participated from Chelsea in Boston. It is also worthwhile to note the contribution of Sam Bukler of Detroit (a native of the village of Chocieszow), and the brothers Avraham and Moshe Kamper of Toronto, Canada.

Translator's Footnotes

1. I have not been able to identify this street in a modern map of the Brownsville area of Brooklyn. It is likely that street names have changed over the decades. The English spelling I used is transliterated from the Hebrew, and may not be exact.https://www.jewishgen.org/Yizkor/Ratno/rat300.html - f1r
2. A Jewish Canadian poet, born in Ratno. See http://en.wikipedia.org/wiki/A._M._Kleinhttps://www.jewishgen.org/Yizkor/Ratno/rat300.html - f2r

The Ratno Heritage in Cuba

by Levi Shapira

Translated by Jerrold Landau

Information about the Book of Ratno that is to be published shortly reached me under particularly difficult circumstances. I am wheelchair-bound, and speaking and writing are difficult for me. However, I wanted to express, and not only in a few lines, my thoughts and feeling about receiving this information.

Fate led me to the country of Cuba in 1937. I, like many others, felt the lack of prospects in the lowly state of life in Ratno, and possibly already prophesied to my heart about the storm that was to come shortly. I found refuge in a country that was not a center of Jewish immigration, the State of Cuba, which was not yet under the dictatorship of Fidel Castro. Despite the fact that Cuba was not thriving economically at that time, I studied the trade of diamond polishing and earned enough from my livelihood and even more. After some time, I tried my hand in business, and I was successful in that realm as well. Our Ratno tradition accompanied me through all of the revolutions and changes that took place in Cuba. I felt duty bound to participate actively in the development of Jewish communal life in that country, that had a small Jewish community. What did we not do there?

Levi Shapira

We built Jewish schools, and set up a theater building, a communal library, and a cultural hall, etc. The Ratno heritage commanded me, even if it did not express itself literally, to participate in all national and Jewish activities. I felt this blinding obligation even more strongly after the tidings of Job regarding the extermination of the Jewish community of Ratno by the Nazis and Ukrainians reached us. Even after the Cuban revolution that brought the guerilla fighters, Fidel Castro and his cronies, to power, we continued to concern ourselves with the character of Jewish life in Cuba. At first, I too was among those who hoped for greatness and goodness from the Socialist guard. The majority of the Cuban Jews left the country. From the 15,000 Jews, only about 2,000 remained, but those who remained did not despair. We had to concern ourselves with a Jewish school for the approximately 150 Jewish children, a synagogue, and the Jewish community. The government permitted us to establish a synagogue, and even the non-religious saw a need to go there to worship. In this manner, they demonstrated the existence of a Jewish community. We concerned ourselves with a shochet (ritual slaughterer) mohel (circumcisor), and for matzo on Passover in order to celebrate the Holiday in accordance with its regulations. Even the library remained open, and we gathered there at set times for discussions on current events. When there was no teacher for the Jewish school, I volunteered to serve as a teacher even though I had no training for this. However, it seemed to me that I, as a Ratner who had received a Jewish-nationalistic education in the town, was commanded to worry about the future, and to ensure that the golden chain would not be severed. After a great deal of effort, I succeeded in receiving an exit permit from Cuba. The government authorities looked kindly upon me as someone who had been active in the revolution, and permitted me to travel to Israel. However, they denied me the right to take out my money and belongings. I left that country empty-handed, without one cent, but I thanked the Divine providence that I succeeded in seeing the State of Israel that had been established by generations of pioneers, including pioneers from Ratno. I felt very bad that I had not been among those myself. I attempted to build a life in strange countries, but had not built up my own country. Due to my serious illness, I have not had the opportunity to feast my eyes on all the charm of our Land.

Ratners in Israel

Translated by Jerrold Landau

Elboim, Emanuel (Manes), the son of Yitzchak and Miriam, was born in 1908. He immigrated to Argentina at the age of 20. Emanuel made aliya in 1963. He lives in Rishon LeZion. He worked as an agent for Tnuva in Rehovot. He married Tova (née Prigal). His children are Yitzchak and Rachel.

Ahal, Ruth, the daughter of David and Gittel Greenstein, was born in 1910. She was a member of Hechalutz Hatzair, and went through hachshara in the Tel Hai Kibbutz in Lida. She made aliya in 1934. She settled in Haifa and studied in a program for registered nurses. She was widowed from her husband Yaakov of blessed memory. Her occupation was a nurse. Her children are Oded (a chemical engineer) and Dalia (a clerk).

Balter, Tzipora, the daughter of Shimon and Sara Rosenberg, was born in 1915. She made aliya in 1935. She married Aryeh. Her children are Shlomit (a secretary) and Moshe (a lawyer). She is a housewife.

Bender, Yaakov, the son of Avraham and Frida, was born in 1922. He was a member of Beitar. He enlisted in the Russian army in 1941. He made aliya in 1943 with a unit of the Polish Army (Andrius). He is married to Bat-Sheva. Their children are Ehud, Aryeh and Aliza. He owns a carpentry shop in Rishon LeZion. He was a member of the Haganah and participated in the War of Independence and Kadesh Operation[1] at the rank of sergeant.

Blitz, Leah, the daughter of Yaakov and Ada Hochman, was born in 1940. She survived the Holocaust and made aliya with her mother and brother in 1946. She was educated in Kfar Batya. She is married to Yosef, and their children are Tzvi and Yaakov. She is a teacher.

Grabov, Zeev, the son of Pesach and Batya, was born in 1918. He was a student of Tarbut and a member of Hashomer Hatzair. He immigrated to Argentina in 1936 and was active there in the field of education, the united appeal, and Hashomer Hatzair. He made aliya in 1950. He married Pnina (née Buber). He works as a supervisor in Kupat Cholim in the Sharon Area directorate. He is active in the community, especially in representing the cities of Volhyn. His children are Avinoam, Yifat, and Gili.

Gotttesman, **Yafa** is the daughter of Avraham and Rivka Bronstein, was born in 1927. She survived the Holocaust as a member of the Diadia Petia partisan unit. She works in special education. She is married to Menachem, a native of Czechoslovakia.

Goldman, Sara, the daughter of Aharon and Henya Papir, was born in 1913. She was a student at the Tarbut Gymnasium of Kowel and a member of Hechalutz Hatzair. She went through hachshara in the Tel Hai Kibbutz in Bialystok and Lida. She made aliya in 1933 with her husband Shmuel Goldman. Their children are Aharon (a physics professor), Edna (a teacher), and Bruria (a journalist).

Grabov, Yaakov, the son of Pesach and Batya, was born in 1921. He was a student of Tarbut and a member of Hashomer Hatzair. He went through hachshara in Rovno. He is a Holocaust survivor who fought with the partisans in the forests and with the Red Army until the conquest of Berlin. He received various medals of excellence. He made aliya from Poland in 1960 with his wife Harriet and two sons: Arnon (who fell in the Six Day War), and Gavriel. His two daughters, Batya and Michal, were born in Israel. He owns a café.

Goizen, Henya, the daughter of Berl and Tova Karsh, was born in 1916, was a student of Tarbut and a member of Hashomer Hatzair. She went through hachshara in Bialystok. She made aliya in 1947. She is married to Reuven, and their children are Yona and Micha. She is a housewife.

Givoni, Charna, the daughter of Yitzchak and Golda Greenstein, was born in 1913. She was a member of Hechalutz Hatzair. She went through hachshara in the kibbutz in Bialystok and made aliya in 1935. She joined Kibbutz Naan, moved to Holon, and worked in the Ludzia factory. Her husband Aryeh was active in the trade union in Holon.

Gefen, Zelda, the daughter of Berl and Henya Feintuch, was born in 1913. She was a student of Tarbut and a prime activist in Hashomer Hatzair. She went through hachshara in Zamosc and made aliya in 1937. She married Mordechai Gefen, one of the first people to make aliya from Ratno. Formerly, she worked in their farm in Kfar Sirkin. Their children are Aviva (a high school teacher), Israel (a sports instructor) and Henya (a kindergarten teacher).

Greenstein (Belgalei), Yafa (Sheindel) , the daughter of Yosef and Chana of blessed memory, was born in 1914. She was a member of Hechalutz Hatzair and Hechalutz. She went through hachshara in Kosow, made aliya in 1939, and joined Kibbutz Ein Hayam. She married Abba Belgalei of blessed memory, and they set up their home in Kiryat Motzkin. Their children are Yossi and Mira.

Goldman, Shmuel, the son of Shamai and Breindel, was born in 1913. He was one of the founders of Hechalutz Hatzair in Ratno and an activist in the pioneering movement in Poland. He made aliya in 1933 and joined Kibbutz Ayelet Hashachar along with his wife Sara. He served as a member of the city council of Rishon LeZion and as secretary of the workers council. He was an activist of the Mapai (Labor Party) and one of the heads of the cooperative center. He was a director of the Amron factory.

Gefen, Mordechai, the son of Israel and Yenta Weinstock, was born in 1910. He was a member of Hechalutz, and went through hachshara in Klesowa. He made aliya in 1929 as the first oleh from Ratno. He joined Kibbutz Givat Hashlosha. He was a guard[2], a member of the Haganah and active in various areas. He was one of the first founders of Kfar Sirkin along with his wife Zelda Feintuch, a Ratno native.

Gendelsman, Tova, the daughter of Yehuda and Leah Bokser, was born in 1923. She was a member of Komsomol. She left Ratno in 1941, and was in the Soviet Union throughout the entire period of the war. She made aliya from Poland in 1957 and joined Kibbutz Ein Shemer. She is married to Yosef and their children are Leah and Pnina. She works on the kibbutz.

Gorodetzki, Zlata, the daughter of Mottle Klein, was born in 1900. During her youth, she belonged to the Poale Zion party. She was widowed from her husband Chaim of blessed memory, a civil engineer. She made aliya in 1978.

Droog, Moshe, the son of Avraham and Reizel, was born in 1908. He is a graduate of the Tarbut Gymnasium and was a member of Hashomer Hatzair. He made aliya in 1934. He is one of the heads of Hamashbir Hamerkazi and the consumers' cooperative. He is married to Bella, a nurse. Their children are Nitza M.A., Dan – an engineer, and Avraham, a practical engineer[3].

Dorner, Dvora, the daughter of Yitzchak and Susia Teitelbaum, was born in 1914. She was a student of Tarbut and a member of Hechalutz Hatzair. She went through hachshara in Krynki and Bialystok. She endured all the tribulations of the war in hiding places and forests with the partisans. She made aliya with her husband in 1948 in a Ha'apala[4] ship.

Drook, Leah, the daughter of Asher and Rivka, was born in 1911. She was a member of Hechalutz Hatzair and made aliya in 1939. She was the sole survivor of her family. She was a member of Kibbutz Alonim. Her son and two grandchildren live in Kibbutz Alonim.

Held, Eliezer, the son of Fishel and Rachel, was born in 1901. He was active in the General Zionist Youth and went through hachshara in the Kibbutz of the General Zionist pioneers in Opatów. He made aliya in 1938. He was a clerk at the Hamashbir Hamerkazi, and the Amizan Company. He is widowed from his wife Roza. He was a member of the Haganah. His daughter Dvora is married to Dan Naot, a lecturer in the Technion in Haifa.

Horwitz, Henya, the daughter of Yitzchak and Miriam Elboim, was born in 1915. She was a student of Tarbut, and was a member of Hechalutz Hatzair. She went through hachshara in Krynki and Bialystok, and made aliya in 1935. She is a counselor of a school for special needs children. She is married to Shlomo. Her children are Ilana, Amiram (an accountant), and Sharona (a bank clerk).

Hochman, Zeev, the son of Yaakov and Ada, was born in 1939. He survived the Holocaust with his mother and sister. They made aliya in 1946. He was educated in Kfar Batya. He works in the aviation industry. His children are **Chagit and Yaakov.**

Wiener, Avraham, the son of Eliahu, was born in 1900. He survived the Holocaust and made aliya in 1950. He is a member of a cooperative workers' settlement (moshav ovdim) in the south of Israel.

Wilk, Aryeh, the son of Chaim David (a shochet) and Chaya, was born in 1922. He escaped to Russia at the outbreak of the war, and served in the Russian Army. He made aliya in 1945 and settled in Rishon LeZion. He served in the police for 30 years. He is married to Ziva, and their children are Chaim and Dalia.

Waks, Batya, the daughter of Hershel and Esther Chana Miller, was born in 1914. She went through hachshara in the religious kibbutz in Otowochek [Otwock], and made aliya in 1934. She is a widow. Her children are Refael and Moshe. She lives with her son in Kibbutz Lavi.

Vernik, Shlomo, the son of Yehuda Leib and Rivka, was born in 1918. He was a student of Tarbut and a member of Hashomer Hatzair. He is a Holocaust survivor. He escaped from a labor camp, arrived in the forests, and joined the partisans. He served in the Russian Army under the command of generals Fedorov and Zhukov. He made aliya in 1947 and fought in the War of

Independence. His is married to Nechama. He works as an accountant. His children are Avraham (an engineer), and Aryeh (a practical engineer).

Zandweis, Chaya, the daughter of Asher and Chasia Leker, was born in 1910. She was a member of Hechalutz, and went through hachshara in the Tel Hai Kibbutz of Bialystok. She made aliya in 1936. She is married in Tuvia. She worked for the General Kupat Cholim. Her daughter is Drora.

Zesak, Eliahu, the son of Chaim and Chava, was born in 1916, and was a student of the Tarbut School and a member of Hashomer Hatzair. He went through hachshara in the Kibbutz in Tshenstochov [Częstochowa]. He worked as a technician in a cooperative in Emek Chefer. He fought with the partisans in the forests during the war. He made aliya in 1950. He participated in Operation Kadesh. His children are Chaim (a bank manager), and Yoav (a flight supervisor).

Chayat, Israel, the son of Yehoshua and Susia, was born in 1913. He was a member of the Haoved (working) movement. He survived the Holocaust. He was in the German labor camps and was even taken to be hanged. He jumped off a bridge into a frozen river to save himself. He fought together with the partisans and served in the Russian Army. He was active in the Bricha[5], lived in Argentina for some time, and made aliya to Israel in 1949. He worked as an accountant in a building materials company. He participated in the Operation Kadesh. He is married to Miriam, and their children are Yechezkel (a dentist), and Asya (a lawyer).

Ternblit, Shraga, the son of Wolf–Leib and Yocha, was born in 1915. He was a member of Hashomer Hatzair and went through hachshara in Vilna. He made aliya in 1935. He was a member of the Haganah and fought in the War of Independence. He is married to Shoshana. Their children are Zeev and Amiram. His occupation is a builder.

Trigobov, Chana, the daughter of Yosef and Rivka Avrech, was born in 1913. She was a member of Hechalutz and went through hachshara in Radzibilov. She made aliya in 1934 and worked in the Defense Ministry. Her husband is Yechhezkel.

Tikuchinsky, Miri (Papir), the daughter of Aharon and Henya, was born in 1928. She made aliya with her mother and the children in 1935, and moved to Kibbutz Ayelet Hashachar. She was a student of a nursing school and serves as the chief nurse in the Shaar Menashe Hospital. Her husband is Aharon. Their daughter Esther is a high school teacher in Beer Sheva.

Yarkoni, Baruch, the son of Chaim and Hinda Greengarten from the village of Zabolottya near Ratno, was born in 1911, immigrated to France in 1930, and later made aliya and settled in Kibbutz Naan.

Yarkoni, Mordechai, the son of Chaim and Hinda Greengarten. He was born in 1913, made aliya in 1938, and is a member of Kibbutz Naan.

Yonosovich, Chaya, the daughter of Yitzchak and Golda Grabov, was born in 1912. She was a member of Hashomer Hatzair and went through hachshara in Chelm and other places. She made aliya in 1939, and spent some time in Kibbutz Mesilot. She is married to Israel and their children are Rama and Yitzchak.

Cohen, Yehudit, the daughter of Yehuda–Leib and Malka Sandiuk, was born in 1914, was a student of Tarbut and a member of Hashomer Hatzair. She went through hachshara in Ludmir. She made aliya in 1935 and settled in Kibbutz Mesilot. She is widowed from her husband Moshe. Her children are Avishai, Rachel, and Eliahu.

Raf, Mordechai, the son of Noach and Malka, was born in 1915. He was a member of Hashomer Hatzair and went through hachshara in Baranovich. He made aliya in 1938. He enlisted in the Hebrew settlement's police force, and served as a communications officer in the Safed Police Force with the Jewish Agency dealing with "illegal" immigrants. He later became an X–ray technician. He was a member of the Haganah and was a defender of Mount Scopus during the time of the siege of Jerusalem. He participated in the War of Independence, Operation Kadesh and the Six Day War.

Kagan, Yehuda, the son of Nachum and Esther (Klara), was born in 1922. He was a member of Beitar. He is a Holocaust survivor. He fought in the partisan ranks and served in the Russian Army. He participated in the War of Independence and Operation Kadesh. He visited the Soviet Union at the beginning of the 1970s. He was arrested there and sentenced to ten years of prison. He was formerly a construction worker and currently owns a vegetable store.

Liberman, Eliahu, the son of Yaakov and Bilha, was born in 1921. He was educated in the Tarbut School and was a member of Hashomer Hatzair. He was a student at a trade school in Brisk. At the time of the Russian conquest in 1939, he travelled to study in Russia and enlisted in the Red Army. After much wandering, he made aliya in 1948 with his wife Chaya. He worked in the

Ha'Malachim Cooperative and currently works in military manufacturing. He served in the Israel Defense Forces. Their children are Bilha, Yael, and Leah.

Levidov, Elka, the daughter of Aharon and Henya Papir, was born in 1916, was a student of Tarbut and a member of Hechalutz Hatzair. She went through hachshara in Kosow and made aliya in 1935. She was a member of Kibbutz Ayelet Hashachar. She was married to her husband Moshe, an employee in the trade union of Tel Aviv, and is widowed. Her children are Aviva and Idit, both teachers.

Lavie, Simcha, the son of Asher and Chasia Leker, was born in 1913. He was a student of Tarbut and a member of Hechalutz Hatzair. He went through hachshara in Klesowa. He made aliya in 1932. He worked in agriculture and building, and later in manufacturing and marketing. He is married to Lilit. He served in the army and fulfilled various duties in the defense apparatus. Their children are Yigal (an aeronautical engineer), Asher (an electrical engineer), and Rachel.

Marin, Dov, the son of Pesach and Malka, was born in 1920. He was a student of Tarbut and a member of the Beitar movement. He made aliya in 1938. His wife is Nechama. He enlisted in the British Army at the beginning of the war, and served in the Israel Defense Forces as a Master Sergeant. He fought in the War of Independence and the Yom Kippur War. Their children are Ziva and Amitai.

Marin, Daniel, the son of Zusia and Sheindel, was born in 1909. He served in the Polish Army during the war and made aliya in 1945. He worked in the Moshav Beit Chanan and was active in the economic issues of the moshav. He was widowed from his wife Tzipora of blessed memory. His daughter is Nava.

Marder, Shmuel, the son of Binyamin and Chana, was born in 1913. He was a member of Hechalutz Hatzair and went through hachshara in Klesowa. He was one of the first olim from Ratno – in 1932. He worked in building and road paving. He was one of the founders of the Cooperative Kibbutz in Haifa and one of the promoters of the Hebrew workforce in the Port of Haifa. He was a member of the Haganah and participated in the War of Independence. Currently, he works as a clerk in the tax clearance office. His children are Binyamin, Avi, and Giora.

Nir, Avraham, the son of Aharon and Henya Papir, was born in 1923. He made aliya in 1935 with his mother, brother and sisters after their father was murdered in the forests of the Ratno area. He joined Kibbutz Ayelet

Hashachar. He was sent to the Mikve Israel Agricultural School. He became an expert in the citrus division, and worked in growing citrus fruits. He is married to Zehava. He was a member of the Haganah and Palmach, and participated in the breaking of the siege of the Atlit Camp. He participated in the wars of Israel and served as a captain in the Israel Defense Forces. Their children are Ayala and Arik.

Arif, Dvora, the daughter of Yitzchak and Golda Grabov, was born in 1910. She was a member of Hashomer Hatzair and went through hachshara in Hrubieszow. She made aliya in 1935. She was a member of Kibbutz Mesilot. She is married to Nisan, and their children are Avraham, Aya, and Gideon.

Flanzman, Ethel, the daughter of Yaakov and Frida Gutman, was born in 1907. She made aliya in 1936. She is married to Avraham. His occupation is an X–ray technician. Their children are Yaakov and Dani.

Perlmutter, Shlomo, the son of Asher and Merida, was born in 1927. He was a student of the Tarbut School. He was a Holocaust survivor. He escaped to the forests and joined the partisans of General Feodorov. He studied in Moscow, and earned the acquaintanceship and friendship of the great Jewish writers there. He made aliya in a Ha'apala ship in 1946. He is a graduate of the University in Jerusalem. He was a high school principal and history teacher. He is married to Shoshana and their children are Miri, Dorit, and Oshrit.

Puchter, Bilha, the daughter of Itzel and Odel Ternblit, was born in 1906. She is a widow and bereaved mother. She spent the wartime years in the forests and in partisan units. She made aliya in 1948, and is a housewife.

Papir, Eliahu, the son of Aharon and Henya, was born in 1918. He made aliya with his family members to Ayelet Hashachar. He later moved to Kibbutz Gimel of Hashomer Hatzair. He worked in agriculture after he left the kibbutz. He was married to Tova of blessed memory. Their children are Drora (a teacher), Dalia (a medical research doctor), and Asher (a clerk).

Friedlander, Shimon, the son of Shlomo–Tuvia and Esther, studied in the Yeshivas of Brisk and Mir, and is an ordained rabbi. He made aliya in 1936. He serves as a rabbi in Tichon Beit/Gimel in Tel Aviv, as well as a vice principal of a school. He served as the rabbi of the Berdichevski Synagogue in Tel Aviv. He is married to Tzipora and their children are Yehuda (a professor of literature) and Esther (a teacher).

Feintuch, Eliahu, the son of Berl and Henya, was born in 1912. He was a member of Hechalutz Hatzair and went through hachshara in Baranovich. He made aliya in 1934 and worked in drilling water wells in the Mekor Hamayim cooperative in Herzliya. He enlisted in the Hebrew Brigade during the war and served for five years. He joined the Haganah. He is married to Herzlia and their children are Dov and Boaz.

Elboim, Tova, the daughter of David and Gitel Prigal, was born in 1907. She married Emanuel Elboim and immigrated to Argentina in 1922. She made aliya with her family in 1963. She is a housewife.

Kotler, Yechezkel, the son of Yitzchak Hirsh and Mindel, was born in 1922. He was a member of Hashomer Hatzair. He served in the Russian Army during the Second World War. He made aliya in 1948. He participated in the Kadesh Operation. He works as a truck owner. His children are Tzvi and Rachel.

Kamintzky, Shmuel, the son of Aharon–Yosef and Bella, was born in 1888. He was the only survivor of his family, thanks to his Ukrainian friends who gave him refuge. He made aliya in 1949, and lives in Petach Tikva. Until his retirement, he worked at sharpening work tools.

Kamintzky, Ben–Zion, the son of Herzl and Chasia, was born in 1927. He was a student of the Tarbut School and a member of Hashomer Hatzair. He found a hiding place with Ukrainians during the war years. He made aliya in 1949. He is a teacher. He studied at university in Jerusalem. He is married to Pnina, and their children are Reuven and Asaf. He fought in Operation Kadesh and the Yom Kippur War.

Karsh, Pnina, the daughter of Yehuda Leib and Rivka Vernik, was born in 1912. She went through all the tribulations of the war. She is widowed from her husband Yitzchak Shapira, who fell during the war as a soldier in the Red Army. She made aliya in 1947 with her daughter Raya. She remarried Ben–Zion Karsh and their son is Yehuda.

Kamintzky, Isser, the son of Yitzchak and Dintza, was born in 1908. He lived in Argentina from 1924 and was active in the appeals, the funds, and the Poale Zion party. He made aliya in 1973, and works in the Amron Factory in Herzliya. He is married to Fanny, and their children are Yitzchak and Eliezer.

Kabashnik, Isser, the son of Yitzchak–Yosef and Henya, was born in 1912. He was a member of Hechalutz and went through hachshara in Dombrowica.

He made aliya in 1932, and always lived in Haifa. He was a member of the Haganah and served in the Israel Defense Forces during the War of Independence. He is married to Frida, and their children are Yitzchak and Nava.

Rozen, Chaya, the daughter of David and Hanche, was born in 1917. She was a student of the Tarbut School and a member of Hashomer Hatzair. She went through hachshara in Czestochowa and made aliya in 1938. She is married to Moshe. The family business is flower growing. Their children are Pinchas, Charna, and Nitza.

Stoltzman, Rivka (Melnik) was born in 1913. She was a member of Hechalutz Hatzair and went through hachshara. She made aliya in 1939, and is a member of Kibbutz Maayan Tzvi.

Schwartz, Sara, the daughter of Yosef and Breindel Ginzburg, was born in 1913. She was a member of Hechalutz and went through hachshara in Klesowa. She made aliya in 1935. She is married to Yehuda and their children are Dalia (a high school teacher) and Yosef (a librarian).

Steingarten, Elchanan, the son of Yaakov and Bat–Sheva, was born in 1926. He was a student of the Tarbut School. His brother Aryeh was murdered by the Nazis at the beginning of the Nazi occupation, and the rest of his family made aliya in 1947 on a Ha'apala ship. He was active in Etz"el and participated in all of Israel's wars. He is a captain. He is married to Batya, and their children are Yitzchak and Aryeh Ben–Zion. His work is with a shoe shop in Kiryat Ono.

Shkolnik, Ada, the daughter of Herzl and Chasia Kamintzky, survived the Holocaust with her two children on account of the protection she found with Ukrainians in the villages of the region. Her children Zeev and Leah were part of the Youth aliya in Kfar Batya. Her husband Yaakov Hochman from Ratno perished in the Holocaust. She remarried in Italy, and her husband died.

Shechter, Charna, the daughter of Chaim Topolovsky, was born in 1914. She was a member of Hechalutz Hatzair and went through hachshara. She made aliya in 1938 and lives in Haifa.

Stern, Moshe, the son of Isser and Rachel, was born in 1909. He was a member of Hechalutz and went through hachshara in Klesowa. He made aliya in 1930. He was a foreman in Solel Boneh, and one of the first residents of Kfar Sirkin. He served in the Hebrew Hashomrim police force in the village for four years. He was active in the Haganah. Their children are Avi, Dvora, and Israel.

Shapira, Levi, was born in 1910. He immigrated from Ratno to Cuba and made aliya to Israel in 1980.

Breshchinski, Yafa, the daughter of Zusia and Esther Geller, was born in 1919. She was a member of Hechalutz and went through hachshara in Vilna. She passed the war years in the Vilna Ghetto. She made aliya on a Ha'apala ship in 1945. Her husband is Yaakov and their children are Aviv and Esther.

Mokotov, Malka, the daughter of Zusia and Esther Geller, was born in 1917. She was a member of Hechalutz and went through hachshara. She made aliya in 1938. She is widowed from her husband Tzadok. Her son is Yuval.

Translator's Footnotes

1. A term for the 1956 Sinai Campaign. See http://mfa.gov.il/MFA/AboutIsrael/History/Pages/The%20Sinai%20Campaign%20–%201956.aspx https://www.jewishgen.org/Yizkor/Ratno/rat300.html - f313-1r

2. See https://en.wikipedia.org/wiki/Notrim https://www.jewishgen.org/Yizkor/Ratno/rat300.html - f313-2r

3. See https://en.wikipedia.org/wiki/Practical_engineer https://www.jewishgen.org/Yizkor/Ratno/rat300.html - f313-3r

4. See https://en.wikipedia.org/wiki/aliyah_Bet https://www.jewishgen.org/Yizkor/Ratno/rat300.html - f313-4r

5. See https://en.wikipedia.org/wiki/Bricha https://www.jewishgen.org/Yizkor/Ratno/rat300.html - f313-5r

Ratners who Died in Israel

Translated by Jerrold Landau

Avrech, Yosef and Rivka, the parents of Aryeh and Alter of blessed memory, and, may she live, Chana Trigobov. They made aliya at the request of their son Aryeh of Kibbutz Yagur in 1936, and lived there with their son.

Avrech, Aryeh, the son of Yosef and Rivka, was born in 1909. He was a member of the Hechalutz headquarters in Warsaw. He made aliya in 1932 and joined Kibbutz Yagur. He was killed in a work accident on the kibbutz in 1948.

Avrech, Alter, the son of Yosef and Rivka, was born in 1924. He made aliya with his parents in 1936, and joined Kibbutz Yotvata. He was killed in a work accident at the Dead Sea in 1948.

Brustein, Pnina, the daughter of Reizel and Avraham Droog, was born in 1913, made aliya in 1936, and joined Kibbutz Givat Hashlosha. She died of cancer in 1969. Her son Hillel lives on Kibbutz Hagoshrim and her daughter Shoshana lives in Givat Hashlosha.

Gutman, Moshe, the son of Yaakov and Freida, was born in 1909 and made aliya in 1932. He was one of the founders of Kfar Sirkin, and was active in the Organization of Ratners and Yad Labanim. He died in 1981.

Goldstein, Batya, survived the Holocaust and died in 1981.

Grabov, Avraham, the son of Yitzchak and Golda, was one of the activists of the Pioneering Movement. He made aliya in 1936, joined Kibbutz Ramat Hakovesh, and was murdered in 1939.

Grabov, Refael, the son of Pesach, immigrated to Argentina, and made aliya to Israel from there. He died in 1980.

Greenstein, Moshe, the son of Yosef, was born in 1915. He made aliya in 1935 and joined Kibbutz Ayelet Hashachar. He died in 1979.

Drezner, Pnina, the daughter of Malka and Pesach Marin was born in 1912 and made aliya in 1935. She was a member of Kibbutz Givat Hashlosha and later moved to Haifa. She died of cancer in 1980.

Held, Roza, (née Rivlin), the wife of Eliezer Held died in 1969.

Weintraub, Chaya, the daughter of Mendel, was born in 1913. She was a member of Hashomer Hatzair. She lived in Ramle.

Weinstock (Gefen), Yenta, was born in 1880. She made aliya in 1935 and helped her son Mordechai set up the farm in Kfar Sirkin. She died in 1947.

Taub, Feiga, the daughter of Sheindel and Zusia Marin, was born in 1913. She made aliya in 1938 and joined Kibbutz Mesilot. She died in 1947.

Yanover, Mordechai, the son of Bracha and Israel, was born in 1910. He was one of the founders of Hechalutz Hatzair in Ratno. He made aliya in 1935, and was a member of Kibbutz Ayelet Hashachar. He moved to Ramat Gan after his marriage. He died in 1979.

Cohen, Yaakov, was the son of Avraham the shochet.

Lifschitz, Pnina, the daughter of Sheindel and Zusia Marin, was born in 1915, and made aliya in 1939. She ran a Magen David Adom station. She was killed in an automobile accident in 1964.

Lifschitz, Avraham, the son of Pnina and Mordechai, was born in 1945. He was killed in an automobile accident in 1964.

Feiglis, Chana and Eliezer, died in Argentina and were buried in Israel.

Papir, Henya, made aliya after her husband was murdered by a robber in the forest in the region of Ratno. She lived with her eldest daughter Sara in Ayelet Hashachar and later in Rishon LeZion. She died in 1947.

Kamintzky, Herzl and Chasia were Holocaust survivors. They made aliya in 1949.

Rozen, Fishel, the son of Berl, was born in 1915, and made aliya in 1937. He was a member of Kibbutz Shefayim. He was lost track of in 1938, and we do not know what his fate was.

Rozen, Pinchas, the son of Moshe and Chaya, was born in 1938. He was killed in an accident.

Rosenthal, Pnina, the daughter of Itzel and Odel Ternblit, was born in 1913, and made aliya in 1938.

Schwartz, Hershel, was born in 1900. He was a Holocaust survivor. He made aliya in 1950, and died in 1981.

Shoshani, Miriam, the daughter of Israel and Yenta Weinstock, was born in 1916. She was one of the founders of Hechalutz Hatzair. She made aliya in 1935 and died on August 24, 1983.

Steingarten, Yaakov and Bat–Sheva, were the parents of Leibel who was one of the first Nazi victims in Ratno. They were Holocaust survivors. They made aliya in 1947. Yaakov died in 5742 (1982) and Bat Sheva in 5741 (1981).

Steingarten, Israel, the son of Yaakov and Bat–Sheva, was born in 1923. He was a Holocaust survivor. He served as a captain in the Israel Defense forces. He died in 1969. He was married to Annette, and his daughters are Ariella and Eti.

Steingarten, Israel, the son of David and Matel, was born in 1911. He was educated in the Tarbut Gymnasium in Kowel. He was exiled to Russia. He made aliya in 1949. He is a graduate of the Hebrew University. He died in Jerusalem in 1976. He was married to Misia, and his children are David and M

Avraham Grabov at training as member of the Haganah

Avraham Grabov

by Moshe Kliger

Translated by Jerrold Landau

Avraham was born in the Ukrainian village of Rokita in Volhyn (Poland)[1]. His parents moved to the nearby town of Ratno when he was four years old. It had two rows of houses, and one could see the second row from the first row. With a few steps, you would be standing on the bridge over the Pripyat outside the town, and from there, one would enter the fields. The town endured a wave of disturbances when Avraham was a child. During his childhood, he saw the sights of blood and fire: Jews being murdered, frightened Jews fleeing for their lives through meadows and forests to find refuge from the hooligans. His oldest sister took her life in her hands to save her father and her family members. These were days of confusion and perplexity. The gentile working at the train harassed her and threatened her life, and she stood up for her honor and her life. She jumped off the train as it was moving and escaped into the forest. The deed of the sister was a childhood experience that accompanied him all his life, like a burning pain that planted the seeds of revenge. It was a command and an oath – to Jewish might and pride.

He was the youngest child of a large, wealthy family in the town. Warmth, love, generosity, and relative calm was the atmosphere of the house. He was the youngest child and beloved by everybody.

The world of the town was small. Its people were few. It had few stores, and the merchandise in the stores was meager. "Grey skies and muddy puddles." "The shreds of blue skies, clear, so painful." – However, the world of "I" is large and broad. The questions of reality, essence and purpose, life and death. The questions were many. One came after the next. There was no solution. From where is the energy to bear all this? Sadness and pain. The uncertainty consumes all the good parts of the soul. At times complacency celebrates its victory: "Liberation cessation." However, the strong, fine youth, in whose image there was somewhat of the village gentile – with flowing youthfulness, and with the spring–like living spirit. Deep inside, he deliberated over the philosophy of nihilism and meaninglessness of life. Life has so many colors! Avraham had a youthful spirit, with a tendency toward mischief and games. If some amount had been taken from him, much still remained: laughter, sunlight, and joy. All of this was with a full breath.

Who can tell what the words – the Land of Israel, the pioneer, Klosowa – meant to a Jewish child in the towns of Volhyn? Is there any expression for the love bound up in them? With great longing, a daydream, the whisper of these names was like the whisper of Mother or the name of a beloved girl. With the tearful prayers of Mother and Father, the crystal tears also came to the eyes of the child. The number of prayers and the Bible inculcated the desire and longing for the Land. The Hebrew pioneers who left the town and their parents' homes with revolutionary songs and "Choliastra nihilism" continued the dream and forged the way. Klosowa was the wonderful island in a remote corner of Poland, next to the border. Its land was rocky. The Jews worked there like gentiles, sang songs of storms and revolutions, mocking the young ones, and the "orderly" life, for they were taken by songs of tomorrow, for the Hebrew revolution.

No Jew will again be embarrassed by work, and no Jewish young man or daughter of Israel will be embarrassed by wearing rags on their body and rubber boots on their feet. The Klosowa group raised the face of the towns of

Volhyn. The Land of Israel, the pioneers, Klosowa – made the soul grow wings. The way was exposed. There is a way.

Avraham, the 15–year–old youth, "flew" to Gruschew. However, the small agricultural farm was calm. In the winter, his friends returned to their parents' homes, and only few remained. The calm was great. Everything was narrow – this was not the song that enchanted him. This is not the song that summoned him to leave his parents' home and to go. Avraham returned to his town, and set out to Klosowa after a few months – to the difficulties, and to the large, noisy group.

He was attracted to the hard work. Through it, he saw a redemption from the bountiful powers of the body and the soul. He had a great desire to struggle with the "strong ones," to see with his flesh that which was frightening and holy with the birth of the new reality; to see the hands that were injured and wounded; to enlist the energy, all the energy. The "light" work did not attract his heart. Quarrying rocks, working alongside "nature" in the sawmill, in paving roads in the Land – this was his way.

In the Hechalutz seminar in 1930 – he was quiet, and turned inwardly, due to the younger people who were among the participants. The Hechalutz Hatzair group at the seminar was caught up with clarifications of the questions of the movement. Experiences were forged in meetings, in conversations among friends, in evenings of song – exciting and engaging. The Hechalutz Hatzair newspaper appeared near the end of the seminar. The driving force behind its renewal was the group of youths of the movement at the seminar. They also participated in it in a significant fashion. The attention of both the members and the counsellors captured Avraham's spirit. He, who was quiet in conversations and introverted, suddenly shone before everyone, surprising them. The poet was exposed. He published an internal newspaper for the chapter, called "Bituyim," even before he went on hachshara. Some of his articles were copied in "Lehavot", the newspaper of Hanoar Hachalutzi His language was that of a visionary. Even the abstract was tangible. His expression was clear, pure, and independent and forged from his "heart and rock." His written expression, like his oral expression (they were very similar), was always forged with internal content. All the pain and creative angst, with enthusiasm around every word and faithful to human reality, always came through in his words. His language – the language of poetry – was not borrowed. He was always original.

From that time on, Avraham more than anyone else was the person who lived the realities of the movement, always wandering around from city to town, and from town to a remote village, with his strong, oppressed journeys. Every step was strong, and every step was deliberate. An abundance of love transported him to children, to the masses of youth of our nation, abandoned and left to the street and emptiness. He organized, collected, and attracted people with the warmth of his personality, with his fire of internal truth. He easily broke down the barriers between himself, the stranger, the guest, between children and the youth groups, being close to them, loving them. He radiated and imbued his environment, sang with devotion, fascinated people with his strong, masculine voice. We were all the same age, but he, Avraham, had youth in his makeup. Throughout all the years of his activity in the movement, in hachshara, and also in the Land, he earned warmth, great love, and open and hidden reverence.

(From the booklet in memory of Avraham)

Right to left: Aryeh Avrech, Moshe Kliger, and A. Grabov

"Love strong as a stone of Klosowa, and as a stone quarried from Jerusalem, to which I will eventually cleave."

"To weep secretly, alone but not to veer off this path."

Translator's Footnote

1. Currently Ukraine.https://www.jewishgen.org/Yizkor/Ratno/rat317.html - f318-1r

Our Brother Avraham

by Chaya

Translated by Jerrold Landau

Avraham was the youngest brother in the family, but he was also the splendor of the family. We were blessed through him, and we were proud of him. It seems to me that all of Jewish Ratno was blessed through him. His praise was in the mouths of everybody. He was an autodidact. He was able to sit for many hours and peruse books that interested him, just as he was able, along with his close friend Avrech, to deliberate and debate important issues of the day for hours. He did not make his peace with the existing society, with its means of operation, and with the modus operandi of many Ratno natives. I remember that he once asked me in a letter from Warsaw, "What is new with you? You are certainly by now already wearing high heels!"... For him, high heels were a symbol of rootlessness, the Philostratus[1] of youth, the pursuing of style.

I will never forget the bitter day when the news of his murder reached us after a delay. I found no comfort at home. It was Friday, and I felt the need to be together with friends. I went to the chapter of Hashomer Hatzair at night, even though at that time (after three years of hachshara, when I came home only to wait for the certificate or information about the confirming of my "illegal" aliya), I did not visit the chapter frequently, because people of my age were no longer active in it. I recall very well Golda Droog, who was the head of the chapter at that time. She was a talented youth with great energy, and everybody related to her with great esteem. Golda understood my soul at that time. She did not leave me for even one minute. She attempted to encourage me, to free me from my terrible mood, and to be with me. I felt a certain easing of my mood when I was with her.

I remember that the news of the murder of Avraham was published in Heint, but they tried to keep it from us for some time. Father went to the post office to receive a letter sent by one of Avraham's friends, containing details about what had taken place. A Tisha Be'Av[2]atmosphere of despair settled upon the house. We all waited for greatness from this youngest member of the family. Who had imagined that this would be his end?

Translator's Footnotes

1. A reference to the philosopher http://en.wikipedia.org/wiki/Philostratushttps://www.jewishgen.org/Yizkor/Ratno/rat317.html - f319-1r
2. A major summer fast day commemorating the destruction of the Temples as well as other tragedies throughout the centuries.https://www.jewishgen.org/Yizkor/Ratno/rat317.html - f319-2r

Avrech

by Aryeh Pialkov

Translated by Jerrold Landau

Alter Avrech, Aryeh's brother, who was killed in a work accident

Aryeh Avrech and his family in Yagur

He was born in the year 5669 – 1909 in Ratno. He arrived in the Land on the 15th of Tammuz, 5691 – June 1931. He was a graduate of the pioneering movement, and one of the best of its actualizers and builders. He was a man of culture who loved books. He was dedicated with enthusiasm and diligence to every job and task that he took upon himself. His hands were expert in every type of work. He worked in the sheep flock for many years, and spent many hours a day shepherding, milking, and shearing. Even then, he did not leave behind a good book. For a time, he worked at counselling youth who had made aliya. Later he edited the diary of the Yagur farm, and imbued it with the best of his style and broad knowledge. He worked in a deciduous forest during his latter years. He was crushed and seriously injured while dismantling a new sprayer. He died a few hours later. About him it is said: If the legend of the 36[1] is accurate – he is one of them. The library building in Kibbutz Yagur is called Beit Avrech in his name.

About his Personality

In the book "Sefer Klosowa," Aryeh Fialkov tells about four emissaries from Klosowa who visited the town. The third one was Aryeh Avrech.

The impression of the first two visitors in the town and in the chapter was noticeable for a long time. Those in the know whispered: this time the man of the book, the man of the spirit, the man of culture of Klosowa, is coming. Thus, Avrech was perceived even before he came, but the matter was still not grasped appropriately: What does it mean? He won't speak? He won't respond to questions and issues?

Then he arrived, with his simple garb, his modest demeanor, and his quiet manner of speaking. They surrounded him, as usual. But he – was not usual. He minimized his speaking.

He listened a great deal. His conversation exuded warmth, and he smiled goodheartedly. During the first break, the group tried to direct him as they did with those who came before him. First he was to speak, then he would respond to questions, which were so many and bothersome, and who can respond to them and straighten things out if not for the emissary of Klosowa? Indeed, Avrech tried to do so, but he immediately realized that this was not within his power. His responses and explanations were terse and to the point. It seemed as if he was trying to hurry to exit from these complexities, in order to start to deal with issues that were closer to him. There was indeed a certain disappointment in the audience of members: what would happen to the irksome questions? Apparently, Avrech did not perceive this. He was in his own element. He took out a book, "Masada" by Lamdan[2], and read from it. He took out a second book, "BaGalgal" by Shlonski[3], and also read and explained it. The youths were a bit surprised. They were not prepared for this. However, Avrech continued with his reading in proper taste, with emphasis, with explaining sentences and ideas with emotional but restrained enthusiasm – he had intended specifically this. This was the main thing – in the work of "we have a small hand with five fingers," with the stubbornness of the maapilim[illegal immigrants] of "Masada" and with the pioneering creativity in the Land.

This is how it was throughout the time of the visit. There were few discussions devoted to ideology, and more about literature on life, on work, and on the dedication that exists in the Land. He read from a memorial book on chalutzim who fell while on guard duty in the Land. Incidentally, he talked about the complex journeys over seas and lands through which the chalutzim carried out their immigration.

The esteem and relationship grew after a few discussions. Many connected with him in love and reverence. His visit had a special value. He directed the attention more inwardly, and the means for this was Hebrew poetry.

Yosef Avrech with his son Alter and wife at Kibbutz Yagur

Translator's Footnotes

1. The legend that there are 36 hidden tzadikim (holy men) in every generation.https://www.jewishgen.org/Yizkor/Ratno/rat317.html - f321-1r

2. See http://en.wikipedia.org/wiki/Yitzhak_Lamdanhttps://www.jewishgen.org/Yizkor/Ratno/rat317.html - f321-2r

3. See http://en.wikipedia.org/wiki/Avraham_Shlonskyhttps://www.jewishgen.org/Yizkor/Ratno/rat317.html - f321-3r

My Native Land

by A. Avrech

Translated by Jerrold Landau And I am a prayer, my native land, my native land!
Please accept my meager offering –
I will bring myself to you,
To wet and fertilize with my sweat and blood
The clods of your earth, dried from the heatwaves.

I will fall down as a servant before your locked gates,
Let me put as a yoke on my neck –
To go with the plow on the dewy morning,
And to return along with the sheep in the evening.

Like Jacob when he crossed the Jordan
I will come to you and plead:
Please take me in, do not spit me out
Oh Mother Earth!

(Written on the day of his Aliya to the Land of Israel, 16 Tammuz 5691 – 1931)

Pnina Brustin (nee Droog) of blessed memory

by Mordechai Gefen

Translated by Jerrold Landau

Pnina Droog in Givat Hasheloshah

Pnina was born in Ratno in 1913 to a Zionist family with many children, the Droog family. The Jews of Ratno were unable to permit themselves to send their children to the high school in the district city of Kowel, but the Droog family was an exception from this perspective. They sent Amalia and her brother Moshe, may he live long, to Kowel to continue their studies at the gymnasium. The home of the Droog family in Ratno was a sort of meeting place for the studying youth in the town. The mother succeeded in creating a warm family atmosphere in the house, and made sure that none of her children would venture far from the bosom of her family. The path for pioneering actualization was forged during the 1930s by isolated pioneers in Ratno. It was not easy to uproot oneself from the patriarchal family life of a small town. The parents were indeed enthusiastic Zionists who educated their children in the path of Zionism. However, they simultaneously guarded the integrity of the family. Many people thought that the first to make aliya to the Land of Israel would be from among the poor folk who had nothing to lose. This was not the reality. The first to break through the fence were specifically people from well-off families. They are the ones who were beacons for actualization in the youth movements of the town. Pnina was the pioneer from the Droog family who went out to hachshara and made aliya to Kibbutz Givat Hashelosha in 1934.

When I visited her in Givat, she told me about the difficulties that she encountered, and stressed to me that being separated from her family in Ratno caused her great suffering. Despite this, she participated enthusiastically in kibbutz life, and her dedication to the kibbutz society knew no bounds. She also conducted an investigation into why I had left the kibbutz. I visited her often, and I was proud of her and her path when I saw how she had become rooted in kibbutz life, for we were relatives.

I recall my visit to her after she had become ill and undergone surgery. She had become very weak, and I chastised her for neglecting her own wellbeing and working hard despite her weakness. She answered me with simplicity: "Mottle, it is possible that you are correct, but you will not change me. This is how I am and this is how I will remain for all the days of my life."

The Image of Pnina

Translated by Jerrold Landau

We were neighbors in the town and I knew her from the Tarbut School. The large house of the Droog family was always a visiting place for any passer-by from Hechalutz and Hashomer Hatzair, where any visitor would be received pleasantly. Pnina had gone through Hechalutz Hatzair, whereas her brothers and sisters had gone through Hashomer Hatzair. Pnina was always concerned with all the household needs, and played her part in receiving guests. She hosted the guests of the family politely and with a smile, winning over the hearts of everyone. Even her young sisters obeyed her. I remember her always laughing in the Hechalutz chapter. At times, her laughter disrupted the activities of the chapter, but they always forgave Pnina for they appreciated her naturalness and simplicity. When she made aliya to the Land and arrived in Givat Hashelosha, she became serious: she accepted kibbutz life as something natural, about which one does not complain. She was always concerned that she was not doing enough for the kibbutz and that perhaps there was something else with which she could fill her daily quota of work, in her role in Haganah (defense) or in other areas of communal and social activity on the farm. In conversations with her about various problems of the group, I always felt that everything that Pnina said came from the heart and from concern for others. Pnina took ill. In one of my last visits to her, I sat next to her, and we discussed all types of problems. The parting was difficult. I did not want Pnina to sense that I knew about her bitter fate. I talked with the nurses and personnel workers of the division. They all valued her and her refined character. Despite her great suffering, she did not make their work more difficult. Therefore, she received the best care from the workers. Some praised her for her honesty, conscience, dedication and love for her fellowman.

We, the natives of the town, were always proud of Pnina. In our eyes, she symbolized the goodness of the town, both in the Kibbutz and in the society. She left behind a vacuum. We will always remember her.

Pnina Droog as a tractor driver in Givat Hashelosha (1937)

Moshe Greenstein of blessed memory

by Shmuel Goldman

Translated by Jerrold Landau

Moshe was born on the 17th of Adar 5675 (March 10, 1915) in Ratno. His father Yosef was a merchant of forestry products. He was a Hassid of Karlin – one of those who saw in Hassidism salvation for the longings of the soul and desire for redemption. He joined the Hechalutz Hatzair youth movement and found his home in that movement. He joined the ranks of the kibbutz movement with dedication and faithfulness. He was active in the chapter, in the summer camp, and in hachshara. He finally succeeded in realizing his dream – he made aliya to the Land of Israel and joined Kibbutz Ayelet Hashachar, which took in the members of the Tel Chai Hachshara Kibbutz of Poland, whose members set their goal, while still in the Diaspora, to settle the Upper Galilee. How great was my joy when I met Moshe on that Kibbutz after a separation of several years.

We were like dreamers in our new home. We breathed the experience of returning to our homeland, to our soil. We were enchanted by the landscape that unfolded before our eyes. If there is an expression to the feeling of absorption of aliya, it is expressed in its full glory here in Ayelet Hashachar.

Moshe was absorbed nicely into the work. He was blessed with expert hands and diligence. He took to the work and camaraderie in the new social group, as if he had grown up within it. He was a quiet man, pleasant to his fellowman, good hearted, and attentive to everybody. He always searched for the good and the positive, and he found such. He was content with himself and with the path of his life. He loved the kibbutz, and his heart rejoiced with every advancement he made. He loved his friends and his friends loved him.

In our final meeting, when I saw him sitting outside next to his house, full of pain and sickness, in a tone of satisfaction as his eyes were widening and sparkling, , he told me about the dedication and concern expressed by the members of the kibbutz to him, and he offered praise and appreciation for the Kibbutz society.

He fulfilled his way in his Kibbutz home for 46 years. He will be missed by me and by very many members of the Kibbutz.

He died on the 17th of Shevat, 5739 – February 14, 1979.

Yisrael (Srulik) Steingarten

Translated by Jerrold Landau

Yisrael Steingarten, the brother of Elchanan, went through the same tribulations as did his parents and brother. After the liberation, he was prominent in the underground activities in Italy. Chaim Lazar discussed this in one of the publications of the Museum of Fighters and Partisans (booklet 10).

"At the end of the winter of 1942, the Banderowches also organized themselves, and set up their camp in the forests. These were nationalist Ukrainians who were fed up with the German promises to establish an independent Ukraine. They fought the Germans, Russians, and Poles. First and foremost, however, they poured out their wrath upon the Jews who were hiding in the forests or other places. The Banderowches began to track the steps of the partisans. They were forced to move their location every few days. One night, the partisans went out for an activity to obtain food, and they noticed that the farmers were more brazen than usual. They quickly discovered that the Banderowches were in the village. As they were preparing to retreat, Yisrael's three friends with their hands raised and guns pointed at them, were already being guarded by two Banderowches,. When they noticed Yisrael leaving one of the houses, they started to shoot at him. Yisraelik lay down next to the fence and shot toward them. One of them fell dead, and the other fell down from fear. Yisraelik's friends took advantage of the confusion, jumped on their horses, and began to gallop toward their base. Yisraelik also began to flee, lying down on the ground on occasion and shooting backward toward his pursuers who were firing at him. When the Banderowches gave up on catching up with him, Yisrael found himself alone in an unknown area. After a bit of sleep, he entered the home of one of the farmers and forced the farmer to take him to the area where his base was located. The partisans who reached the base before him had told everyone that Yisraelik had fallen in battle, and one other partisan was wounded. To everyone's surprise, Yisraelik appeared in the camp with his weapons. From that time, masses of Jewish fighters began to join the partisan camp.

Yisrael volunteered to be a guerrilla. First of all, he wanted to strike at the enemy. Second, he wanted to provide backing for his family, and justify their existence among the partisans. There was no guerrilla action or battle in which he did not participate. Even on the threshold of liberation, he did not respond to the urging of his father to hold back somewhat and take more care.

— — — On January 7, 1944, they met up with the Red Army. Yisrael's parents remained in a town near the city of Rovno, whereas Yisrael and his brother Elchanan, along with the entire partisan brigade, continued to participate in all types of actions and battles. After some time, his parents set out for Kiev, where the head partisan and Ukrainian command was located, so that they could receive news on their son. The fragments of information that arrived contradicted each other, until his brother Elchanan finally succeeded in tracking him down. The mother traveled to the town of Terszow, where rumor had it that Yisrael was located. She met her son and succeeded in persuading him to move to Kiev, where the family was located at that time. In the meantime, news began to arrive in Kiev about the possibility of aliya to the Land via Romania. Under pressure from his family, Yisrael agreed to take on a position of train inspector. In this task, he greatly helped with the escapes that were starting at that time.

In February 1945, the Steingarten family reached Lublin as partisans, and were brought to the "escape depot." They remained in Romania for several months, and then in Hungary and Austria, with their destination being Italy. Once in Italy, they were sent to the south of the country, to the Santa Cesarea Camp. There, the Steingarten family, including their father Yaakov, joined a pod of the Beitar organization, and a chapter of the Revisionist party.

Chaim Lazar relates that Yisraelik quickly became one of the pillars of Beitar in Southern Italy, with its many camps. When the first representatives of Etz'el (Irgun Tzvai Leumi) arrived in Italy, Yisralik became one of the activists. Then he was appointed as the Etz'el commander for the entire district of northern Italy. He was sent to Belgium in 1947, as responsible for the Etz'el activities there. A chapter of Etz'el activists existed in Belgium under the leadership of a young woman Annette, who was appointed to this position by the representative of the organization in Europe. When Yisraelik arrived in Belgium , he began to develop activities that spilled over the borders of that country. He set up additional cells of Etz'el in Antwerp and Liege. He collected money, amassed weapons, developed activities, conducted publicity through posters, forged connections with newspapers, etc. He also visited other European countries and established connections with all the Etz'el centers in Europe. After a year of living in Belgium, the police tracked his path, and he received an order from the authorities to leave Belgium. After spending several months in France, he returned to Belgium with a forged passport in order to gather his people and bring them to the Altalena ship. Annette, who was later to marry him in Israel, was among them. After he made aliyaaboard the Altalena, Yisrael joined the Israel Defense Forces. He participated in the War of Independence as a captain, and served as vice commander of a brigade.

After he was released from the army, he began working at the Remet building company. He died of a heart attack in 1969.

Yisrael Steingarten

Mordechai Yanover of blessed memory

by Shmuel Goldman

Translated by Jerrold Landau

He was the elder in the group of youths – the first ones of Hechalutz Hatzair. His spiritual leanings, his relationships of friendship that he nurtured, and his love of the youth – with all these traits, he became a counselor and educator of the movement at its outset. His personality is reminiscent of the "Matmid" of Bialik.

He learned and read without stop, and he then tried to impart to his charges everything that he had learned on his own. Through him, we became familiar with the classicists of Hebrew Literature. He also succeeded in drawing us near to authors such as Brenner, A. D. Gordon, Yitzchak Lamdan, and others. He especially loved the "Masada" work of Lamdan, and our group was named after that work.

From his early youth, Mordechai bound himself with the pioneering movement, through which he saw the solution to the problems that were bothering us. Therefore, to the best of his ability, he imparted the pioneering values into the Hechalutz and Hechalutz Hatzair movements. Among other things, he was the force behind the publication of an internal newspaper called "Bituyim." He ensured that many children would have their writing published in that newspaper, so that they could express the feelings and desires of their hearts. I recall the words of farewell that he said to the members who went out to Hachshara. He encouraged us and served as an important force in our journey. Despite his physical weakness, he too went to Hachshara and prepared himself for aliya.

When he reached the Land, he joined the Ayelet Hashachar Kibbutz. Since I came to that kibbutz some time before him, I was able to follow his absorption into the kibbutz from the first day that he was there. I saw him more than once returning from work with wounded hands, but he never complained or asked for easier work. He fulfilled every task given to him by the Kibbutz in the best possible way. His chief aspiration was to be a worker of the land, rooted in the soil. He was among the volunteers for external work in helping other kibbutzim. He was not weakened by the difficulties of acclimatization in his work in the kibbutz in the Jordan valley. Our paths separated with the passage of time. We each went to our own work path, and our meetings were rare.

His work outside the confines of the Kibbutz was not easy, when he was burdened with the yoke of a family. However, he succeeded in serving as an accounting director in a Histadrut institution, and he earned great respect as a person of a high cultural level, who knew how to maintain proper human relationships with everyone with whom he lived and worked.

Those of us who went through the Hechalutz Hatzair movement will always guard his memory as someone who shone and influenced our path and our development during the time of our youth.

Arnon–David Grabov Writes to his Mother

Translated by Jerrold Landau

Arnon David Grabov of blessed memory

Mother, don't be surprised that I am writing to you this time in Polish[1]. I know that Father has been drafted and there will be nobody to read this letter to you, and you will have to wait for the arrival of Uncle Zeev. There is another reason for this: I want you to understand every word that I am writing to you with the light of a pocket flashlight.

Father and Gabi[2], as I have said, have been drafted. Father knows what a war is: three years with the partisans and two years in the Red Army weakened his character. How great is my pride to be his son! Gabi too has already tasted the taste of tension when he jumped out of an airplane for the first time. After I met him at my base he said to me, "At first, when you are floating between heaven and earth, you forget completely that you exist. It is not you who is jumping, but rather someone else. However, from the moment that the parachute begins to open, the fear dissipates, and the only thought that you think is "mother earth." How secure is a person when his foot treads upon the ground that perhaps he might soon have to defend with all his might..."

I also went through my first immersion in fire when I participated in the Samua action[3]. You recall, Mother, when I came home in the middle of the darkness of night, and the first thing that I asked you, before I kissed you, was, "Mother, I need a bath!" I had to wash everything off me... I did not speak much at that time, but I felt that you knew what I endured. At night I dreamed that I was alone in a room, with only one candle burning. Suddenly, the candle started to flicker, and then it went out. Endless darkness and quiet pervaded. I woke up and recalled that a bomb fell upon my commander, injured his head, and he slowly weakened. We returned from Samua, and I managed to visit you for several hours. That was the night that you were very worried that I had not spoken much to Grandfather, Grandmother, and you. You noticed the sadness on my face. The next day, you read in the newspaper about the raid on Samua, in which the death of the captain was described. Then you understood the meaning of the silence.

It has now been several weeks since I have been at home. How are you?

I met Gabi a few days ago, and he is satisfied. It is too bad that I did not meet with Father, and see him in his Israel Defense Forces uniform. I feel that I am in a good situation. We receive many good things from various people, as well as letters from young children who encourage us to protect them. My heart aches when I read these letters. I know what will happen to these children if, Heaven forbid, our enemies win. But such a thing will not happen and will not be! Every one of us is prepared to give everything for the honor of the homeland... You remember when I was six years old: I attended the Polish school and was the only Jew there. Once, a child called me a dirty Zyd. I knew that I was a Jew. You and Father told me that. As a reaction to the shame, I threw onto his face the piece of bread with jam that I loved so much. How great at that time was the sacrifice that I gave to protect the honor of my nation, since as a punishment I did not receive another piece. Is it not true, Mommy, that this is funny? But now, when I read the letters of the children, I am prepared to give my life and my great love for them. However there is one thing that I ask, do not mourn or weep over me. Be strong!

Today I received a package with all sorts of sweets as well as a letter in Yiddish. I read it with difficulty, with the help of some of my friends. In the letter, the woman writes that she is very afraid. She had been in Auschwitz, and her four children along with her husband were murdered. She arrived in the Land after many tribulations and succeeded in building a family. She has young children. She trusts the Israel Defense Forces, and prays for our wellbeing every evening. Tears flowed from the eyes of all the armed men.

Mother, is this not enough to give us enough strength to fight with all our might against those who rise up against us?

Dear mother! You must be strong. What will happen will happen. Know that I am going to protect and fight for something that is just, the likes of which does not exist in the world. The seven years that I have been in the Land seem to me like 70. I connected with the Land so much! When I return from the army, I will take you with me so that you can get to know all the wonderful places where I fought. I never thought that our small Land is so beautiful and wonderful. We go out every day to protect this Land. We have no other place in the world! How does Grandmother say it? At times one must pay a very high price in order to merit to live in honor. This time, who knows what fate will bring. Be strong. Lots of kisses to all of you.

To you with love,

Translator's Footnotes

1.
2. There is a footnote in the text as follows: Written originally in Polish.https://www.jewishgen.org/Yizkor/Ratno/rat317.html - f328-1r
3. There is a footnote in the text as follows: The name of his younger brother.https://www.jewishgen.org/Yizkor/Ratno/rat317.html - f328-2r
4. Samua is a village in the southern West Bank. It was under Jordanian control prior to the Six Day War in 1967.https://www.jewishgen.org/Yizkor/Ratno/rat317.html - f328-3r

Arnon–David Grabov

Translated by Jerrold Landau

He made Aliya to Israel with his parents in the year 1960 when he was 12 years old. He studied in a school in the Neveh Oz neighborhood next to Petah Tikva, and excelled as a good student and an excellent sportsman. He was drafted into the army when he was 18 years old and volunteered for a paratrooper unit. He graduated with a course in communications and endured his first battle next to the Jordanian town of Samua. He spoke to his mother by telephone a day before the outbreak of the Six Day War and asked her to be appropriately strong should something happen to him that night. Among other things, he told her , "I am going out to protect my Land regarding a matter of justice and propriety, for we have no other place in the world other than this land of ours."

He fell in battle next to Gaza at the age of 19 on the first day of the Six Day War, June 5, 1967. In a conversation between Arnon–David's father Yaakov and Major Yechiel Amsalem of blessed memory (Arnon–David's commander who fell in battle along with him), the commander told him that he was proud to be the commander of a battalion that included soldiers such as Arnon–David, and that his father too should be proud of such a son.

Moshe Gutman of blessed memory

by S. Lavie and M. Gefen

Translated by Jerrold Landau

Moshe Gutman of blessed memory

Yoram Gutman of blessed memory, the son of Moshe and Tzipora

The memory of my friend Moshe Gutman is connected with the early days of the Herzliya Moshava. Herzliya then consisted of low, white houses that appeared as glistening pearls in the background of scenery that included the sea, vegetation, and sand dunes. With my first steps on the ground of Herzliya, I said in my heart: I am bound to you forever. Later, when I met four friends who were natives of Ratno (Mordechai Gefen, Moshe Stern, Shmuel Marder, and Moshe Gutman) who preceded me in aliya to the Land, I was full of praise for Herzliya that embraced me as a mother and a sister.

It seems that all of these praises did not fall upon deaf ears. On a cloudless morning, or perhaps it was an evening after work, Moshe Gutman appeared in my room with a heavy bundle, and declared mischievously, "I have come to partake of your Garden of Eden."

We lived and worked together for a period of time. Moshe was a few years older than me. He had richer life experiences than I had, and he also knew the Israeli reality better than I did. He was a friend and brother to me, eased the difficulties of my acclimation significantly, and even helped assuage the feelings of loneliness that tend to afflict a person in a strange environment. Various circumstances caused our paths to diverge after that. Moshe returned to Petach Tikva, to his three friends and to the way of life that he followed for approximately 50 years: founding a building company, volunteering for the guard brigade on the railway line, building Kfar Sirkin and Hitnachalut, and establishing a family.

Moshe became ill with a malignant disease and fought it. When he found out that I had been hospitalized due to a heart attack, he got in touch with my household, took interest in my situation, and even expressed interest in visiting me. The news of his death reached me when I was still bound to my sickbed. I was saddened that I could not perform the final good deed of escorting him to his eternal rest, but I will always remember him positively.

About Moshe of blessed memory by Mordechai Gefen

I was a friend and neighbor of Moshe for more than 60 years. This began in Ratno, in the cheder of Yudel the teacher, continued in the Tarbut School, in the pioneering movement, and later in Kfar Sirkin, where we both were among the founders of the village. It can be said that we were both nurtured by the same roots, and even saw the same visions of disaster and torment that overtook the Jews of Ratno. There was an incident where the Ukrainians made slanderous accusations to the Russians about Moshe's father, claiming that he was a profiteer. He was sentenced to hanging, but the rope attached to his neck tore twice. The hangmen regarded this as the hand of fate, and let him be. Many people left their stamp on Moshe and they brought him to the realization that there was no future for the Jews of Poland, and that the only way to ensure a different life was aliya to the Land of Israel and joining the labor movement. He went out to pioneering hachshara and made aliya to the Land of Israel in 1931.

He worked for some time at the Mekor Hamayim Company that drilled wells in Herzliya. This work was considered dangerous in those days, when the bore went down 40 meters or more. Later, he worked in the orchards of the Sharon. In a later period, he studied the building trade and joined the Solel Boneh building company in Petach Tikva. In 1936, he joined the first group that settled Kfar Sirkin. This was the stormy period in Moshe's life. He built farms without limit, working during the day on the scaffolding of buildings, and performing guiding and defense tasks at night. Moshe was active in all the institutions of the village, and when the first survivors of Ratno began to arrive after the Holocaust, he acted to the best of his ability to offer help to the survivors and to establish the organization of Ratno Natives - work that he continued until his last day.

Pnina Drezner of blessed memory

by Nechama Meril

Translated by Jerrold Landau

Pnina Drezner

Miriam Shoshani (Weinstock) of blessed memory

She was born in Ratno into the home of a faithful Zionist. From her early youth, she was active in the ranks of the youth, and when she got older, she went out to hachshara in Klesowa, where she became known for all of her fine traits, and earned general appreciation. She made aliya in 1935. Her first stop in the land was Kibbutz Givat Hashlosha. During the disturbances of 1936, she volunteered to help Kibbutz Ramat Hakovesh, and was very active in the Haganah. One of her aims in life was to bring her family members to the Land. Among others, her brother Dov, my current husband, made aliya through her efforts. Pnina tried to impart the feeling of a warm home and literally acted as a mother to the Holocaust survivors. Her assistance to her fellowman was one of the values in which she immersed herself as well as her family. She was very alert to the suffering of her fellowman, and did everything she could to help. She would help without saying anything. When she got sick with a severe, malignant disease, she bore herself with strength and privacy, as she fought her illness. She was not subdued even when on her sick bed. She continued her tasks to the best of her ability, showed interest in everything happening in Israel, and attempted to not speak about her suffering and illness. Our sages stated that a person can be understood from his pocket, his cup, and his anger[1]. I will add an additional feature to this list: also through a person's illness. Anyone who did not know Pnina when she was well was able to know her and testify to her goodness even during the time of her illness. It is about people such as this that Bialik based his well-known poem: "Let my lot be with you."

Translator's Footnote

1. In Hebrew, the three words sound similar: kiso, koso, kaaso. It refers to how a person relates to money, how a person acts when under the influence of alcohol, and how a person controls his anger.https://www.jewishgen.org/Yizkor/Ratno/rat317.html - f331-1r

Miriam Shoshani (Weinstock) of blessed memory

by Mordechai Gefen

Translated by Jerrold Landau

During the early 1930s, a young girl stood out in the arena of Zionist and pioneering activity in the town. She was quiet, introverted, and had pleasant mannerisms. Along with this, however, she was a dynamo who was prepared to do everything for the movement to which she belonged - Hechalutz Hatzair.

Indeed, she was bothered when I decided to make aliya to the land and did not heed the pleas of my mother to remain in Ratno and continue to help with the family livelihood after my father died. I knew in my heart that it was possible to depend on my younger sisters, and especially Miriam, who was graced with a business sense. Indeed, that is the way it happened. I made aliya in the midst of the disturbances of 1929. My heart was concerned for what was going on with my family in Ratno, but from the letters I received, I found out that Miriam was carrying on to the best of her ability.

In 1935, I brought my late mother and my sister Miriam to the Land of Israel. She established a warm household in Afula, and along with her husband, may he live long, she did everything to educate her son and daughter and to ensure their future. I am certain that Yisrael and Batya appreciate everything that their mother did and sacrificed for them.

On her gravestone in Kfar Tavor, it was fitting to engrave the words of the poet Ch. N. Bialik, "Let my lot be with you, the modest ones of the world, the discreet ones, who live their lives in secret, modest in their thoughts and adventures -- -- -- they call out, and you - and it was not told to you, oh prominent ones - and you did not know."

In Memory[1]

by Shmuel Goldman

Translated by Jerrold Landau

In memory of my father Shamai, my mother Breindel, my brother Aharon and my sister Sheindel who were murdered by the Nazis

Where is the burial place of my dear mother and father? On which of the terrible days of killing was the thread of their lives cut short? Where were they killed - in the Krymno Ghetto or in some other killing field? Who will reveal this terrible, holy place to my eyes? My soul and my spirit are bound to it, where is it?...

My brother and sister were killed in the thick forests of Zabrodze. I was told that they were seen walking in those fields armed with weapons - my strong, brave, brother who was 23-years-old at the time he was murdered; and my sister, the youngest child of my parents, flowering in her beauty, who was 17-years-old at the time she was murdered. Oh G-d of vengeance, tell me, did they take revenge on their murderers before they gave up their pure souls, how did they fall, where are they buried, and on what day did their souls ascend - will I never know these answers?...

We were five, and I alone survived. I am bereaved of my father, mother, brother and sister. I am the sole survivor of a large family of many roots - a family of those who studied Torah and fulfilled its commandments. They were Hassidim of Karlin, faithful to the Rebbe. They were rooted in their Hassidism, believing and faithful to its values and essence. They were a wonderful blend of Jewish scholars, who were also attuned to the ways of the world. They absorbed into their essence the good and beautiful aspects of the changing ways of the world brought with them, and exerted their influence. Everything was uprooted and is no more, could this be?...

I saw them for the last time on October 23, 1933. I took leave of them as I set out on my journey to the Land of Israel. I hoped that we would be reunited in our Land. We exchanged many letters on that topic. However, the circumstances of the times, of poor health, and of other such matters disrupted the realization of their desire to make aliya to the Land, and pushed it off to when circumstances would improve for them. Could anyone have imagined that the end of Polish Jewry was approaching, and that the fire was already consuming the ground upon which they were walking?...

... Thus, we were suddenly placed against the horror in its full cruelty. Terrible waves of murder also enveloped and flooded the holy community of Ratno. Everything was destroyed, uprooted and annihilated, and the masses of our martyrs were tortured and murdered in the light of the day, in the view of the shining sun...

"The sun shone, the acacia blossomed, and the slaughterer slaughtered."[2] ... The survivors were only very few, distraught in their loss and bereavement, wandering along with us in the darkness of the days and asking why and for what reason?

... My dear, good father, refined in soul and noble of spirit, with a sharp mind and clear way of thinking. Your quiet, calming voice has been silenced. Your heartwarming, engaging gaze has been shut. How do I regret that I parted from you so young, and did not drink sufficiently of your wonderful wellsprings.

... I will never again see the noble face of my mother, etched with furrows of sorrow over her children who died while still in their youth. Her tall, thin stature was bent with worry and fear over those who remained alive, with their illnesses and travails of growing up... How strong was your desire to make aliya to the Land and be together with us here. Did you yet sense the knife fluttering above their heads?...

My dear brother and sister, you were the faithful support of our parents at the time of their old age. You were dedicated to them and concerned about them, and for this, I always blessed you. You are dear, innocent souls, and my soul and spirit are bound to you forever.

Tel Aviv, October 1952

Translator's Footnotes

1. "This article is not in the original Yizkor Book, and was added in to the online translation at the request of Dr. Goldman."https://www.jewishgen.org/Yizkor/Ratno/rat317.html - f331b-1r
2. This is a line from the Hebrew poem "In the City of Slaughter" by Chaim Nachman Bialik.https://www.jewishgen.org/Yizkor/Ratno/rat317.html - f331b-2r

Name Index

D

E

F

G

H

I

J

K

L

M

N

T

V

W

Y

Z

www.ingramcontent.com/pod-product-compliance
Lightning Source LLC
Chambersburg PA
CBHW082008150426
42814CB00005BA/261
* 9 7 8 1 9 3 9 5 6 1 8 9 3 *